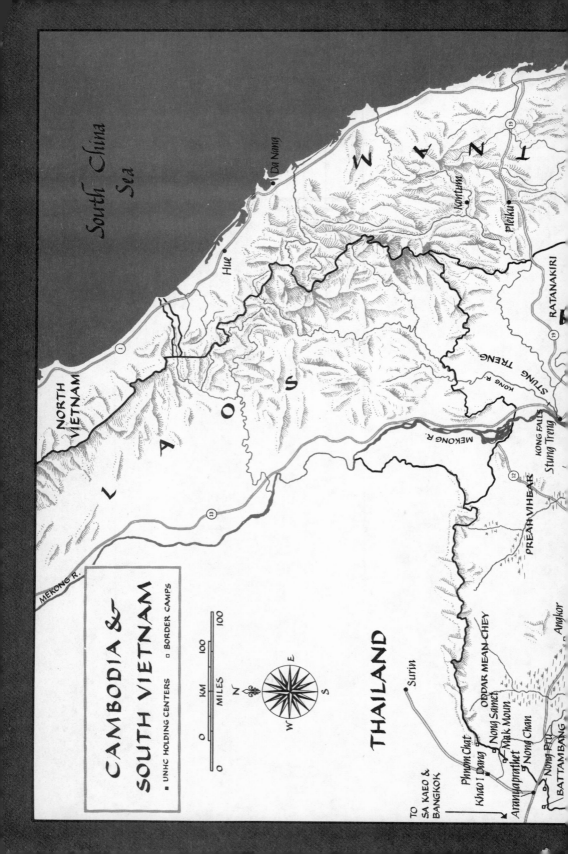

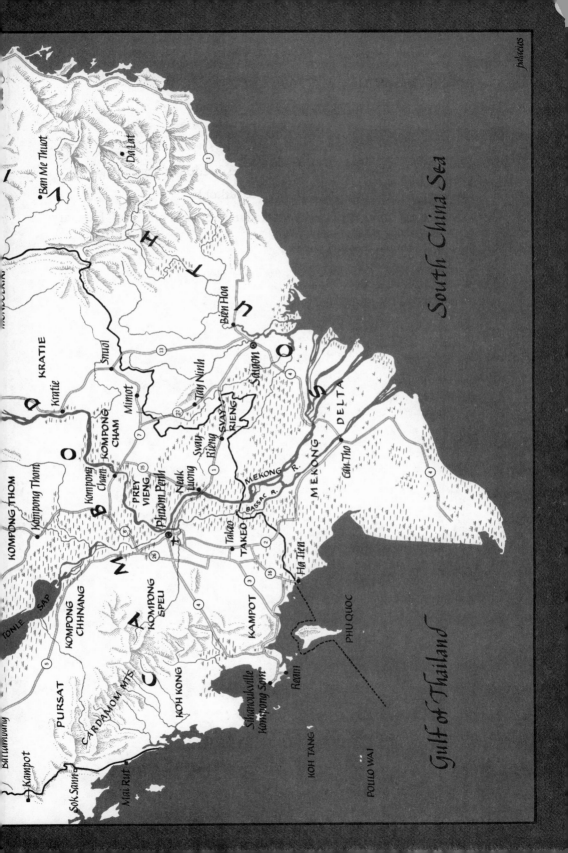

South China Sea

Gulf of Thailand

MONGOLIEN

I
N
D
O
C
H
I
N
A

• Ban Me Thuot
• Da Lat

• Biên Hoa

KRATIE
• Kratie

Snuol

① ③

• Tay Ninh

Saigon ⊛

④

Mimot

KOMPONG CHAM

⑦

②②

SVAY
RIENG

Svay
Rieng

①

MEKONG R.

MEKONG
DELTA

Cần Thơ

④

KOMPONG THOM
• Kompong Thom

KOMPONG
CHAM
• Kompong
Cham

⑮

PREY
VIENG

Neak
Luong

Phnom Penh

⑥

⑦

BASSAC R.

• Takeo

TAKEO

②

• Hà Tiên

⑯

C A M B O D I A

⑥

⑳⑥

KOMPONG
CHHNANG

KOMPONG
SPEU

③

④

KAMPOT

PHU QUOC

TONLE
SAP

PURSAT

CARDAMOM MTS

KOH KONG

Sihanoukville
Kompong Som

• Ream

⑤

• Battambang

• Kampot

Sok Sann •

Mai Rut •

KOH TANG ◦

POULO WAI

OTHER BOOKS BY William Shawcross

Sideshow: Kissinger, Nixon and the Destruction of Cambodia

Watergate: The Full Inside Story (coauthor)

Crime and Compromise: Janos Kadar and the Politics of Hungary
Since Revolution

Dubcek

The QUALITY *of* MERCY

Cambodia, Holocaust and Modern Conscience

With a Report from Ethiopia

William Shawcross

A TOUCHSTONE BOOK
Published by Simon & Schuster, Inc.
NEW YORK

FOR
MICHAL

This Touchstone Edition, 1985
Published by Simon & Schuster, Inc.
Simon & Schuster Building
Rockefeller Center
1230 Avenue of the Americas
New York, New York 10020

TOUCHSTONE and colophon are registered trademarks of Simon & Schuster, Inc.

Designed by C. Linda Dingler

Manufactured in the United States of America

10 9 8 7 6 5 4 3 2 1
10 9 8 7 6 5 4 3 2 1 Pbk.

Library of Congress Cataloging in Publication Data

Shawcross, William
    The quality of mercy.

    Bibliography: p.
    Includes index.
    1. Kampuchea—History—1975. 2. Refugees—
Kampuchea. 3. Food relief—Kampuchea. 4. Political
atrocities—Kampuchea. I. Title.
DS554.8.S54   1984   959.6'04   84-1353
ISBN 0-671-44022-5
ISBN 0-671-60640-9 Pbk.

ঔঃ Contents

The quality of mercy is not strained,
It droppeth as the gentle rain from heaven
Upon the place beneath: it is twice blessed:
It blesseth him that gives, and him that takes.
'Tis mightiest in the mightiest, it becomes
The thronéd monarch better than his crown:
His sceptre shows the force of temporal power,
The attribute to awe and majesty,
Wherein doth sit the dread and fear of kings;
But mercy is above this sceptred sway,
It is enthronéd in the hearts of kings,
It is an attribute to God himself,
And earthly power doth then show likest God's
When mercy seasons justice.
                    —William Shakespeare
                    The Merchant of Venice

❧ Prologue

On the day after Leonid Brezhnev died the back page of *The New York Times* carried a huge advertisement that exulted, *"We told America about the death of President Brezhnev before most of Russia learned of it."* The advertisement was placed by Satellite News Channel and promised, *"Give us eighteen minutes. We'll give you the world."*

The flood of instant information in the world today—at least in the Western industrialized world—sometimes seems not to further, but to retard, education; not to excite, but to dampen, curiosity; not to enlighten, but merely to dismay. Archibald MacLeish once noted, "We are deluged with facts but we have lost or are losing our human ability to feel them."

MacLeish compared the speed and plethora of modern communications with the way in which the world learned of Napoleon's retreat from Moscow. The news was brought to New York by MacLeish's grandfather, months after the event. The story was carried on the front page, but its effectiveness derived from the one man's telling of it.

Similarly, I recall Admiral Nelson's own dispatch—carried in *The Times* of Wednesday, October 3, 1798—modestly and exquisitely announcing to the First Sea Lord his victory over the French at the battle of the Nile two months previously.

> My Lord, Almighty God has blessed His Majesty's arms in the late battle, by a great victory over the Fleet of the Enemy, whom I

attacked at sunset on the 1st of August, off the mouth of the Nile. The Enemy were moored in a strong line of battle for defending the entrance of the Bay [of Shoals], flanked by numerous gunboats, four frigates and a battery of guns and mortars on an island in their Van; but nothing could withstand the Squadron your lordship did me the honour to place under my command. Their high state of discipline is well known to you, and with the judgement of the captains, together with their valour and that of the officers and men of every description, it was absolutely irresistible. Could anything from my pen add to the character of the Captains I would write it with pleasure but it is impossible.

And that was all.

Today the battle of the Nile or the retreat from Moscow might have been covered live or at least endlessly commented upon as it took place—or it might have been almost ignored. Either way, covered or uncovered, it would soon have been superseded. The exiled Czech writer Milan Kundera pointed out, in *The Book of Laughter and Forgetting,* that "the bloody massacre in Bangladesh quickly covered the memory of the Russian invasion of Czechoslovakia; the assassination of Allende drowned out the groans of Bangladesh; the war in the Sinai desert made people forget Allende; the Cambodian massacre made people forget Sinai; and so on and so forth, until ultimately everyone lets everything be forgotten."

In Kundera's vision the destruction of memory is both the function and the aim of totalitarianism. He is correct—and for pointing it out the Czechoslovak *apparat* "forgot" him—he was deprived of his citizenship. But memory is being destroyed in democratic societies as well. Our sense of impotence seems to grow in direct proportion to the spread of our knowledge. And so, in self-protection, does our sense of indifference, or at least our ability to recall, to identify. Who among us is aware that between 1979 and 1982 six new wars began in the world and only two ended, four million people and forty-five nations were engaged in combat that killed unnumbered millions? And who among us, being aware, knows how to deploy that knowledge?

In 1981, during the week in which there were reports of eight thousand dead in an Iranian earthquake, newspapers and television around the West were consumed in reporting the attempts to reach a small boy who had fallen down a well in Southern Italy. The earthquake was another in the long litany of catastrophes, in which personal involvements were so hard to feel. With the child's solitary anguish millions identified. "It's nobody's fault," said his mother when rescue efforts failed through incompetence. "No government works."

Archibald MacLeish again: "We all know with the head now, by the facts, by the abstractions. . . . Why we are thus impotent, I do not know. I know only that this impotence exists and that it is dangerous, increasingly dangerous."

MacLeish believed that the endless accumulation of mere facts about the world was no way for men to master their experience of "this darkling earth." At the same time, however, there is an arbitrary and often capricious imbalance in our "accumulation of mere facts." Some areas of the world are bathed in the glare of publicity, from some there are only glimmers of light, and others are in total darkness.

The problem is older and wider and deeper than merely the plethora of today's communications. In his book *Language and Silence,* George Steiner wonders about the "time relation" of events. While Jews were being murdered in Treblinka "the overwhelming plurality of human beings, two miles away on Polish farms, 5,000 miles away in New York, were sleeping or eating or going to a film or making love or worrying about the dentist. This is where my imagination balks. The two orders of simultaneous experience are so different, so irreconcilable to any common norm of human values, their coexistence is so hideous a paradox—Treblinka is both because some men have built it, and almost all other men have let it be—that I puzzle over time. Are there, as science fiction and Gnostic speculation imply, different species of time in the same world, 'good times' and enveloping folds of inhuman time in which men fall into the slow hands of living damnation?"

It is one purpose of this book to ask how the inhabitants of "good" time do or do not relate to those incarcerated and often murdered in the "enveloping folds of inhuman time." Another is to examine the work of some of those humanitarian organizations that the world has created in an attempt to bind its self-inflicted wounds. And a third is to explore a little the extent to which the memory of the inaptly named *Holocaust* has affected our perception and our imagination when hearing distant cries for help.

To these ends I have chosen to look in particular at the world's reaction to the plight of Cambodia.* Other writers might have tried to explore the same themes in the context of another contemporary disaster. To this extent my choice is arbitrary; Cambodia happens to be a place in which I have been interested for a number of years. But I think Cambodia has an importance beyond itself, because there in its fragile heart paraded, throughout the 1970s, many of the most frightful beasts that now stalk the world. Brutal civil war, superpower intervention carelessly conducted from afar, nationalism exaggerated into paranoid racism, fanatical and vengeful revolution, invasion, starvation and back to unobserved civil war without end.

* I have generally used the names Cambodia and Cambodian, rather than the titles given it by its most recent governments, Democratic Kampuchea and The People's Republic of Kampuchea, or Kampuchean.

1 ⁂ In Phnom Penh

My earliest political memory, if "political" is an adequate word, is
preserved on fragile discs. They are 78-rpm recordings, and as a
child I was fascinated by them, because the voice was that of my father, speaking with both gravity and scarcely controlled emotion.
The terror of his words seized me. There was one record in particular to which I often listened; my father had written in ink across the
label the strange word "Dubno." For a long time I could not understand how or why my father should have seen such things.

On 5th October, 1942, when I visited the building office at Dubno,
my foreman told me that in the vicinity of the site Jews from
Dubno had been shot in three large pits, each about 30 metres long
and 3 metres deep. About fifteen hundred persons had been killed
daily. All of the five thousand Jews who had still been living in
Dubno before the pogrom were to be liquidated. As the shooting
had taken place in his presence, he was still much upset.

Thereupon I drove to the site, accompanied by my foreman,
and saw near it great mounds of earth, about 30 metres long and
2 metres high. Several trucks stood in front of the mounds. Armed
Ukrainian militia drove the people off the trucks under the supervision of an SS man. The militia men acted as guards on the trucks
and drove them to and from the pit. All these people had the regu-
lation yellow patches on the front and back of their clothes and thus
could be recognized as Jews.

My foreman and I went directly to the pits. Nobody bothered
us. Now I heard rifle shots in quick succession from behind one of

the earth mounds. The people who had got off the trucks—men, women and children of all ages—had to undress upon the orders of an SS man, who carried a riding or dog whip. They had to put down their clothes in fixed places, sorted according to shoes, top clothing and underclothing. I saw a heap of shoes of about 800 to 1,000 pairs, great piles of underlinen and clothing.

Without screaming or weeping, these people undressed, stood around in family groups, kissed each other, said farewells, and waited for a sign from another SS man, who stood near the pit, also with a whip in his hand. During the fifteen minutes that I stood near I heard no complaint or plea for mercy.

I watched a family of about eight persons—a man and a woman, both about fifty, with their children of about one, eight and ten, and two grown-up daughters of about twenty to twenty-four. An old woman with snow-white hair was holding the one-year child in her arms and singing to it and tickling it. The child was cooing with delight. The couple were looking on with tears in their eyes.

The father was holding the hand of a boy about ten years old and speaking to him softly; the boy was fighting his tears. The father pointed to the sky, stroked his head and seemed to explain something to him.

At that moment the SS man at the pit shouted something to his comrade. The latter counted off about twenty persons and instructed them to go behind the earth mound. Among them was the family which I have mentioned. I well remember a girl, slim and with black hair who, as she passed close to me pointed to herself and said, "Twenty-three."

I walked around the mound and found myself confronted by a tremendous grave. People were closely wedged together and lying on top of each other so that only their heads were visible. Nearly all had blood running over their shoulders from their heads. Some of the people were still moving. Some were lifting their arms and turning their heads to show that they were still alive. The pit was already two-thirds full. I estimated that it already contained about a thousand people.

I looked for the man who did the shooting. He was an SS man, who sat at the edge of the narrow end of the pit, his feet dangling into the pit. He had a tommy gun on his knees and was smoking a cigarette.

The people, completely naked, went down some steps which were cut in the clay wall of the pit and clambered over the heads of the people lying there, to the place to which the SS man directed them. They lay down in front of the dead or injured people; some caressed those who were still alive and spoke to them in a low voice. Then I heard a series of shots.

I looked into the pit and saw that the bodies were twitching or the heads lying motionless on top of the bodies which lay before them. Blood was running away from their necks. I was surprised that I was not ordered away, but I saw that there were two or three postmen in uniform nearby.

The next batch was approaching already. They went down into the pit, lined themselves up against the previous victims, and were shot.

When I walked back round the mound I noticed another truckload of people which had just arrived. This time it included sick and infirm persons. An old, very thin woman with terribly thin legs was undressed by others who were already naked, while two people held her up. The woman appeared to be paralyzed. The naked people carried the woman around the mound. I left with my foreman and drove my car back to Dubno.

On the morning of the next day, when I again visited the site, I saw about thirty naked people lying near the pit—about thirty to fifty metres away from it. Some of them were still alive; they looked straight in front of them with a fixed stare and seemed to notice neither the chilliness of the morning nor the workers of my firm who stood around.

A girl of about twenty spoke to me and asked me to give her clothes and help her escape. At that moment we heard a fast car approach and I noticed that it was an SS detail. I moved away to my site. Ten minutes later we heard shots from the vicinity of the pit. The Jews still alive had been ordered to throw the corpses into the pit; then they had themselves to lie down in this to be shot in the neck.

These words, these images, came from the diary of a German engineer, Herman Graebe.* They were part of the evidence produced by

---

*Herman Friedrich Graebe was manager of a branch of a German building firm in Sdolbumaw in the Ukraine, from September 1941 till January 1944. His firm had a contract from the Army Construction Office to erect the prosecution at the Nuremberg Trials. My father, the British Chief Prosecutor, was repeating them in his closing speech to the Tribunal. Eventually I understood that, and I realized thankfully that he had not been at Dubno to watch these terrible, casual killings himself. But throughout my childhood the horror of the place was a troubling refrain. I never expected and obviously never wished to see such sights myself. But in Cambodia I saw something of the kind.

After the Khmer Rouge Communists won power in Cambodia in April 1975, they immediately emptied the towns at gunpoint, expelled all Westerners, renamed the country Democratic Kampuchea, and closed it to almost all the world outside. Refugees began to come to the Thai-Cambodian border. They brought terrible stories of hardship, of disease, and of vicious, arbitrary mass murder.

The Vietnamese had originally backed the Khmer Rouge and, till 1978, they effectively denied the truth of the refugee stories, but relations between the two countries had deteriorated into open warfare, and at the very end of 1978 the Vietnamese invaded Cambodia. The Khmer Rouge apparat, including the party leader, Pol Pot, fled to the west of the country. The Vietnamese installed a new administration under a former Khmer Rouge officer named Heng Samrin, who had earlier defected to Vietnam. Several months later, in 1979, when Cambodia appeared to be on the edge of an appalling famine, the Vietnamese began to allow a few Western journalists and aid officials into the country. They saw a school in which the Khmer Rouge had imprisoned and tortured some of their victims—the Vietnamese had now arranged it as a museum—and they were shown mass graves into which victims of Khmer Rouge terror had been cast. "Echo of Auschwitz" declaimed the London *Daily Mirror*. A massive aid program was mounted by the United Nations and by private organizations throughout the Western world.

I applied for a visa to visit Cambodia myself. In the summer of 1980 a letter, typed on flimsy plain paper, arrived by sea mail from the Ministry of Foreign Affairs in Phnom Penh. It invited me to the country.

---

grain-storage buildings on the former airport at Dubno. Graebe frequently visited the building sites.

I flew to Bangkok and arranged a passage with the International Committee of the Red Cross (ICRC), whose cargo plane carrying relief supplies was the only flight from Thailand to Cambodia. Among the other people on the plane (a military Transall lent by the French government) were a burly Australian Red Cross courier, a Swiss pharmacist from the Red Cross, and a young American woman working for a small aid agency called Operation California.

The last time I had been in such a military aircraft was in South Vietnam. It belonged to the U.S. Air Force, and it carried pallets of ammunition to be dropped to a government enclave surrounded by Communist troops. This time similar pallets were carrying drugs, and the crew wore red crosses instead of military badges. On the flight deck there was bonhomie as the French pilots drank Thai Mekhong whisky and rum mixed with black coffee. They no doubt needed it, for they had been up since 2 A.M. and had already made one round-trip flight to Phnom Penh that day.*

The direct route due east from Bangkok to Phnom Penh takes only forty minutes' flying time. But for over a year now the Vietnamese, citing military security, had continually refused to allow the ICRC relief plane to fly over western Cambodia. Instead, the plane had to arc out south across the Gulf of Thailand, turn north over the delta of South Vietnam and then back west toward Phnom Penh. The flight took more than two hours; the additional cost in fuel—to say nothing of efficiency—was considerable. The Vietnamese were now also demanding $150,000 as payment for flying over southern Vietnam; the ICRC was resisting this. The Vietnamese had suggested that such problems might be resolved by direct discussions between the aviation authorities of Thailand and the Heng Samrin regime. But, since Thailand did not recognize that regime, the Thai government refused any direct contact. The relief program abounded in such political difficulties.

Eventually, the plane crossed over the frontier between Vietnam

---

* It was one of the ironies of this relief operation that the daily ICRC flight to Vietnamese-controlled Phnom Penh had been made on a succession of Western military planes lent for the purpose. One of the crews was from Air Alaska; they had previously been with the U.S. Air Force, and had flown in B-52s over Indochina. They knew the terrain well.

and Cambodia at the Parrot's Beak, a piece of Cambodian land that juts into Vietnam only thirty-five miles from Saigon. As we began to descend we could see craters left by bombs from B-52s and other airplanes, white against the green soil. The plane came down along the Mekong river; it was in flood from the monsoon rains and covered thousands of acres of land with its brown and fertile silt.

I was nervous. I was about to land in a country in which I had been peripherally involved, as a writer, for a number of years—a country that seemed to have been cast into the outer reaches of hell and only barely retrieved. Now I was to meet some of the people who had endured, in all its agony, the disaster about which I had been writing from afar. That was chastening, even awesome. We flew over a corner of the town, close to the gilded Royal Palace, and landed in a sudden sharp squall of rain. The plane was boarded by a smiling Cambodian soldier who took our passports.

Usually foreigners were met at the airport by a guide from the ministry concerned with them. There was no one from the Foreign Ministry to meet me. But, to my surprise, standing at the steps was a young American in a smart black safari suit. He strode forward to greet his compatriot. He was the head of her relief agency, Operation California.

"They've just discovered another mass grave," he called. "Shall we go see?"

I drove into town in the Volkswagen minibus of the ICRC. On our way we stopped to leave plasma and drugs from the plane at the Seventh of January Hospital, named after the day in 1979 on which the Vietnamese army reached Phnom Penh. This was the former Chinese Hospital; in April 1975 it had been a place of terrible squalor, crammed with wounded and dying soldiers and civilians for whom there had been almost no drugs and no care in the last months of the war. The Khmer Rouge had burst in, as into all the other hospitals, and forced people at gunpoint to take up their beds and walk.

In power, the Khmer Rouge had banned Western drugs and had smashed equipment, while doctors and nurses, like all educated people, risked execution. Since their invasion of January 1979, the Vietnamese had sent their own medical teams, but had allowed only a handful of other medical teams, all from the Soviet bloc, into the country. Now the hospital was just about functioning again, but throughout the country there was still a terrible shortage of medical personnel as well as of drugs and equipment.

The road became more crowded as we approached the town center. Most people were on foot; some were cycling; others were riding in new Japanese and British trucks bearing the emblem of UNICEF or Oxfam. Outside the Hotel Monorom, which had recently been reopened, there were people selling cigarettes. I was welcomed warmly by the woman running the hotel, Madame Sophan; in another time she had been trained as a hotelier in Strasbourg. She had spent the Khmer Rouge years trying to conceal this fact as she worked in the fields.

My guide from the Foreign Ministry finally arrived. Sam Peng, a slight, nervous man, had been a teacher before the war and the revolution. He too had spent the Khmer Rouge years in the fields, in terror lest his past be discovered. He telephoned the press section at the Foreign Ministry to ask permission to take me to see the mass grave. It was granted, and we set off in a little Russian Lada car after the group from California.

The road out of town was crowded with peasants carrying firewood to sell in Phnom Penh. The graves were in fields beyond a village just outside the city. The driver turned left off the road and up a track by the village; he parked the car under a large tree and lit a cigarette. Sam Peng and I climbed out and were at once surrounded by laughing children who, knowing what we had come to see, scampered ahead of us along a damp path that wound through fields and scrubby trees.

We came to the pits. About six had been excavated; there were, said the villagers, many, many more. The remains had been carefully arranged in a shocking open-air exhibition. Several hundred skulls had been neatly piled together. Femurs and limbs were in separate piles. Many of the wrists were still bound together with cord or wire, as they had been when the people were forced to kneel on the edge of the pits while Khmer Rouge soldiers clubbed them in the back of the neck. Many of the skulls were blindfolded.

These murders had apparently taken place at the very end of 1978 as the Vietnamese swept in from the east to expel the Khmer

Rouge. Flesh still clung to the hip joints and its terrible sweet-sour smell hung over the fields, so thick as to be almost a pall.

The people from Operation California were taking many photographs of the scene and, rather guiltily, I did so too, stepping gingerly around the muddy graves. Later I discovered that such was my nervousness, I had forgotten to put film into the camera.

The head of the village committee came to talk to us. His name was Lap Kuon; he was thirty-two. Until 1975 he had been a student. Under the Khmer Rouge he had worked in the fields. Now he was concerned about food supplies for the village. When I asked him why the Khmer Rouge had killed all these people, he replied: "It's Maoism. Pol Pot was acting on orders from China, which wanted to destroy Kampucheans and replace them with Chinese." This, a Vietnamese propaganda explanation of the Khmer Rouge terror, was one I was to hear often in Cambodia.

As we drove back to Phnom Penh I sat silent, shaken, in the back of the car. I was reminded of the long-ago story of Dubno, and I could only think of the arbitrary and the awful way in which the world is at all times divided into contiguous layers of war, peace, misery and joy.

That evening I had supper on the sixth floor of the Monorom Hotel, which had been an empty shell in an empty city while the people whose bodies I had just seen were being clubbed to death a few miles away. Now Madame Sophan had already managed to create a rather fine establishment. The menu was neatly typed on cards; we ate pork and potatoes and drank Vietnamese beer. Afterward I set off along Phnom Penh's main street, Monivong Boulevard, for the other hotel, where most of the international aid personnel were quartered.

There was no street lighting; Phnom Penh's electricity was still erratic and as yet supplied little more than the hotels and a few government offices. But the area outside the hotel was lighted by dozens of candles burning on tiny stalls at which people were offering single cigarettes or single slivers of grapefruit for sale. The candles were protected in glass jars and threw flickering shadows on the faces of the vendors, who smiled and laughed as they saw me.

Outside the railway station, dozens of "cyclopousse" drivers slept on their rickety bicycle rickshaws as they awaited the train. The station, built under French rule in the 1930s, towered above them, imposing if not beautiful. The railway system had virtually collapsed during the 1970–75 war. Now trains were running, if irregularly, to Kompong Som, the country's only deep-water port, where both the international relief agencies and ships from the Soviet bloc were unloading relief supplies. There was another line to Battambang, the largest town in the west of the country. Trains returned from there crowded with traders bringing scarce consumer goods—cloth, soap, cigarettes, pins, sugar, nails, bicycles, fishhooks—acquired on the black market at the Thai border. It was for these traders that the cyclopousse drivers waited patiently, sometimes for days.

Beyond the station were dilapidated homes in which people seemed to be camping rather than living. Families had hammocks strung between the pillars of the houses, food was being cooked over little fires on the pavement, small children scampered around naked, playing on bits of old furniture which had been cast out of the homes and taken no further. A large dilapidated building with flaking red stucco had been the country's principal medical school; its few personnel were now trying to restore some order to the country's shattered medical services.

A little farther on, I came to an open space the size of a football field. It was quite empty and there was nothing to suggest that anything had ever been there. But, in fact, until 1975 the Roman Catholic cathedral, built by the French in the 1930s, had stood here. The Khmer Rouge had had the entire cathedral razed and every stone carted away. Article 20 of their constitution, promulgated in 1976, declared: "Every Cambodian has the right to worship according to any religion. Reactionary religion, which is detrimental to Democratic Kampuchea and the people of Kampuchea, is absolutely forbidden."

More important to the people than the razing of the cathedral and the destruction of other Catholic churches in Phnom Penh was the organized assault upon Buddhism that this article justified. For centuries Buddhism had been the glue which, together with the monarchy, held Cambodian society together. All over the countryside the Khmer Rouge expelled bonzes from their wats, smashed the Buddhist images and turned the wats into stores. Many bonzes were killed; all others were forced to exchange their saffron for black cloth and were forced to work like everyone else in the fields.

Leading off from where the cathedral had stood was a tree-lined avenue that went to Le Phnom, the tree-covered hillock from which the city takes its name. On this avenue stands the country's main hotel, a splendid crenellated building which has known as many recent lives as Cambodia itself. Built by the French in the thirties for their *colons* and *stagiaires,* it was known as Le Royal. In the relatively fortunate 1950s and 1960s, when Prince Sihanouk kept most of his country out of Vietnam's growing war, it was Cambodia's most gracious inn, where tourists and French planters supped on Chablis and fabulous fish from the Mekong river and the Great Lake. After 1970, when Sihanouk was overthrown by his Prime Minister, General Lon Nol, a republic was declared and the hotel was renamed Le Phnom. I went there in late 1970; the food was still marvelous, but the tourists had begun to go to Bali instead of Cambodia. As the war spread like a stain across the land, the hotel became home to Western war correspondents who filled its rooms with typewriters, cameras, whisky and illusions, and drove every day in rented Mercedes to bloody battles.

Under the Khmer Rouge the hotel remained for the most part empty. In 1979, the hotel was renamed the Samaki—"Solidarity" (with Vietnam)—and was opened just before the first international aid officials arrived that summer.

By now, they had made the bare rooms quite comfortable for themselves and their files, but the corridors and halls of the Samaki that first night seemed empty, dim and echoing. In a glass case by the front door stood a small stuffed dog, its teeth bared. Many of the people I wished to see were in a meeting, but upstairs a young man from Oxfam–America offered me a beer and said he was worried that flooding might lead to serious losses in this year's rice harvest.

As I walked back to the Monorom a large truck drew noisily up beside me. Two Cambodians looked down from the high cab. One of them asked me, in French, if I wanted to go for a ride. I said, Why not, and climbed in. The man sitting next to me seemed to be about thirty-five; he had the sort of black cowboy hat that Cambodians often wear, and not too many teeth. He would like to visit me at my hotel, he said, but the Vietnamese would arrest him—no Cambodian was supposed to talk to foreigners without permission. I had the impression that he did not care greatly for the Vietnamese. "People should only come to a country if they are invited by the foreign ministry, like you," he said.

He was the boss of a gang of workmen repairing a warehouse, he said. There were some Russians there. A Russian had given him a badge—it was of Lenin—and this was a Russian truck. But it was no good; it did only one kilometer to the liter—not like the Japanese machines.

By this time we were far from the center of town; the streets did not even have the glimmer of camp fires. I confess I found it a little uncomfortable. Who were these men, and why were they putting themselves at risk by entertaining a foreigner in their truck? Eventually I suggested that we return to the hotel. They agreed at once, and we splashed through the stinking refuse of a large street market where huge rats jumped out of old straw baskets and garbage before the loom of our lights. After warm handshakes they dropped me off in front of the Monorom; the guard was dozing in a deck chair and took no notice.

My room was hot and airless. I turned on the creaking ceiling fan and opened the window. From the street below came the mingled smells of dung and wood smoke. A train whistled in the dark, and I wondered whether the long wait of the cyclopousse drivers had finally been rewarded. It was then that I noticed that my shoes were caked with mud from the mass graves outside Phnom Penh. Horrified, I tried to scrape and rub it off without actually touching it, but there was no water in the tap. So I covered the mud with shoe polish. When I finally fell asleep on my first night in this terrifying place, I was pursued by dreams in which the mud from my shoes seemed to be caking the entire room.

2 ⁋ In Cambodia

At breakfast my first morning in Phnom Penh—coffee, papaya and omelet—one of the waiters in the Hotel Monorom stopped to talk about his life in recent years. He said that until the Khmer Rouge victory in 1975 he had worked at the airport. The Khmer Rouge had sent him and his family south to Takeo. He had been dispatched into the forests on a woodcutting detail, and twelve of the thirty members of the team had died of fever.

Their trips into the forest lasted two or three months at a time. While there they were guarded by the "base people"—the uneducated peasants who had been the Khmer Rouge's most dependable forces; these were not armed, but they reported anyone with whom they were dissatisfied to the Khmer Rouge cadres, the *Angkar,* or organization, on their return to the village. The worst period of killings was 1978, when cadres from another region of the country were sent to take over his area. Previously it had been controlled by cadres from the Northwest—"They killed only an average number of people. But the cadres from the Southwest killed all over the place." He said that he saw the Southwestern leader Ta Mok—who was one of the most ruthless of the Khmer Rouge leaders and who was still, in 1980, one of Pol Pot's principal aides—drive up in a car. "He watched us work. People whose oxen were in poor shape were bashed in."

Another waiter, who had been deported to the west of the country from Phnom Penh in 1975, said that for the "new people"—as those expelled from the towns in 1975 were called—food was terribly short in 1976 and 1977. No one was allowed to forage in the abundant countryside; cadres distributed food. "Ten people would have just one small tin of rice. We looked for crabs in the forest, but if anyone was caught he would have his fingers cut off. We were not allowed to take fruit from the trees; you could be killed for that. Each year became worse. By 1978 they were killing base people as well as new people."

When Vietnam invaded at the end of 1978, "we did not know what was happening. Pol Pot forced us into the mountains and forests. I spent four months there. It was a death place." One or two Khmer Rouge were killed in revenge by women with their bare hands. He and some friends managed to make an old radio work by saving batteries thrown away by the Khmer Rouge and using salt to give them some power; they learned that Vietnam was now in control of Phnom Penh.

Finally, he escaped from the mountains and made his way to the capital. He too was lucky; his wife and children, who had been in a mobile work brigade, had also survived. He sold fish and noodles in the market till December 1979 and then was taken on the hotel staff. "The truth is even stranger than when I just say it. Everyone in Cambodia has this sort of experience. It's not because they like things now that they say these things of Pol Pot, but because of their experiences. It's all so clear, but one cannot even talk about it or explain it in words. Anything bad you write about Pol Pot will be true," he said to me. I asked why it had happened, and he replied, "Pol Pot wanted to kill the people, especially the new people. They had no other idea." For these waiters, as for almost everyone else, the Vietnamese invasion had been a true liberation.

When my guide arrived, he announced that we would go this morning to Kompong Speu, a town only about twenty miles down the road to Kompong Som, Cambodia's only deep-water port. I might, he said, be able to see a food distribution and thus witness the excellent way in which the government was getting international food aid to the peasants.

We threaded our way through the little horses and carts bringing wood and vegetables into the town, and then sped on down Route 4. It had been constructed by the United States in the 1950s, before the growing pressures of the Vietnam war had led Prince Sihanouk to denounce United States aid and to break relations with Washington. It had been built well and was now the country's only road in reasonable condition.

We passed several convoys of new Japanese and British trucks bearing the emblems of UNICEF and Oxfam respectively. By now UNICEF had provided more than a thousand trucks, and Oxfam nearly two hundred. Some were coming from Kompong Som laden with sacks of rice. Others were returning empty. Some were clearly being used as buses and were crowded with both civilians and soldiers, who grinned and waved as we overtook them. Along the side of the road, Vietnamese soldiers squatted quietly on their haunches. Most of the little villages through which we passed had small stalls in which fruit was sold.

The town of Kompong Speu was almost invisible. It had been obliterated during the 1970–75 war, particularly in the fierce final battles between the Khmer Rouge and General Lon Nol's retreating child soldiers, who fought with extraordinary bravery in the first three months of 1975. The town had been left almost empty after the Khmer Rouge victory, and since then the forest had grown up to reclaim the bourgeois villas, rather as it had reclaimed the temples of Angkor Wat after the collapse of the great Angkorian dynasty in the middle ages. There was almost no one to be seen. At one crossroads we came upon a family selling cigarettes and loaves of French bread. I reached into my bag and blew up a balloon for a four-year-old child; he was astonished.

We drove out of the ruins along a cart track and then walked deeper into the woods. We were going to another mass grave, which had been excavated some months ago. There was no smell here; the neat piles of bones, carefully arranged for photographers, were bleached white by the sun, grass was overgrowing them. We walked past the grave to a clearing in which a few bamboo huts had recently been built and where an old schoolhouse remained. Children were playing with tin cans, a group of women were preparing rice. I climbed a long stone staircase to the temple behind the village clearing. The heads had been knocked off all the Buddha images inside the wat, and an attempt had been made to scrape some of the religious paintings off the stonework.

In the temple an articulate young man who was now the teacher in a nearby village school spoke of how Pol Pot had arrested his father for eating a piece of sugar palm outside of communal meal time. As punishment he was forced to work in a mine field. He was blown up.

On the way back to the car we talked with a young peasant couple who were happily carrying their tiny new daughter home in their ox cart. Farther on we came across a convoy of about six ox carts, each one carrying a sack of United Nations fertilizer, which the peasants had just been given by local officials. They were smoking leaves and eagerly took the cigarettes I offered.

By now my guide was impatient; he wanted to get back to Phnom Penh in time for me to take him and the driver to lunch at the Samaki Hotel. We drove quickly back to the city. To my astonishment the hotel offered a four-course meal. The menu was folded into a large card that turned out to be an invitation to a party given by a U.S. Embassy aid official in 1963. While Frank Sinatra sang from a cassette recorder, my guide and driver attacked tomato salad, tinned paté, fish, roast beef and vegetables with the determination of men who had, for years, known deprivation.

At other tables were men and women from many of the aid agencies—Europeans, Indians, Latin Americans, from UNICEF, the Food and Agriculture Organization, World Food Program, World Council of Churches, Oxfam, and many more. They ate here for the convenience—the food was bad as well as overabundant. The only aid officials not in the dining room were the Swiss from the International Committee of the Red Cross; they had their own supplies, along with drugs and plasma, flown in from Bangkok, and almost always they ate in their office upstairs.

Most of Cambodia's roads now lie across the land like ribbons crumpled by an angry child. I traveled south to Kampot; it was just eighty miles away, and the journey took us nine hours, crawling around ditches, potholes, rubble, and poorly filled trenches cut across the roads by one of the many armies that had fought along them in the last ten years. Every town along the road had been blasted away by war; in place of concrete homes and wooden-stilted houses were only shacks and wrecked buildings in which people were attempting somehow to reorder their lives.

Much of the history of the decade lay along that road. The carcasses of American trucks and armored personnel carriers, supplied to General Lon Nol during the 1970–75 war; bomb craters filled with stagnant water and mosquitoes; twisted remains of concrete bridges with Bailey bridges flung haphazardly across them; grandiose canals and embankments constructed by the Khmer Rouge with slave labor; relics of towns and villages, some almost all gone, others half standing like roughly cut stubble in a plowed field.

In the wreckage of the town of Tram Khnar we happened on a distribution of rice donated by Japan. The man in charge was worried that this year might be worse than last, because they did not have enough seed and there was not enough rain.

Two smashed and open shops had been made into a primitive infirmary; people lay within listless and with little care. A woman rushed forward in the hope that I was a foreign doctor and could help a relative suffering a hugely swollen jaw for months without attention. The hospital director showed me upstairs a crate of drugs and equipment that he had received from the ICRC; they were still very short of beds and drugs and equipment, he said. Malaria was a problem—people often contracted it when they went into the hills to collect firewood to sell in Phnom Penh.

On we went, carefully crawling over decrepit bridges, through the onetime town of Ang Tasom. Here boys were selling sarongs that had been bought in the black market on the Thai border. The government had distributed food only once in the whole year, said villagers.

Kampot was described in a 1966 Shell Guide, which I found in the market in Phnom Penh, as "a pleasant small town on the Tuk Chhou river . . . When you have gone over the bridge, turn right and go up a narrow road across a lot of little bridges and you will come to a delightful picnic spot on the river; the fishing is good there, and little boys stand on the rocky waterfalls ready to grab the fish as they leap across. There are four cinemas in Kampot, and some lovely old houses covered with bougainvillea along the shady, flower-lined riverside road."

Now most such scenes were only memory. Half the town was in ruins. The hospital still stood, its one hundred beds filled with almost two hundred patients. There were ten trainee nurses, but not a single doctor. The operating theater was spotless but bare. The nurse in charge gave me a list of drugs and equipment he needed; back in Phnom Penh I handed it to Dominique Dufour of the ICRC, who took it with a sigh and a promise to do what he could.

In the archaic textile factory an old man named Kau Nhep told me that he had been a technician here in the Lon Nol years and he spent his time under Pol Pot in the fields. Somehow he had managed to get fifteen of the 69 looms in the plant working—for the few hours every evening that the town had electricity. Did I know Oxfam? he asked. An Oxfam man had come months ago, promising to help restore more machinery, but he had heard nothing since. He hoped the Oxfam man would be back.

I was taken for the night to the government guesthouse, a fine villa that had survived the last ten years; I learned, without pleasure, that until 1979 it had been used as the home of provincial Khmer Rouge dignitaries. Unlike the hospital, the place had many mosquito nets, and an excellent, large meal was cooked for me, my driver, my guide and two young men from Phnom Penh who had been sent to organize unions in the local administration. In the dusk, the town's loudspeakers were playing the new national anthem. Like that of the Khmer Rouge, it demanded a fierce resistance to the destruction that was a traditional Cambodian fear:

> The people of Kampuchea make up a resolute force,
> determined to destroy the enemy.
> We draw our strength from our unity and stand ready
> to shed our blood for victory.
> The Kampuchean army marches valiantly forward, setting
> adversity at defiance,
> To destroy the despots who threaten our people
> with extermination
> And bring prosperity to the heroic Kampuchean people!

The Kampuchean people, fighting stubbornly will make
the enemy pay his debt of blood!
The blood-red flag with the towers is raised and
will lead the nation to happiness and prosperity.

This is the official translation, but I doubted, as I heard the rendering
fill the soft night sky of Kampot, whether the actual Khmer words
would have rendered it more lyrical.*

Eventually, just as the town's generator was dying at 9 P.M., the Governor of Kampot came to see me. He was a former teacher, he said; he had been in the fields under Pol Pot and had fled to Vietnam in 1977. In July 1978 he had been set to work helping to form an army from the Cambodian refugees in Vietnam. He fought in the liberation.

He said that he had left his wife and children behind when he fled; he feared they were now dead. I said that I hoped this was not so. Perhaps I should not have said this, for he became rather angry. "Do you believe Pol Pot killed people or not?" he asked through an interpreter. "Of course," I replied, and once more I asked, "Why did the Khmer Rouge happen?"

He replied, "Pol Pot's principle was to kill intellectuals and students, also merchants, also members of the Sihanouk and Lon Nol administrations and technicians, also foreigners, monks, upper workers, soldiers."

"But why?" I asked.

"Because Pol Pot sold the country to China," came the reply.

"But I was told that China wanted Khmer soldiers to kill the Vietnamese," I said.

"Pol Pot killed all those who opposed him," came the reply.

* The Khmer Rouge anthem contained the words,

"Bright red blood which covers our fields and plains,
Of Kampuchea, our motherland!
Sublime blood of workers and peasants,
Sublime blood of revolutionary men and women fighters!
The Blood changing into unrelenting hatred
And resolute struggle,
On April 17th, under the flag of the Revolution,
Free from Slavery!"

"What does selling Kampuchea to the Chinese really mean?" I asked.

"During Pol Pot there was a Chinese presence in Kampuchea. They wouldn't even drink our water—only in cocoa—because they knew there were corpses in the wells. I saw them at Prey Nop, while I was a peasant and I saw them drinking only cocoa."

Government propaganda seemed intent on establishing that the crime of the Khmer Rouge was "genocide" and that the criminal was Pol Pot, acting on Chinese orders. People rarely blamed either their individual suffering or that of the country on "the Khmer Rouge," never on "the Communists." Instead, a single demonic Chinese agent, or at best a small gang, was responsible for all the horror. "Pol Pot killed my father" or "When Pol Pot sent me into the fields" was how people recalled their lives.

The reasons seemed clear. If the crime was indeed "genocide," then there could not be much room for argument. In the world today, particularly in the Western world, the term arouses instant dread and guilt. And if, at the same time, it was the work of one maniac under alien control, then the system that the Vietnamese and the Khmer Rouge shared, Marxist-Leninism, could be exonerated—even while the *révanchisme* of Vietnam's old enemy, China, was excoriated.

"China's plan was to have the Cambodians and the Vietnamese die fighting each other; then when we were weak they would take over all Indochina," another official told me.

"That was what the Americans used to say that China wanted in the sixties," I reminded him. "Then the Americans were right," he replied.

On another trip out of Phnom Penh I went to the eastern province of Kompong Cham, where much of the most bloody history of the past ten years had been enacted. My thought was to go to one small village near the Vietnamese border and talk to people about all that had happened—about the way in which the Vietnamese Communists had usurped sanctuaries to escape American troops in South Vietnam; about the American bombing of those sanctuaries which had begun in 1969; about the spread of the war after the overthrow of Prince Sihanouk in March 1970 and the American invasion that followed it; about the increase in the fighting and the growing cruelty of the growing Khmer Rouge; about life after the Khmer Rouge victory in 1975; and about the terrible famine that we in the West were persuaded was racking Cambodia in 1979.

I set off with a different guide and driver and with Ben Kiernan, a Cambodian-speaking academic from Australia. During the first two and a half years of Khmer Rouge rule Kiernan had publicly cast much doubt on the refugees' horror stories. He changed his mind in 1978 and, unlike many apologists, had publicly acknowledged his mistake. Now the Heng Samrin government had given him and his Cambodian wife permission to stay several months in the country to research the history of the Khmer Rouge. He was a fine traveling companion.

Villagers along the scarred road to Kompong Cham said mournfully that hundreds of hectares of the new rice crop planted with seed provided by the international relief program had been swept away by floods. They were also suffering a plague of rats; the poison sent by the West was not strong enough.

At one point the Vietnamese had provided a small ferry to take vehicles over the flooded rice fields to bypass a huge break in the road. But the waters were receding, and the ferry could carry only one truck and a couple of cars at a time. So only about fifteen trucks a day were passing along Cambodia's main road to the north and east.

Our little Lada shared this makeshift ferry with an ancient Chinese truck and a brand-new Mercedes. This belonged to the Polish ambassador, a suave and clever man, who declared that he was the author of several books, one on the Treaty of Rapallo and another on Lithuania. He had been in Cambodia in 1954, just after Sihanouk won independence from France, as part of the Polish contingent to the ill-fated International Control Commission, which had been set up by the Geneva Conference on Indochina and was supposed to supervise Cambodia's neutrality. He did not tell me why he was now traveling to Kompong Cham, but I learned later that it was to discipline the Polish medical team working under the auspices of the ICRC. Its members had made no secret of their fear and loathing of the Cambodians; the ambassador was supposed to persuade them to be more pleasant and to work harder.

After the ferry our guide produced from under the seat an M-16 rifle and hung out of the window brandishing it: "Pol Pot," he said reassuringly. We came to a crossroads where a few bamboo shacks were grouped. Back in the sixties this had been the bustling little market town of Skoun. In the 1970–75 war it had been constantly fought over, bombed and shelled. Now the concrete houses were all gone; one would hardly know they had ever existed.

Kompong Cham, the capital of eastern Cambodia, had hardly fared any better. There was now a thriving market offering for sale pots and pans from Vietnam, sarongs, soap, bicycle parts, batteries, toothpaste. But half the town lay in wreckage, and much of the rest had simply been swallowed up by the encroaching forest. It had been savaged by war continually through the last decade. In 1970, when people here heard of the overthrow of Prince Sihanouk by General Lon Nol, they had seized Lon Nol's brother, torn out his liver, cooked it and passed the morsels around. Hundreds marched on Phnom Penh to protest the coup. Lon Nol troops shot at them; we met several men who had then immediately left for the jungles to join the infant Khmer Rouge.

We went to see the governor, Preap Pichey. He had been a Communist since the 1950s. Back in the sixties his allegiance was still secret and he worked as a teacher. After Sihanouk's overthrow, he said, he became an "information cadre" in the Khmer Rouge. "My job was to educate the people to like the revolution, to fight the U.S.A. and Lon Nol." Asked how successful he had been and what effect the war had had on the Khmer Rouge revolution, he replied, "People hated the Americans and Lon Nol. The Khmer Rouge had to win, because the people were so angry. Their homes and buffalo were destroyed. And the Americans were living in America all the time, ten thousand kilometers away. That created more anger. Why did they have to come and do that? Most people joined our army after 1970. If an elder son was killed in bombing then a younger son joined the army. If all sons, then the father."

The Governor would allow us to go only a few miles farther east, not to the border. The ferry across the Mekong was pulled by a UNICEF tug. On board were traders with their bicycles, children selling grilled shrimps and pineapple slices, young Vietnamese soldiers in a UNICEF truck, and a couple of ancient Cambodian army trucks laden with food, including cans of Oxfam edible oil, apparently bound for a Cambodian army camp. On the other side, the road was only a track. Beside it stilts of spacious old houses stuck into the sky; the houses were gone, and people squatted in straw huts along the muddy road.

By contrast the Khmer Rouge Eastern Zone headquarters in the rubber-plantation town of Suong—now taken over by Heng Samrin officials—was palatial, with fine, classical lines and excellent carpentry.

We were met by local officials, who gave us a huge lunch, at which many kilos of rice, bowls of fish soup, fried chicken, green vegetables and pineapple slices were consumed. The district chief, a man called Mon, exuded menace. Like the governor of Kompong Cham he had been a Khmer Rouge cadre until shortly before the Vietnamese invasion. Indeed, he had been a subdistrict chief in this very same area.

The Heng Samrin regime was made up in part of Communists who had long been loyal to, and often lived in, Hanoi, in part of non-Communists who had survived under the Khmer Rouge (almost no non-Communist Cambodians had been able to return from exile in the west), and in part of former Khmer Rouge. Some of these had defected to Vietnam in 1977, others only a few weeks before the Vietnamese invasion at the end of 1978, and some had even been "turned around" after the invasion. Not all Khmer Rouge cadres were equally responsible for the massacres that had taken place; it was evident that some areas and some periods had been far more brutal than others. But the Vietnamese had conducted very little "de-Nazification" of Cambodia. This, it seemed, was another reason for concentrating all responsibility for the Khmer Rouge crimes on the personality of Pol Pot himself.

When I asked Mr. Mon what he knew of the mass murders, he said that he knew nothing. "When people were taken away we were told they were going to study," he said. "Who took them away?" I asked. "Security cadres from the Central Zone," replied Mr. Mon, as he took another large helping of rice and chicken.

After lunch we went to see a mass grave in the Chup rubber plantation, which had been heavily bombed by the U.S. Air Force during the 1970–75 war. As we were led by soldiers in single file into the trees, it occurred to me that we must have looked like those who were taken—such a very short time ago—to be murdered here. As elsewhere, people had been cast into B-52 bomb craters. To see the skulls and the femurs and the clothing lying discarded in the craters under the quiet nave formed by the silver-pillar trees was to contemplate a fantastic and terrible marriage of destructive forces.

The suffering of the Cambodians and the courage with which they were trying to rebuild something of their lives were constantly moving. It was clear that there were now many more women than men (according to some estimates 65 percent of the population were women). Many men had several wives, and a baby boom was taking place. Once I came around a corner in Phnom Penh, and there, standing on the curb, was a young woman. One hand was on her brow in perplexity and concern. In the other, she cradled a newborn infant which looked far too tiny to live. I gave her all the money I had on me, which was not much, and she burst into laughter. I was afraid it would not help her or her child for long.

On another occasion, I was walking toward the Samaki Hotel in the midday sun. The street was deserted when an old man, dressed poorly, drove his pedicab over to talk quietly under a tree. His hair was gray, his face was lined, and he looked at least sixty-five. He said he was forty-nine. He had been a schoolmaster in the sixties, he said. Under Pol Pot, of course, he had worked in the fields, and when the Vietnamese came he tried to go back to teaching. "But I stopped after eight months, Monsieur, because I love liberty and it is not possible now . . ." His voice trailed off.

"My son is twenty-seven and he is in the government," he said. "He and I don't talk to each other. We have different routes. Sihanouk, Lon Nol, Pol Pot, Heng Samrin, I like none of them. But whoever gives me liberty is my father. I want just to be a poet, Monsieur. I write secretly." And then he smiled, adjusted his hat and cycled away. I, a free man in his country, was able to go into the Samaki Hotel and drink a beer with UNICEF's Russian staff member, whom everyone took to be KGB.

In the Phnom Penh market I bought a sarong and some incense. The stall keeper wrapped my sarong in paper covered in typing. When I opened it I discovered that she had used files from the Ministry of Justice in Sihanouk's day; she had a whole pile of them. The incense was more brightly wrapped—in bank notes of the Lon Nol era, stuck together to make bags.

My driver told me how greetings had changed with regimes. Under Sihanouk, people would say to friends they had not seen for some time, "How many children have you?"; under Lon Nol, "Are you in good health?"; under the Khmer Rouge, "How much food do you get in your cooperative?"; under Heng Samrin, "How many of your family are still alive?"

Once, on a trip out of Phnom Penh, we set off in an old hulk, guarded by several heavily armed militia men, from the wreckage of what was once the market town of Kompong Trabek. Our destination was the island village of Peam Montea, close to the Vietnamese border, part of the country that the Communists had always controlled and that was frequently bombed by United States, South Vietnamese and Cambodian warplanes during the war.

Today happened to be a feast day, and as we approached the island several long canoes, each with a crew of about twenty paddlers, and with men in lurid wooden masks standing in the prow, shot out to greet us. They came alongside and stood up, waving their paddles and cheering. Our boat steamed into the mud and we waded ashore through a huge crowd of people clapping and smiling. We were the first foreigners, bar Vietnamese, to have been there for at least a decade.

The village resembled the one attacked by American helicopter gunships blaring "The Ride of the Valkyries" in the film *Apocalypse Now*. Indeed, an old woman to whom we talked spoke of the way in which the helicopters would come roaring up the river below the level of the palms to rake the village with fire. (Throughout the countryside I was astonished by the detail with which people recalled the bombing. They remembered not only when they were attacked, but also the sorts of planes that had attacked them. Frequently we were told that the bombing had driven people to support the Khmer Rouge in the early seventies.) But mostly, she wanted to talk about Khmer Rouge rule from 1975 to 1978. Stretching up her hands and crying, she described how her three sons had been murdered. The

Khmer Rouge soldier who had killed them was still living nearby. He had not been punished. She wished someone would kill him too.

After lunch we joined in the boat races. Five times we paddled to a bend in the river, turned and then raced down, with the coxes and the coaches shouting *"Muoi Yo"* ("One More") as we stabbed the water with the thick staves which served as paddles. After each exhausting race, we turned back upstream to a bend in the river where the water met the low and level rice fields that stretched out of sight, green with the hope of harvest. There we would turn, stabbing the water once more, each stroke prodding the old boat forward with a leap.

After the races, we motored back up the river as lightning began to tear the evening sky. Eventually, after several breakdowns, we reached Kompong Trabek, and our driver insisted that we rush back through the early night to Phnom Penh. At the Samaki Hotel, the aid officials were having a party. Members of the Russian medical team were being thrown into the swimming pool, and the Swiss secretary from the ICRC was gently persuading a Vietnamese soldier who was bemusedly watching these proceedings to dance with her.

I told my guide that I wanted to see Tuol Sleng. This was the former Phnom Penh high school, which the Khmer Rouge had converted into a prison and interrogation center, and the Vietnamese had now made into a museum. He told me I needed the permission of both the Foreign Ministry, which had approved my visa, and the Information Ministry, which ran the museum.

The Foreign Ministry was housed in what was formerly the Buddhist Institute. I waited in a bare reception room until I was joined by a young man named Chum Bun Rong, the head of the press department. Mr. Bun Rong was charming and helpful. Of course I could visit Tuol Sleng, he said. We drove to the Ministry of Information, where my guide disappeared and came back with written permission.

We set off down Monivong Boulevard, the broad central avenue designed by Sihanouk and named after one of Cambodia's kings. Here too people appeared to have installed themselves only temporarily in the houses and old shops. It was as if, after all the forced movement and mayhem of the last ten years, no one was now willing to trust any arrangement, any home, to be permanent. In the side roads there were immense piles of rubbish. Cars were rusting where they had been dumped when the Khmer Rouge emptied the city and smashed machinery in April 1975.

We turned right, off the main road, and then right again, down a pretty, leafy lane. We stopped in front of a complex of three plain buildings, built in the early sixties by the Sihanouk government as one of the city's principal high schools. Now over the gate was a sign, TUOL SLENG EXTERMINATION CENTER. We were met by a young student called Dara, who spoke good English and was retained as a guide. About sixteen thousand people had been brought to Tuol Sleng, and only five were known to have escaped alive in the confusion as the Vietnamese army stormed the city in early 1979; one of them, Ung Pech, was now the museum's curator.

Most of the people brought to the prison had been Khmer Rouge cadres on whom the Party had turned, as Communist parties so often do to their own. Whereas straightforward "class enemies" tended to be executed in the fields without ceremony, the party leadership was determined to extract confessions from its own members accused, for whatever reason, of treason—which almost always meant collaboration with Vietnam, with the CIA, or with both.

The classrooms on the ground floor of the first building had all apparently been used as torture rooms. In each was a metal bed frame to which victims had been strapped, a school desk and chair for the interrogator. In each there was also an old U.S. Army ammunition box, into which prisoners were supposed to defecate, and petrol cans, into which they were to urinate. Each cell also had a large photograph of the room as the Vietnamese had apparently found it after their invasion. The Khmer Rouge had departed with such speed that decaying corpses were found bound to the bed in several cells. These bodies were buried in graves in front of the building.

In one of the classrooms was a blackboard on which, the guide said, were written instructions to the prisoners on their behavior under interrogation. Underneath it was a translation into English:

1. You must answer in conformity with the questions I asked you. Don't try to turn away my questions.

2. Don't try to escape by making pretexts according to your hypocritical ideas.
3. Don't be a fool for you are a chap who dares to thwart the revolution.
4. You must immediately answer my questions without wasting time to reflect.
5. Don't tell me about your little incidents committed against the propriety. Don't tell me either about the essence of the revolution.
6. During the bastinado or the electrisisation you must not cry loudly.
7. Do sit down quietly. Wait for the orders. If there are no orders do nothing. If I ask you to do something you must immediately do it without protesting.
8. Don't make any pretexts about Kampuchea Krom in order to hide your jaw of traitor.*
9. If you disobey every point of my regulations you will get either ten strokes of the whip or five shocks of electric discharge.

In the next block the classrooms had been subdivided by crude brick partitions about eight feet high into tiny cells for individual prisoners. Each was manacled by the ankle to a shackle large enough to take a ship's anchor set in the floor. Each lived here awaiting his interrogation, torture, confession and death.

In another room a huge pile of black clothing lay displayed along one wall in direct imitation of the museum at Auschwitz. I was told these were the dead prisoners' clothes. Also in this room was a heap of typewriters, plates, cooking utensils and a broken photocopier, which the guide said had been found there.

The most terrible of the exhibits were the photographs. The Khmer Rouge had abolished much of what we think of as modern bureaucracy—except, it seemed, in that area of government with which they are most closely identified, repression. The prisoners at Tuol Sleng had almost all been photographed—either on arrival at the school, or after their grisly deaths. The Vietnamese had found the negatives and taken them away for enlargement, and the pictures were now displayed around the walls.

* Kampuchea Krom is the Cambodian name for the Mekong Delta, which used to be part of Cambodia and is now in Vietnam, and which the Pol Pot leadership coveted. Presumably, anyone accused of having a Kampuchea Krom accent would be declared a Vietnamese spy.

There were photographs of bodies lying strapped to the metal beds, of others cast on the floor with their throats cut. But the studies of the arrivals were the most poignant. They had been stood or seated before a draped sheet, as in a photographer's studio. For the most part their faces were blank, but some attempted a tentative, slightly hopeful smile, as if they wished to believe that by wooing the cameraman they might, somehow, obtain mercy. There were men, there were women, and there were a lot of children. They had apparently been brought here when their parents were arrested. Some had been photographed with their mothers, some were alone. They were of all ages. Sometimes their faces showed a merciful incomprehension, but often they were as rigid with terror as their elders. All had been murdered.

Upstairs in the school the files were kept. These were almost the only Khmer Rouge documents to which the Vietnamese had allowed foreigners access; nothing from the party leadership was available. At Tuol Sleng there was a translation, written in pencil, of Lenin's *On the State* and of an East German book called *Who's Who in the CIA,* which is merely a list of American names and addresses. The other files were filled with confessions. All were laboriously taken down in longhand, and some were then retyped as, one after another, these prisoners of the Party had been forced to admit to monstrous and absurd crimes. There were pages and pages of confessions in folders signed by those who admitted to having secretly betrayed the revolution for years by working for the CIA or the Vietnamese. There were elaborate charts and card indexes cross-referring different "traitors" and groups of "traitors."

The fantastic nature of the confessions is illustrated by that extracted from John Dewhirst, a young Englishman who was captured along with two friends on their yacht in the Gulf of Thailand. The confession began, "My name is John Dawson Dewhirst, a British citizen. I am a CIA agent who officially works as a teacher in Japan. I was born at Newcastle-upon-Tyne, England, on 2 October 1952. My father was a CIA agent whose cover was headmaster of Benton Road Secondary School."

Dewhirst declared that he himself was recruited to the CIA at the age of twelve by a friend of his father named Edward Fraser.

"He was a colonel in the CIA and as a cover was an executive on the Shell-BP oil company." According to Dewhirst, his father was a CIA captain whose duty was to report on Communist teachers in the Newcastle district. He had been paid $1,000 for his son's induction into the agency.

After being tortured, Dewhirst and his friends, like almost everyone else at Tuol Sleng, were murdered. One of the most prominent Khmer Rouge officials murdered in Tuol Sleng was Hu Nim, who, like many of his peers, had become a Communist in Paris in the late fifties and early sixties. He had then spent eight years in the Khmer Rouge maquis, and he was Minister of Information in the Khmer Rouge government until his arrest in 1977.

In his "confession," Hu Nim was compelled to declare that he too had been "an officer of the CIA" since 1957, working toward

> the construction of capitalism in Kampuchea . . . completely toe-ing the line of the American imperialists. . . . On the surface it seemed that I was a "total revolutionary," as if I was "standing on the people's side." . . . But, in fact, deep in my mind, the essence was service of the American imperialists . . . I wrote a thesis for my law doctorate which even took a progressive stand. . . . These were the cheapest acts which hid my reactionary, traitorous, corrupted elements, representing the feudalist, capitalist, imperialist establishment and the CIA . . . I'm not a human being, I'm an animal.

Hu Nim was "crushed to bits" in July 1977.

Just as the Khmer Rouge had attempted to impose a fanatical and brutal perspective upon the country, so the Vietnamese had since devised another order of unreality. In one room at Tuol Sleng the new sanitized history of the Cambodian revolution was displayed in texts and old photographs. There were pictures of Mao Tse-tung with Pol Pot to emphasize the evil of that connection and the complicity of Vietnam's own great enemy to the north in the crimes of the Khmer Rouge. There were many blurred photographs of hitherto obscure Cambodian Communist cadres, whose roles were now being exaggerated so as to demonstrate that the party had had a tradition of true Marxist-Leninism and of international solidarity with Vietnam, which the Pol Pot group had sought to extinguish by murder. There was nothing to suggest the extent of Vietnam's own past support for the Khmer Rouge revolution.

In the account of the end of French colonial rule in the 1950s and the growth of the country in the 1960s there was not one single reference to Prince Norodom Sihanouk, who had in fact led his country for twenty-five years. The Prince not only had negotiated independence from France but also had managed, till the end of the sixties, to keep Cambodia largely out of the growing war in Vietnam. During the 1970–75 war in Cambodia he had been titular leader of the revolutionary forces, living in exile in Peking without real power, but officially recognized by Hanoi and many other governments as the true head of state of Cambodia. After the Khmer Rouge victory in 1975 he had returned to Phnom Penh; his usefulness over, the Khmer Rouge stripped him of office and kept him under close house arrest in the almost empty city. As the Vietnamese tanks drew close to Phnom Penh he was flown out in a Chinese airliner and was dispatched to New York at once by the Chinese to denounce the Vietnamese attack at the United Nations. He had excoriated both the Vietnamese and the Khmer Rouge. Now he was yawing around in uncertain limbo between Peking, Paris and Pyongyang, while at home he had been removed from history.

"Why is there no mention of Sihanouk?" I asked my guide.

"On the advice of the experts," he replied.

"What experts?" I asked.

"Vietnamese experts," he said.

One entire wall of this room had been made into a map of Cambodia—perhaps fourteen feet high and as many wide. On glass eight inches in front of the wall the rivers and lakes of the country were painted blood red. Behind the glass, arranged in the shape of the country, were hundreds of skulls collected from a nearby mass grave. This was another contribution by the Vietnamese experts.

3 ❦ Views from Outside

When does disaster become "Disaster"? How is it that bad news can be long ignored and then suddenly reach such a state of critical mass as to become an international *cause célèbre?*

In April 1945, a correspondent of *The Times* of London reached Belsen and wrote: "It is my duty to describe something beyond the imagination of mankind." One of the British officers charged with the relief of the camp wrote that he could "never have imagined" what it was like. The news from Belsen, from Dachau, from Auschwitz was a tremendous shock when it was broadcast around the world in 1945. Yet its essence was hardly new.

In spring and summer 1979 foreign correspondents were able to visit Cambodia. They were similarly shocked by the evidence they found of Khmer Rouge atrocities. Their reports from Tuol Sleng prison, their photographs of piled skulls and mass graves had an enormous impact as they were flashed around the world. But, again, the news was hardly new. Notwithstanding the differences in scale and nature between the two crimes, there are many, not always reassuring, parallels in the way in which the outside world reacted to contemporary accounts of Hitler's war against the Jews and Khmer Rouge terror inside Cambodia between 1975 and 1978.

Hitler had pledged since the early thirties to rid Europe of Jews. Yet, as has since been well documented, at no time did the scale of the response outside Nazi Europe match our knowledge of the disaster within. In the late thirties the United States and most western European countries were hostile to the idea of accepting Jewish refugees. Indeed, in 1936 the League of Nations High Commissioner for Refugees, James G. McDonald, actually resigned in protest at the failure of the rest of the world either to put pressure on Germany to alter its racist policies or to grant haven to the victims of those policies.

After the German annexation of Austria and the persecution of Austrian Jews that followed, President Franklin D. Roosevelt called an international conference to discuss how the refugees could be resettled elsewhere in the world. But when the conference finally opened at Evian on Lake Geneva in July 1938, it became very clear that few countries were willing to do much for the Jews. Holland and Denmark were generous, but Australia announced that it had no racial problem now and did not intend to import one. New Zealand would not lift its restrictions. The United States agreed to accept just its full quota of 27,370 immigrants from Germany and Austria. The British delegate declared that while it had always been British tradition to offer asylum to people persecuted for their religion or race, Britain was densely populated and engaged in a difficult fight against unemployment; there was very little room in Britain itself, and no sanctuary within the Empire sprang to mind.

The spirit of Evian continued. In the summer of 1939 the ship *St. Louis* carrying 930 Jews from Germany to Cuba was refused permission to land them in Havana, despite the fact that they had landing certificates. From Havana the boat people sailed to Miami; they were not allowed to land. Eventually Belgium, France, Holland and Britain agreed to accept them. For all except those taken to England, the sanctuary was short-lived. Similarly, in February 1942, 767 Jews on board the Rumanian ship *Struma* drowned off the coast of Turkey after the British refused to allow the unseaworthy vessel to land in Palestine.

The Nazi effort to exterminate the Jews began on a massive scale in 1941. Details began to filter out of occupied Europe almost at once. They came in letters to neutral Switzerland and Sweden, in intelligence reports garnered in or from the USSR, in radio intercepts, in examination of railroad movements, in reports from refugees and couriers. And yet the details were never fully assimilated. They never reached critical mass. Much the same thing happened, I believe, with Cambodia after 1975.

In 1942 Jan Karski, a member of the Polish resistance, made his way by a dangerous and complicated route out of central Europe, into neutral territories and thence to England and the United States. He had actually been inside a death camp. His reports are staggering if looked at today. Yet they created rather little stir at the time. When Karski visited Felix Frankfurter, the Supreme Court Justice, to tell him what he had seen, Frankfurter replied, "I do not believe you." Karski not unnaturally protested. Frankfurter replied, "I do not mean that you are lying, I simply said I cannot believe you."

Frankfurter might as well have said, "I do not want to believe you." Few people do want to believe tales of atrocities; resistance to them is a natural defense mechanism. And the more awful the speculations, the greater the resistance.

There were other reasons why the news of the fate of the Jews was so hard to accept. The first was that Allied propaganda in the First World War had been filled with lies; it had tried, often successfully, to persuade people that the Germans were carrying out widespread massacres of civilians, that Belgian babies were being slaughtered and turned into soap, and so on. In March 1916, the London *Daily Telegraph* reported that 700,000 Serbs had been gassed to death. This report was widely believed. But it was untrue, and its untruth was subsequently revealed. In June 1942, it was the *Daily Telegraph* that first reported the massive gassing of the Jews. By awful coincidence the number given was once more 700,000. This time the story was not widely believed. Similarly, propaganda, the fear of propaganda and the excuse of propaganda all played their part after 1975 when stories of atrocities in Cambodia began to reach the West.*

---

* One of the organizations most conspicuous in its failure to heed the plight of the Jews was the International Committee of the Red Cross in Geneva. Its knowledge was extensive, yet the ICRC consistently refused to make any public statement, let alone protest.

In November 1941 the Swiss minister in Bucharest sent a private letter to a senior ICRC official about persecution of Rumanian Jews; he wrote that "the Armenian massacres which shook the European conscience at the begin-

. . .

For most of the 1970–75 war in Cambodia it was the policy of
the American administrations to say as little as possible about the
role of the United States in Cambodia. There were very few on-the-

---

ning of the century were a mere child's play in comparison." Underlying the
policy, he wrote, was the "physical destruction of the Jews." Next year, a
delegate returned from a trip to Hungary and Rumania and reported on *"les
massacres les plus atroces."* The ICRC now began to hear the name of
Auschwitz; the head of the Slovak Red Cross wrote that the deportees there
were never heard from again.

By the autumn of 1942 about two million Jews had been murdered and
so many reports had been received that the ICRC felt compelled to consider
whether it should make its information public. An official drafted a bland
statement that said merely that civilians should be humanely treated. Others
in the organization did argue that this was hardly adequate. But not only
were they ignored, in the end even the bland draft was rejected—on the
grounds that it might be seen as a violation of the organization's neutrality.
So the ICRC made no public statement. Privately, senior ICRC officials did
begin to inform other organizations of what they knew.

In an attempt to explain if not justify this decision after the war was
over, the ICRC in 1948 published a remarkable booklet that gave no details
whatsoever, but instead contained the following observations: "Critics objected: 'At least, in view of certain too flagrant violations of humanitarian
principles, you should have protested and appealed to world opinion.'

"Protest? The International Committee did protest—to the responsible
authorities. It had too many occasions to protest. A whole department of the
Committee's work was to make one long series of protests: countless im-
provements in the camps, for example, were due to steps of this kind.

"Public protest and denunciation would have been of no avail. No protests and no threats have ever changed methods of barbarism or lessened the
destructive power of modern weapons. . . . Every man to his job, every man
to his vocation. That of the Red Cross is to nurse the wounded where it can,
with the means at its disposal. For the Committee to protest publicly would
have been not only to outstep its functions, but also to lose thereby all chance
of pursuing them, by creating an immediate breach with the government concerned. The Committee would thus have abandoned to their fate the very
people whom it wished to save.

"The same critics observed further: 'It would have been good for your
prestige.'

"Prestige is an idea which does more often harm than good. The Committee's prestige is not worth the loss of a single human life—not one! Besides,
no one will ever be saved by the prestige of the idea whose handmaiden that
institution must be. The prestige of the Red Cross idea lives not by words,
but by deeds—by deeds which are, after all, the most eloquent of all protests."

record statements by President Nixon on Cambodia, almost none by his aide Henry Kissinger. The most memorable—and it was important—was Nixon's declaration that aid to Cambodia was "the Nixon Doctrine in its Purest Form." Throughout the period, White House instructions were, as State Department officials in Phnom Penh later said, "Keep the show on the road and out of the press." The U.S. Embassy in Phnom Penh not only gave little help to correspondents, it also tried to frustrate their work.

From the White House's point of view this was sensible enough —those years of warfare saw the destruction of Cambodian society and the rise of the Khmer Rouge from its ashes, in good part as a result of White House policies. I attempted to document this process in my previous book; although it is not repeated in detail here, it should not be "forgotten."*

---

* One of the principal contentions in *Sideshow* was that careless policies of the White House, in particular of Richard Nixon and Henry Kissinger, were in good part responsible for the disasters that befell Cambodia in the 1970s.

Until 1969 Prince Norodom Sihanouk had managed to keep most of Cambodia out of the growing war in Vietnam by collaborating with the Vietnamese Communists and, to a certain extent, with their enemies. He allowed the Communists to land supplies at the port of Sihanoukville and to truck them across his country to its eastern border. There he had tolerated their construction of "sanctuaries" from the fighting in South Vietnam. This was an undoubted violation of Cambodia's proclaimed neutrality.

In 1969, the White House ordered a campaign of B-52 bombardment of these sanctuaries. This was done without the advice and consent of Congress. The true records of the missions were burned, and false records were inserted in the Pentagon's own computers. The bombing was illegal. Sihanouk did not protest.

The bombing helped to spread the Vietnamese Communists further into Cambodia, thus alienating right-wing members of Sihanouk's government from his rule. In March 1970, while Sihanouk was abroad, he was overthrown in a right-wing *coup d'état* led by his Prime Minister General Lon Nol. The extent of U.S. participation in this coup is a matter of dispute. The United States immediately began to deal with the new regime. In Peking, Sihanouk formed a United Front with his former enemies, the small Cambodian Communist group known as "les Khmers Rouges," in alliance with Hanoi.

South Vietnamese attacks across the border increased at once and the Communists moved further into Cambodia. At the end of April 1970 the U.S. army invaded eastern Cambodia to attack the sanctuaries. By the time the American troops withdrew at the end of June, the war had ineluctably

Many newspaper editors and television networks played by the United States government's rules and treated Cambodia as a "sideshow." (The term was first used, correctly, by Bernard Gwertzman of *The New York Times*.) There were few full-time correspondents in Phnom Penh during the war. There were, however, many stringers, a lot of whom were young and were appalled by the destructiveness of the war, in particular by the widespread bombing and the flood of refugees off their land into the towns; they hoped for a victory by the other side, the Khmer Rouge led nominally by Prince Norodom Sihanouk. Their work was supplemented by full-time correspondents of newspapers and networks who made visits from Saigon or Bangkok. They too wrote moving, often angry descriptions of United States policy and its effects upon the country.

Through 1974, however, as more and more reports of Khmer

---

spread, and from now on Cambodia was an integral if subsidiary part of the war in Vietnam.

Between 1970 and 1975 Cambodian society was destroyed. The war overturned an overwhelmingly peasant society. Almost half the population fled their fields for the sanctuary of the towns; the population of Phnom Penh grew from about 600,000 to well over two million. Lon Nol's army was expanded and equipped with American military aid and equipment, but despite the bravery of many soldiers it was forever bedeviled by corruption and incompetence. The Khmer Rouge also grew. In 1970 they had numbered only a few thousand, under the leadership of a small inbred group of French-educated Marxists, who had fled Sihanouk's autocracy and taken to the maquis during the sixties. From 1970 onward, with the exiled Sihanouk as their figurehead, with Hanoi and China both providing arms and other supplies (and the Vietnamese, at first, supplying support troops) and with the forces of nationalism unleashed by the war at their command, the Khmer Rouge became an increasingly formidable army. Between 1970 and 1973 they were subjected to a massive American bombing campaign which was ended only by act of Congress in August 1973. Their casualties are thought to have been huge. As the war continued, their policies became increasingly cruel, and refugees to Phnom Penh spoke with horror of the way in which they seemed determined to restructure society.

At the same time, relations between the Khmer Rouge leadership and Hanoi deteriorated as traditional Khmer suspicion of Vietnamese ambitions to create an Indochina federation dominated by Hanoi took precedence over any Marxist solidarity. Hanoi was unable to compel the Khmer Rouge to take part in the 1973 Paris Peace Agreement. After that, the United States made scant effort to find any solution—such as the return of Sihanouk ahead of the Khmer Rouge—to the bitter civil war.

Rouge brutality began to seep out of the growing areas that they controlled, some journalists began to wonder whether postwar reconciliation would be as easy as they had hoped. In March 1974, the Baltimore *Sun* correspondent wrote of "the incomprehensible brutality of the Khmer Rouge communists"; the *Washington Post* reported on how the Khmer Rouge were "restructuring people." Sydney Schanberg of *The New York Times* wrote about the joy with which refugees escaped Khmer Rouge control at Kompong Thom. James Fenton wrote in the *New Statesman* of the fear with which some Khmers were beginning to talk of the other side. In the fall of 1974, journalists learned of Sar Sarsdam, a village near Siem Reap, which had been burned by the Khmer Rouge and in which, according to Catholic Relief Services workers, over sixty peasants had been brutally killed. Old women were reported to have been nailed to the walls of their homes before being burned alive. Children had been torn apart by hand.

Even so, there were few journalists in Phnom Penh who wanted to believe the blood-bath theory. It had been invoked so often by United States officials in defense of a policy with which most of those same journalists disagreed, that there was a tendency in the final days of the war to dismiss the United States Ambassador John Gunther Dean and other officials who harped on Sar Sarsdam as hawks who wished to prolong the war. Martin Woollacott of the *Guardian* later recalled with pain that some journalists sang a little song to the tune of "She Was Poor but She Was Honest":

> Oh will there be a dreadful bloodbath
> When the Khmer Rouge come to town?
> Aye, there'll be a dreadful bloodbath
> When the Khmer Rouge come to town.

When the Khmer Rouge did come to town, in April 1975, only a few foreigners remained in Phnom Penh. Closeted in the French Embassy they watched, at first more astonished than appalled, as the victorious young army began to empty the entire city at gunpoint. Hospital patients, refugees, schoolchildren, all had to take one of the main roads out of the city. Most of the Cambodians in the Embassy were ordered to leave its supposed sanctuary and to trek into the countryside as well. The foreigners were then trucked to the Thai border. From then on, the Khmer Rouge closed Cambodia almost completely from the outside world and embarked upon one of the most radical and bloody revolutions in history.

For the next three and a half years the few thousand refugees who managed to escape to Thailand were the principal source of news about the country. They told from the start a consistent story— of deaths from starvation and exhaustion during the evacuation of Phnom Penh; of forced evacuation of almost all the towns after Phnom Penh; of relocation into new villages or work zones; of inadequate food supplies and nonexistent medical care; of a rule of terror conducted by young boys with AK-47s on behalf of a shadowy, all-powerful organization known as Angka. Refugees spoke of people being shot, clubbed to death or buried alive for disobeying orders, asking questions or in some other way infringing the rules that Angka laid down. Among the dreadful tales they told were those of babies being beaten to death against trees.

Accounts of such atrocities began to appear in the Western press in the summer of 1975. In London, early reports were by Bruce Loudoun and John McBeth in the conservative *Daily Telegraph,* the paper which had reported German atrocities wrongly in World War I and correctly in World War II. In July, Henry Kamm wrote a long article in *The New York Times,* and the paper ran an editorial comparing the Khmer Rouge policies with "Soviet extermination of kulaks or with the Gulag Archipelago." Kamm was one of the few journalists on a major newspaper to cover the Cambodian story throughout.

Clearly, Cambodia was not ignored. Its travails received far more attention than those of, say, East Timor, Burundi or the Central African Republic, to mention just three other contemporary disasters. Nonetheless, it was some time before many reporters came to accept that terrible events were taking place in Cambodia. Just as few people had wished to believe in the elimination of the Jews until the evidence was thrust before them, so many people wished not to believe that atrocities were taking place in Cambodia after the Khmer Rouge takeover. This was especially true among reporters who had reported the war negatively from the Lon Nol side, hoping for the victory of the others. Far from eagerly seeking, let alone fabricating, evidence of Khmer Rouge atrocities, they shrank from it.* Others believed, at least for a short time, that the refugees were unreliable, that the CIA was cooking up a blood bath to say, "We told you so."

I had made one brief visit to Cambodia in 1970, just a few months after Prince Sihanouk had been overthrown and before war had really engulfed the country. During the course of the 1970–75 war I had tried to follow what was happening and when the refugees began to come out in the summer of 1975 I started to try to discover what their stories meant, who the Khmer Rouge were, and why they might be behaving thus.

At the end of 1975 I visited China, which was emerging as the one foreign country to enjoy close relations with the government of Democratic Kampuchea, as the Khmer Rouge had renamed Cambodia. In Peking a deputy foreign minister of the People's Republic assured me blandly that the refugee stories were meaningless and that all was well under the new revolutionary leadership.

From China I made my way to Thailand. I had expected the right-wing administration of Thailand to be anxious to exploit the refugee stories for their propaganda value. However, the procedure for obtaining permission to visit refugees along the border was complicated, involving numerous passes from different government offices in Bangkok and still more from the local authorities in the border town of Aranyaprathet.

The refugees whom I eventually met talked of the unrelenting rigor of life in Democratic Kampuchea, and they spoke of the fear in which the Khmer Rouge were held. None of those to whom I spoke had actually witnessed massacres themselves, but almost all

---

* Thus, for example, at the end of 1975 *Newsweek* published a story that cast doubt on the atrocity stories. Early in 1976 *The Sunday Times* of London did the same. (One of the paper's Paris correspondents, Edith Lenart, had filed a story based on interviews with Khmer refugees who had reached Paris and corroborated the atrocity stories; it was never published.) The *Far Eastern Economic Review,* which offers the most comprehensive coverage of the region, did not at first give credence to the atrocity stories, except in an occasional article by a contributor. The *Daily Mirror* of London, which had published constant, angry attacks upon the American war effort, published little on the Khmer Rouge until 1979.

claimed to have seen the bodies of people murdered by the Khmer Rouge. Some said that anyone associated with the Lon Nol regime risked being savagely killed. Others said that those with education faced death. They spoke of being ruled by children with AK-47s.

Although it was hard to find a rationale for the Khmer Rouge conduct that the refugees described, their testimony was the same as that given to other people along the border. And their stories rang true; I just could not believe that these people had invented their tales or that they were simply being manipulated by the CIA or by Thai military intelligence. Refugees fleeing dictatorships—Stalin's USSR, Hitler's Europe, Pinochet's Chile, Husak's Czechoslovakia—have all been reliable witnesses of the states they left behind. It seemed to me that whatever the numbers who had died in Cambodia since the Khmer Rouge took over, the regime was using terror as a means of social control.

After leaving the camp I went to the bridge at Aranyaprathet. It crosses a narrow stream that forms the border between Cambodia and Thailand at this point. Once the bridge linked Cambodia with the world to its west. Since the Khmer Rouge takeover it had, like the entire country, been closed. It was overgrown now. Just across the bridge a single young Khmer Rouge soldier dressed in black stood stiffly, his checkered scarf around his neck, an old rifle straight at his side. Beyond him lay the empty Cambodian border town of Poipet, only the wind in the deserted streets, and beyond that the terrifying, incomprehensible brutality that the refugees described. I shuddered to think how close and yet how unreachable this area of darkness really was.

At that time one of the few journalists doing sustained research among the refugees was Anthony Paul of the *Reader's Digest*. I listened to some of the interviews he had recorded; they were seriously done. Eventually, however, his work was incorporated by the *Digest* into a book—*Murder of a Gentle Land,* co-authored by John Barron—which was diminished by its reliance on propaganda. It suggested that one cause of the Khmer Rouge violence might be the fact that one of its leaders, Khieu Samphan, was alleged to be impotent. The United States bombing and the destruction of Cambodian society between 1970 and 1975 were all but forgotten. Nonetheless, the refugee accounts gathered by Paul have stood the test of time and eventual firsthand verification.

In February 1976, *Le Monde* published a series of articles about life under the Khmer Rouge by a French priest, François Ponchaud, who had lived for years in Cambodia and had a closer understanding of the country's culture and history than most foreigners. Ponchaud's book *Cambodge Année Zéro* was published first in France in 1977, and elsewhere in 1978. It was the first serious attempt to describe and to analyze what was taking place in Cambodia.

Through 1976 and 1977 and especially in 1978 the Western press's coverage of Cambodia increased. Nonetheless, the issue never reached critical mass. I did not write enough myself. And there was no broadly based campaign of protest in the West as there was, say, over abuses of human rights in Chile.

One reason for this was the skepticism (to use a mild word) displayed by the Western left toward the stories coming out of Democratic Kampuchea. That skepticism was most fervently and frequently expressed by Noam Chomsky, the linguistic philosopher at the Massachusetts Institute of Technology. He asserted that from the moment of the Khmer Rouge victory in 1975 the Western press colluded with Western and anti-Communist Asian governments, notably Thailand, to produce a "vast and unprecedented" campaign of propaganda against the Khmer Rouge.* Many left-wing academics and

---

* Chomsky declared:

　　Three features of the propaganda campaign with regard to Cambodia deserve special notice. The first is its vast and unprecedented scope. Editorial condemnation of Cambodian "genocide" in the mainstream media dates from mid-1975, immediately following the victory of the socalled "Khmer Rouge." After that time the western media were deluged with condemnation of Cambodia.

　　A second major feature of the propaganda campaign was that it involved a systematic distortion or suppression of the highly relevant historical context as well as substantial fabrication—the grim reality evidently did not suffice for the needs of the propaganda.

　　A third striking feature of the campaign was the constant pretense that the horrors of Cambodia were either being ignored except for the courageous voices that seek to pierce the silence or that some great conflict was raging about whether or not there have been atrocities in Cambodia.

journalists took the same line. The Washington-based pressure group Indochina Resource Center, which had determinedly opposed the American war effort, now threw itself energetically into the defense of the Khmer Rouge against what it saw as vicious calumny in the media. Two of its directors, Gareth Porter and George Hildebrand, published a book, *Cambodia: Starvation and Revolution,* which was in effect an apology for Khmer Rouge behavior.* Such apologies by the Western left—and by many prominent American antiwar activists, Joan Baez being a notable exception—continued until Vietnam itself began publicly to denounce the Khmer Rouge.

Vietnam took a long time to do so. Through 1975, 1976, and 1977, relations between Hanoi and Phnom Penh deteriorated, with border skirmishes turning to open warfare. Most of the provocation appears to have been carried out by the Khmer Rouge. Nonetheless, so long as there was a chance of negotiating a settlement with Phnom Penh relative to their border and other disputes, Vietnamese spokesmen continually disregarded the stories told by the refugees

* As late as May 1977 the Center wrote to me to ask for any information I had on "CIA-operated radio stations designed to spread 'disinformation'—especially with regard to Cambodia. CIA operatives in Thailand and their debriefing of Cambodian refugees . . . Possible contacts the CIA might have with reporters . . . in Thailand or other reporters who were in Cambodia . . . As you can tell, we are interested in possible United States attempts to spread 'disinformation' about Cambodia. We don't know for sure what is really going on inside Cambodia either. But judging from the conflicting reports appearing lately, together with what we now know about such U.S. attempts in Vietnam, we think we have good reason to be suspicious." Even after firsthand evidence of Khmer Rouge atrocities became widely available in 1979, some left-wing ideologists continued to maintain that newspaper articles in the 1975–79 period were blatant propaganda. Thus an Australian academic, Gavin McCormick, writing in 1980 in the *Journal of Contemporary Asia,* declared that

> the Kampuchean question is shrouded in a dense fog of prejudices, distortions, propaganda, and half truth. The Western media and intelligence worked hard on Kampuchea. But, and here is a tragic irony, it becomes increasingly likely that some of the most malicious fantasies of propagandists, conceived with little or no regard for truth, may actually be close to the truth. This is a difficult and unpalatable conclusion.

McCormick thus seems to be attempting to vindicate the fact that he and others, in what he calls "the movement of solidarity with the peoples of Kampuchea and Indochina as a whole," denied for so long the terrible suffering of those people.

in Thailand and publicly endorsed the Khmer Rouge regime.*
The far larger number of refugees who fled to Vietnam had remarkably similar tales, but until 1978 they were kept silent by Hanoi.
Where Vietnam went, its socialist friends went also. Throughout the
period, the Soviet and East European press published articles favorable to the Khmer Rouge, and gave no credence to the refugee reports.

In such circumstances, one might have expected the United
States government to be quick to exploit the refugee stories out of
Cambodia and to argue that they gave *ex post facto* justification of
the United States adventure in Indochina. In fact, it did not. There
were many reasons. War weariness and the anxiety to look away
from Indochina was one. Henry Kissinger and Gerald Ford asked
that there be no recriminations about the war. Their pleas were
heeded and, as a result, there was no examination, either. Later
Jimmy Carter was concerned that his human-rights crusade break
new ground by attacking right-wing regimes as well as traditional
left-wing opponents. Under Carter the State Department's Human
Rights Bureau did much good work, but it barely noticed Indochina.

United States relations with both Thailand and China also had
considerable impact.

After April 1975 relations within the region began to change

* For example, on April 9, 1977, Hanoi attacked the United States for
launching "a slanderous campaign against the socialist countries to discredit
them and sap their influence. Colluding with the Thai reactionaries, the
United States has conducted several armed attacks against Laos and Cambodia." On April 16–17, 1977, the Vietnamese leadership offered fulsome
praise to the Khmer Rouge on the occasion of the second anniversary of the
capture of Phnom Penh. Thus a message from Le Duan, general secretary of
the Party's Central Committee, to Khieu Samphan and Pol Pot, ". . . under
the leadership of the Cambodian Revolutionary Organization and in the traditions of ardent patriotism and industry, the heroic people of Cambodia over
the past two years have upheld the spirit of self reliance and have overcome
many difficulties. . . . The Vietnamese people warmly hail these fine achievements of the fraternal Cambodian people . . . On this great occasion, the
Vietnamese people sincerely thank the fraternal people of Cambodia for your
vigorous support and precious assistance to our revolutionary cause, and sincerely wish you many more and still greater successes in building an independent, united, peaceful and neutral, nonaligned, sovereign, democratic and
territorially integral Cambodia."

extraordinarily rapidly as the powers moved to fill the apparent vacuum created by the American defeat in Indochina. The Thai government, which had actively helped the United States prosecute its war, felt, for that very reason, particularly vulnerable to the Communist victors. Bangkok's attitude toward the Khmer Rouge was deeply ambiguous. Its fiercely anti-Communist ideology profited from exposure of Khmer Rouge atrocities. But the strategic implications were different. As often in the past, the Thais saw the Vietnamese as a greater threat than the Khmers, a race whom the Thais have traditionally seen as a buffer against Vietnam.

Back in 1975, the poor relations between the leadership of the Khmer Rouge and that of Hanoi were not well documented in the press. But it was well known to United States and, presumably, Thai intelligence; in researching *Sideshow,* I found CIA and Defense Intelligence Agency reports of the tensions stretching back as far as 1970. Moreover, fighting between the victorious Communists in the two countries broke out along the border and over offshore islands as early as May 1975. This information was available from satellite surveillance.

Immediately after the Khmer Rouge victory in April 1975, the Thai government attempted to improve relations with the new government in Phnom Penh. This attempt continued, with interruptions, throughout the three and a half years of Khmer Rouge rule. Thus, while the Thai press busily recounted Cambodian refugee horror stories, Khmer Rouge and Thai officials exchanged cordial visits. Thailand even forced some refugees back across the border to almost certain deaths.* And throughout the period, Washington was attempting to support most Thai government policies.

* After the Khmer Rouge victory on April 17, 1975, Thailand recognized the Khmer Rouge "as the sole and legal government of Cambodia," saying it hoped this would "promote good will, friendship and understanding with Cambodia." Other members of the Association of Southeast Asian Nations (ASEAN) followed suit. The Thai Prime Minister Kukrit Pramoj announced on April 19 that Thailand would assist Cambodia with as much food and medicine as the new regime needed to rehabilitate the country. A few days later Thailand agreed to return to the Khmer Rouge six Armored Personnel Carriers brought to the border by fleeing Lon Nol troops. On April 23, 1975, the Thai foreign minister announced that Thailand would send an ambassador to Phnom Penh as soon as an air service was resumed. After the United States government used its bases in Thailand for operations intended

At the same time China's status in the region was changing dramatically. Throughout the war the Chinese government had supported Hanoi, the Khmer Rouge and the Pathet Lao. The USSR had

---

to recapture the American container ship *Mayaguez* from the Khmer Rouge in May 1975, the Thai government ordered those bases closed.

Throughout the rest of 1975, relations between Thailand and Democratic Kampuchea continued to improve, particularly after diplomatic relations were established between China and Thailand. In October 1975, Foreign Minister Ieng Sary of Democratic Kampuchea flew to Bangkok for talks on establishing normal and even friendly relations between the two countries. (He came in a Chinese Boeing and was visited every day at his suite in the lavish Erawan Hotel by the Chinese ambassador.) On October 30, 1975, the Bangkok *Post* reported "under a friendly atmosphere and with discussion on future cooperation and no reference to the past, Thailand and Cambodia yesterday agreed to normalize relations. . . . At a press conference at the Erawan Hotel, Ieng Sary said that he had asked the Thais to return all refugees. Asked about reports that some refugees who had returned had been killed, he said that most of the refugees had fled the country because they had some penalties to pay, so that any statement made by them was unreliable. The two countries promised to resolve any border disputes by peaceful means."

An official Thai-Cambodian Liaison Committee was established at Aranyaprathet and Poipet on November 17, 1975, and official trading between the two countries was resumed on August 30, 1976. At the end of November 1976 a group of Cambodian refugees was handed back across the border to the Khmer Rouge; there were reports that these refugees were all immediately executed by the Khmer Rouge.

Relations deteriorated at the end of 1976, following a bloody coup by extreme right-wing sections of the Thai military in October 1976. By the end of the year the new Thai junta was giving more help to anti-Communist Khmer Serei (Free Khmer) guerrillas along the border. Border consultations were dropped by Phnom Penh. In January 1977, Khmer Rouge troops attacked three villages in a disputed area of the border just north of Aranyaprathet.

Relations between Bangkok and Phnom Penh began to improve again after General Kriangsak Chamanand, a relatively moderate military figure, became Thai Prime Minister in October 1977. Kriangsak restored the emphasis on national rather than ideological priorities in foreign policy. Support for the Khmer Serei was cut back. In February 1978, just after skirmishes turned into open warfare between Vietnam and Democratic Kampuchea, Thai Foreign Minister Uppadit visited Phnom Penh. Henry Kamm recorded in *The New York Times* that when Uppadit returned to Bangkok, "reporters at the airport were struck by Mr. Uppadit's effort to say nothing unkind about Cambodia. He volunteered a comment that reports about conditions in Cambodia since the Communist victory might have been exaggerated. Asked about his impression of life in Phnom Penh, Mr. Uppadit said it had seemed like a normal city."

aided the Vietnamese and the Lao revolutionaries, but had given scant support to the Khmer Rouge. After April 1975 China began to withdraw support from Vietnam, a country which it has traditionally tried to subjugate. Vietnam strengthened its links to China's own principal foe, the USSR. Simultaneously Peking increased its support for the Khmer Rouge regime even as that regime moved into a state of hostility with its own former ally, Vietnam. The Chinese also embarked upon a diplomatic offensive among the non-Communist countries of Southeast Asia, an area where hitherto they had had no relations at all. Remarkably effective links were quickly established with Thailand.

This whole realignment, which was designed in part by the Chinese, if not by the Southeast Asian countries, to "contain" Vietnam and which was far more complex than such a thumbnail sketch suggests, was at least tacitly endorsed by the United States.

One of the priorities of the Carter Administration was normalization of relations with China. Normal relations with Vietnam, an ambition of Assistant Secretary of State for East Asia and the Pacific Richard Holbrooke, was a much lower priority in the White House. For obvious reasons, it was not much of a vote winner; and it was rendered politically impossible by Hanoi's insistence until mid-1978 that the United States pay war reparations as part of any agreement and by Congressional opposition to almost any form of aid to Vietnam.

These strategic considerations—particularly the importance that was being attached in Washington to the views of both China and the Association of Southeast Asian Nations (ASEAN)—seem to have discouraged the United States government and other Western nations from leading any "vast and unprecedented" propaganda campaign against the Khmer Rouge between 1975 and 1978. In Bangkok I found that the U.S. Embassy was surprisingly reluctant to help reporters discover what was going on under the Khmer Rouge, still less to share information.

In January 1977 Khmer Rouge troops swooped into Thailand across the disputed border just north of Aranyaprathet and attacked three

Thai villages. They slit the throats of children, murdered pregnant women and departed leaving piles of dead behind them. Photographs of the bodies were published around the world, and for the first time there was visible firsthand evidence of the conduct with which the refugees had charged the Khmer Rouge.

The improvement of relations between Thailand and Democratic Kampuchea was interrupted. But two things were extraordinary about this. First, the interruption was only temporary; it was soon set aside by Thailand. Secondly, the Khmer Rouge regime did not deny that its soldiers were responsible for the murders. Instead it claimed that the villages in question were actually part of Cambodia and that the Thai protest was therefore an interference in Cambodian affairs.*

Despite the fact that news items about the atrocities were carried widely by the Western press, Western governments still limited their expressions of outrage. A young Englishman encountered directly the lack of public interest they displayed. Robert Ashe, who worked with a British Christian relief agency for Cambodian refugees along the Thai border—long before it became fashionable—sent off a series of letters to the British and American governments urging they take action over Khmer Rouge conduct.

To President Jimmy Carter he wrote, "Working amongst the refugees I often hear stories of the brutal revolution that has racked the country since 15th April 1975 . . . if only ten per cent were true, it is still a horrifying picture of life for those people left alive in Cambodia. . . . I urge you to take up the cause of the innocent Cambodian people . . ."

Ashe received no reply from President Carter or the White House. Almost three months later he received a cursory response from Charles Twining, the political officer and "Cambodia watcher" of the U.S. Embassy in Bangkok, who was, in fact, personally ap-

---

* The Foreign Ministry in Phnom Penh asserted: "The measures taken by the Government of Democratic Kampuchea in its own territory are answerable to the absolute sovereignty of Democratic Kampuchea. The Government of Democratic Kampuchea expresses its indignation at the groundless note of the Thai Government which constitutes an interference with the internal affairs of Democratic Kampuchea and a provocation against Democratic Kampuchea . . ."

palled by Khmer Rouge behavior. "We fully agree with you that the attacks [on the Thai border] were reprehensible and merit world-wide reprobation. We have been asked to express Washington's appreciation to you for having taken the time to write to the President on the subject."

Ashe also wrote to Ivor Richard, the British permanent representative to the United Nations, to ask whether the U.N. knew of the atrocities in Cambodia and what it was doing to investigate and condemn them.

In response he received a letter from N.R. Jarrold of the Foreign Office's U.N. department, who pointed out that British government ministers had twice mentioned Cambodia in the Houses of Parliament in 1976. Neither exchange indicated any sense of urgency by the British government.

Mr. Jarrold observed that "We have not thought it right to raise this question at the United Nations. I am sure that we could not help potential victims if we were to do so: and, if the Cambodian authorities believed that the West was orchestrating a campaign against them, they might respond by withdrawing even further into the isolationism from which there are at present some signs that they want to emerge."

This did not satisfy Robert Ashe on the Cambodian border. He wrote again to the British government. This time he received a reply from a junior minister, Lord Goronwy Roberts, who explained that Britain had not taken the Cambodian question to the U.N., because any resolution condemning Khmer Rouge conduct was bound to fail and such a failure would only reinforce the Khmer Rouge. However, "There have recently been signs that the Cambodians may be emerging from their present self-imposed diplomatic isolation. As they do so, they will become more aware of the impact of their behavior on world opinion. We shall do what we can to encourage the learning process."

Another individual to become increasingly concerned was Jean Lacouture, a French socialist intellectual and specialist on Indochina. In March 1977, in a review in the *New York Review of Books,* he gave an emotional endorsement to François Ponchaud's *Cambodge Année Zéro,* which thus far had been published only in France. (Lacouture's review had been published first in French in *Le Nouvel Observateur,* a Paris periodical.)

"Ordinary genocide (if one can ever call it ordinary) usually has been carried out against a foreign population or an internal minority," Lacouture wrote. "The new masters of Phnom Penh have invented something original, auto-genocide. After Auschwitz and the Gulag, we might have thought this century had produced the ultimate in horror, but we are seeing the suicide of a people in the name of revolution—worse, in the name of socialism." Lacouture felt that "François Ponchaud's book can be read only with shame by those of us who supported the Khmer Rouge cause." He was almost alone in acknowledging such a sense of shame.

His apology obtained wide circulation and much comment, particularly in the United States. Unfortunately, in his haste, Lacouture had made a number of errors. These did not alter either his or Ponchaud's assessment of the Khmer Rouge, but they were seized upon by Noam Chomsky, who circulated them widely. In a subsequent issue of the *Review,* Lacouture corrected himself. Not all those who had reported his *mea culpa* published his corrections. Chomsky used the affair as part of his argument that the media were embarked on an unjustified propaganda blitz against the Khmer Rouge.

As a third example, a single United States Congressman, Stephen Solarz, held hearings on "Human Rights in Cambodia" in the summer of 1977 before a subcommittee of the House Foreign Affairs Committee. What was perhaps remarkable was that this was the first time that any such Congressional hearing had been held. All the witnesses at the first hearing were journalists or academics; no United States government official testified. At a later hearing that summer, the Assistant Secretary Richard Holbrooke and the Bangkok Embassy's Cambodia watcher, Charles Twining, did testify. Whatever their personal repugnance for the Khmer Rouge, their statements were measured and certainly no part of a propaganda blitz against Democratic Kampuchea.

Finally, in 1978, Cambodia did become something of an international issue. It happened after and partly because the bitter but surreptitious border disputes between the Khmer Rouge and their former Vietnamese allies broke into public warfare and violent recrimination. Massive abuse of human rights alone had failed to win worldwide attention in the way that open schism and warfare within the Communist bloc did.

Part of the reason was that Vietnam and its allies in the Soviet bloc now directed their own considerable propaganda resources toward blackening the reputation of the Khmer Rouge. Now, in a complete reversal of its propaganda, Hanoi endorsed the most dreadful of all the accounts. Thus, for example, it declared that "The entire Cambodian nation now faces genocide" and that the "Pol Pot–Ieng Sary clique has already executed several million Cambodian people," and that Cambodia was "a land of blood and tears, hell on earth." Hanoi radio also began to broadcast excerpts from François Ponchaud's book *Cambodge Année Zéro* and from the *Reader's Digest* account, *Murder of a Gentle Land*. Vietnamese propaganda began what was to be a long campaign to equate Pol Pot with Hitler.

This was the first-ever war between two Communist states. Zbigniew Brzezinski called it a "proxy war," fought by Cambodia and Vietnam, on behalf of their respective patrons, China and the USSR. This phrase appeared at the time to underplay the real national differences between the two sides in favor of superpower concerns. But even if the war began from local causes, each side's great-power backer soon adopted and thereby expanded its cause to embrace its own priorities.

Evidently anxious finally to secure normal relations with the United States, Vietnam now dropped its claim to war reparations. It was too late. United States policy, under the influence of Dr. Brzezinski, was moving closer toward normalizing relations with China. And now that Vietnam was openly at war with China's protégé, Democratic Kampuchea, reconciliation with the old enemy held even less attraction in Washington.

However, even as the United States moved closer toward the Khmer Rouge's patron, China, so at last Washington and its allies began to play a more aggressive role in denouncing the crimes of the Khmer Rouge themselves. One important reason may have been that, without much governmental support, public interest in Cambodia had finally reached such a point that it could not be ignored but had rather better be embraced.

In early 1978 a group of Norwegian politicians, academics and journalists arranged a hearing on Khmer Rouge atrocities. Somewhat to everyone's surprise, President Carter—who had previously made almost no mention of Khmer Rouge conduct—sent the Conference a statement declaring that the Khmer Rouge were "the world's worst violators of human rights."

Almost at the same time the Canadian Foreign Ministry compiled a hurried dossier of refugee allegations. And the British government—despite serious misgivings in the Southeast Asian department of the Foreign Office, which was concerned lest Thailand and the other ASEAN countries be upset—raised the matter at the United Nations Commission on Human Rights. The British delegate asked for an inquiry into the situation in Democratic Kampuchea.

Despite the fact that the Soviet Union was now, along with Vietnam, publicly denouncing Khmer Rouge atrocities, the Soviet delegate to the Commission vigorously opposed the British request. Soviet refusal to accept the notion that the Commission should inquire into the affairs of any member states—save South Africa, Israel and, after 1973, Chile—has rendered the Commission singularly ineffective for most of its life. In 1948 the Commission had drawn up the Universal Declaration of Human Rights, which was proclaimed by the General Assembly and has been seen by individuals all over the world as both a prayer and a promise. Eleanor Roosevelt observed that "a curious grapevine" would carry its words around the world even (perhaps especially) to those deprived of information or liberty by their governments. But millions of those people were betrayed by the geopolitics that controlled the Commission's work.

The U.N. Human Rights Commission was established by the U.N.'s Economic and Social Council in 1946. Its problems reflect in fine detail those of the entire U.N. system. Unlike the members of the European Human Rights Commission, who are relatively free of government pressures, members of the U.N. Commission are their countries' delegates. From the start, many of them, particularly those from the Soviet bloc, cited Article 2, Paragraph 7 of the United Nations Charter, which could be interpreted as saying that violations of human rights were "matters which are essentially within the domestic jurisdiction of any state." In 1947 the Commission actually adopted a self-denying ordinance that "it had no power to take action in regard to any complaints regarding human rights."

Throughout the fifties, desperate messages from individuals and groups were sent from all over the world to the Commission; they were, quite literally, ignored. In 1959 the Commission was empowered to send complaints—known in U.N. terms as "communications"—on to the governments concerned, but not to follow them up or comment.

In the sixties, the new majority of the U.N. moved, with Soviet support, to consider white racism in South Africa—a human-rights abuse that the West had preferred to condone. In 1961 and 1962, the General Assembly established special committees on both colonialism and apartheid with unprecedented powers of investigation. Their creation showed how a majority could override Article 2, Paragraph 7, the "domestic jurisdiction" clause of the charter. In 1967 and 1968 the Commission set up an ad hoc group of experts to examine first South Africa and then the one other target whose investigation was becoming politically acceptable—Israel. Most important of all, in 1967 the Commission was empowered "to make a thorough study of situations which reveal a consistent pattern of violations of human rights, *as exemplified by* the policy of apartheid" (emphasis added). It was a hopeful moment; the opportunity provided by the words "as exemplified by" was seized by defenders of human rights in lands other than South Africa. But the new procedures were not embarked upon courageously. In 1971 well-documented "communications" alleging genocide in Bangladesh were dismissed. In 1972 torture in Greece was thrown out. Only in 1973 were eight cases even really considered; these alleged "consistent patterns of gross violations of human rights" in Brazil, Guyana, Burundi, Indonesia, Tanzania, Britain (Northern Ireland), Iran and Portugal. In the end nothing was done. Amnesty International condemned this as "an ignominious abdication of the Commission's authority to promote respect for and protection of human rights and individual freedoms. . . . The present rules of confidentiality are an undisguised stratagem for using the U.N., not as an instrument for promoting and protecting and exposing large-scale violations of human rights, but rather for concealing their occurrence."

In 1974, procedures, precedents and confidentiality were set aside when a special committee was set up to examine human rights abuses under the military junta in Chile. This group issued a devastating report in 1975. Few other victims were as fortunate as the Chileans. In 1978, for example, when estimates of the number of Cambodians who had died ranged between one and three million, the Commission could agree only that the allegations should be presented to the government in Phnom Penh for comment.* The eventual response was a Khmer Rouge tirade of abuse against all those who dared to criticize Democratic Kampuchea. Since then, the Commission's procedures have been further improved, from the point of view of the victims, but the situation remains uncertain. For example, in 1981 the Commission decided not to censure the terror conducted by the Ayatollah Khomeini's regime in Iran. But in 1983 the Commission condemned continuing violations in Cambodia, West Sahara, Afghanistan, East Timor, El Salvador, Guatemala, Poland, Iran and Bolivia.

The image of Cambodia that one had in 1978 was both horrible and imprecise. Under the growing threat from Vietnam, the government in Phnom Penh was beginning to make some links to the rest of the world. A group of Scandinavian ambassadors from Peking made a brief visit to Phnom Penh; they said they found it a "ghost city." They were appalled. So was a group of Yugoslav journalists; their film of empty towns was chilling despite the caution of its commentary.

* This action excited some incredulity. In an essay entitled "Cambodia: An Experiment in Genocide," in *Time* Magazine, David Aikman, a former correspondent in Phnom Penh, declared:

> Somehow, the enormity of the Cambodian tragedy—even leaving aside the grim question of how few actually died in Angka Loeu's experiment in genocide—has failed to evoke an appropriate sense of outrage in the West. . . . The U.N., ever quick to adopt a resolution condemning Israel or South Africa, acted with its customary tortoise-like caution when dealing with a Third World horror: it wrote a letter to Phnom Penh asking for an explanation of charges against the regime.

At the same time, refugees said that the killings were getting worse and worse. Under the threat of Vietnam, the Khmer Rouge were embarking on widespread purges. *The New York Times* published an editorial entitled "The Unreachable Terror in Cambodia," which reflected some of the despair that the visions of Cambodia from the outside world evoked.

> The magnitude of disaster numbs the mind. . . . We have said little about the war because we do not know what outcome to prefer. A Vietnamese victory that places Hanoi's puppets in control of Cambodia would probably have its own unfortunate consequences for Cambodians. And while denouncing the Khmer Rouge's reign of terror is easy, we are unable to suggest ways in which the United States and other countries might apply pressure against the offending regime. There appears to be no way, short of war, to influence the policies of Pol Pot and his colleagues.

That thought occurred also to Senator George McGovern; he actually speculated about the possibility of an international invasion of Cambodia. At a hearing of the Senate Foreign Relations Committee he declared that the Khmer Rouge record made the Nazis "look very tame by comparison." He asked, "Do we sit on the sidelines and watch a population slaughtered or do we marshal military force and put an end to it?" He thought that "we ought not dismiss out of hand" the possibility of international action, preferably by the U.N. "One would think the international community would at least condemn the situation and move to stop what appears like genocide."

McGovern's question was not well received. His former allies in the antiwar movement were stunned that this most doveish Senator could be proposing armed intervention in Indochina. From the right there was contemptuous dismissal; the *Wall Street Journal* told liberals that since their policies had led to the present horrors they should now keep quiet about Indochina.

But McGovern's question was serious. How can or how should the international community react in the face of the knowledge that a government is massacring its own people? Where do human rights supersede those of sovereignty? What lesson, if any, can be derived from the world's inaction over the murder of the Jews? How can we now meet the promise of "never again" made in 1945? Or, to return to the problems of knowledge and awareness, which I mentioned in the prologue, what obligations does awareness of a continuing disaster impose upon the world community? Is the spread of our knowledge making us blind? Or are we, like the blinded Gloucester in *King Lear,* still able to "know how this world goes" because we can "see it feelingly"?

These were all questions that the fate of Cambodia in the 1970s prompted. It did not encourage ready answers.

4 ✥ A Liberation

One answer to those questions was provided, for different reasons, by Vietnam. At the end of 1978 it invaded Cambodia, drove its former Khmer Rouge ally out of Phnom Penh and installed its own client regime, which it named The People's Republic of Kampuchea. Finally, the "unreachable" terror had been reached.

But this was not the answer that Western governments had sought. Cambodia had been liberated from the east, by those same Vietnamese Communist forces that had always been suspected of wishing to topple dominoes, had defeated the United States in 1975, had harshly imprisoned without trial at least 200,000 people since 1975, were now compelling scores of thousands more to take to the sea in boats, and were formally allied with the Soviet Union. Suddenly, sometimes subtly, sometimes not, the way in which the Western world saw the problem of Cambodia began to change. The liberating nature of the Vietnamese invasion was almost completely obscured by its aggressive and strategic implications. "Hanoi on the rampage" and "Hanoi's power play" is how *Time* Magazine described the invasion, quoting in its headlines the reaction of an unnamed senior American official—"an abhorrent regime overthrown by an abhorrent aggression."

Hanoi itself rendered such a reaction inevitable. The Vietnamese had helped the Khmer Rouge to power and had, until 1978, disregarded the refugee stories. Their invasion now was strategic, and had nothing to do with human rights. The Vietnamese Foreign Minister

Nguyen Co Thach later told Congressman Steve Solarz, "Human rights was not a question; that was their problem. We didn't go along with the McGovern proposal. We were concerned only with security."

Now, far from acknowledging that the invasion raised international issues of legitimate concern to Cambodia's other neighbors, indeed to the world community, the Vietnamese first denied that they had any troops in the country at all and then declared that the matter was "irreversible" and of no concern to anyone else. Had Hanoi instead proposed an international conference or United Nations participation in discussing Cambodia's future much of the agony to come might have been avoided.

After Cambodia itself, the country most obviously and most immediately affected by the invasion was Thailand. Thai attitudes were to play a crucial role in the development of the crisis to come. In good part those attitudes were shaped by the historical relations between Thailand, Cambodia and Vietnam. Each of those relationships has been characterized by varying degrees of mistrust and both the Thais and the Vietnamese have used Cambodia as a focus of that mistrust.

During the Angkorian empire, the Khmers extended their suzerainty over vast areas of Southeast Asia, including the Mekong Delta, Laos, Thailand, Burma and Malaya. After Angkor began to collapse in the thirteenth century, the Siamese (Thais) expanded their kingdom into Cambodia from the west, while in the east the Vietnamese moved southward from China toward the Mekong Delta and then west. Having ruled the entire area, successive Cambodian princes had to seek aid from and pay tribute to either the Vietnamese or the Siamese who competed and fought with each other for influence over Cambodia.

The Khmers feared both of their more populous neighbors. But occupation by the Siamese was mitigated by the fact that they had the same religion and cultural background as the Khmers. Khmer-Vietnamese relations, by contrast, involved a sharp cultural clash between Indian-influenced and Chinese-dominated views of society; they were much more brutal and bitter. Unlike the Siamese, the Vietnamese regarded the Cambodians as "barbarians" and tried to eradicate Cambodian customs in the areas they seized. For similar reasons of cultural disparity, the Siamese and the Vietnamese exhibited great distrust of one another; Siamese commanders continually warned of the risk of Vietnamese plots in Cambodia. One 1842 report explained a defeat as due to the "tricky thinking of the Vietnamese."

By the middle of the nineteenth century, Cambodia was on the verge of disappearing and was saved only by the French, who, having colonized Vietnam, imposed a protectorate on Cambodia; this lasted until France granted independence to King Norodom Sihanouk in 1953. Like other Cambodian kings before him, Sihanouk subsequently tried to play off his Thai and Vietnamese neighbors, and their conflicting ideologies, in order to preserve his territory. He had a large measure of success until his overthrow in 1970.

Alone of the countries in the region Thailand, which now has a population of about 46 million, was never colonized. Thus, there has been no outside interference in the country's monarchy, which remains its focal point, particularly among the peasantry, which constitutes a large majority of the people. Thailand has a plethora of political parties, but for decades politics have been dominated by the military. During the 1950s, '60s and early '70s, a succession of generals formed close links with the United States, and Thai troops fought the Communists in Indochina.

Nonetheless, parliamentary politics remained alive in Bangkok and in 1973 the military regime was overthrown after massive student demonstrations against it. Three years of democratic government followed, but they were ended in October 1976 by a bloody military coup in which hundreds of students and other civilians were killed.. Hundreds more young people fled to join the Thai Communist Party, which had Chinese support, in the hills and forests.

The leaders of the coup claimed that their action was necessary, to defend the monarchy against Communist conspiracy both at home and abroad. But the repression that the new regime instituted was too much even for many of those soldiers who had installed it, and in November 1977 a group of middle-ranking officers known as the Young Turks helped to overthrow the regime in favor of a new government under General Kriangsak Chamanand.

Kriangsak pledged, and actually began to institute, a much more moderate, liberal regime. It was one that allowed more freedom of movement, of the press and of debate than in probably any other country in South East Asia.

The government's critics could still point to the corruption that greases economic and political life, to the number of journalists who have been intimidated and even killed for trying to expose it, and to the enormous disparities that still exist between rich and poor. Wealth is ostentatiously displayed in Bangkok, particularly among powerful Chinese families, and the government itself acknowledges that ten million peasants still live in absolute poverty. Nonetheless Thailand is a society that is continually growing—per capita income increased eightfold in the twenty years to 1983—and for the majority of people standards of living have improved. In 1983 the World Bank called it "one of the success stories of the developing world over the past two decades," especially in terms of economic growth and alleviation of poverty.

The Vietnamese capture of Phnom Penh in January 1979 was greeted in Bangkok with fear similar to that which the fall of Indochina had occasioned for the Communists four years earlier. Indeed, for many ordinary people the fear was perhaps greater still—the experience of Communist rule in Indochina, particularly in Cambodia, was unlikely to have made many Thais more sanguine about the prospect of such government in their own country. For this reason, as well as because of the pattern of history, the idea of accepting a Vietnamese takeover of Cambodia was not one that had very widespread appeal in Thailand in early 1979.

Some Western diplomats later suggested that Thailand's best chance of influencing the outcome would have been to invade Cambodia from the west as Vietnam crossed from the east. The west was virtually undefended and had the Thai army occupied Battambang and the fertile rice lands around it, Vietnam might have been compelled to negotiate. Equally, however, the Vietnamese might have driven the Thais back.

Through its ally, China, the Khmer Rouge Government of Democratic Kampuchea sent a message to the Secretary General of

the United Nations—of which, of course, it was still a member—
asking for a special meeting of the Security Council to discuss the
invasion. The Thai government gave permission to the Khmer Rouge
Foreign Minister Ieng Sary to cross Thailand en route to Peking.
He was picked up at the Cambodian border by Thai army helicopter,
flown to Bangkok and put on board a scheduled flight to Hong Kong.

In a first-class cabin, being plied with champagne, went the man
who, until a few days before, had been reviled as a leader of one of
the most vicious regimes in the world—a regime, moreover, that
prided itself on abjuring most of that world.

Until now the Khmer Rouge leadership had been mass mur-
derers. Now they were also a government that had been overthrown
by a regime seen as a surrogate of the Soviet Union. It was a change
that they began at once to exploit with great diligence. Indeed, the
alacrity with which, Chinese petty cash in hand, they took to the
trappings of that same Western civilization that they had affected
to deplore was astonishing.*

As the Vietnamese army had closed upon Phnom Penh the Chinese had also managed to extract Prince Sihanouk from the house
arrest in which the Khmer Rouge had held him for the last three
years. He was flown to Peking and greeted with considerable honors.
Silence has never been one of the Prince's trademarks, and now, after
such a long and frightening incarceration, he burst into speech, giving
a superb and typically idiosyncratic six-hour press conference. He
called upon the Voice of America correspondent in Peking to thank
him for all VOA's broadcasts about Cambodia in recent years. He
asked *Newsweek*'s correspondent, James Pringle, "Are you Art
Buchwald? I so appreciate Art Buchwald, and you look almost like
him." He said that he had lived well enough in Phnom Penh—
"Look, I am fat"—but several of his family had been killed. He also
roundly denounced the brutality of the Khmer Rouge. They had, he
said, denied Cambodians "the basic rights of humanity: the right to

* In June 1979, the *Le Monde* correspondent, Roland Pierre Paringaux
took the same flight as Ieng Sary to a meeting of the Non Aligned Nations
in Colombo. He noted that while thousands of Ieng Sary's followers and the
civilians under their control were starving in Cambodia, Ieng Sary himself,
again traveling first class, spent a large amount of money on cigarettes, alcohol
and perfumes.

be loved, to choose your wife freely and to be with your wife and children all the time; to have classical justice with lawyers; to be judged publicly."

But Sihanouk reflected also the ambiguity that many Cambodians and many other people felt or would come to feel about the Vietnamese invasion and that would render the prolonged crisis so painful. Cambodians have always feared Vietnamese territorial ambitions. Cambodia was now being swallowed by Vietnam, Sihanouk said, and much though he hated the Khmer Rouge, he was prepared to demand, in the name of their government, that that be resisted. "I am not a member of the Khmer Rouge team," he said. "They are courageous fighters for . . . I cannot say freedom, but for national independence and territorial integrity." He warned that after Cambodia, the Vietnamese would "swallow" the rest of Southeast Asia. He was flown to the United Nations.

At the Security Council the Soviets demanded an adjournment until the new foreign minister of the government of "the People's Republic of Kampuchea" could arrive. The Chinese declared that Soviet conduct was "preposterous and despicable." Everyone knew that Democratic Kampuchea was a legitimate member of the U.N., and here was Prince Sihanouk to represent it. "It is indefensible for puppet regimes to appear before the Council," stated the Chinese.

The U.S. Ambassador Andrew Young—whom Sihanouk had embraced, saying that the United States was now a defender of Cambodian neutrality—declared, "I daresay this is as interesting a session as we have had for some time." He said that "we have here a representative of a government recognized by the General Assembly and so should proceed with the agenda as adopted."

The Kuwaiti ambassador thought the situation was "tragic" rather than "interesting." "Rome is burning, children are being orphaned, women widowed, and we haggle. From 1970 to 1975 my government consistently supported Prince Sihanouk as the embodiment of the people of Kampuchea. Even under these circumstances we believe Prince Sihanouk is the embodiment of the people of Kampuchea." Eventually the Council agreed, despite Soviet anger, to hear Sihanouk. As a concession to the Soviets, Vietnam and Cuba were also allowed to attend the session.

Sihanouk made an eloquent plea for Cambodia, which he declared Vietnam was trying to swallow "like a boa constrictor." And he compared himself with Charles de Gaulle in 1940. "We will never surrender," he declared. "We may lose everything but we will never lose our national honor."

The Vietnamese representative, Ha Van Lau, then gave a moving account of the misery of life under the Khmer Rouge—"unique in living history, a living hell." Outside the chamber Ha Van Lau was less impassioned, more cynical. According to members of the Singapore delegation, he said to Tommy Koh, Singapore's representative, "Why do you make such a fuss over Cambodia? The world will have forgotten in a week." In this the Vietnamese made a rare misjudgment. Hanoi's occupation of Cambodia and the country's representation at the U.N. would remain an international issue for years to come. At the end of this session, the Security Council resolution calling for withdrawal of Vietnamese troops from Cambodia was vetoed by the Soviet Union.

In response to the invasion, Japan and the European Economic Community immediately cut off economic aid to Vietnam, and the United States moved to restrict those few loans that had already been extended by international institutions such as the International Monetary Fund and other projects funded by United Nations specialized agencies.

China had already taken a position of absolute opposition to the Vietnamese conquest. In the past—particularly during Sihanouk's rule in the 1950s and '60s—Cambodia had seen China as a natural protector against encroachment by either Vietnam or Thailand, a role China had been glad to fulfill. Sihanouk and Zhou Enlai had a close relationship, and although China was evidently uncomfortable with Khmer Rouge excesses, it was the regime's only effective ally while it was in power. The Chinese were not now prepared to tolerate the Vietnamese overthrow of the Khmer Rouge. When Ieng Sary was flown to Peking he was apparently given specific instructions to start a resistance.

Much later, in 1982, the foreign ministry of the Vietnamese-controlled government in Phnom Penh published what were alleged to be documents captured from the Khmer Rouge. One appeared to be the transcript of a conversation between Ieng Sary and the Chinese leaders Hua Guofeng and Deng Xiaoping in January 1979 after Ieng Sary was flown to Peking. The Chinese rebuked him for the sectarian policies the Khmer Rouge had pursued while in power and urged that the Khmer Rouge now create a united anti-Vietnamese front including Prince Sihanouk and other non-Communist resistance groups.

The Chinese agreed to provide the Khmer Rouge with a radio station and then Deng asked Ieng Sary, "How are we to supply you with money? Send it to Bangkok? Or to Kriangsak? Or deposit it in Thai banks? You can withdraw it at any moment. We can deposit five million dollars subject to withdrawal at any moment. We can deposit it in Thai banks, or leave it with the Chinese embassy, or the Kampuchean embassy in Thailand."

"We'll take it from the Chinese embassy in Bangkok," replied Ieng Sary, with a clear understanding of the manner in which Thai politics often works.

At the end of January, Deng Xiaoping traveled to the United States to set the seal on the normalization of relations with Washington, which had been completed in December 1978. He was the first Chinese Communist leader ever to visit America, and he threw himself with gusto into the occasion. In Texas he wore a ten-gallon hat and rode around in a stage coach. Throughout he denounced his former ally, Vietnam.

Deng also made a point of visiting Sihanouk. The Prince had taken refuge in a New York hospital in order to escape the Khmer Rouge escort with whom the Chinese had sent him to New York. He had secretly summoned Andrew Young, America's ambassador to the U.N., and asked him for political asylum in the United States. However, Deng induced the Prince to return to China and to play a role in the anti-Vietnamese resistance that he had instructed Ieng Sary to set up.

Soon after Deng's return to Peking, China launched an attack on the northern provinces of Vietnam to "punish" the Vietnamese for their invasion of Cambodia. It was bound to seem to have Washington's imprimatur. Only four years after the Americans were de-

feated by the Vietnamese with the help of China, China with at least
the foreknowledge of the United States, was itself trying to cow
Vietnam.*

Two wars between Communist states were now taking place,
China versus Vietnam and Vietnam versus Democratic Kampuchea.
During their four-week occupation of northern Vietnam, the Chinese
embarked on a wide swathe of destruction. But they did not manage
to damage Vietnamese main-force units, which remained grouped in
defensive positions a little farther south around Hanoi.

Throughout this time, the details of what was actually taking place
in Cambodia under Vietnamese occupation were scarce. Having first
denied their presence there, the Vietnamese were now strictly limiting foreign access to the country.

For the overwhelming majority of the Cambodian people the
invasion meant freedom. The Vietnamese made no attempt to contain people in the collective villages into which they had been corralled by the Khmer Rouge. Indeed, they encouraged people to go
home. In the weeks that followed the invasion, the roads of Cambodia were filled with hundreds of thousands of people crossing and
crisscrossing the country. Thin, poorly dressed, often with no possessions at all, they were searching among the awful wreckage of
recent years for their families, for friends, for their old villages—for
some traces of the past on which to build the future.

Fighting between the Vietnamese and the Khmer Rouge was
continuing. Crops—the main rice crop of the year—were being seized

---

* In his memoirs, Jimmy Carter asserted that Deng had mentioned the
proposed invasion but that he, Carter, had tried to discourage it. "He claimed
to be still considering the issue, but my impression was that the decision had
already been made. Vietnam would be punished." Zbigniew Brzezinski records in his memoirs that he wanted to avoid having the United States criticize China as an aggressor in Vietnam. "Accordingly, I developed a proposal
that the United States should criticize the Chinese for their military action
but should couple that criticism with a parallel condemnation of the Vietnamese for their occupation of Cambodia, and demand that both China and
Vietnam pull out their forces. I knew that such a proposal would be totally
unacceptable to the Vietnamese and to the Soviets, and hence would provide
a partial diplomatic umbrella for the Chinese action without associating the
United States with it, thereby permitting the United States to adopt publicly
a somewhat critical position."

or burned. The Khmer Rouge were attempting to build up their strength by forcing groups of people, sometimes whole villages, into the forests and hills, where some of them would be conscripted into the army. They were building bases in the mountains close to the Thai border.

As a result, Vietnamese troops were also coming closer and closer to Thailand. The Vietnamese attempted to assure the Thais that there was no threat to Thailand. The government in Bangkok publicly professed neutrality between the two warring groups of Communists. But, in fact, Thai help was soon being extended to the Khmer Rouge, who were still the legal government of Cambodia, recognized by the U.N.

In mid-January the Thai Foreign Minister announced that the Thai Red Cross would be allowed to provide medical care for wounded Khmer Rouge soldiers who came to the border. This was being done, the Foreign Minister then insisted, "on purely humanitarian grounds. We are a Buddhist country. How can we let wounded men die in front of us without giving them the necessary help?"

On Sunday, March 4, as northern Vietnam was sitting out the Chinese invasion, a small contingent of Vietnamese troops briefly invaded Thailand at Aranyaprathet. The Thai army reacted somewhat chaotically; road blocks were flung up and truckloads of troops careened around the border. Within hours all was quiet again, but the incident established once and for all for the Thai government and many ordinary Thais that the Cambodian buffer—which had existed ever since the French cast their protectorate over Cambodia in 1864—was gone and there was now nothing and no one between Thailand and Vietnam save those Cambodians who were prepared to fight the Vietnamese.

From now on it would be an important part of Thai policy to encourage the growth of all manner of guerrillas along the border. Anti-Communist groups on a limited scale had existed since 1975. Often they were little more than bandits, smuggling teak and gems and occasionally sniping, to little effect, at the Khmer Rouge. Now it was suggested that, instead of fighting the Khmer Rouge, they should cooperate with their former enemy against the Vietnamese. This evolving policy, building up the Khmer Rouge to hinder Vietnamese consolidation of Cambodia, was conceived with Chinese help, was underwritten by ASEAN, and was at least tacitly endorsed by Thailand's allies in the West.

For Thailand the policy was not really inconsistent; the Thais had sought normal relations with the Khmer Rouge through most of the period since 1975. But, for Thailand's Western friends who in 1978 had taken up the case of Khmer Rouge atrocities, the policy involved more than the usual hypocrisies and ambiguities associated with political and strategic choices. The paradox was particularly complicated for those international humanitarian organizations that were hoping that now they could finally bring assistance to the Cambodian people. The agency most immediately affected was the United Nations High Commissioner for Refugees (UNHCR).

Like sands shifted by restless winds, refugees spill today across the globe. They constitute a Fourth World, one whose inhabitants have no representation and over which they have no control. No one even knows how many refugees there are; some estimates say ten million, some twelve million, a few even up to eighteen million. Whatever their number, they are among the symbols of the twentieth century. Armenians, Russians, Germans, Jews, Central Europeans, Hindus and Muslims in the Subcontinent, Palestinians, Hungarians, Cubans, Biafrans, Bengalis, Vietnamese, Lao, Cambodians, Chileans, Czechoslovaks, Ethiopians, Somalis, Ugandans, Salvadorans, Afghans—just a partial list of nationalities provides a mournful litany of disaster.

The first international official solely responsible for refugees was Fridtjof Nansen, the polar explorer. In the 1920s, under the auspices of the League of Nations, he provided travel papers, known as Nansen Passports, for at least one and a half million White Russians and later also for Armenians and Greeks. By the time he died in 1930, Nansen had come to personify the refugee cause and had given the refugee's predicament a meaning all over the Western world that it had never before enjoyed. But after his death the newly created High Commissioner for Refugees, also under the aegis of the League, was able to do much less well on behalf of the Jews—simply because few governments would back him.

During the Second World War, the U.N. Relief and Rehabilitation Agency (UNRRA) was created as an office of the Allied powers to deal with some of the consequences of the total warfare—starvation, disease, flight, national bankruptcy. It was probably the broadest and most effective disaster-relief agency ever formed—at one time it employed almost 50,000 people, and over its existence it spent $4.25 billion on food supplies, medical supplies and programs, industrial and agricultural reconstruction, and aid to refugees—in Greece, Yugoslavia, Albania, Czechoslovakia, Poland, Italy, Austria, Finland, Hungary, Ukraine, Ethiopia, China, the Philippines and Korea—8.5 million in all.

After the defeat of the Nazis, many refugees voluntarily returned to their homelands. Others had no wish to go back to territories now controlled by the Soviet Union. Nonetheless, the Western allies, to their lasting shame, shipped back to Stalin many scores of thousands of Soviet citizens who had been captured by the Nazis. Almost all were either murdered or incarcerated. The Russians insisted that only war criminals would not wish to return home, and when the idea of a new agency to help refugees was debated at the new United Nations in San Francisco, Moscow refused to support any organization that was not solely concerned with repatriation. It was one of the first clear breaks between the USSR and its wartime allies.

At the end of the forties, a new flood of refugees out of Soviet-controlled Europe, the migration of millions of people between India and Pakistan and the problems of Palestine showed that other agencies were desperately needed. The Palestinians evicted from Israel were taken under what was to prove the permanent wing of the United Nations Relief and Works Association (UNRWA). The International Refugee Organization had a brief existence, and then in 1950 a new Office of the High Commissioner for Refugees (UNHCR) was created.

In 1951 UNHCR produced the U.N. Convention relating to the status of refugees. Its terms referred only to events occurring in Europe before January 1, 1951. A refugee was defined as

> Any person who, owing to well-founded fear of being persecuted for reasons of race, religion or nationality, membership of a particular social group or political opinion, is outside the country of his nationality and is unable, or owing to such fear, is unwilling to avail himself of the protection of that country; or who, not having a nationality and being outside the country of his former habitual

residence, is unable, or owing to such fear, is unwilling to return to it.

In 1967 the Convention was amended by a Protocol that removed its limitations of time and geography. This meant that from now on all refugees, not just those created by the Second World War, could come within the protection offered by the 1951 Convention. The Convention and Protocol remain the principal international instruments for defining, protecting and aiding refugees today, except in Africa where a Convention passed by the Organization of African Unity in 1969 is rather more generous to African refugees in that it widens the concept of persecution, refers specifically to asylum and makes explicit the mechanism for voluntary repatriation.

The spirit of the conventions is that every person is entitled to freedom from persecution and that he or she will receive recognition and assistance from the international community to effect that freedom. At the same time, no person can or should be forcibly repatriated (the technical term is refoulement) to his or her own country, the source of his or her fear of persecution. UNHCR's principal task is to protect such rights of refugees. Its task is obviously made more difficult when it is operating in countries which have not ratified the Convention or the Protocol. By the end of the 1970s only seventy-eight states had ratified the Convention and only seventy-two the Protocol. Thailand had ratified neither.

Separate words for exile, migrant and refugee do not exist in the Thai language. All Thai words for such people tend to imply that their stay in Thailand might be permanent, an impression that successive Thai governments have been anxious to avoid. Nonetheless, since 1945 Thailand has experienced and has offered various forms of asylum to different waves of refugees. About 11,000 Kuomintang supporters of Chiang Kai-shek escaped through Burma and Laos after the Communist takeover of China in 1946; these aging warlords and their followers still live in camps in northern Thailand, often dealing in opium. There are also about 40,000 Vietnamese who came either in the late 1940s or after the French defeat at Dien Bien Phu in 1954. Thirty thousand people fled the fighting in Burma in 1959. After the Communist victories in Indochina in 1975, about

160,000 Indochinese crossed their borders into Thailand. Most of them were placed in camps financed by the United Nations High Commissioner for Refugees but run by the Ministry of the Interior. Voluntary agencies provided additional services, such as medical care and training.

From the point of view of the Thais (and other non-Communist Southeast Asian countries), a containable situation became intolerable with the growing exodus of Vietnamese boat people at the end of 1978 and the Vietnamese invasion of Cambodia. By the beginning of 1979, more than 100,000 Vietnamese had fled increasingly harsh policies at home to reach other Southeast Asian shores. The numbers were growing exponentially. In one six-week period, 40,000 boat people arrived off the tiny island of Pilau Bidong off the Malaysian coast. No one knew how many more had died in the attempt; some contemporary estimates put the number at half those who had survived. The governments of first asylum were expressing more and more impatience. The prime minister of Malaysia warned in January that no more would be allowed to land. The Thai Prime Minister General Kriangsak Chamanand warned that no refugees from either Vietnam or Cambodia would be allowed to enter Thailand, as "we have too many already."

Early in January 1979, Poul Hartling, a former Danish prime minister who was now the U.N. High Commissioner for Refugees, sent a telegram to General Kriangsak offering UNHCR help in dealing with new Cambodian refugees fleeing the fighting between Vietnamese and Khmer Rouge troops. The offer was ignored. Instead, Thailand labeled these new arrivals "illegal immigrants" and confined them to camps separate from those who had arrived before the Vietnamese invasion. Even relatives who had come hoping to join those who had fled before were kept apart. The government attempted to keep not only journalists but also all international aid officials away from them.

The Bangkok office of the High Commissioner was run at this time by an Englishman called Leslie Goodyear, who was always cautious in his dealings with the Thais. He accepted the government's argument that this new wave of refugees (about 3,500 came from Cambodia in the first three months of 1979) threatened Thai security since their loyalties were not known. He argued to UNHCR headquarters in Geneva: "So long as there is no threat of forced return to Cambodia it is considered wise to allow the Thai authorities sufficient time to fully satisfy themselves of the non-involvement of these arrivals and thus to quieten their fears of a new major refugee problem. . . ." Goodyear knew that the Thais do not welcome external pressure.

Goodyear said that very little information was available on what had happened to many of the new arrivals. By then, numerous small groups of people were being forced back into Cambodia. UNHCR was aware of some such incidents, but it made no effective protest, despite its duty to protect refugees from such forcible repatriation.

The limits of UNHCR's effectiveness were shown in April, when a Vietnamese offensive pushed thousands of Cambodians, combatants and civilians, over the Thai border.

On April 12, 1,728 new "illegal immigrants," most of whom had relatives in the old pre-1979 refugee camp at Aranyaprathet, were loaded by the Thai military onto buses. They were told they were being taken to another camp. Despite informal protests by UNHCR officials both at the border and in Bangkok, they were driven to the border and forcibly handed over to anti-Communist, Khmer Serei soldiers. Many of them were old people, women and children; they were marched off into the forest at gunpoint. A week later two men from the group escaped and told relief officials that two hundred of the refugees had already died.

At another such incident on April 16, the UNHCR field officer, David Taylor, attempted to intervene with the military to protect individual refugees from being driven back. The incident was written up in melodramatic fashion by the newspaper Bangkok *World*. The Thai government complained about Taylor's behavior, saying it infringed Thai sovereignty.

By mid-April, the Vietnamese offensive against Khmer Rouge positions west of Battambang had pushed between 50,000 and 80,000 people into a narrow strip of land just south of Aranyaprathet. About 25,000 were thought to be soldiers, the rest were civilians, most of whom had been unwillingly corralled by Khmer Rouge troops. The only escape route was into Thailand, and groups of civilians sought refuge. Wherever possible the Thai military forced them back to the border. UNHCR field officers reported this to Bangkok, Bangkok to Geneva. From Geneva Poul Hartling cabled Prime Minister Kriangsak once again to offer help. Again the offer was ignored.

In the third week of April, the Thai military gave permission for a group of about 8,000 Khmer Rouge soldiers to force a much larger group of Cambodian civilians—more than 50,000 of them—to trek twenty miles or so along the Thai side of the border, to evade Vietnamese forces and then rejoin another Khmer Rouge unit inside Cambodia.

A long train of dusty, disheveled, terrified and emaciated men, women and children was marched south under Khmer Rouge control and Thai army supervision. Western reporters and aid officials were there; hundreds of civilians constantly begged to be allowed to stay in Thailand to be saved from the Khmer Rouge and the war. Their requests were rejected. The whole group was driven back into Cambodia.

In the first week of May 1979, UNHCR was made aware of another terrible incident. A diligent UNHCR official, Ove Ullerup-Peterson, heard that in Buriram province 826 Cambodians had been removed on April 15. The Thai district officer was unable to give any information, "as the matter was under the responsibility of the army." Ullerup-Peterson learned, however, that they had been taken in buses about 230 kilometers to another part of the border. Peasants in the last village before the border saw the buses pass through full and return empty. Refugees in another camp then reported that the Cambodians had been ordered out of the buses and made to walk for two and a half hours "to a large mountain, which had a steep cliff on one side, 150–200 meters high. The whole group was pushed over by Thai soldiers and killed."

Throughout these events it was UNHCR policy not to protest officially to the Thai authorities. Leslie Goodyear argued constantly that to do so would only anger the Thais and make them still more intolerant of refugees. Unfortunately, humanitarian organizations are often forced into such a policy of least resistance against intransigent governments. But some of Goodyear's junior colleagues in the Bangkok office were fiercely critical, at least among themselves, of this attitude. They argued that Thai officials were running rings around

UNHCR—giving hints that if only the organization were polite then better treatment would be meted out to the refugees. In fact, nothing of the sort was occurring. Goodyear's dilemma was unenviable.

All this time, UNHCR and the International Committee of the Red Cross (ICRC) were trying to persuade the Thai government to allow them to set up a proper program of assistance to the refugees. The Thais insisted that any such program must have "no strings attached"; in other words, they would not agree to stop forcible repatriation. They urged the ICRC to start a program inside Cambodia so as to deter people from leaving the country in the first place. In fact, the ICRC, along with UNICEF, had sent frequent messages to the government in Phnom Penh asking permission to come and determine what sort of relief was required, but as yet there had been no reply.

On May 3, High Commissioner Poul Hartling finally reacted to the reports of forced repatriation. He wrote a private letter to Prime Minister Kriangsak in which he spoke of "a matter of the utmost gravity. . . . Recent reports indicate that large groups of Kampucheans are seeking at least temporary asylum in Thailand. Many are entirely innocent victims of events of which they had no control. They fear, and the experience of others has proved, that if returned to Kampuchea at present, they would face unbearable suffering and quite possibly death. May I appeal to you to let such persons stay in Thailand so that their lives might be saved." The letter had no obvious effect. On May 7, the Bangkok *World* reported that 250 refugees were pushed back into Cambodia the day before, despite their pleas to stay and their fear of being killed by the Khmer Rouge. "Soksam Ol, twenty-three, revealed himself as a former student after crossing into Thailand. 'If the Khmer Rouge get me they will cut me into pieces,' he said."

Thai soldiers said the refugees were going to be pushed back. "Asked who would be waiting on the other side, the soldiers said: 'Khmer Rouge.' Thai officers ordered newsmen out of the area before the trucks departed." Leslie Goodyear forwarded this report to Geneva, noting, "According report eyewitness statement substantially correct. Press men not allowed film."

Some refugees were luckier. In the middle of May, Kurt Waldheim, the Secretary General of the U.N., was due to visit Bangkok, and the government, for a time, relaxed its rules on new arrivals from Cambodia. In the second week of May about four thousand "illegal immigrants" were allowed to cross the border near Aranyaprathet.

Waldheim came to Aran on May 13. Relief officials on the border including David Taylor of UNHCR, John Naponick, an American doctor, Peter Baltsensberger of the ICRC, and Robert Ashe, the British relief worker, decided to present to the Secretary General the details of what had been happening. They encouraged the refugees at the old camp at Aranyaprathet to make speeches dwelling on the forced repatriation of their relatives among the group of 1,728 who had recently been repatriated. Thai officials were infuriated. Taylor received death threats; UNHCR subsequently removed him from the border and failed to replace him for several months.

Waldheim apparently was impressed. At a dinner with Prime Minister Kriangsak on May 14, he raised the matter and asked the Thai government not to push more refugees back into Cambodia. In response, Kriangsak said that the Thai authorities were not pushing people back but merely trying to "persuade" them to return. Kriangsak proposed what he called a "pragmatic" solution—the U.N. should provide Thailand with food and money for the refugees but they would remain under Thai control.

Then another guest, the Minister of the Interior, General Lek Naeomali, emphasized that what Thailand required was money not words. Money in the hand.

The Prime Minister added that food for the new arrivals should be bought in Thailand. It would be distributed by Thais. He did not want any foreign relief officials in the field. "Send the supplies to us. We will do it." Then, in a remark which summed up what officials in third-world countries often feel about international humanitarian agencies, he said, "Refugee officials are wonderful but unrealistic and only look at one aspect." This was a clash of priorities which was to occur again and again throughout the Cambodian drama, as through many others.

All this time the crisis both within Cambodia and along its border with Thailand was overshadowed in the Western world by the drama of the boat people, fleeing and being expelled now in scores of thousands from both northern and southern Vietnam. Scarcely a day went by without news of a frail overloaded craft sinking under the weight of its passengers or the fury of the sea, of the survivors of a pirate attack telling of murder and rape, of merchant ships passing by imperiled boats, of refugees being forced away from the beaches of Malaysia, Singapore, Indonesia. The visions that the boat people inspired, and the guilt that they evoked in the West, particularly in the United States, obscured most other crises from the imagination.

The Thai press was filled now with daily denunciations of the refugees and the hypocrisy of the West in accepting only a few of them. Prime Minister Kriangsak complained constantly to Western ambassadors and others that the world was interested only in the boat people and did not care what happened along the Thai-Cambodian border. The Thai military became even more exasperated than the Prime Minister. One subsequent UNHCR internal history noted that "the Prime Minister was under considerable pressure from various groups within the Thai political and military circles, as well as external pressure from China as regards Thailand's overt stance of 'neutrality' in the face of what was considered a clear position of aggression on the part of the Vietnamese government." On one occasion, Kriangsak said to this author that the Cambodian refugees "were conceived by U.S. policies during the 1970–75 war, and were delivered by Vietnam. Why should they be left on our doorstep?"

On the morning of Friday, June 8, 110 buses pulled up at the border site of Nong Chan, a few miles north of Aranyaprathet, where several thousand refugees were now camped in fields. Thai soldiers in the buses told the refugees they were being moved to another, better camp.

Some refugees seemed to believe what they were told and were happy enough to leave the squalid, overcrowded conditions of Nong Chan. Others were not; one woman, who had walked out of Cambodia to Nong Chan with her three children only a week before, said later that she was terrified when the Thai soldiers began to herd them into buses.

The buses first drove west, away from the Thai border. This

calmed the refugees and raised their hopes. Then the buses turned north and finally, after a long journey, they turned east, back toward Cambodia. There was silence in the buses.

At the same time refugees were also being taken from the Wat Ko camp inside the town of Aranyaprathet. These were the people whom Kurt Waldheim had visited; his blessing had evidently conferred no protection.

When they heard what was happening, UNHCR officials and diplomats from the American, French and Australian embassies descended on Aranyaprathet. They tried first to stop the movement and then to rescue those who had already been accepted for resettlement. They were not allowed into the Wat Ko camp but had to stand on the edge and call out lists of names. Some refugees, who had no idea what was happening, were afraid to come forward. Others could not understand the way the foreigners pronounced their names. Eventually about 1,500 of the 6,000 Cambodians there were rescued.

Most foreigners were then ordered out of the town. Buses were drawn up. Thai soldiers told the refugees they were being taken to a transit camp to await resettlement. Many refugees had to be beaten by the soldiers before they climbed fearfully into the buses.

Loaded with Cambodian refugees from temporary camp sites all over eastern Thailand, hundreds of buses converged on a mountainous region of the northeastern border near the temple of Preah Vihear, whose ownership had long been a source of bitter dispute between Thailand and Cambodia. They arrived, with military precision, after dark.

The border had been sealed off by Thai soldiers; the area was flooded with troops. The refugees were ordered, busload by busload, to walk back into Cambodia. They were told that there was a path down the mountains but that on either side of it there were mine fields. They were also told that on the other side the Vietnamese army was waiting to welcome them. Thai soldiers also said, "Thai money will not be valid in Kampuchea; we ask you to make a voluntary contribution to our army."

The path down the mountains became steeper, the jungle thicker. Dozens, scores of people fell onto mines. Those with possessions had to abandon them to carry their children down. One group of refugees desperately pooled whatever valuables they had left, filled two buckets with them and walked back up toward the Thai soldiers, carrying a white flag. The soldiers took the buckets and then opened fire on the refugees.

For days this operation went on. Altogether, between 43,000 and 45,000 people were pushed down the cliffs at Preah Vihear. It took three days to cross the mine field. Water was very hard to find. Some people had salt. Very few had food. The Thais had distributed at most a cup of rice per person before the buses were emptied.

One refugee who finally managed to escape back to Thailand told UNHCR officials: "The crowd was very dense. It was impossible to number the victims of the land mines. The wounded people were moaning. The most difficult part of the walk was near the dead bodies. Tears I thought had dried up long ago came back to my eyes— less because of the sight than from the thought that those innocent people had paid with their lives for their attempts to reach freedom in a world that was too selfish."

That world knew what was going on. The story of Preah Vihear was well reported by both journalists and diplomats even as it was taking place.

Henry Kamm wrote dramatic, moving accounts in *The New York Times*. So did Roland Pierre Paringaux in *Le Monde*. On June 11 Jean Christophe Oeberg, the Swedish ambassador, cabled Stockholm: "What should have been long predicted is now fact—forced repatriation. No protests or insubstantial threats will change the Royal Thai Government's mood. The decision has been taken in the conviction that the international community has shown a notorious lack of interest in this question. . . ."

At lunch with Oeberg on June 14, Kriangsak said that the decision had been imposed upon him by Supreme Command. Nevertheless, he was pleased at the international furore it had aroused. At last Thailand was receiving attention. A few days later Kriangsak told Ilter Turkman, an Assistant Secretary General and a special envoy from Kurt Waldheim, that he had public support for the repatriation. It would be stopped only if Turkman promised that all the Cambodians involved would be resettled in other countries. Turkman was unable to give such assurance.

Through the rest of June and early July the refugees remained stranded in the no man's land of Preah Vihear. They received a little food and water from Thai villagers, but not nearly enough. The Vietnamese army, which was close by on the other side, also gave them some food, but was very hesitant about allowing them through.*

What did the U.N. High Commissioner for Refugees do on their behalf? From Geneva there was silence. From Bangkok, inaction.

On July 6 Leslie Goodyear, the head of UNHCR's Bangkok office, called a meeting of foreign ambassadors to discuss the general refugee crisis. UNHCR has a primary responsibility to try to protect refugees from just such assaults as were now taking place at Preah Vihear. In his prepared introduction Goodyear made a brief reference to the fate of the 45,000. Turkman advised that forced repatriation was "a delicate political matter requiring much prudence."

Oeberg interrupted to ask just what UNHCR was doing for the 45,000. According to UNHCR files, "Mr. Turkman replied that the U.N. has not come up with any feasible programme as of yet, although efforts were now being made by various governments that have approached the Thai Government on a bilateral basis. He stressed that multilateral means of dealing with the problem seemed inappropriate at this given moment." Leslie Goodyear said that UNHCR was, of course, "prepared to help in any way," and he repeated that "the lack of public statements over this issue might be a sign that 'best efforts' are now being made quietly."

Eventually about two thousand people were rescued with the help of the U.S. Embassy and UNHCR, but UNHCR's over-all inaction appalled mid-level officials in its Bangkok office. Several wrote to Geneva to complain. This disaster proved to them that the policy of trying not to offend the Thais had failed; silence over the April re-

* Jean Christophe Oeberg attempted to organize a rescue operation. He obtained Thai permission for the Swedish Red Cross to take supplies across the border to the survivors. He then tried to get similar permission from the Vietnamese or Cambodian authorities. The Vietnamese first agreed and then refused, saying that aid could not be sent across the border but must go via the sovereign government in Phnom Penh. This would never reach Preah Vihear in time to save anyone.

patriations had encouraged, not deterred, the repatriation of the 45,000. The previous High Commissioner, Sadruddin Aga Khan, would have been on the border beating drums back in April, they said.*

The International Committee of the Red Cross, by contrast, did protest the repatriation of the 45,000 at Preah Vihear. The Thai government angrily rejected the protest. As a result, the ICRC delegate, Francis Amar, had to be recalled to Geneva; he was replaced by François Perez.

While pointing out UNHCR's failure to protect these refugees, one must remember that the one authority that might have been able to force the Thais to halt the repatriation at Preah Vihear was the U.S. government. Yet the Embassy in Bangkok did not strongly protest the action by the Thais despite the attempts, by Leslie Goodyear, among others, to persuade it to do so. Embassy officials later acknowledged that their reaction was too weak. The Ambassador Morton Abramowitz said subsequently that his reticence was caused by fear of undermining Kriangsak. "We asked the Thais to stop. They refused. We took the view that if the government had been forced to stop in midstream, Kriangsak could have been brought down by the military. Also we hoped that the refugees would be able to get back. We didn't realize how awful the geography was."

And so it was that these refugees, ordinary people of all classes fleeing the awful past, the bloody present and the very uncertain future of Cambodia were forced back. At the same time, Khmer Rouge troops were allowed to remain in well-hidden enclaves along the southern section of the border.

Though the forced repatriation at Preah Vihear did direct international attention toward Thailand's refugee problems, Cambodia was

* UNHCR had still failed to appoint a field officer to replace David Taylor at Aranyaprathet, and the post of Regional Protection Officer in Bangkok was also vacant. On July 31 a junior UNHCR official, Graeme Lean, after visiting the border, reported to Leslie Goodyear that it was impossible to tell how many refugees there really were or what the Thais were doing to them. "At the risk of being repetitive," he wrote, "there can be no hope of UNHCR offering a respectable level of succor or protection until a new field officer is assigned to the area."

not much discussed at the Geneva Conference on Indochinese refugees in mid-July. The Conference was convened in response, above all, to the crisis of the boat people.

By this time there were 350,000 Vietnamese waiting in camps in the Philippines, Thailand, Malaysia, Singapore, Indonesia and Hong Kong for the rest of the world to decide what to do with them. The countries of first asylum had complained with increasing bitterness that until now the developed world had not done enough. Just as the Thais had pushed the Cambodians back over the cliffs at Preah Vihear, so other Southeast Asian countries (except Hong Kong) had been towing boat people back out to sea and casting them adrift once more. A Malaysian minister, Dr. Mahathir bin Mohamad, Prime Minister by 1983, caused consternation in the Western press when he threatened that Malaysia would shoot any more boat people who tried to land.

Over the meeting, and frequently invoked, hung the ghost of the Evian Conference forty-one years before, when the world community had failed to offer refuge to Jews fleeing Nazism. Delegates at Geneva were beseeched by Vice-President Walter Mondale not to repeat the tragedy of Evian.

They did not do so. Nonetheless, during the two-day conference it became clear that there was great confusion in the West over the dilemma that the boat people posed. Many Western delegates used the meeting as a forum for berating Hanoi. But it was not always clear just what was so offensive about Vietnam's conduct.

Did we wish Vietnam to close its doors entirely and, like East Germany, shoot those people who tried to escape? Or was it that Vietnamese officials were often charging exorbitant fees for allowing people to leave?

Did we object to the unseaworthy nature of the boats and the fact that so many people drowned at sea? Or was it the fact that by releasing people in such huge numbers from the dictatorship that we condemned, the Vietnamese were testing the limits of our humanitarianism, the sincerity of our criticism of their abuse of human rights?

In an appeal for the Indochinese refugees, the writer John le Carre said, "They face us as the living witness of our rhetoric" during the war. Certainly guilt, particularly in the United States, was a large part of the emotional response that the boat people engendered. So was the memory of the Jews, and of ships like the *Struma* and the *St. Louis*.

Several delegates at Geneva asserted that no country has the right to export forcibly a section of its population that it considers racially or politically undesirable. But did that mean that other nations should collude in an attempt to stop it from doing so? At Geneva that did seem to be one sense of the meeting, and the French, with American and British backing, persuaded the Vietnamese to agree to a "moratorium" on departures of the boat people.

Kurt Waldheim, in his summing-up, announced this as a great achievement. But it seemed an astonishing solution, and it was greeted with horror by many members of the UNHCR staff. Returning to the Evian analogy, one said that it seemed rather like asking Hitler to hang on to the Jews, for the time being at least.

At the same time, however, the meeting did result in a significant increase in the number of resettlement places offered in the developed world. Two hundred sixty thousand new places were pledged in particular by the United States, Canada, Australia and France. As a result, pressure on the countries of first asylum was eased, and they ceased to make public demonstrations of forcing boat people back out to sea.

By the end of 1983 the West would have admitted about one million refugees from Indochina.* But it did not solve the problem. Through 1983, boat people were still setting out in thousands from Vietnam. The difference was that international concern had long since shifted to other areas of misery.

* Approximately 130,000 Vietnamese went to the United States after the Communist victory in 1975, and 260,000 ethnic Chinese refugees from Vietnam went to China from 1978 onward. By the end of 1982, 816,280 Cambodians, Lao and Vietnamese had been resettled in the West. By far the largest number—481,660—went to the United States.

5 &: Fears of Famine

From January 1979 onward, UNICEF and the International Committee of the Red Cross—both of which had programs in Cambodia until the Khmer Rouge victory in 1975—made repeated requests, by cable and through their offices in Hanoi, for permission to visit Cambodia.* They told Vietnamese officials that they wished to assess Cambodian needs and the most appropriate way in which the international organizations could help. The Vietnamese response was that all such matters must be referred to the sovereign government in Phnom Penh. They met regularly with the new Cambodian ambassador in Hanoi. But from Phnom Penh there came no reply.

The freedom to leave the cooperatives in which the Khmer Rouge had confined them and to search for their former homes was one of the most important benefits that the Vietnamese invasion conferred upon the Cambodian people in early 1979—but it did not accord with the rhythms of the country's agricultural life, which

* Apart from making private communications, the ICRC on January 4, 1979, issued a public statement:

CONFLICT IN CAMBODIA—ICRC OFFERS ITS SERVICES

Geneva (ICRC)—Greatly concerned at the fighting in Cambodia and anxious to ease the suffering inflicted on civilian and military victims, the International Committee of the Red Cross (ICRC) has decided to remind all the parties involved of the provisions of the Geneva Conventions and to offer them its services.

In particular, the ICRC hopes to visit the prisoners and to receive a full list of all persons captured.

the previous nine years of war and revolution had already almost destroyed.

Cambodia has two main rice crops. The minor one is planted toward the end of the year, when the monsoon rains are beginning to cease, and is harvested in February and March, during the dry season. Stocks of seed are then needed for planting the main crop soon after the monsoon starts again in May. This crop is harvested in December and January. In early 1979 hundreds of thousands of people abandoned the dry-season crop that they had just planted, in favor of going home. Much of the crop was lost. And much of that which was harvested in still-contested areas was destroyed by one side or the other. By April most reports reaching the outside seemed to show that there was very little prospect of the main 1979 crop being planted at all.

Very few visitors from the West were then being allowed into Phnom Penh. One exception was Jean Pierre Gallois, the Agence France Presse correspondent in Hanoi. He wrote:

> The Cambodia that survived Pol Pot is like a dismembered body trying to return to life. Its economy is shattered, its communications severed. Millions of acres of rice paddies have been abandoned. . . . In Phnom Penh itself there is no drinking water, no post or telephone, no transport, no registry office, no money, no markets. . . . The city is so silent that bird song has a sinister ring to it. . . .

In late spring 1979, Hanoi began to allow a few Western sympathizers briefly into Phnom Penh. But still no one from ICRC, UNICEF or any other international humanitarian agency was allowed to go there. From the outside, Nayan Chanda of the *Far Eastern Economic Review* wrote on the basis of reports reaching Vientiane,

> Kampuchea today is described by recent visitors and refugees as a country after a holocaust. In this parched land abandoned towns are littered with skeletons and the debris of war, and hundreds of thousands of tired and dazed people crisscross the country seeking missing relatives and trying to reach their native villages.

Chanda noted that the writ of the regime installed by the Vietnamese did not yet run very far and reported that many foreign observers monitoring Kampuchea's development are concerned that if some order and stability are not restored and measures [are not] taken to plant rice in the few weeks before the monsoon, the country may face a severe famine.

However, officials of the U.N.'s Food and Agriculture Organization in Rome told Henry Kamm of *The New York Times* that "they knew of no contingency plans at their headquarters and were making no plans at the regional level for an effort that would require long preparation . . ."

One of the diplomats following the problems of Cambodia most closely from Thailand was the Swedish Ambassador Jean Christophe Oeberg. Oeberg was an unconventional ambassador; he rarely minded making his views widely known even if they were not very politic. His affection for free speech had earned him the nickname "Jean Catastrophe" among some journalists and diplomats.*

Oeberg was an emotional man; during 1979 he, like his friends Morton Abramowitz, the United States ambassador, and Jean Soulier, the French ambassador, reacted with great passion to the unfolding crisis of Cambodia. After a visit to the Cambodian border in April, Oeberg cabled Stockholm that the lack of planting "could lead to . . . catastrophic famine . . . a national catastrophe of unexpected dimensions. . . ."

Oeberg's cable and his suggestion that Sweden attempt to alert world opinion was taken seriously in Stockholm. The Foreign Ministry cabled its embassies in fifteen countries to see if others shared Oeberg's perceptions.

In Paris the Quai d'Orsay said that it had no information. This was despite the reports from the *Le Monde* correspondent in Bangkok, Roland Pierre Paringaux, similar accounts from French missionaries along the Thai-Cambodian border, and cables from the embassy in Bangkok.

From Tokyo the embassy replied that the Japanese thought

* During 1978 Oeberg and his wife had made a brief trip to western Cambodia at the invitation of the Khmer Rouge. They had seen no signs of terror, and Oeberg had publicly said so on their return to Bangkok. This directly conflicted with the evidence of the refugees which was finally being taken up in the U.N. Human Rights Commission. The Swedish government disowned Oeberg's statement and rebuked him.

Oeberg's fears alarmist. In Ottawa there were no plans for any relief operation. Nor in Canberra. From Peking the Swedish embassy reported that the situation was clearly bad, but there was no precise information. In Brussels, Common Market officials were not aware of any real problem. They said the EEC could not act unless the country in question was a signatory of the Lomé Convention or unless a request came from an international organization.

In New York Swedish officials talked with the U.N. Development Program. This had had no request from Phnom Penh, but the Khmer Rouge government of Democratic Kampuchea, still the holder of the U.N. seat, was asking for assistance. In Rome, officials of the World Food Program said that they were waiting on a possible appeal from Kurt Waldheim. They asked whether Sweden could provide food in a hurry if it was needed; Sweden said yes.

The American view was confused and confusing. In Bangkok Ambassador Abramowitz agreed with Oeberg that the reports from the border were alarming. He too was predicting famine and urging action from Washington. But the National Security Council under Zbigniew Brzezinski was critical of action that would help the Vietnamese. The National Security Council usually preferred positions that were sympathetic to Vietnam's enemy, China. The State Department was more flexible; Secretary of State Cyrus Vance had already testified to Congress on the possibility of food shortages in Cambodia. At a dinner at the Chinese Embassy in Washington in early May, Richard Holbrooke, the Assistant Secretary of State for East Asia and the Pacific, told the Swedes that Vance had ordered State to see whether United States food could be channeled through the U.N. to Cambodia despite existing legislation preventing the export of United States supplies to either Vietnam or Cambodia. Even so, officials of the Senate Foreign Relations Committee who made inquiries at State were told that there was no great risk. And the State Department's intelligence bureau, INR, sounded almost sanguine in the face of journalistic queries. It seemed that, whatever the private concerns, public policy at this stage was to downplay the danger.

However, the most important factor was that neither the Vietnamese government nor its client in Phnom Penh was urgently or effectively seeking massive food aid for Cambodia in the spring of

1979. No appeal had been made to the U.N. Indeed Hanoi and Phnom Penh maintained through early 1979 that little or nothing was amiss with food supplies inside Cambodia.

It later became clear that at this stage quantities of bilateral aid were arriving in Cambodia. It came from Vietnam and its allies, notably the USSR, some East European countries, and Cuba. The exact amounts have always been difficult to determine. (It later also became clear that Vietnamese troops had indulged in a good deal of looting of Cambodia in their first few months there.)

Then, on April 23, Hanoi published a statement said to have been distributed by S.P.K., a news agency established by the Vietnamese in Phnom Penh. It was delivered by one Neou Samoun, described as a member of the Central Committee of the "National United Front of National Salvation of Kampuchea," President of the "Kampuchean Peasants Association for National Salvation," and also "Head of the Agricultural Service." He was speaking of the 1979 rice-planting plans.

He attacked the destruction of agriculture wrought by the "fascist Pol Pot–Ieng Sary administration," but declared that, since January, agricultural production was being restored. Samoun said that 1.8 million hectares of land had already been cultivated in the first four months of 1979. This was impossible—in 1970, before the war disrupted agriculture, 2.2 million hectares had been planted through the course of the entire year. "The people will have sufficient food for the main season and next year," Samoun promised. He made no request for aid.*

Despite such complacency, cries of alarm continued during May 1979 from the Bangkok press corps and some diplomats. On May 6, Henry Kamm wrote in *The New York Times,* "Cambodians are

---

* Samoun said that the Pol Pot–Ieng Sary clique had destroyed many seed stocks as they fled, but, "our country is relying mainly on its own resources and on this basis also receives aid from the socialist countries and other friendly countries of the world, notably the people of Vietnam. . . . With these advantages, which are very fundamental, combined with the ardent patriotism, intelligence and traditions of hard work of our people, and with the glorious traditions of Angkor, we are sure of great success in this year's rainy-season rice-growing campaign."

once more addressing a mute question to the world: Who will feed a nation whose food has been largely destroyed by war and whose future food supply can hardly be planted while fighting continues?" His own answer was that "those who have followed Cambodian events are not optimistic about government actions when the issue at stake is Cambodian lives."

UPI reported that "the tragic nation of Cambodia faces a deadly famine that could kill thousands and send a million new refugees fleeing to Thailand, Indochina observers believe." Keyes Beech, the *Los Angeles Times* correspondent, wrote that Cambodia now faced "the specter of mass starvation." It was inevitable unless rice was planted at once. Beech said that the question of how to respond posed a grave moral problem for the West, especially the United States. He quoted a United States source as saying that from the United States point of view, there were "no good guys." If they gave rice to the Vietnamese it would be rewarding aggression. The Heng Samrin regime "wouldn't last ten minutes without Vietnamese military backing." And the Khmer Rouge were now murdering anyone who accepted a grain of rice from the Vietnamese.

At this time Jean Pierre Hocke, the Director of Operations of the International Committee of the Red Cross—one of the most powerful figures in the organization, and one of the most effective of all the aid officials who came to deal with Cambodia—visited Bangkok. In response to queries from diplomats and journalists about what the ICRC was doing for Cambodia, he replied that they had been trying since January to make contacts in Hanoi with the new regime in Phnom Penh; ICRC had a standing request for permission to visit Phnom Penh, but there had as yet been no reply. The ICRC stood ready to carry out whatever operation it could in terms of its mandates under the Geneva Conventions.

The International Committee of the Red Cross is one of the oldest, is certainly the best known, and is perhaps the grandest of the international organizations designed to help relieve suffering in times of warfare. Much of its work is both secret and vital.

The organization dates its foundation to the battle of Solferino in 1859. A young Genevois entrepreneur, Jean Henri Dunant, who happened to be there, was appalled at the lack of care for the wounded. On returning to Geneva, he published a book called *A Memory of Solferino,* in which he called for the establishment of a civilian medical corps to tend the wounded of both sides on the battlefield.

The notion that enemy wounded or prisoners should be treated humanely was not new—the ICRC claims to be able to trace it back to Cyrus the Great—but it was not in any sense guaranteed. Perhaps the first time that a large public became aware of the conditions in which the wounded lingered or died was the Crimea, when the correspondent of *The Times* reported on their atrocious suffering from cold, mud and gangrene, and Florence Nightingale became, almost overnight, a European legend.

Nightingale disagreed with Dunant; she feared that the formation of civilian medical services would relieve from states part of the burden of going to war. Nonetheless, in 1863 delegates and doctors from sixteen European countries attended a conference in Geneva and agreed to establish private national societies linked with one another and to work as auxiliaries to the Army Medical Service. They and their equipment were to be protected by a distinctive sign, a red cross on white ground—the Swiss flag in reverse. The next year the First Geneva Convention, guaranteeing the care of the sick and the wounded on the battlefield, was adopted.*

The Red Cross movement then grew with remarkable speed and quickly became synonymous with humanitarian rescue operations through much of the world. It has three components: the ICRC itself, which is the guardian of the Geneva Conventions; the League of Red Cross Societies, of which there are now about 123; and the International Conference of the Red Cross, which meets every four years to establish guidelines for the movement.†

---

* The signatories included Baden, Belgium, Denmark, France, Hesse, Holland, Italy, Portugal, Prussia, Spain, Switzerland and Württemberg. Great Britain, Russia, Saxony, Sweden and the United States also attended the conference, and their accession, as well as that of all other states, was encouraged. The Holy See then acceded and so did Turkey—in Moslem countries the memory of the Crusades remained, and the red cross was replaced with a red crescent. The United States ratified the Convention in 1882, Japan acceded in 1886, Siam in 1895 and China in 1904.

† The International Committee of the Red Cross (ICRC), the initiator

During the First World War, the ICRC turned its attention to prisoners of war as well; for the first time prisoners and their families were able to correspond, and some two million parcels were delivered to prisoners. After the war the ICRC assisted in the repatriation of refugees, and its tracing service continued to work with the newly established Nansen office on behalf of refugees. Then its responsibilities were widened to embrace the prevention of disease and the improvement of public health.

In 1929 two new conventions, expanding ICRC's duty toward wounded soldiers and prisoners of war, were signed. In the middle-thirties a new draft Convention intended to protect civilians in wartime was devised. But diplomacy does not move fast on matters to which diplomats or politicians accord no priority; when the Second World War commenced in 1939, the draft had still not been approved.

The ICRC's own official history acknowledges that "the Second World War was to put the International Red Cross to an infinitely harder test than the war of 1914–1918." Its principal failure was, as already noted, its inability to do anything on behalf of the Jews. On other matters it was more successful. Its 180 delegates worked effectively on behalf of many prisoners of war. But they were unable to do anything for Axis prisoners held by the USSR, or vice versa, because the USSR had not ratified the 1929 Convention. This meant that the Axis was no more bound by the treaty with regard to Moscow than Moscow was to them. Elsewhere, 36 million parcels were shipped and 120 million messages were transmitted. Medical supplies were delivered to suffering civilians, and seriously wounded or

---

of the movement, is a self-perpetuating private Swiss organization. It is financially and legally independent of the rest of the movement.

The League was founded in 1919 to coordinate the health work of the national societies. One of the League's most important functions is to channel contributions made by other societies and governments in response to an appeal by a national society.

The International Conference of the Red Cross includes representatives of the ICRC, the League and one government and Red Cross delegation from every country in which there is a national society. The national societies must operate according to its principles. In 1965 it laid those down as humanity, impartiality, independence, voluntary service, unity and universality.

sick prisoners of war were exchanged, as were some categories of civilians. After the war was over, the ICRC helped to find or reunite some thirty million people on the files of its tracing center at Arolsen in Germany, a service that still operates today.

In 1949 the first three Geneva Conventions, covering the care of sick and wounded members of the armed forces on the battlefield and in shipwrecks, and the treatment of prisoners of war, were revised once again. At the same time a fourth Convention, relating to the protection of civilians in wartime, was added. This prohibited violence to life and person, the taking of hostages, outrages to human dignity, including any form of discrimination and execution "without previous judgement pronounced by a regularly constituted court affording all the judicial guarantees that are recognised as indispensable by civilised peoples." This new Convention clearly extended the scope of the organization enormously. It enabled the ICRC to become much more directly involved in the succor and care of the general population in time of war or other disaster.

In the first twenty years after the Second World War, the ICRC remained a select and rather small Swiss organization, relying on the principles of neutrality and confidentiality to try to see that the Conventions were implemented. But since the Nigerian civil war, where it was involved for the first time in large-scale civilian relief on both sides, its concerns and the scope of its activities have grown enormously. New Protocols were added to the Conventions in the middle seventies, and these made the organization both more acceptable and more relevant to the nations of the Third World. But it still attempts to carry out its traditional functions, like the exchange of prisoners of war and the visiting of political prisoners. Indeed, Jean Pierre Hocke, who joined the organization at the time of Biafra, considers that prison visits remain among the ICRC's most important functions. "A visit gives people back their humanity for a time," he says.

In Indochina the ICRC was active during the American period of the war. When the Khmer Rouge captured Phnom Penh in April 1975, its delegates attempted to make the Hotel Phnom a neutral haven. The Khmer Rouge had no time for such niceties. All foreigners and their Cambodian friends then took refuge in the French Embassy. The Khmer Rouge ordered most of the Cambodians to leave the Embassy and march, like everyone else, into the countryside. The ICRC was unable to help them; in anguish the Cambodians and their foreign friends, spouses and lovers were separated. A Khmer Rouge officer said to one delegate, "For you, it's tomorrow." "What—to Peking?" asked the ICRC delegate, hoping for an airplane. The officer smiled and drew his finger across his throat. In the event, the foreigners were trucked to the bridge at Aranyaprathet, which was then closed behind them.

After 1975, ICRC remained in Hanoi, with François Zen Ruffinen, who had been in Phnom Penh till 1975, for much of the time the delegate. It was involved in relief operations, and its other tasks included the repatriation of foreigners who had been caught in Saigon by the sudden victory of the Communists. Gradually it managed to return more than eight thousand people to their homes. These included Indians, Pakistanis, and Yemenis, but the bulk of them were overseas Chinese with Taiwanese passports. In early 1979 the ICRC also facilitated the exchange of prisoners between China and Vietnam after China's punitive expedition into northern Vietnam.

Throughout the period, Cambodia remained closed to the ICRC, as to all other humanitarian organizations. Zen Ruffinen attempted to make contact with the embassies of Democratic Kampuchea in both Hanoi and Vientiane; there never was any response. The Vietnamese were no more helpful to him. Until the fighting between the two countries broke into open warfare in 1978, Vietnamese officials absolutely refused to discuss the subject; publicly, indeed, they were still supporting the Khmer Rouge. However, once the break between the two former allies became public, the Vietnamese government allowed the ICRC to visit Khmer Rouge prisoners of war in southern Vietnam; Zen Ruffinen was shocked by their condition. Like those he had seen in 1975, "they seemed on the limits of humanity."

In the first quarter of 1979, after Vietnam's invasion of Cambodia, Zen Ruffinen constantly sought permission in Hanoi for an ICRC mission to visit Phnom Penh. The response was either that he should approach the Phnom Penh government direct or that relief supplies should simply be delivered to Ho Chi Minh City. Like his UNICEF colleague in Hanoi, Zen Ruffinen insisted that a mission must first be sent to assess the country's actual needs. Humanitarian relief operations are difficult enough to mount in the best of circumstances. Without direct, firsthand assessment of people's needs and customs and the logistical problems, they can become impossible.*

When Kurt Waldheim visited Hanoi at the beginning of May, he too raised the issue of food for Cambodia. Later he said that the Vietnamese were not very helpful. They merely referred all his questions to the Heng Samrin regime in Phnom Penh, just as the Chinese referred everything to the Khmer Rouge. He said that he had even considered trying to break the deadlock by using air drops of food over Cambodia. The trouble was that the food would be seized by the troops on either side. A briefing paper prepared for the Secretary General's office noted:

> As regards possible international relief operations to deal with the existing and expected serious food shortages in Kampuchea, the difficulty is that there are no supply routes into Kampuchea other

* Subsequently, the ICRC and UNICEF received considerable criticism for having insisted on visiting Phnom Penh before mounting a relief program. In defense of their caution, aid officials pointed out that for any disaster relief operation to be effective, needs have to be precisely identified. For example, food habits vary, and even in emergencies people are reluctant to turn to food they do not know—the USSR sent considerable quantities of maize to Cambodia in 1979–80, and many hungry people refused to eat it. Medicines are even more difficult; on the Indian subcontinent Chloroquine and Nivaquine are the standard antimalarials, but it was found that they were useless in Cambodia in 1979—the parasites were different. ICRC officials argue that many medicines will do more harm than good unless they are properly prepared and dispensed. Moreover, drugs have to be adapted to the state of medical equipment available; injections may be more efficient than tablets, but if sterilizers are unavailable, then syringes are likely to spread viral hepatitis and other diseases.

Once objectives are defined, logistical problems need to be solved. If a proper assessment cannot be made of the state of roads, bridges, ports and means of transport, then bottlenecks of relief goods occur almost at once. This was one of the most serious problems to develop in Cambodia.

Thirdly, no relief operation can succeed unless the people concerned are closely associated with it and it corresponds to their needs and wishes.

These were the principal reasons why both the ICRC and UNICEF insisted that before they could mount a relief operation some sort of mission must go to Phnom Penh to make contact with the authorities and to assess the needs and the means. One of those concerned said, "Apart from the question of principle involved—and clearly there was one—it would have been totally impracticable to handle relief to Cambodia through a third party, namely Vietnam."

than those controlled by Viet Nam. Viet Nam has de-emphasized shortages both in Viet Nam and in those areas in Kampuchea controlled by it, although there are indications that she barely manages to supply its own troops, leaving Kampucheans to fend for themselves.

Nonetheless, during May, Vietnamese attitudes toward aid from the Western world seemed to change. A few more Western journalists, notably Wilfred Burchett, a longtime sympathizer of Hanoi, were allowed briefly to Phnom Penh; they brought out the first glimpses of Tuol Sleng prison, which the Vietnamese were transforming into a museum. Two French Communist doctors were also able to make a short trip to Cambodia; they returned to speak with horror of the extent of the devastation and the country's needs. Then the ICRC office in Hanoi was informed by the Vietnamese Foreign Ministry that its request for permission to send a survey mission to Phnom Penh was being "carefully considered"—but still no invitation was given.

At the end of May 1979, the Executive Board of the United Nations Children's Fund (UNICEF) met in Mexico City for its annual review of programs. After a good deal of discussion, it announced that it intended to collaborate with the ICRC's plan to send a survey mission to Cambodia. On the basis of the ICRC report, UNICEF would contribute medical and other supplies and equipment. "For a further phase of assistance, UNICEF would be prepared, when this is practicable, to send a mission to examine emergency measures as well as possible cooperation in the rehabilitation of services for children."

UNICEF was created by the U.N. General Assembly in 1946 as a temporary, three-year body. Its name was the United Nations International Children's Emergency Fund, and its mandate was to help children who had been "victims of aggression" and to assist "child health purposes generally"; it did so principally in Europe and China. The organization met a need that no one would deny; by 1949 it was giving food every day to five million mothers and children, and was clothing two million children. It was the first U.N. agency to send help to the Palestinian refugees, and in 1949 it became the first such body to respond to a natural disaster, when it sent aid to the victims of an earthquake in Ecuador. In 1950, the General Assembly changed the emphasis of UNICEF's mandate to give it responsibility for "nursing and expectant mothers" and "emergency and long-term needs of children," particularly in developing countries. Three years later the General Assembly voted to continue UNICEF's existence indefinitely; the name was changed to the United Nations Children's Fund, but the acronym remained the same.

Since then it has become one of the best-known and most popular U.N. agencies. It has also been among the most effective and has avoided the bureaucratic sloth that afflicts some of its sibling agencies; UNICEF's staff and overhead costs have been kept relatively lean. It is funded by voluntary contributions from governments in both the industrial and the developing world, from nongovernmental organizations, from individual contributions and from such activities as the sale of greeting cards. Like the Red Cross, UNICEF has its own national societies on which it places considerable reliance.

UNICEF is unique among U.N. agencies in that its mandate deals with a particular age group, rather than a particular field such as health or education. And unlike other U.N. agencies, UNICEF has a certain independence from the General Assembly; it is governed by an executive board on which thirty nations are represented, and its mandate allows it to operate on behalf of mothers and children in countries whose governments the General Assembly has not recognized. Unlike any other U.N. agency, it can operate in any country without the approval of other governments. It is hard to overestimate the value of this flexibility. In the case of Cambodia it was vital.

Ninety-five percent of UNICEF's assistance goes to support development projects such as immunization campaigns, mother-and-child health services, clean-water systems and sanitation, training of teachers, health personnel and social-welfare workers, equipment for schools, nutrition programs and prevocational training. But because women and children are the first victims of both natural and man-made disasters, emergency relief is also a major UNICEF responsibility. In both Nigeria and Bangladesh, UNICEF was active in restoring mother-child health services and in restoring primary education.

UNICEF's cohesion and sense of self was undoubtedly helped by the fact that by 1979 it had had only two executive directors in its entire history. Both (at the insistence of the major donor, the United States) had been American, and the second, Henry Labouisse, was now nearing the end of his term. Labouisse had always taken a keen interest in Indochina; UNICEF had long been involved in South Vietnam, Cambodia and Laos, and in 1973, over the opposition of the Nixon Administration, it opened an office in Hanoi. As a result of this initiative and its subsequent work there, Labouisse himself was personally on good terms with Prime Minister Pham Van Dong. In May 1979 he hoped that this would help enable UNICEF to gain access to Cambodia.

In Mexico City, UNICEF's executive board decided that the initial funding of any relief effort in conjunction with the ICRC would be from UNICEF's emergency reserves. But Labouisse also appealed for contributions to a new special fund for Cambodia. He set one million dollars as the target. In weeks to come this would seem very small beer.

A few days later, before word of UNICEF's decision had been officially delivered to Hanoi, the Vietnamese foreign ministry summoned Bertram Collins, UNICEF's representative in Hanoi and François Zen Ruffinen, the ICRC delegate, to separate meetings. Officials told them once again that Cambodia required assistance and advised them to contact the Cambodian embassy, with a view to delivering food to the port of Ho Chi Minh City.

Not until the end of June was there any further movement. Then UNICEF and ICRC officials were once more summoned to the foreign ministry in Hanoi, and each was invited to send an official to Phnom Penh the following week. A few days later the Cambodian ambassador to Hanoi, Chea Soth, bicycled around to the UNICEF and ICRC offices and said that the Heng Samrin government would like them each to send a delegate to Cambodia in July.

In Geneva, Henry Labouisse and Alexander Hay, the President of the ICRC, at once agreed that a joint ICRC-UNICEF survey mission be sent, but quietly. UNICEF-Geneva cabled its Bangkok office to say that Labouisse and Hay had decided "that as far as possible we will avoid any publicity—for obvious reasons—in the press. . . . We do not plan to issue at this date any press communiqué."

This policy of discretion was perhaps inevitable, given the fact that Democratic Kampuchea (the Khmer Rouge) was still recognized by the United Nations as the legal government of Cambodia, but over the weeks and months to come, it was to result in both organizations suffering great abuse for their apparent inaction on behalf of the suffering Cambodians.

At last, in early July, the first written request from Phnom Penh itself for international aid arrived in the West. It was signed by Hun Sen, a former Khmer Rouge officer, who was Foreign Minister in the new regime installed by the Vietnamese, and it was addressed to the World Food Program and other U.N. organizations. The letter, dated July 3, 1979, was an urgent appeal for aid. It stated that under the Khmer Rouge about three million of Cambodia's 7.25 million people had died—either through lack of food, physical or mental torture, or execution. The four million surviving Cambodians were suffering from malnutrition, and famine now threatened 2.25 million of them. Hun Sen asked that the World Food Program immediately start to deliver 108,000 tons of rice or wheat flour together with vegetable oil and sugar to Cambodia. The letter did not invite any of the international organizations to Phnom Penh, but asked that all arrangements for delivery be made with the Cambodian ambassador in Hanoi.* (The entire text is included in the Notes.)

It was now that the diplomatic *danse macabre* that was to swirl endlessly around the relief operation began in earnest.

UNICEF and ICRC's discreet agreement to visit Phnom Penh did not escape the attention of the government of Democratic Kampuchea, the Khmer Rouge. On the contrary. Jean Pierre Hocke, ICRC's Director of Operations, received an invitation to meet Khieu Samphan, the President of Democratic Kampuchea, at the government's mission in Geneva. Hocke, a man who is both well read in philosophy and experienced in the horrors of modern government, was astonished by Khieu Samphan. Like so many of the Khmer

---

* In its original French, Hun Sen's letter stated, *"De ce qui procéde, il resulte que la famine menace plus de 2 millions de nos compatriotes. . . . Les besoins de secours immediate pour 2.250.000 personnes menacées par la famine sont les suivants. . . ."* The letter calculated that 162,000 tons of rice were needed to feed 2.25 million people 12 kilos each for a period of six months. Kampuchea itself would try to provide 54,000 tons. Hun Sen was, therefore, requesting 108,000 tons of rice plus 8,100 tons of vegetable oil and 15,000 tons of sugar from the World Food Program.

Rouge leaders, Khieu was highly educated in France, and he has a remarkably mild appearance. He now asked that the International Committee of the Red Cross should resume contact with the Kampuchean Red Cross in the territory controlled by Democratic Kampuchea. Hocke asked why the ICRC had had no replies to all its attempts to enter Cambodia while the Khmer Rouge were in power. There had been no such thing as a Red Cross society then. Khieu Samphan refused to respond.

Similarly, the UNICEF-ICRC initiative excited a chillingly elegant letter of complaint from the Khmer Rouge permanent representative to the United Nations. On July 10, 1979, His Excellency Thiounn Prasith, now housed in Mitchell Place, New York, wrote to Labouisse to insist that a visit by UNICEF to Phnom Penh would constitute "implicit recognition of the regime installed by Vietnamese aggression." Nor could it help Kampuchean children, he wrote, for it would be used as part of the Vietnamese plan to exterminate the Kampuchean people. On the other hand, he declared, the government of Democratic Kampuchea was ready to accept aid so that it could nurse the suffering caused by the Vietnamese aggression.

Thiounn Prasith followed his letter with a visit to Labouisse's office. Thiounn and his two brothers, who were also in the Khmer Rouge hierarchy, had been among the most brilliant Cambodian students in Paris in the 1950s. Like Khieu Samphan, he has a mild, sophisticated appearance—though in his case this is sometimes belied by flashes of evident viciousness.

Labouisse, who found such representations from the Khmer Rouge bizarre, if not painful, told him he understood his view about the Vietnamese, but UNICEF's task was to help children in need whatever the political circumstances. He quoted UNICEF operations in Nigeria-Biafra and on both sides in Cambodia and Vietnam before 1975. He said that the proposed mission to Phnom Penh was purely exploratory and that aid would be given only to mothers and children on the Heng Samrin side. "I said that if his government wishes us to send someone to explore the situation in territory controlled by his government we would be glad to consider it. He said he would pass this information on to his government."

Later in July Thiounn Prasith returned to see Labouisse again.

He made the same complaint about aid to Phnom Penh, and Labouisse gave the same reply. Thiounn Prasith then said that if UNICEF wanted to help children under the government of Democratic Kampuchea, it could contact Mr. So Hong, a foreign-ministry official of Democratic Kampuchea, who was in Thailand.

"The Ambassador could not give me Mr. So Hong's address," Labouisse wrote to his Bangkok office, "but said he could be reached through the Thai foreign ministry. Apparently he comes into Thailand from time to time—or he may reside there, for all I know. All of this is a very unorthodox approach." Labouisse suggested that the Bangkok office try to reach So Hong, "in order to find out whether we could do something for needy children under the jurisdiction of the Pol Pot regime. Depending on that 'feeler,' we can decide what to do next."

6 ❦ Joint Mission

For its special envoy to Phnom Penh, the International Committee of the Red Cross chose François Bugnion, a lawyer and an experienced delegate, who had just been involved in the ICRC's successful negotiation of prisoner-of-war exchanges between Vietnam and China. UNICEF chose Jacques Beaumont, a Frenchman with long field experience. He had been stationed in Indochina before 1975, and since January 1979 he had been trying to persuade the Vietnamese mission to the U.N. to allow UNICEF into Cambodia. Over the years to come, Beaumont, a man of wit, intelligence and tenacity, would become one of the principal architects and engineers of the entire Cambodian relief operation.

Beaumont and Bugnion arrived in Hanoi on July 11, 1979. They had to wait another six days before being allowed to fly into Phnom Penh. Together with Victor Umbricht, a Swiss U.N. official who was on a mission to Vietnam for Kurt Waldheim, they were the first representatives of the United Nations or the ICRC allowed into Cambodia for over four years. None of them had any idea of what the real needs of the country were, why the invitation had finally been extended, or what sort of reception would be given them. They were disappointed to be told by the Vietnamese that they would be allowed to stay in Cambodia for only forty-eight hours. They did not think this was adequate to assess the country's needs.

Their first impression of Cambodia was of overwhelming emptiness. On the short flight from Ho Chi Minh City they peered out of windows. Almost all the fields below seemed to be untilled (they should by now have been well planted if there was to be a 1979 main-season crop), villages looked deserted, no boats were to be seen on the rivers.

Phnom Penh airport appeared abandoned. In the town itself shops and houses were ransacked, the streets were littered with rubbish and wrecked cars. It seemed that only a few thousand people had managed to make their way back into the capital; they were living the lives of scavengers. Thousands more were not being allowed into the city but were being held in terrible conditions in camps along the outskirts.

Beaumont and Bugnion were taken to the Seventh of January Hospital—named after the day on which the Vietnamese captured Phnom Penh. There were only three doctors for over eight hundred patients, half of them on the floor. No sheets, no soap, no sterilizers, no surgical equipment, one tray of drugs, many of them pre-1975 and useless, no food except rice soup. They were shown an orphanage where hundreds of children were in a pitiful condition, without food, without drugs, near death.

One blind sixteen-year-old girl heard their voices, pulled herself up and greeted them in Cambodian fashion, with her hands before her face. They wept. And they were shown Tuol Sleng, the torture center; they found it quite horrific.

On this first trip they were lodged in the government guesthouse. Everything was ramshackle. Water and electricity were intermittent, food was very scarce. Their interpreters from the Foreign Ministry seemed so weak from lack of food that they occasionally fainted. Bugnion and Beaumont shared with them whatever food they had brought. They handed over two suitcases filled with 200 kilos of drugs to officials from the Ministry of Health, who had tears in their eyes as they carried them away. One said, "For almost five years we have seen thousands and thousands of our people dying, while we were unable to give them any assistance. Now we are becoming doctors again."

Every Cambodian to whom they talked had a horror story to tell about life under "Pol Pot"; everyone, it seemed, had lost at least one member of his family, by murder, starvation or disease. They were told how "intellectuals," bourgeois and anyone connected with the Lon Nol regime would be beaten to death. Everyone praised the coming of the Vietnamese.

To their disappointment the aid officials were not allowed to travel widely. In fact, they made just one trip of about thirty miles to the town of Kompong Speu, which had been almost completely destroyed. There conditions were, if anything, even worse. Agriculture seemed to be at a standstill. They were told that thousands of draft animals had died, there was no fertilizer or tools. Children in the school and the orphanage were clearly suffering terrible malnutrition.

Cambodia's needs were evidently vast, but, to Beaumont and Bugnion's frustration, they were able to have detailed or substantive talks with almost no one. Perhaps no one in the government itself had any real idea of what the country's needs now were. In any case, there was absolutely no way they could tell just how much food or fuel or medical care had already been provided by Vietnam or the socialist bloc, and they felt they could not make even an informed guess of just what the country most needed—apart from food, of course.

They saw Hun Sen, the twenty-seven-year-old foreign minister. He was so ill with dysentery that he had to leave the room every few minutes during their conversation. Hun Sen had spent most of his adult life in the Khmer Rouge, until he defected to Vietnam during the summer of 1977. He had lost one eye during the war. His knowledge of the rest of the world was understandably sketchy; Beaumont had to explain to him just what the United Nations actually was. When they asked him about setting up a relief program, he said they should just deliver food to the revitalized Cambodian Red Cross or to the Vietnamese Red Cross. The head of the Cambodian Red Cross during the Lon Nol period, a formidable and graceful woman named Madame Phlek Phiroun, had survived the Khmer Rouge and had been reappointed. She attended this meeting but said nothing; it seemed to them that she was not supposed to speak.

At the end of their brief visit, Beaumont and Bugnion met President Heng Samrin; he did not impress them. He too had been an officer in the Khmer Rouge, until he defected to Vietnam in 1978.

He spoke only in general terms, but repeated, with no trace of self-consciousness, that "two million people are starving as a consequence of the Pol Pot time." He also acknowledged that "we are not well organized among ourselves. Please understand our problems. Please be our interpreters to the world."

Like almost every foreigner who visited Cambodia after them, Beaumont and Bugnion were so moved by the plight of the country that they were more than willing to accept Heng Samrin's request. But when they asked to be able to remain in Phnom Penh to assess Cambodia's needs more accurately, Heng Samrin refused. The two men submitted a draft relief program.

Appalled by the visible legacy of the Khmer Rouge, awed by the apparent scale of the relief operation required, and depressed by the cursory nature of their trip, they flew back to Ho Chi Minh City, uncertain whether they or anyone else from the international organizations would be allowed back into Cambodia. Vietnamese officials tried to persuade them to leave, so as to report what they had found to their headquarters and the world. The U.N. Conference on the boat people was about to open in Geneva; the Vietnamese may have hoped that Beaumont and Bugnion's description of Khmer Rouge brutality would help Hanoi's international image. But, worried lest they might never be allowed back to Phnom Penh to make a proper assessment of the needs and logistics, the two men refused to leave. They insisted that their written reports would be enough to engender action. They said they wanted to stay in Ho Chi Minh City until a planeload of drugs could be flown from Bangkok for them to take back to Phnom Penh.

Victor Umbricht returned to Switzerland and wrote a report, which he circulated widely. As the first assessment of Cambodia by a United Nations official, it commanded wide attention. In it Umbricht concluded "the grim and somewhat overwhelming impression resulting from such a tour is one of a country and of a people which have suffered more distress and endured more misery than could possibly have been imagined from this type of civil strife."

He repeated the figures of the Phnom Penh government: "In the past four years, 2–3 million of the population, or up to 45 percent of

a population of 7.5 million in 1975 were either deliberately exter-
minated or perished from physical exhaustion. . . . The remaining
population of Kampuchea faces utter deprivation . . . with famine
an ever present threat. . . . Most of the people are in rags, with no
shoes, and even the government's civil servants have at most one
shirt and one pair of pants."

Apart from malnutrition, pest, tuberculosis, chronic dysentery
and diarrhea, "a staggering number of eye problems are prevalent,
attributable to the fact that most of the men who wore eye glasses
before 1975 threw them away in order to avoid being branded as
intellectuals by the Pol Pot regime, and thereby marked for elimination."

Some humanitarian aid was being provided, notably by Vietnam, and by Cuba, East Germany, and the Soviet Union; but Umbricht concluded that

> Massive international assistance is essential if widespread starvation,
> death resulting from lack of basic health-care facilities, drastically
> shortened life expectancy, etc., are to be averted. Famine threatens
> to engulf the country even now, and the Vietnamese contribution
> of rice is all that is holding back massive starvation.

The tone of Jacques Beaumont's scribbled private notes, sent from
Ho Chi Minh City to New York, was similar.

> Disastrous situation particularly health . . . situation education sec-
> tor below zero but primary schools resuming activities. . . . Kom-
> pong Speu school showing visible sixty per cent at least nutritionally
> deficient children. More than half the children below the nutritional
> level. Kompong Speu rice ration being to date one hundred thirty
> grams rice only (as opposed to a World Health Organization rec-
> ommended minimum of 400 grams per day), no vegetables nor fruit
> in hospital and children ward where more than half in serious mal-
> nutrition. . . . Am I authorized in view this zero situation to pre-
> sent limited proposals to be airlifted through already identified
> channel in my presence?

Beaumont thought the figure of three million dead was

> more or less true. Therefore the Vietnamese army was and is still
> welcomed as liberator of the nightmare. There is a real psychosis

Pol Pot-Yeng Sari [sic], which after six months is still in their minds: they are traumatized. We have not seen anybody (even a peasant illiterate family) which has not lost by death, or simply lost, part of the family.

Beaumont could not say whether the Vietnamese would ever now return Cambodia to the Cambodians, but without them today the country would continue to collapse. "No money, no resources, no rice fields cultivated (we estimated 5% maximum from the border to Phnom Penh and along the 47 km of road we made)." He thought the strain upon Vietnam itself of supporting Cambodia was considerable; Vietnam itself was facing a massive food shortage and many ordinary Vietnamese had had their meager rice rations cut from 15 to 13 kilograms of rice a month.

At the same time François Bugnion sent a memo to ICRC headquarters in Geneva in which he outlined the draft relief program which they had already submitted to the Phnom Penh authorities on July 17. It consisted of both food and medical aid. All distribution would be carried out by the reconstituted Cambodian Red Cross, according to ICRC principles. He thought the initial emergency-relief program would have to last about three months and would need an eight-person ICRC team in Phnom Penh—including a delegate, a nutritionist, a pharmacist, a transport coordinator, a doctor, a relief administrator, a secretary and a radio operator.

Bugnion thought the radio was essential. Without it, coordination of ship and aircraft movements would scarcely be possible. After all, communications between Cambodia and the rest of the world were literally nonexistent.

Communications are often determined by politics. During the Vietnam war South Vietnam had probably been more closely linked by satellite to the United States and thence to the rest of the Western world than any other country. Cambodia's links to the West had been less sophisticated, but they had functioned. After the American defeat in Vietnam the plugs were literally pulled, while the Khmer Rouge themselves deliberately severed almost all links with the world outside. Now, in the summer of 1979 there was no telephone at all out of Phnom Penh—bar the Vietnamese army land line and radio. At the same time it was very difficult to telephone the outside world from Ho Chi Minh City. One route lay through Singapore, but since

Vietnam owed Singapore money, Singapore would not take any calls. The other route to the West, via Hanoi and Moscow, was usually unobtainable and almost always inaudible.

Bugnion suggested that radio messages out of Phnom Penh be transmitted uncoded in French, that the government be informed of frequencies and hours of transmissions and be given copies of all messages. Nonetheless, he realized that it was a touchy subject "which will require much diplomacy and persuasion." In the event it would prove almost fatally contentious.

In Ho Chi Minh City, Bugnion and Beaumont did not easily obtain permission to ship drugs from Bangkok through Ho Chi Minh City to Phnom Penh, despite Vietnamese assurances of assistance. Bugnion flew up to Hanoi to plead with the Cambodian ambassador, Chea Soth, that they be allowed back into Cambodia. The ambassador said he would do what he could.

In Bangkok the supplies were quickly assembled—some of them came from UNICEF's vast warehouse called Unipac in Copenhagen— but three times at the end of July and the beginning of August the Vietnamese authorities canceled the shipment. Beaumont, an emotional as well as a shrewd man, was upset by such delays and cancellations, as well as by the difficulties of communicating with the world outside. But eventually their flight was cleared and on August 9—almost three weeks after their first two-day trip—the two men flew back into Phnom Penh bearing with them 4.4 tons of emergency medical supplies, the first consignment of international aid to reach Cambodia since 1975.

As with any plane arriving in those days, everything had to be unloaded by hand; there were no forklift trucks at the airport. Nevertheless, within hours the drugs were being used in hospitals and orphanages in Phnom Penh. They were very quickly exhausted. Beaumont later reported to New York that this first planeload of drugs was much welcomed "as a proof of our good will, understanding and efficiency." On August 10, the two men submitted a more detailed program.

This time Beaumont and Bugnion were able to stay eight days in Cambodia. They were housed at the old Hotel Phnom which had just been reopened as the Hotel Samaki—"Solidarity" (with Vietnam). As in the guesthouse where they had stayed on their previous trip, conditions were rough. Next to them were the Cuban and Polish ambassadors.

Beaumont thought that the hospitals in Phnom Penh were slightly better organized than they had been three weeks before. But they still had almost no drugs. Anemia and other diseases seemed to be on the increase. In the orphanages children were eating banana shoots and rice soup.

It was clear to Beaumont and Bugnion that any relief operation would be enormously difficult. For one thing the roads were in terrible condition and almost no vehicles seemed to have survived the Khmer Rouge. The Ministry of Health had just one ambulance, no trucks. The Ministry of Transport had just two trucks to each province. None of the ministries had typewriters, and even pens and paper were hardly available to most ministries. Furthermore, after four years of terror and isolation, few Cambodians had any understanding of the immense practical and logistical, not to say political, problems of organizing a relief program from the outside.

One of the most helpful Cambodian ministers was Ros Samay, Minister of Economy. (He was later purged and disappeared.) Ros Samay agreed to allow nonstop relief flights from Bangkok to Phnom Penh rather than via Ho Chi Minh City. However, these could not be direct; "for reasons of security," they would have to fly in a wide arc out over the South China Sea and then over Vietnam before looping back to Phnom Penh.

Beaumont and Bugnion were still unable to get permission for a permanent office in Phnom Penh. This was depressing. The government had requested help in saving over two million people from imminent famine. Proper teams, adequately supported, would be needed to meet such a disaster. After their trip, Bugnion cabled Geneva: "Regret results still insufficient. We must be patient and understand difficulty our interlocutors who have no experience of collaboration with international institutions." Jacques Beaumont cabled New York:

> I am convinced that the only viable solution is the opening of a ICRC delegation with means of logistics, transport, radio plus the reopening ASAP of a UNICEF office. To liaise permanently with

a newly born government characterized by extreme goodwill, extreme ignorance of many things and poor intellectuals—average proportion of survivors being ten per cent—many badly affected their health but willing to learn and solve enormous problems. . . .

In another message written at night in his bare room at the Hotel Samaki, Beaumont detailed the successes and the problems they had so far encountered with the first shipment of aid. Through it all shone his exuberance and enthusiasm for the operation:

I am now writing at the light of a candle. . . . Any office equipment should foresee at least for the beginning its own generator for safety reasons; last time, we had no electricity for 22 hours! . . . but water at least once a day. Things are improving rapidly. . . . Fortunately ICRC gives automatically a candle to delegates, and I got one in Geneva. . . . No more candle. . . . To my request for another candle, I received a bottle of hot water. . . . A new world. The problem is that the "expert" in hotellerie assigned to my floor does not speak anything known to me (Russian and Vietnamese), and I cannot locate the Cambodian counterpart must be sleeping somewhere. . . . Mosquitoes all over, my mosquito net has holes. . . . But they are all very gentle, including the "expert" who makes "my" cigarettes. I begin to establish Packing Lists 1 to 4. End at 5:10 A.M.

Beaumont and Bugnion were surprised to find a good many other foreigners were coming to town at this time. Indeed the two aid officials had to leave to make way for them. But few of these visitors were tending the sick or the starving. Instead they were witnessing a "People's Revolutionary Tribunal for the Trial by Genocide Committed by the Pol Pot-Ieng Sary clique." According to the government, five hundred Cambodians and foreigners attended it. Fairly elaborate preparations were made for the foreigners. Beaumont and Bugnion noted that a fleet of empty cars was driven up from Ho Chi Minh City. The Vietnamese number plates were exchanged for Cambodian plates. A squad of pretty Vietnamese girls was also brought. They were outfitted in Cambodian sarongs and had their hair redone in the Cambodian fashion. For the duration of the trial they were to be the "Cambodian" staff at the Hotel Samaki. With hindsight, it seems reasonable to ask why the Vietnamese could not feed an orphanage of starving children, if they could stage such an elaborate trial.

Some of the evidence produced at the trial was valuable, and many of the Cambodian witnesses provided moving firsthand accounts of the ordeal they and their country had endured. But at times its atmosphere of the trial was reminiscent of Moscow in the 1930s. Thus, for example, the statement of Hope Stevens, described as "Co-chairperson of the National Conference of Black Lawyers of the United States and Canada." He appeared as defense counsel for Pol Pot and Ieng Sary. He opened his statement by declaring, "I have not come from halfway around the world to give approval to monstrous crime nor to ask for mercy for the criminals. No! A thousand times No!"

After emphasizing the importance of a fair trial and the presumption of innocence, Stevens declared:

> It is now clear to all that Pol Pot and Ieng Sary were criminally insane monsters carrying out a program the script of which was written elsewhere for them. So that, if it were left to me and the other lawyers of the world who are present here, you would not have only Pol Pot and Ieng Sary and their agents and willing vassals standing judgement here; in fairness to them we would have beside them, as fellow accused, the manipulators of world imperialism, the profiteers of neocolonialism, the fascist philosophers, the hegemonists, who are supporting Zionism, racism, apartheid and reactionary regimes in the world—all these would be standing there with the false socialist leaders of fascist China, awaiting the verdict and sharing the sentence. . . .

In conclusion he said, "Honorable Chief Justice and the Courts, we and the world await your verdict. *'Let right be done.'* "

Pol Pot and Ieng Sary were found guilty and sentenced to death by a regime in which many of their erstwhile lieutenants were now in nominal power.

On August 26 the first man from Oxfam arrived in Cambodia. He was Jim Howard, Oxfam's technical officer, a bluff engineer with socialist opinions and strong emotions.

Oxfam, founded in 1943 as the Oxford Committee for Famine Relief, is one of the most formidable private British relief agencies.

Since it was set up in order to send food to Greek children starving under Nazi rule, it has become almost an integral part of British life. Indeed some of its staff would say it was in danger of becoming too much of a British institution. Almost every medium-sized town in England has an Oxfam shop, which will typically be run by an elderly woman giving her time for free. There are over six hundred such shops; they sell handicrafts produced by Oxfam projects around the world, and secondhand clothes and other goods brought in by Oxfam supporters.

Oxfam's annual budget is £15–£20 million—small compared with many of the larger American voluntary organizations, but the largest overseas aid agency in Britain. Most of its funds are spent on development rather than emergency work. It has projects in about eighty different countries and in many of them it has acquired a reputation for financing sound, small-scale schemes such as well drilling, teaching carpentry, literacy courses, building village pharmacies, or training nurses.

In July 1979, Oxfam was approached by the two French Communist doctors who had been allowed to make a short visit to Phnom Penh in the spring and who had formed a special group, the "Committee for medical and health aid to the people of Cambodia." They asked Oxfam to participate in sending a planeload of supplies to Phnom Penh. Oxfam agreed to help underwrite the mission and had sent Jim Howard along with it.

Howard found the devastation of Cambodia beyond belief.

> Visited small clinic at Kilometer 7 [he noted in his log], absolutely no drugs or medicines—serious cases of starvation—clearly just dying for lack of food. One young woman who had just aborted lying on a filthy bed—the bloody remains put in a plastic bag by the side of her—she was still haemmorrhaging badly. The hundreds of children were all marasmic—much skin disease, baldness, discoloured hair and great fear in the whole population.

At an orphanage in the Providence High School, he found

> five hundred children, many starving and too weak to stand . . . [In a clinic], for the first time I saw an adult cry. The lack of tears had been noticeable to me over the week—people seemed too hurt

to cry. The adult was in fact the woman doctor in charge of the clinic and when she realised we were there as friends and had brought in modest relief supplies—her lips and hands quivered and we were all shattered by the tragedy of it all. The thing she mentioned through her tears was the filthy rags many of her patients were clothed in and she couldn't help them with clothes and other simple human needs. She said that coloured cloth was needed to allow people to dress and be human again. She said there was much malaria—dysentery—starvation.

At the Seventh of January Hospital, Howard described

terrible conditions—children in bed in filthy rags dying with starvation—no drugs—no food. . . . The T.B. allied to starvation gives the people a Belsen-like appearance. In one ward a boy of thirteen tied down to the bed because he was going insane—many children now orphans . . . The face of one small boy of eighteen months was in a state of destruction by what appeared to be infected skin and flesh which had broken down under severe kwashiorkor—his eyes full of pus, held in the arms of his five-year-old sister . . . I find this sort of thing very tough to take—and this situation must be applicable to hundreds of thousands of Kampuchean people today.

Out on Route 4:

The villages visited all contained starving people and clearly many of the people I saw couldn't possibly survive several more months on what they had available. Most had a tiny rice ration of 3 kg. per month—and they were eating wild tree pods and cooking banana stems. This was starvation at the worst Biafra level.

Of the Tuol Sleng prison, Howard reported:

Quite horrific—like Auschwitz. Photographs of hundreds of prisoners photographed both alive and dead by Pol Pot to prove they were dead.

Both Cambodian and Vietnamese officials assured Howard that there was absolutely no obstacle in the way of any humanitarian aid. He decided that, together with UNICEF and the ICRC, Oxfam must at once participate in a major relief program for Cambodia.

Howard's report became available to journalists in Britain in early September. Its dramatic warning followed a *New York Times* dispatch from the Pulitzer Prize-winning reporter Seymour Hersh in Hanoi. This was an interview with Beaumont and Bugnion, and it began,

> United Nations and Red Cross officials have said in interviews here and in Ho Chi Minh City that 2.25 million Cambodians were facing imminent starvation. The officials . . . also described the widespread starvation as only one element of what seemed to be the near-destruction of Cambodian society under the regime of the ousted Premier Pol Pot. "I have seen quite a few ravaged countries in my career, but nothing like this," an official said.

All these and other reports came together and began to create a sense of spellbinding horror. Every Westerner who was allowed to make a brief, strictly controlled visit to Phnom Penh in July and August 1979 was overwhelmed by the extent of the destruction, by Khmer Rouge brutality and by the country's needs. On the basis of what they all saw it would have been humanly impossible for them to question the government's claim that three million Cambodians had died under the Khmer Rouge and that famine now threatened to wipe out over half the four million survivors. The scale of the disaster, both past and impending, was such that almost everyone who came out of Cambodia—and many who merely read what they said—began to talk of the country in terms of "The Holocaust." It seemed the only appropriate comparison. The warning that there could be "two million dead by Christmas" began to echo around the world like a curse.

7 ☙ Washing of Hands

While Jacques Beaumont and François Bugnion were attempting to set up a relief program in Phnom Penh, their colleagues in the Bangkok offices of UNICEF and the ICRC were meeting secretly with representatives of Democratic Kampuchea in Thailand. The Khmer Rouge too wanted food.

Throughout the spring of 1979 the Vietnamese had concentrated on securing the principal towns and roads of Cambodia. It was only after April 1979, with the onset of the rainy season, that the Vietnamese began to establish broad military control of the plains. As they did so, the Khmer Rouge, often driving large numbers of captured civilians with them, retreated into the infertile and malarial mountains close to the Thai border.

Groups of these people and others not under Khmer Rouge control began to appear along parts of the border in the summer of 1979. From Bangkok the World Food Program, the operational arm of the U.N.'s Food and Agricultural Organization in Rome, shipped about one thousand tons of food to the border. With a grant from the U.S. Embassy in Bangkok, Catholic Relief Services did the same.

By the middle of August it was clear that growing food shortages in Cambodia and a renewed Vietnamese offensive were pushing hundreds of thousands more Cambodians toward the Thai border. Some but not all of these were under Khmer Rouge control.

These developments rendered the negotiation that Jacques Beaumont and François Bugnion were conducting in Phnom Penh far more complicated. Indeed, at times it seemed as if the growing crisis along the Thai border might even prevent UNICEF and ICRC from mounting their relief program inside Cambodia itself.

The Khmer Rouge government of Democratic Kampuchea still, of course, held Cambodia's seat at the United Nations, though Vietnam and its allies were preparing to challenge that when the General Assembly convened in September. Thus, the Khmer Rouge were in a position to request assistance from U.N. agencies and had already done so. In August and September 1979 their requests became more pressing. Thailand encouraged these requests.

Since January 1979, Thailand's policy, directed by the Prime Minister General Kriangsak Chamanand, had been based on the notion that 200,000 Vietnamese troops across its border in Cambodia posed an unacceptable threat. Assurances from Hanoi that Thai sovereignty would be respected were not considered relevant. Instead, Thailand was leading the Southeast Asian countries in the ASEAN bloc, trying to thwart Vietnam's historic ambition to control Cambodia. ASEAN's stated policy was to give the Khmer Rouge diplomatic support while urging that an international conference be held on the future of Cambodia to guarantee the withdrawal of Vietnamese troops, elections and neutrality.

At the same time, through 1979 Thailand came to align itself more and more closely with Chinese policy, which was to reinforce the Khmer Rouge military resistance to the Vietnamese in order to "bleed Vietnam white." In return the Chinese publicly guaranteed Thailand's security in that they threatened to teach Vietnam "a second lesson" if Thailand were attacked by Vietnamese forces. And a shadowy agreement was devised whereby the Chinese provided Thailand with oil at favorable prices and, even more importantly, decreased their aid to the Thai Communist Party. (This caused the party great problems and was in part responsible for massive defections to the government side in 1982 and 1983.)

A hint of this deal was given in the captured transcript of conversations between Ieng Sary and the Chinese leadership in Peking in January 1979. Deng Xiaoping's offer to transfer $5 million or more through Bangkok to the Khmer Rouge was quoted in Chapter Four. In another conversation, Chairman Hua Guofeng allegedly said of Thailand:

With regard to the Thai Communist Party, as Comrade Deng Xiaoping has told you, it's not that we don't support their struggle; it's that we must take the over-all situation into account. If Kampuchea is not steady, the Thai party will also wobble. We must pay attention to politics and tactics. Viewing things as a whole, Thailand doesn't want Vietnam to hold Kampuchea, for then their borders would be contiguous . . . but in lending assistance to Kampuchea Thailand cannot act openly as China does. The main point is that it favors Kampuchea; if it wants to keep its action secret we too must keep the veil of secrecy on. So, with regard to the transit of materiel through Thailand, we must keep it secret over a fairly long time, so that Thailand can continue to play its present role.

Just how much Chinese materiel had been secretly transported through Thailand to the Khmer Rouge by the fall of 1979 is impossible to determine. Clearly it had not been enough to avert more and more starvation among scores of thousands of civilians under Khmer Rouge control or even among their own troops.

In Bangkok discreet meetings between international officials and Khmer Rouge representatives were arranged in August by Jean Christophe Oeberg, the Swedish ambassador, after consultations with the American and French ambassadors and Thai Prime Minister General Kriangsak Chamanand. Kriangsak had voiced his concerns to a group of United States Congressmen earlier in the month. He expected famine conditions inside Cambodia to worsen, he said, so that many thousand more people would flee to the Thai border. On another occasion Kriangsak said that while aid to both sides must be for civilians, "we must face the reality that soldiers are hungry too."*

Oeberg said later that his concerns were both humanitarian and political. Thousands of ordinary people in Khmer Rouge areas were

* Kriangsak's position was explained in more detail to officials from the Australian embassy by one of his principal advisers, Dr. Suvit Yodmani. He said Thailand wanted a full-scale debate on Cambodia in the United Nations as soon as the General Assembly began. The Thai military believed that despite their present difficulties, the Khmer Rouge would survive, so long as Chinese support continued. He acknowledged that some members of the Thai government thought that Thailand should not cooperate in any relief program, because the Heng Samrin regime would be the principal beneficiary; but General Kriangsak's position was clear—he wanted to help. For this reason Thailand had agreed to the relief flights to Phnom Penh and to the border operation. But it did not wish to conduct the border operation on its own.

starving and would soon pour into Thailand. Unless something was done, the Thais would push everyone back. It was hard for Mort Abramowitz to act, he said, without the United States seeming to be aiding the Khmer Rouge, but he did not have that problem.

And so, under Oeberg's roof, ICRC and United Nations officials began to discuss humanitarian relief operations with first a Khmer Rouge official, So Hong, and then the Khmer Rouge Foreign Minister Ieng Sary. The Khmer Rouge claimed that they controlled a million people who urgently needed relief supplies. They promised that the international organizations would be allowed to monitor the distribution of food and medical supplies sent to their areas. Kriangsak told Oeberg that Thai Supreme Command would organize the transport from Bangkok to the border. François Perez, ICRC's chief delegate in Bangkok, agreed with Ieng Sary that the first delivery would be on August 29.*

ICRC's Geneva headquarters had already approved this operation in principle. But the meeting between Perez and Ieng Sary coincided with François Bugnion's return from Phnom Penh to Geneva bearing passionate firsthand witness of the atrocities of the Khmer Rouge. He was appalled by the idea of the ICRC sending any aid to the Khmer Rouge. (He had a furious row with Oeberg while in transit at Bangkok airport.) As a result of Bugnion's passion, Geneva ordered Perez to delay the first shipment of supplies through Thailand to the Khmer Rouge areas at least until two more planes of supplies had been sent to Phnom Penh and the Heng Samrin regime had agreed to the opening of permanent UNICEF and ICRC missions there.

Accordingly, on August 27 François Perez told Thai Supreme Command that the border operation had to be delayed. Kriangsak was displeased. He was prepared for supplies to be shipped into

* The first of these secret meetings was on August 17 between Sture Linner, an FAO official who had just returned from Phnom Penh, François Perez, Roberto Esquerra-Barry of UNICEF, and So Hong of the Khmer Rouge. So Hong had been secretary general of the Foreign Ministry in Phnom Penh while the Khmer Rouge were in power. He was now a liaison official responsible for aid in Bangkok. Later he returned to Cambodia to become a division commander. The meeting between François Perez and Ieng Sary took place on August 22.

Phnom Penh, but they must be balanced by supplies to the border as well.

On August 29 Perez and UNICEF officials met again with Ieng Sary, who declared that the million-or-so civilians under Khmer Rouge control needed immediate help. Perez said that ICRC wanted to conduct a survey of Khmer Rouge areas before anything was delivered. Negotiations with Phnom Penh were going slowly, he said. He did not want to upset them by starting deliveries to the Khmer Rouge side first. Oeberg asked, "Are you just going to let these people die?" After the meeting, Oeberg suggested to Abramowitz that it was time the Americans started "banging the table" in Geneva.

Abramowitz had been reporting the danger of famine since the spring. In July, Cyrus Vance had called for an international relief program for Cambodia, but since then the State Department had done little. Now Washington began to move. In the last week of August, Vance wrote to the Canadian, Australian, Japanese, Common Market and other governments, asking them to endorse any ICRC appeal for Cambodia. At the same time, the State Department instructed United States embassies around the world to start making an issue of Cambodia. Washington was asking not only for funds but also for pressure to be put on Vietnam to allow a large-scale relief program to the interior to begin.

It was becoming clear to the international organizations that with United States interest rising, their ability to offer Cambodia a huge relief program was rising too. Charles Egger, UNICEF's experienced Deputy Executive Director, cabled from New York to Jacques Beaumont—who was in Bangkok awaiting Vietnamese permission to fly with the second of the Joint Mission's planeload of supplies to Phnom Penh—"to look also at wider dimension going much beyond UNICEF/ICRC resources." This was because "there is increasing realization in UN secretariat that serious situation may demand much greater effort." At the same time, however, Egger voiced growing concern about publicity. "We must absolutely show more restraint on public information in all places and levels and only report on action in the process of immediate execution. Further releases to be co-ordinated between Bangkok-Geneva-New York."

In Rome two days later, Edouard Saouma, the Director General of the U.N.'s Food and Agriculture Organization, summoned the permanent representatives of the United States, Britain, the Netherlands, Argentina, France, Sweden, Canada and Australia. He began by saying that on the basis of the report by Sture Linner, the FAO man who had just returned from Phnom Penh, he was now convinced that "the situation is extremely desperate and could lead to the final elimination of the Kampucheans as a distinct people." (Linner's report had also stressed that the Vietnamese were in total control of the Heng Samrin government and that the Cambodian officials in Phnom Penh were utterly powerless. Linner was even convinced that the original July 3 letter from the Cambodian Foreign Minister requesting food aid, was actually written in Hanoi.)

Saouma acknowledged that he had had requests for food from both the Heng Samrin regime (the Hun Sen letter of July 3) and the Khmer Rouge in early July but had not acted before, because he felt he needed some guarantees against its diversion to troops. That risk still existed, but the humanitarian crisis was now so acute that he felt obliged to go ahead regardless. He was not proud of FAO's tardiness in Biafra, he said.

Saouma now proposed, with the donors' agreement, to ship 2,000 tons of food to Cambodia—half to Phnom Penh and half to the Thai border. It would all be distributed by the ICRC and UNICEF to civilians only. He planned to issue no press release about this experiment.

Sweden was especially pleased at this proposal. Australia agreed in principle but wondered whether the Heng Samrin regime would actually allow food to go to civilians on both sides of the war. Canada—which had already allocated all its food aid for the current fiscal year—said that its attitude would depend on the success of this first experiment.

Saouma's proposal and the donors' support, even qualified, marked the start of the massive aid program to Cambodia. Charles Egger cabled the UNICEF office in Bangkok to say that since donors were already coming forth with large sums, UNICEF should expand its proposals. But he was still worried about the immense diplomatic problems the operation posed and the paradox of the press. "Regarding public information next delicate phase will be return of mission from Kampuchea. . . . While having to steer carefully disciplined course we must also be open-minded to tremendous help media could give us in support in a wider appeal for Kampuchea at the appropriate moment."

On August 31, U.N. Secretary General Kurt Waldheim told Henry Labouisse, UNICEF's Executive Director, that he was under great pressure from the donors to take much stronger initiatives on Cambodia. Several countries, including the United States and Canada, were urging him to have Cambodia debated as soon as the General Assembly met in mid-September. They were also urging him to make a vigorous personal intervention in favor of food aid to both sides at once.

Waldheim told Labouisse that he wanted to designate UNICEF the lead U.N. agency in a general relief program in Cambodia. Charles Egger, Labouisse's deputy, pointed out that there were problems. First, UNICEF and ICRC were already operating together. In some ways ICRC was the stronger partner—more attuned to emergencies (UNICEF is a development agency) with a better logistics base, good communications, and a strong headquarters, able to concentrate manpower resources. UNICEF's strength, by contrast, is in the field. Egger also stressed that UNICEF must preserve its humanitarian character and its emphasis on reaching mothers and children. If UNICEF did become the lead agency, it might be asked by the Phnom Penh government to do far more than its mandate allowed.

Despite these objections, Waldheim confirmed UNICEF as the "lead agency" in Cambodia, cooperating closely with the ICRC. But Waldheim never formally defined what "lead agency" meant in these specific circumstances. Nor did he invest it with any real authority, let alone with the power of the purse. The role was to cause UNICEF endless problems.

By early September, the Thai government was expressing more and more alarm at the movement of desperate people toward its border. The Bangkok press was daily filled with stories of thousands of dying Cambodians about to invade eastern Thailand. A U.S. Embassy survey, labeled "Restricted Use Only, Not for Attribution," but handed to embassies and some relief agencies, made chilling reading. It said that between 100,000 and 200,000 hungry Cambodians were now pressing against the Thai border, together with 160,000 a little farther back in Cambodia. The health of those in Khmer Rouge areas was "extremely grave," with thirty to sixty people dying every day. People were getting from the Khmer Rouge only 1-plus milk tins of rice a week; there was no medicine. For the time being Khmer Rouge, Vietnamese and Thai troops were preventing these people from reaching Thailand, "but the combination of their already desperate situation and the expected Vietnamese offensive will probably lead to most of them attempting to seek sanctuary in Thai territory sometime during the next one to four months."

Prime Minister Kriangsak warned that, unless Thailand received substantial economic aid, no such sanctuary would be given. But by this stage any attempt to force the refugees back once they had crossed into Thailand would have caused an international uproar very damaging to Thailand. On September 11 the Thai cabinet formally agreed to work with the international organizations in a massive relief effort along the border and inside Cambodia itself. Air Vice-Marshal Siddhi Savetsila, then the Secretary General of the National Security Council, was appointed to run the operation. After the cabinet meeting he told journalists that the Cambodians across the border "will die if we do not aid them"; they might be allowed temporary asylum in Thailand and "when the situation improves they will be sent back."

Throughout the ensuing drama, Thailand's policies would be determined by a mix of humanitarian, political, military, strategic and even sometimes commercial concerns. This is not unusual; man-made disasters are rarely defined in strictly humanitarian terms. Within Thai ruling circles there were very different perceptions as to how Thailand should best respond to the crisis. Indeed, it was rare that the views of the Prime Minister's office, the National Security Council, the Foreign Ministry, the Ministry of the Interior, the Supreme Command, and the First Army headquarters near the border coincided. Their differences at times rendered the work of the relief organizations more difficult still.

But during the drama Siddhi would be one of the most consistent players. Mild-mannered and studious, he appeared more like a scholar than a military man. In September 1979, he was already Kriangsak's principal foreign-policy adviser; he would soon also become foreign minister. His task during the Cambodian relief operation was to reconcile the Thai military's national-security demands with the humanitarian needs of the Cambodians. This was at times almost impossible, but Siddhi achieved a great deal on behalf of the Cambodians. "I have never met a foreign minister who consistently displayed such humanity, let alone for another people," said Jean Pierre Hocke of the ICRC later.

In September 1979, Thai officials constantly insisted that the cabinet's decision to allow aid to be sent from Bangkok to Phnom Penh did not constitute recognition of the Heng Samrin regime. As for the border, all aid must pass through Thai official channels. Supplies to both sides must be internationally supervised and monitored so as to prevent their diversion from needy civilians to soldiers. That requirement was, of course, part of the organizations' mandates. It would, however, prove impossible for them to fulfill, either in Thailand or Cambodia itself.

Meanwhile, the relief agencies were losing momentum in their operation in Phnom Penh. At the end of August the Cambodian embassy in Hanoi told UNICEF officials that many Cambodian officials were abroad or were "otherwise engaged" and, so, perhaps no plane or officials could be received now. On August 29, Beaumont, Bugnion and an ICRC doctor, Dominique de Ziegler, took off from Bangkok with their second plane-load of supplies; it carried 20 tons. They had not received prior permission to land, let alone stay.

Both permissions were granted, but this, their third trip, became increasingly frustrating. They found that no decision had been made on the relief program that they had submitted on August 10. Many members of the tiny government and bureaucracy were indeed away. Some were in Eastern Europe. Others were in Havana at the Sixth Conference of Nonaligned Nations. The Vietnamese Prime Minister Pham Van Dong was there; so was Kurt Waldheim. Dong told Waldheim that the famine in Cambodia was "extremely grave" and that a full-scale relief operation must be mounted at once.

The seating of the Cambodian delegation was one of the main issues of the conference. Eventually, the participants refused to accept the credentials of either Heng Samrin or the Khmer Rouge, but decided to leave the Cambodian seat vacant.*

In Phnom Penh, unable to negotiate with government officials, Beaumont and Bugnion tried to visit many hospitals, dispensaries and orphanages to demonstrate the extent to which they were able and willing to collaborate with the people. Dr. de Ziegler instructed

* Under Prince Sihanouk, Cambodia had been one of the original twenty-five members of the nonaligned movement, along with Nasser's Egypt, Nkrumah's Ghana, Nehru's India, Tito's Yugoslavia. Of those independent nationalists only Tito now remained in the movement.

The Havana conference (which was to be Tito's last) was in fact a serious challenge to his moral leadership of the movement and the concept of nonalignment that he embodied. The Cubans sought to ban the Khmer Rouge altogether from Havana, but the Yugoslavs refused. Tito had no affection for the Khmer Rouge, but Yugoslavia, like many other Third World countries, had no wish to legitimize the invasion of a small nation by its larger neighbor and so continued to support the Khmer Rouge claim to represent Cambodia.

Khieu Samphan, the Khmer Rouge president, had been taken from the border by the Thai military to Bangkok. From there he flew to Belgrade and waited while the Yugoslavs in Havana negotiated a visa for him. Eventually this was agreed. But the Cubans billeted him in a small house outside Havana. Heng Samrin, by contrast, was welcomed with the full honors due a head of state.

In his opening address Castro declared that Heng Samrin's government was the only legitimate government of Cambodia and "we endorse Vietnam's friendly solidarity with that fraternal country." He added, "With all our energy we condemn the genocidal government of Pol Pot and Ieng Sary. Three million dead accuse them." He found it "inexplicable" that "efforts are being made to condemn Vietnam for its legitimate defense against aggression, and the fiction is maintained that Pol Pot's bloody government, an affront to all mankind, still exists."

Nonetheless, because of opposition from Yugoslavia, Singapore, Indonesia and Malaysia, the conference was unable to agree on the seating of the Heng Samrin regime in place of the Khmer Rouge. Instead, the Cambodian seat was left vacant. Interviewed by journalists in his distant villa, Khieu Samphan proposed a new National United Front, led by Sihanouk, to fight the Vietnamese. He even promised that once the Vietnamese had been expelled, there would actually be "direct, secret elections by universal suffrage in Cambodia."

Many of the officials of the Heng Samrin government who had traveled to Havana remained there after the conference's completion to await the opening of the U.N. General Assembly in New York.

Khmer doctors and set up a Supplementary Feeding Program at the orphanage which had so appalled them during their first visit. Ordinary Cambodians whom they met always begged them to stay, and they used to find notes in their laundry, or pushed under their doors, begging them on no account to leave. For many people, it was clear, the mere presence of the outside world after four years of being severed from it offered some protection against terror.

But Beaumont and Bugnion began to detect more reserve on the part of officials. And it also became clearer that the Vietnamese were making their own policy regardless of Cambodian feelings. In one memo back to headquarters, Beaumont described "the paternalistic/ maternalistic even almost colonialistic attitude" of the Vietnamese officials in Phnom Penh. He and Bugnion were not now certain whether the Vietnamese even wanted them to operate in Cambodia; the signals seemed to keep changing.

On September 7 the Vietnamese shipping agency finally gave clearance for use of the Cambodian port of Kompong Som. On September 9 the third UNICEF-ICRC flight, carrying 41 tons of food and medicines, arrived in Phnom Penh. Then Beaumont and de Ziegler were allowed to make a brief trip to the town of Kompong Chhnang, at the southeast corner of the Great Lake. This was the first real trip out of Phnom Penh since July. It was, Beaumont wrote, "very well organized and without any notice to the field (therefore no time for preparation). . . ." In his report he made no mention of any sign of famine.

On the other hand, UNICEF was told by the Vietnamese that no international aid agency would be allowed to open offices in Ho Chi Minh City to facilitate the Cambodia program. Several requests for visas for other aid officials were denied. Twice the UNICEF man in Ho Chi Minh City arrived by plane and was ordered to leave at once. On September 18 Peter Baltsensberger, whom ICRC had designated to replace Bugnion, was also refused permission to land when he arrived on the fourth of the Joint Mission's relief flights.

Then Beaumont and Bugnion themselves were actually given exit visas. They protested volubly that this was tantamount to expulsion. This led to a three-hour meeting at the Vietnamese embassy with Mrs. Phan Thi Minh, the Director of International Organizations from the Vietnamese Foreign Ministry. She appeared condescending toward the Cambodians, and her purpose seemed to them to be to mediate with the Phnom Penh authorities but also to see that maximum pressure was maintained on the Joint Mission.

Close to despair, François Bugnion cabled ICRC headquarters in Geneva: "Majority government still absent from Phnom Penh. In spite of our written and verbal *démarches,* still have no news about future aid operation and are not able to make the slightest prediction on its development. . . ." Referring to the Vietnamese role, he said, "Since 7 September several indications seem to show pressure from a third party [Vietnam] to have the joint mission expelled or at least reduced to one delegate from each organization."

Similarly, Beaumont wrote to New York, "We all take this 'waiting' period with difficulty knowing that people are dying and that we could do more."

Efforts to make progress in Phnom Penh were not helped by events in either Thailand or New York. On September 17, ICRC and UNICEF made their first visit to the Khmer Rouge areas along the border. This was the trip that had been arranged with Ieng Sary in August, and it was conducted, under conditions of extreme secrecy, with the help of the Thai army. The team consisted of François Perez, the ICRC chief delegate to Thailand, a doctor and a UNICEF nutritionist.

At the border, the Thai army handed them over to Khmer Rouge officials, who led them several kilometers into the country on foot and on elephant. What they saw of human misery surpassed even what their colleagues had seen in and around Phnom Penh. In this one area alone there were about ten thousand people—they were mostly women, but with them were about 2,000 men and 2,000 children—in whom life barely flickered. Some were undoubtedly families of Khmer Rouge soldiers. Others had been dragged by the Khmer Rouge into the mountains after the Vietnamese invasion. Almost all were suffering from a virulent strain of cerebral malaria, and all were terribly malnourished. In one forest area people were living only on bark, bamboo shoots and a little watercress.

The three international officials spent the night just inside Cambodia. They were nauseated by the spectacle of debilitation and death. It was evident to them that, whatever the political considerations, here were thousands of innocent civilians who desperately needed help. They handed out 850 kilograms of dried milk and medicines, which they had brought with them, to Khmer Rouge officials. "In all my 17 years of work with the United Nations I've never seen another group in need of greater further assistance," wrote the UNICEF nutritionist, Angskar Welle, on their return to Bangkok.

For fear of the reaction of the government in Phnom Penh, UNICEF and the ICRC did all they could to keep the border trip concealed. The next day UNICEF issued a press release announcing the fourth relief plane to Phnom Penh, carrying 3.7 tons of medicines, 1 ton of kitchen equipment and bicycles, 6.7 tons of milk powder, 2 tons of sugar, 9 tons of enriched flour donated by Sweden, 8 tons of fish protein supplied by Norway, and 10 tons of surgical equipment and medical supplies. At the end, the release merely mentioned that UNICEF and ICRC were also "pursuing efforts to reach other parts of Kampuchea where women and children are in desperate need of medical and nutritional assistance." It was not until a week later, when even the BBC had talked about the trip to the Khmer Rouge areas, that UNICEF finally agreed to give the Associated Press details of what had been seen. The regime in Phnom Penh immediately protested strongly against this "violation of sovereignty."

In New York the thirty-fourth session of the General Assembly opened on September 18. As usual, a credentials committee was appointed to examine the credentials of all delegations. Vietnam and its Soviet-bloc allies were intent on challenging the Khmer Rouge credentials and proposing that Heng Samrin represent Cambodia.

By way of compromise, Congo, one of the countries on the committee, proposed that the seat be left vacant—as at Havana. The Russians agreed that such a compromise was possible. But China would have none of it, nor would Pakistan. Panama supported Congo, the United States repeated its "abhorrence" of the government of Democratic Kampuchea but said the only issue was "the validity of credentials," and these fulfilled the requirements. Senegal agreed that the U.N. should not ratify invasion. Eventually the committee recommended that the General Assembly accept the Khmer Rouge credentials.

An eight-hour debate, involving complicated parliamentary procedures, followed in the Assembly itself. Delegate after delegate excoriated Pol Pot and Ieng Sary, while Ieng Sary himself sat smiling quietly at the back of the chamber. Many of the Western and ASEAN delegates asserted they were concerned only that the rule of law be upheld by seating the Khmer Rouge. They pointed out that the United Nations charter is based on the principle of noninterference and that U.N. membership has never been granted or withheld on the basis of respect for human rights. If it were, a large proportion of the governments presently there would have to leave. The precedent that would be set for the expulsion of Israel, if the Khmer Rouge were to be expelled, was a concern that exercised many delegates at this and future sessions.

Other delegates pointed out that earlier in the year Tanzanian forces had installed a new regime in Uganda with scant international protest and that few governments complained in 1971 when a new government was created in Bangladesh as a result of Indian army intervention. One important difference in the case of Bangladesh was that Indian troops had soon left. Tanzanian troops had taken longer to go. Another difference, in politics if not in law, was that while most of the countries of the region, particularly ASEAN and China, were opposed to the Vietnamese action, most members of the Organization of African Unity had been glad to see the end of Idi Amin. And in the case of Cambodia, many states saw the dark hand of the Soviet Union manipulating events.

An Indian proposal for a vacant seat was rejected and at the end of the debate the Khmer Rouge credentials were accepted by 71 to 35, with 34 abstentions. Many of the delegates who voted for Pol Pot acknowledged that the General Assembly's decision would make the task of the international organizations inside Cambodia more difficult than ever.

After one of the votes, an American delegate, Robert Rosenstock, found someone shaking his hand with great enthusiasm. He looked up and saw that it was Ieng Sary, grinning broadly. "I felt like washing my hand," said the American.

8 &❀ Other Aid

The virtual embargo that the U.N. organizations and the ICRC were still imposing on news of their operations both inside Cambodia and along the border was not helping their public relations or, therefore, their fund raising. Now, when the Western world was, for the first time, becoming aware of the enormity of the horror that had engulfed Cambodia, the two organizations were accused of doing nothing to alleviate it. By contrast, the British-based organization, Oxfam, was open with information.

One of the most negative campaigns against the international organizations was begun in Britain by an Australian journalist, John Pilger, in the *Daily Mirror,* the *New Statesman,* and later on television. Pilger was the *Mirror*'s Indochina writer. While the Khmer Rouge were in power he had not written about their atrocities. In August 1979 he visited Phnom Penh under the auspices of Vietnam Television, which was the only way that Western camera crews were allowed to visit Cambodia, and produced a sensational series of reports about the death of Cambodia, first of all in the mass-circulation *Daily Mirror.*

A rather interesting quality of the articles was their concentration on Nazism and the holocaust. Pilger called Pol Pot "an Asian Hitler"—and said he was even worse than Hitler. On a huge center spread of Tuol Sleng and a mass grave the *Mirror* declaimed, "Echo of Auschwitz," "12,000 died here. The killers, like the Nazis, photographed their victims before and after death," and "Murder, Nazi

Style." Again and again Pilger compared the Khmer Rouge to the Nazis. Their Marxist-Leninist ideology was not even mentioned in the *Mirror,* except to say that they were inspired by China's Red Guards. Their intellectual origins were described as "anarchist" rather than Communist. The torturers in Tuol Sleng were called "a gestapo" and Tuol Sleng itself "might have been copied from the original"—Auschwitz. One article ended by declaring, "A generation ago, while the civilised world still reeled in disgust at Auschwitz, the United Nations was formed 'so that this might never happen again.' It has happened again."

Pilger's reports underwrote almost everything that refugees along the Thai border had been saying about the cruelty of Khmer Rouge rule since 1975, and that had already appeared in the books by the *Reader's Digest* and François Ponchaud. Nonetheless, the reaction to the stories in Britain was as if they were something quite new. (For *Mirror* readers they were indeed new, since their paper had inadequately covered Khmer Rouge atrocities while the Khmer Rouge were in power.) They made Cambodia a real issue for many people who had previously paid it no attention. In Britain and elsewhere they were crucial in galvanizing widespread public support for a massive relief operation.

As with the eyewitness reports from Belsen in 1945, the eyewitness reports from journalists and from aid officials in Phnom Penh in late summer 1979 had far more impact than the previous refugee accounts. Firsthand evidence is often more compelling—and perhaps more easily assimilated—than that which is retold. Another reason, no doubt, was the photographs of Khmer Rouge horrors; today words can be ignored in a way that pictures cannot. (The photograph of the execution of a Viet Cong soldier in a Saigon street during Tet 1968 and that of the naked little girl running down the highway after being napalmed in 1972—for many people these embody the Vietnam war as no article or book can ever do.)

Pilger insisted that the Vietnamese were not placing any obstacles in the way of an aid program. After the Khmer Rouge, the principal target of his criticism was the U.S. Government and he asserted that the West in general was consciously refusing to feed the children of Cambodia because it "would not only mean co-operating with Vietnam, it would also mean displeasing the leaders of the world's newest and richest market, China." He blamed Western governments and the ICRC and UNICEF for the delays in aid reaching Phnom Penh.

This, as previous chapters may have helped to show, was not quite so. The delays were almost all due to the authorities in Phnom Penh.* But neither UNICEF nor ICRC was prepared then to reveal the problems; Pilger's views were widely believed in Britain and elsewhere and, as a result, the offices of UNICEF and the Red Cross received many calls from horrified people who demanded to know why they were letting Cambodians starve. By contrast, Pilger praised Oxfam and suggested that people send donations to its Cambodia relief operation. Oxfam was at once deluged with donations and offers of help, and some, not all, of its officials actually encouraged the notion that the Vietnamese had in no way hindered any relief effort and that Oxfam alone was prepared to help Cambodia live.

In fact, UNICEF and ICRC officials were close to panic at their inability to obtain any agreement from the Phnom Penh government. In Geneva Alexander Hay, the President of the ICRC, a body that depends above all on its neutrality, publicly criticized the Heng Samrin regime and Vietnam. He was backed by the Swiss government, which declared, "Everything points to the fact that the responsible authorities are putting obstructions in the way of large-scale aid operations. . . ." In New York, Henry Labouisse, UNICEF's Executive Director, wrote to Kurt Waldheim to warn that it was proving impossible to establish the sort of team in Phnom Penh that was necessary for such a huge operation and communications were hopeless. "This is a terribly serious situation, and untold thousands are dying

---

* To recapitulate some of the delays: On January 4, 1979, the ICRC made its first public offer of help to Cambodia. Both the UNICEF and the ICRC offices in Hanoi sought permission for visas to assess needs in Cambodia from January onward. It was not until the end of June that the Cambodian ambassador in Hanoi invited them both to send a delegate in July. Two delegates left Geneva a few days later. They had to wait in Hanoi. They submitted a draft plan of action to the Phnom Penh authorities on July 17; this was approved by the ICRC in Geneva on July 22. A more detailed plan was put before the Phnom Penh authorities on August 10. By mid-September this had still not been approved by Phnom Penh.

and millions suffering. It will be most difficult to mount an adequate programme—even with full co-operation. It will be impossible without it." Labouisse urged Waldheim "to again use your good offices to impress upon those having an influence in Phnom Penh the urgent necessity of giving full co-operation to those wanting to help."

Waldheim sent two of his senior officials to meet Ha Van Lau, Vietnam's permanent representative to the U.N. They reminded him that his Prime Minister, Pham Van Dong, had himself promised Waldheim in Havana that the Vietnamese would cooperate fully with the UNICEF-ICRC relief effort. Yet it was not happening. Ha Van Lau claimed that Hanoi could exert only limited influence on Phnom Penh. And he pointed out that the Heng Samrin regime had protested the food across the border.

Waldheim's officials replied that they thought the emergency was so grave that political considerations should be set aside. The donor countries could not fund assistance that would exclude a section of the population, even if it was only a few thousand people. They asked Ha Van Lau to try to expedite matters and to have the fifth ICRC relief flight to Phnom Penh cleared. He promised to try.

On September 21 came the U.N. vote to allow the Khmer Rouge to retain Cambodia's seat. For his part, Prime Minister Kriangsak declared that Cambodia was ravaged by starvation, disease and death and that Thailand could be the base for relief operations. A cable from UNICEF's Bangkok office to New York announced "more reports received telling alarming situation lack food medicines . . . needs for food enormous." On September 23, *The New York Times* reported from the U.N. that "although two million Cambodians are facing famine, the Heng Samrin government in Phnom Penh is obstructing the expansion of desperately needed foreign assistance, according to diplomatic sources here and in Washington."

By coincidence, that very day Beaumont and Bugnion thought they had achieved a breakthrough in Phnom Penh. They met with Ros Samay, the Minister of Economy, who had always been one of the most helpful of the Heng Samrin officials. To their delight, he informed them that their August program and their permanent presence had been approved by the cabinet. They then read back to him the short memo on which they had listed all aspects of the program—ships, food, monitoring, transport, radio, secretarial help. He said yes to each item. Greatly relieved, they sent cables to Geneva and New York. The messages took three days to reach their destinations —and by then everything had changed once more.

September 26 was busy with regard to Cambodia all across the world.

In Hanoi, the party paper, *Nhan Dan* attacked the proposed international aid program as "a cover for intervention and aggression." It declared that the United States was trying to paint "a dark picture" of the Heng Samrin government and to reinstall Pol Pot. More extraordinarily, Hanoi declared that the story of a famine was instigated by "the same people who whipped up the so-called Indochina refugee problem." This reversal of propaganda by the Vietnamese both strained credulity and increased the confusion in the West over what was happening in Cambodia and what Vietnam's attitude really was.

In April, when fears of a famine had first been voiced by Western journalists and diplomats in Bangkok, such concerns had been dismissed by Hanoi and Phnom Penh. In July, however, both Hanoi and Phnom Penh claimed that international assistance was needed to save 2.25 million people threatened by famine.

But now that Western and particularly American interest were becoming aroused, now that food was starting to go across the border as well as to Phnom Penh, and now that the Heng Samrin regime had failed to win the United Nations seat, Vietnam appears to have begun to reconsider the implications of a large-scale international relief operation. *Nhan Dan* declared that Western aid "is only designed to open a way for them into Cambodia and, as such, is a flouting of the U.N. Charter and international law."

In Phnom Penh that same day Beaumont and Bugnion met with Hun Sen, the Foreign Minister. He was markedly less enthusiastic than Ros Samay had been three days earlier. He said there could be no question whatever of ICRC and UNICEF putting food across the border to the areas controlled by the Khmer Rouge. Beaumont sent a note to headquarters saying, "I do not believe that, psychologically, they are ready to understand any support, direct or indirect, given to the other side, which they consider responsible for the incredible suffering of the people."

Later that day in Bangkok, Air Vice-Marshal Siddhi summoned embassies and agencies to a meeting (the second in a week). There he unveiled Thailand's own emergency plan for the Cambodian crisis and solicited contributions to it. He began by saying that, "out of humanitarian concern for the starving and diseased Kampuchean people," Thailand had now adopted a new four-part policy:

1. The ICRC and UNICEF were to be helped to ship assistance from Bangkok to Phnom Penh. But voluntary agencies would not be able to ship supplies from Bangkok to Phnom Penh.

2. UNICEF and ICRC must also push food across the border in the hope that this would discourage at least some starving Cambodians from entering Thailand. Voluntary agencies could be involved in Thailand.

3. Holding centers for the "illegal immigrants" who were allowed to enter Thailand would be built.

4. These new "illegal immigrants" must be resettled quickly; they must be taken out of Thailand over and above the existing quotas for the resettlement of Indochinese refugees.

Siddhi also said that responsibility for distribution of supplies inside Thailand would be in the hands of Supreme Command. The World Food Program should distribute food to sixteen special warehouses the government was creating close to the border; Supreme Command would take the food to the border itself. World Food Program officials agreed. They had no option. Like the Vietnamese, the Thais wanted to minimize the extent to which the international organizations monitored the distribution of the aid they supplied.

Money was the next problem. Siddhi suggested that "for convenience and economy" most relief supplies, including food, be bought in Thailand. Hence cash contributions direct to the Thai government would be ideal. The government would like one million dollars over the next six months to provide assistance to about 260,000 people along the border and in the holding centers.* To

---

* The Thai calculations were based on feeding people 800 grams of rice per day, whereas WFP reckoned that 400 grams was adequate and 500 grams the absolute maximum needed. Such differences perpetually plagued the program and made real accounting almost impossible.

Siddhi's disappointment none of the embassies present came forward with an immediate pledge of funds.

In conclusion, Siddhi declared that relief could not take the place of a political solution, and he urged all those present to support the resolution that ASEAN had tabled for the new session of the General Assembly. This called for the withdrawal of all foreign forces from Cambodia, free elections, and an international conference to decide the country's future.

Some hours later that same day, on the other side of the world in New York, two meetings took place, one in the office of the United Nations Secretary General.

Into Waldheim's office glided Ieng Sary, the Khmer Rouge foreign minister. He thanked the Secretary General for the international assistance over the Thai border and praised the dedication of ICRC and UNICEF officials. Referring to the charges of genocide against his regime, he said merely that "history will judge the issue." At the moment he was not prepared to engage in polemics, he said. It should be remembered, he declared, that "there was great confusion after the liberation of Kampuchea" in 1975. "Whatever the judgment of past events, the problem the country now faced was one of foreign occupation and survival."

Waldheim responded that the U.N. was trying to provide substantial assistance to the Cambodian people. Its success depended on cooperation from the relevant authorities. He deplored the continued fighting. Did Ieng Sary think a debate in the General Assembly would contribute to peace? Ieng Sary said he thought its influence would be only moral; the Vietnamese were not concerned with international opinion.

The second New York meeting, on September 26, took place just up First Avenue at the UNICEF headquarters, where news of the "breakthrough" with Ros Samay on September 23 had just arrived. It was chaired by Henry Labouisse of UNICEF and Jean Pierre Hocke of the ICRC and was intended to inform the major donors of progress. Labouisse painted a terrifying picture of Cambodia. He repeated what was by now almost a cliché (and fortunately an incorrect one)—that there were few children under five. He said that almost all the surviving children were hungry and there were no medical facilities. He was glad to report that Beaumont and Bugnion had been given permission by Ros Samay, the Minister of Economy, to set up a program. Since this had happened after the ICRC-UNICEF mission had gone to the Khmer Rouge areas, he thought it meant that Phnom Penh was prepared, at least tacitly, to agree that aid should go to all civilians in Cambodia.

Obviously Labouisse could know nothing of the meeting in Phnom Penh a few hours earlier, in which Hun Sen had told Beaumont just the opposite—that aid to the border was intolerable.

Labouisse and Hocke asked that news of the "breakthrough" be kept confidential. Then they outlined the program they had in mind. Aid was needed over a six-month period. But the political and logistical constraints were extremely severe. Fortunately, Thailand, previously reluctant, had now agreed to allow Bangkok to be the staging area.

They planned to deliver aid for 2.25 million people for 180 days. At least 30,000 tons of supplies a month would be needed. If capacity could be developed, they hoped to ship altogether 152,000 tons of supplies together with 100 trucks. The cost of the program they had in mind would be at least $17 million and at most $96 million. This was clearly leaving a lot of room for error; and, because of ignorance about conditions, errors were indeed being made. Within weeks, even Labouisse's maximum figure would seem absurdly small. For now the donor response was disappointing. Only the Netherlands made a firm commitment, of $150,000.

Despite the plea for secrecy, ICRC's own headquarters responded to the public clamor for action by issuing a press release that very evening announcing an agreement with Phnom Penh. It declared that both ICRC and UNICEF had been given permission to open offices and start a relief program in Phnom Penh and that their officials would be allowed to monitor the distribution of supplies. The statement said that the "authorities of Democratic Kampuchea" had also agreed to allow relief to be distributed to the tens of thousands of civilians stranded near the Thai border. The statement concluded, with more wishful thinking than realism—"In accordance with the principle of neutrality, the ICRC and UNICEF through their representatives on the spot, will watch that this relief, so essential to the civilian populations, will in no way contribute to the war effort of either belligerent."

The ICRC statement was flashed back to Hanoi within a few hours. It was then denounced by the Heng Samrin regime, whose news agency, S.P.K., declared that the ICRC-UNICEF proposals were "designed to legalize the dispatch of supplies to the Pol Pot–Ieng Sary remnant troops in their opposition to the Kampuchean people." The agency declared that the "so-called assistance to both sides" was merely "a trick to legalize the supply to the Pol Pot elements now in dire straits . . . a trick of using humanitarianism for interfering in the internal affairs of Kampuchea and trying to reanimate the Pol Pot corpse. . . ."

Two days later, on September 28, a typewritten *aide mémoire* from the Foreign Ministry was pushed under François Bugnion's door at the Samaki hotel in Phnom Penh. This was remarkable not so much for its manner of delivery as for the fact that it was the first written document that the aid officials had ever received from the government.

The memo thanked them for the aid already delivered and stated that the Minister wanted them to have permanent offices in Phnom Penh, but only on three conditions:

First, they must submit a precise, detailed program of what they would supply and when. Secondly, they must entrust all distribution to the government, which would then give ICRC and UNICEF reports. Thirdly, they must guarantee not to interfere in Cambodia's internal affairs; in particular they must not give any aid "to the Pol Pot–Ieng Sary clique under the cover of so-called 'aid to all parties.'"

It was obviously the third point that caused most difficulties— there were indeed Khmer Rouge troops along the Thai border and the Thai military wanted them to be fed. But the majority of the people there were civilians who had either been forcibly brought there by the Khmer Rouge or had arrived there in the course of their panic-driven flight. To deny them aid would be to deny the principles of impartiality and nondiscrimination on which the organizations were founded. When the conditions reached New York, Labouisse wrote to Waldheim saying that UNICEF could accept the first two but not the third. "It is hard to believe that anyone would insist that a humanitarian agency undertake to deny aid to starving and ill children." He thought that UNICEF should simply "play down any emphasis on assistance to the northwest." (The "northwest" was the name that the agencies gave to that part of the border where most refugees were concentrated.) UNICEF could not ignore the area; it had always before fed children on both sides of a civil war. In any case, he thought the border program would be quite limited. "I have serious doubts that large quantities can be moved." In this he was, unhappily, mistaken. Thousands more pitiful people were moving every day toward Thailand. By the first week of October the Thai government was already asking for a border program to feed over 350,000 people, to stop their pushing into Thailand in search of food. More and more food was being trucked there by the World Food Program.

Labouisse again asked Waldheim to intervene with the Vietnamese. And he cabled Bangkok: "No comments on future assistance to Pol Pot administered areas should be made. If pressed on this subject, spokesman would state that the situation in the northwest is extremely fluid and conditions extremely difficult—UNICEF's assistance has been very limited. No further details are available."

The quandary in which UNICEF and the ICRC found themselves was not eased by the different approach of Oxfam.

Small independent agencies are often able to move faster than international organizations with more cumbersome procedures or more demanding mandates. After receiving Jim Howard's terrifying report on Cambodia, Oxfam had organized another planeload of supplies with an Oxfam doctor, Tim Lusty, on board. Realizing that planes alone could not possibly meet Cambodia's needs, Oxfam dispatched Guy Stringer, an avuncular former British army officer who was its deputy director general, to Southeast Asia to try to arrange shipping.

When Stringer arrived in Bangkok he learned of the Thai government's decision that only the ICRC and UNICEF could ship supplies either through or from Bangkok to Phnom Penh. A consignment from the World Council of Churches was already lingering in

Bangkok warehouses. Since Oxfam's second supply plane was about to be staged through Bangkok, Stringer went to see Air Vice-Marshal Siddhi. Siddhi said there was nothing he could do, since he had already refused applications for a number of Russian and Polish over-flights. Stringer reported later that he appealed to Siddhi—"as a brother officer and a gentleman"—to let the one Oxfam flight through. Siddhi agreed, "provided I undertook that the meeting with him had never taken place."

Since he could not hire, fill and dispatch barges in Bangkok, Stringer flew down to Singapore. Here he was allowed to go ahead. This was fortunate if not unexpected, because the Singapore government was, if anything, even more steadfast in its opposition to the Vietnamese occupation of Cambodia than the Thai administration. Since Thailand was insisting that UNICEF and the ICRC feed both sides, one might have expected that Singapore would do the same. Presumably because the U.N. organizations and ICRC had accepted Thailand's condition—which was part of their mandates—Singapore was prepared to tolerate Oxfam's unilateral venture on behalf of Phnom Penh. Whatever Oxfam's quota of zeal and rhetoric, the resources it could muster would never equal those harnessed by the U.N. and the ICRC.

This is not to deny the importance of the Oxfam initiative in securing shipping. While Guy Stringer was busy loading the first Oxfam barge in Singapore, UNICEF's Bangkok office called to ask that he should include 200 tons of goods in UNICEF's name. Stringer hesitated. The aid business is probably no more competitive than any other, but it is sometimes a shock to outsiders that it seems no less. Many officials of small relief agencies about to make a coup of the sort Stringer was conducting would refuse to allow any other organization to associate itself in any way. Stringer had not been impressed by ICRC and UNICEF's operations in Bangkok. However, after some heart searching, he decided to cooperate with them. Some of his colleagues in Oxford were chagrined.

When complete, Stringer's load, the first Western aid shipped by sea to Phnom Penh, consisted of 50 tons of sugar, 25 tons of edible oil, 200 tons of white rice, 500 tons of milled maize, 500 tons of wheat flour, 6 tons of assorted seeds, 600 hoes, and the 200 tons donated by UNICEF. The cost of the entire shipment was about $500,000. With a scratch crew and in very high spirits, he set sail.

Meanwhile, Brian Walker, Oxfam's director general, flew to Phnom Penh on Oxfam's third relief plane. Walker, an accomplished fund raiser, had been a businessman in Northern Ireland before he joined Oxfam in 1974. He arrived in Phnom Penh on September 28, just as Beaumont and Bugnion received the *aide mémoire* telling them that they could not work inside Cambodia if UNICEF and ICRC were active on the Thai border.

When Walker's plane landed, one of his staff, Robert Mister, was denied entry and had to fly out with the empty plane. The next day, Walker met with the Foreign Minister Hun Sen; he told Walker that it was quite impossible for Cambodia to accept aid from agencies that were also helping the Khmer Rouge. "Our people would prefer to eat grass or to die than to share aid with Pol Pot," Hun Sen said. He asserted that agencies that insisted on working on the Khmer Rouge side would not be allowed to stay in Cambodia.

Like every other visitor to Phnom Penh, Walker was appalled by the evidence of Cambodia's suffering under the Khmer Rouge and was determined to set up a large-scale aid program to try to meet the present needs. He had already reached provisional agreement with a number of European voluntary agencies to join a consortium under Oxfam's umbrella. It seems that he was now persuaded that if Oxfam agreed, in effect, not to operate in their border areas, it would be allowed to operate in Cambodia. And if the ICRC and UNICEF insisted on helping those along the border, they would be expelled from Phnom Penh. Then, as a result, Oxfam and a few other voluntary agencies would alone have the responsibility of succoring the country itself. The responsibility would be onerous—but the opportunity would be immense.

This impression was reinforced by Mr. Bui Huu Nhan. Mr. Nhan, a friendly and personable man who enjoyed James Bond novels, was the senior Vietnamese liaison officer to the Cambodian foreign ministry. In other words, he gave the instructions. He now told Walker that Oxfam "must stay separate from the ICRC-Unicef program" and "must not cooperate with that programme." ICRC and UNICEF were "helping Pol Pot" and would be asked to withdraw.

Hun Sen repeated these strictures at a second meeting, insisting that Oxfam must not cooperate in any way with ICRC or UNICEF in Cambodia.

In many parts of the world Oxfam is in constant cooperation with UNICEF and ICRC. Walker was not clear whether these relationships had to be severed for Oxfam to stay in Phnom Penh. He asked Mr. Nhan if the strictures referred only to Cambodia. Mr. Nhan said yes.

Walker accepted the government's conditions. He agreed to hand over supplies to the regime, which would distribute them "in cooperation with" Oxfam. He agreed—as UNICEF and ICRC were still refusing to do—that Oxfam would give no aid to what the regime called "the forces of Pol Pot" along the Thai border. And he agreed that Oxfam would "not cooperate" with the ICRC, or with UNICEF in Phnom Penh. He wrote a letter to the Foreign Ministry, apologizing for the fact that Oxfam's first barge might be carrying UNICEF supplies. He reached his understanding on October 7, and he proposed a consortium of voluntary agencies led by Oxfam to begin a huge relief program costing about £2 million a month. He cabled Oxford, "Because of aid across the border to Pol Pot we understand Unicef ICRC have been asked to leave the country. We must not assist any aid programme of that nature and we have been asked not to cooperate with Unicef inside Kampuchea only. Have agreed."

Throughout all this, UNICEF and ICRC were subjected to more and more pressure by the Phnom Penh authorities. Beaumont thought this was due partly to the border operation and partly to Walker's agreement to the authorities' demands. On October 5, Knud Christensen, whom UNICEF had designated to replace Beaumont, was refused permission to enter when he arrived at the airport. Next day, as Walker pursued his agreement, Beaumont was told by the Ministry of Foreign Affairs that he and all UNICEF and ICRC staff must leave the country at once "for consultations" with their headquarters.

Beaumont was sick, as well as exhausted and dispirited. His father had just died. He was anxious to return to Europe for family reasons as well as to New York to consult with Labouisse. Nonetheless, he decided that he had better refuse to leave, lest he never be allowed back. Stalling, he wrote to the Foreign Ministry asking for written confirmation of the instruction. He also wrote to Labouisse expressing fears about Oxfam's agreement; he was worried that Oxfam had agreed to "promise more—and without much supervision"—and to "accept a programme with less monitoring." He added that Vietnamese officials were slandering UNICEF "and, as usual, this (partly) is believed by some of our partners" in other relief agencies. In New York, Labouisse prevailed upon Waldheim to intervene once again with the Vietnamese.* In a letter to Pham Van Dong, written in French, Waldheim referred to their discussion, in Havana, of the food crisis in Cambodia. "You told me then that the situation was extremely grave, that the famine was already widespread and that it was necessary for the United Nations organizations to undertake a relief operation for the people of Kampuchea."

Waldheim assured the Vietnamese premier that the U.N. operation was in no way intended to constitute interference in Cambodian affairs and had only humanitarian ends. "However, the aid cannot be dispatched and delivered if the local authorities do not cooperate fully with the operations and if the organizations involved, particularly UNICEF and the International Committee of the Red Cross, do not have a minimum of personnel and equipment in place. I am counting on your understanding and support in this matter."

The shades of the Nazis were being summoned more and more frequently now. In Geneva, François Bugnion, who had returned from

---

* Waldheim sent Ilter Turkman, an Assistant Secretary General, to see Ha Van Lau, the Vietnamese Permanent Representative to the United Nations. Turkman said that the Secretary General was hoping that the September 23 agreement with Ros Samay would be strictly implemented; he was disturbed by the denial of Knud Christensen's visa. Ha Van Lau said that his government supported the Joint Mission but had only limited influence with the Heng Samrin regime. Turkman asked that Hanoi make a *démarche* at the highest level. Ha Van Lau said that there were difficulties since the whole administrative structure had collapsed in Phnom Penh. Then Waldheim once more dispatched Turkman to Southeast Asia as his special representative to try to find a solution to the crisis before he made his own report to the General Assembly in early November. Turkman bore letters from Waldheim to Prime Ministers Kriangsak and Pham Van Dong. Waldheim thanked Kriangsak for the refuge he was so far giving to Cambodians and promised "I will do everything possible to mobilize additional assistance. Relief assistance to the people of Kampuchea is one of the most important humanitarian tasks the United Nations has undertaken."

Phnom Penh to brief his superiors at the ICRC, likened Cambodia to Buchenwald. He too repeated that there were few children under five, that there were many more spontaneous abortions than live births because of mothers' poor health, and that many of the rare babies born had died in infancy. Agence France Presse reported that his "apocalyptic visions cast a chilly light on the Cambodian Government's foot dragging over aid."

In similar vein Agence France-Presse reported from Bangkok: "All the evidence brought back by refugees, members of relief groups, diplomats and journalists points to one fact: since the Second World War no people has experienced an ordeal as total, as traumatic or as lasting—in terms of the effects still to come—as the one the Cambodians have been experiencing for the past ten years. For once a tragedy cannot simply be reduced to mere statistics."

With such reports in mind, Anthony Lewis wrote in *The New York Times* on October 6, that what the Cambodians had suffered and were still suffering, "justifies a word that should not be cheapened by overuse: *holocaust.*" If nothing were done, two million Cambodians might die. "We do not want to tell ourselves, if the worst happens, that we stood by and wrung our hands." A few days later, Lewis wrote, "In the 1930s and 1940s many of the world's leaders stood by, mute, as a human disaster took place. History has not forgotten. New books continue to record the terrible facts of their indifference. Today, right now, another enormous human tragedy is unfolding. The remnants of the Cambodian people are dying of starvation and disease." He urged that world leaders like Jimmy Carter and Kurt Waldheim act more urgently than they had acted so far. "Just think what the reaction would be if two million Italians were about to starve to death, or two million Jews or, for that matter, two million Russians. But these victims are Cambodians."

The implication was that Cambodians had no lobby in the United States. But the pressure of the stories and the photos from Cambodia, coupled with the increasingly common references to the Holocaust of the Jews, was changing that—in a way which rarely happens for most of the world's benighted peoples.

But at the same time as Western demands for real action grew, so Vietnam was responding in a way which its critics took to con-

firm their worst analysis of Hanoi's actions and intentions. Its officials insisted that aid from Vietnam and other socialist countries had
already alleviated the crisis and that there was no famine at all now.
The Cambodian News Agency, S.P.K., announced that the socialist
countries had so far given "one thousand times" more aid than the
West. Agence France-Presse was told by Vietnamese officials that the
USSR had given Vietnam and Cambodia over two million tons of
food in the past eighteen months; of this, 154,000 tons had gone to
Cambodia since January, they claimed. There is no doubt that considerable aid had come from Vietnam and its socialist partners in the
previous nine months. But no Western official or journalist who had
been into Cambodia had seen any trace of such massive shipments as
were now claimed—nor, indeed, the logistics by which they could
have been distributed.

Then the Cambodian Foreign Minister Hun Sen declared that
not a single Cambodian was dying of hunger and that the food crisis
had been relieved, thanks to the "considerable" aid given, "with no
strings attached," by the socialist world. The situation was not nearly
as "critical" as "exaggerated, ill-intentioned" Western reports of an
"appalling famine" would have people believe, he declared. At the
United Nations, Vietnamese officials held that "there is a food shortage, yes, but not this so-called famine that the West is playing up.
This is a trap to try to supply food and ammunition to the Pol Pot
forces."

Such assertions by the Vietnamese and Cambodian governments
were impossible to tally with the reports of most of those Westerners
in Phnom Penh or with the reports from the border. They led to increasing distrust, by many Western governments, of the motives of
the Vietnamese. From now on, what was actually happening in Cambodia would become a matter of more and more bitter polemics—
which made it even more difficult for an effective relief operation to
be mounted and sustained.

9 ❧ The Program

The first Oxfam barge, towed by the tug *Asiatic Success,* arrived off the Cambodian port of Kompong Som on the evening of October 13. The indomitable Stringer ran up a Cambodian flag, which he had purchased in Singapore. Alas, it turned out to be the Pol Pot emblem and it was later ceremonially burnt on the dockside.

Next morning, a dozen Cambodian officials came on board. They were young and were equipped only with penny notebooks and cheap ballpoint pens. Pinned to their chests were pieces of cardboard on which were written their respective duties—*"Douane," "Santé,"* and so on. Everyone came downstairs and sat around the table, smoking furiously and drinking Coca Cola. The ship's agent passed around the manifest and other documents, and the Cambodians wrote in their notebooks. This rather touching moment reminded Guy Stringer of the court scene in *Alice in Wonderland,* when the jurors write on their squeaky slates.

On the dock to meet this, the first shipload of humanitarian supplies from the West in almost five years, were the Minister of Economy and Reconstruction, the Minister of Health, the Minister of Agriculture, and a senior provincial official—together with two Oxfam people from Phnom Penh. Stringer made a fine speech about the indelible friendship between ordinary British and Cambodian people; Ros Samay, the Minister of Economy—who wore a revolver on his hip—explained that he personally had gathered almost every working truck in Cambodia, plus fifty he had hired from Vietnam, to meet the boat. (The ship's Singaporean crew immediately thought the food was going to be stolen by the Vietnamese; Stringer reassured them.)

There were no forklifts, no cranes, no conveyors in the port. Everything had to be carried off the barge by a ragtag collection of young men and women, boys and girls. They were quite unskilled and were very weak. They had to be fed with food being unloaded from the barge, and they took five days, even under ministerial supervision, to unload the cargo.

Stringer drove up to Phnom Penh, where he visited an orphanage in which five hundred children were without blankets, mats, pencils or anything at all; he decided that Oxfam should order a thousand orphan kits, including blanket, sleeping mat, mosquito net, towel, soap, toothbrush, toothpaste, for each child, together with buckets, cooking pots, baths, pencils, penny notebooks, toys for the group. At the Rusey Keo textile factory the manager chose cotton from the samples Stringer had brought, and Stringer immediately ordered another twenty tons from Singapore, to make 50,000 sarongs. "I ordered in addition some new screen printing material so that new gay designs could be produced to brighten the lives of the women of this town of whom so many are widows."

Hoping that Oxfam's next barge could be brought right up the Mekong to Phnom Penh, Stringer visited the port on the river. The port director was very little more than a boy; there were four small ancient cranes on the dock, and some 120 laborers who could unload about 300 tons a day. Ros Samay encouraged Stringer to bring a boat up the river; so did the ubiquitous Vietnamese adviser, Mr. Nhan, who often came to afternoon tea with the Oxfam people to discuss what they were doing. However, the Vietnamese later canceled permission for Oxfam's second barge to come up the river. When eventually the river transit was arranged, the Vietnamese demanded very high dues.

Stringer also visited an old fishing-net factory. Pulling open the doors of a huge shed, he and his colleague Marcus Thompson confronted row upon row of complicated Japanese fishing-net machines. Naked children scampered around in the gloom. From the back an old man emerged; he introduced himself as Mr. Sok Seng, the chief engineer. He said he had worked here since the time of Sihanouk,

though the Khmer Rouge had banished him to the fields. He turned
out to be the sort of natural engineer who could repair anything with
a hairpin. In halting French he said that with spare parts he could
get one bank of five machines in working order. A perfectionist, he
said he needed many different sorts and sizes of line to make different meshes of net for rivers, seas and lakes, but eventually he agreed
that there was one size that was nearly universal. Stringer promised
to help restore the factory. The old man was clearly happy, and that
evening a little parcel arrived at Stringer's room. It was a tea towel
in which was wrapped a present of four small pieces of dried fish.

On Stringer's recommendations, Oxfam tried to persuade the
Japanese manufacturers to send a man to Phnom Penh to help repair
their machines. The Japanese—whose ideas of humanitarian aid are
often even more commercial than those of most other nations—refused, and an engineer was sent from Scotland instead. Before that
time, several machines had been repaired, nylon line had arrived
from Hong Kong, and the fishing-net factory was in business.

Next Stringer went to see the Minister of Agriculture, Neou
Samoun, who, in April, had declared publicly there was no risk of
famine. He seemed completely out of his depth, but his deputy, Kom
Som Ol, who had been educated in the United States, was very
efficient. In time Oxfam and other foreign relief officials came to
depend upon him greatly. Kom Som Ol estimated that about 570,000
hectares of rice fields had been planted with rice; he thought this
might produce about three months' worth of food in the New Year.
He wanted to sow short-term rice as soon as possible. For this about
a thousand irrigation pumps would be needed. Stringer agreed that
pumps and seed rice should come on Oxfam's third barge.

At the Ministry of Commerce the Minister Taing Sarim was
jovial as he explained that 70 percent of all factories were still
closed; he hoped to start up first textiles, blanket factories, tire factories, a plastics factory and, to Stringer's surprise, a raincoat factory.
At the Seventh of January Hospital, Tim Lusty, Oxfam's doctor, had
set up a supplementary feeding program, but many of the children
were still too weak to hold their mugs or bowls. They needed someone to sit with and care for them all day long; they had no one.

Stringer then went to Phnom Penh's railroad station and found the railroad in a hopeless state of disrepair. The system had only two diesel engines and one of them was broken down. The station itself was littered with burnt pieces of wood and cloth; Stringer was told that on the day the Khmer Rouge fled Phnom Penh they had set fire to a train filled with 200 wounded. He walked along the railway line and wondered how it could be that "these charming people with their good looks and their elegant women had embraced this madness and horror."

In Geneva, Henry Labouisse and Charles Egger of UNICEF met with Alexander Hay and Jean Pierre Hocke of the ICRC. They had agonized discussions about how to reconcile their fundamental principles of impartiality and nondiscrimination with the political demands being made of them by Phnom Penh. The ICRC traces its concept of impartiality back to Henri Dunant's actions on the battlefield at Solferino. It was embodied in Article 6 of the first Geneva Convention of August 22, 1864—"Wounded and sick combatants shall be collected and cared for, to whatever nation they may belong." It was repeated in all the subsequent stages of the Geneva Conventions (1906, 1929 and 1949) and is the real foundation of Red Cross action. For UNICEF, similar considerations applied to the principle of "non-discrimination," which is enshrined in Article 1/3 of the United Nations Charter on which the UNICEF Statute is itself founded.

Now ICRC and UNICEF's senior officials agreed in Geneva that neither organization could ignore principles that were at the heart of its existence. They agreed also that to accept Hun Sen's third demand—that they not feed people on the Thai border—would create a very dangerous precedent and would invite any government involved in a future conflict to bully them into refusing to give assistance to war victims under the control of its enemy. They therefore agreed that they must continue to accept the risk of being expelled from Phnom Penh rather than forfeit their basic principles. This determination was approved at a session in early October of the Red Cross's Council of Delegates, meeting in Geneva. The Council includes delegates of all Red Cross and Red Crescent societies as well as representatives of the League and the ICRC. It accepted the

ICRC's insistence on impartiality in the Cambodian crisis almost unanimously—only Vietnam opposed it. The Red Cross societies of the socialist bloc did not support their Vietnamese ally. They abstained.

Nonetheless, in view of the extraordinary circumstances in Cambodia, the ICRC and UNICEF agreed to go some way to meeting the requirements of the Phnom Penh regime, in order to appear to make some concessions that did not offend their founding principles. Food deliveries to Phnom Penh would be greatly increased, while border operations would not only be conducted in conditions of strict secrecy, but would actually be cut down.

This decision worried UNICEF officials in Bangkok. Thailand had made it abundantly clear that it would not tolerate any relief operation out of Bangkok unless it was aimed at all Cambodians, those on the border as well as those under the control of Phnom Penh. Moreover, the crisis on the border was such that they were actually having to expand, not cut back, their operation. Indeed, they had made their first big delivery of supplies, to 40,000 people living under Khmer Rouge control south of Aranyaprathet at Nong Pru, on October 5. Up to 100,000 more were thought to be close to the border, in terrible conditions. More and more food and medical supplies were being trucked there daily.*

Nonetheless, those were the instructions which were given to François Bugnion of the ICRC before he returned to Cambodia. He flew back to Phnom Penh on the daily relief flight that the ICRC began—with a Royal Air Force Hercules C-130 lent by the British government—on October 13.† With him he took the radio he thought

---

* By October 19 the joint program had delivered to the border 788 tons of food, 4 tons of special children's food, 1 ton of medicines, 600,000 multivitamin tablets, 4.9 tons of soap, 10.5 tons of tarpaulins, 9,600 mosquito nets. For the next month over 2,000 more tons of food were planned. By contrast the Joint Mission had delivered only 233 tons of supplies by air from Europe to Phnom Penh, with another 180 tons from Bangkok.

† The start of the regular C-130 relief flights was crucial. There was no other way of importing Land-Rovers, trucks, forklifts, and other heavy equipment, since at this time there were no unloading facilities at Kompong Som or Phnom Penh ports, nor at Pochentong airport. The plane enabled the Joint Mission to break one of the most serious logistical bottlenecks that had afflicted the operation. Two Land Rovers and an airport forklift truck were brought on the first flight, and about twenty trucks came in the next ten days.

so essential to an effective relief operation. To his dismay it was im-
pounded by the Heng Samrin authorities.

On October 14, Bugnion, together with Beaumont and Knud
Christensen (who had by now been allowed entry) met once more
with Foreign Minister Hun Sen. This was a crucial meeting; it lasted
four hours.

Bugnion talked for an hour and a half about the discussions in
Geneva on the government's September 28 *aide-mémoire*. He explained the Joint Mission's plans for health, educational, logistical
and food assistance. He made it clear UNICEF and ICRC accepted
the first two points of the September 28 memorandum; they had a
definite plan and they would allow distribution to be run by the
government. But point three—no aid through Thailand—was still
causing them difficulty, because their mandate was to help all civilians on either side of a war. UNICEF and ICRC felt for the sake of
basic principles that they had to help the people, most of them innocent civilians, on the border.

Bugnion also reminded Hun Sen that the Thais had given permission for the purchase and shipment of relief to Phnom Penh "on
the condition that transport and distribution take place under the
responsibility of UNICEF and ICRC. The Thai government has decided not to authorize transit under other conditions." If UNICEF
and ICRC were no longer able to work in Cambodia, the Thai government would not allow anyone else to ship aid through Thailand
to Phnom Penh. Bugnion said he presumed that other ASEAN states
had adopted a similar position.

The implication was that unless Phnom Penh accepted the
UNICEF and ICRC presence on the border as well as in Phnom
Penh, it would forfeit not only their aid but also that of all Western
nongovernmental organizations who hoped to operate in the area.
Oxfam, whose first ship had arrived the day before, might no longer
be able to send supplies from Singapore. Where else could they come
from? Hardly Hong Kong, whose well-being was totally dependent
on China. Flights from Europe could perhaps be routed through the
Soviet Union and Vietnam, but no airlift could begin to provide the
quantities for which Phnom Penh was hoping.

The discussion became rather heated. Hun Sen declared, "It is preferable to die from famine, rather than receive poisoned assistance."

Bugnion objected strongly and asked Hun Sen to withdraw this remark. But Hun Sen replied that it was quite accurate—the aid being sent across the border was poison because it fell at once into the hands of the enemy. At this, Bugnion asked for the meeting to be suspended for ten minutes. Outside the room, the minister's interpreter apologized for "mistranslating" Hun Sen's words and agreed that the expression *"aide empoisonée"* would not be used in the future.

When the meeting resumed, Hun Sen said that he understood the difference between bilateral and multilateral aid. "The assistance from socialist countries may be distributed to anyone. Concerning assistance received from international organizations, it is understood that aid must not fall into the hands of the military or government officials." This was a fair reading.

Hun Sen went on to say, "The essential problem is political in nature. . . . The government of Kampuchea is prepared to envisage the loss of thousands of lives in order to safeguard their territorial integrity." But he also said he was glad agreement had been reached on the first two points of the September 28 memorandum, and he suggested that the Joint Mission begin the relief program while discussions on the third point—feeding the border—continued.

Beaumont and Bugnion were much encouraged. It seemed that their mission and program had survived a crucial trial of strength. Bugnion cabled Geneva, "The essential element of the conversation seems to reside in the possibility of disassociating points one and two in the September 28 *aide mémoire* from point three."

The meeting was indeed a turning point. Both sides had made concessions, though on both sides these were tacit. The organizations had effectively dropped their usual monitoring requirements, and for its part the Heng Samrin government seemed to recognize that there was no way in which they could stop the organizations' working along the border. There was no single moment in Phnom Penh in which such compromises were openly made and agreement was explicitly reached. But each side, it seems, had come to realize at about the same time that the international pressures upon it were too great to withstand, and that the cost of maintaining its demands was politically insupportable.*

Neither would publicly acknowledge this. The Heng Samrin authorities continued to denounce aid to the border. And UNICEF and ICRC declared that in the new plan, "as has been the case until now, the representatives of ICRC and UNICEF will regularly be associated with the distribution of relief material forwarded through the two organizations. In this way UNICEF and ICRC will be able to fulfill their responsibilities toward donors and will thereby, in cooperation with the relevant ministries and the Red Cross of Kampuchea, furnish reports on distribution that the two organizations are obliged to present to donors." This was the standard basis for such operations, but neither in Cambodia nor in Thailand would it be achieved.

On the medical side the plan would provide equipment for 60 doctors, 200 nurses, 200 midwives to work in 35 hospitals, 140 district dispensaries and 2,000 village clinics. Twelve of the hospitals would be equipped with specialized equipment, like laboratory material, instruments for the collection and storage of blood for transfusions, instruments for major surgery, ophthalmology, radiology, and so on. A nursing school in Phnom Penh would be furnished to train 300 students. Supplies for 35 orphanages around the country would be provided.

For education UNICEF would provide tools and paint to make blackboards, chalk, exercise books, pens, erasers and other teaching material for 1,300 schools. The Ministry of Education would receive a Duplicating Unit including typewriters, duplicating machines, stencils, ink, paper.

As for food supplies, the program stated that these were "calculated on the basis of 2,250,000 persons in danger of starvation," ac-

---

* On the international organizations, the pressures were from public opinion, particularly in Western Europe, the United States, Canada, Australia and New Zealand, demanding action. The pressures upon the Heng Samrin government and its Vietnamese allies were more political. Hanoi was still seeking international support and recognition of the Heng Samrin regime. Had it finally blocked the Joint Mission's efforts, that support would have become even more remote. In New York, Kurt Waldheim was actively trying to persuade both the USSR and Vietnam itself of this.

cording to Hun Sen's July letter to the World Food Program. It is worth noting that despite their current public propaganda that the risk of famine was now being grossly exaggerated in the West, neither Hanoi nor Phnom Penh objected to this being the basis of the Joint Mission's efforts. Indeed, privately Phnom Penh actually increased this estimate to 3 million people in their talks with the Joint Mission. The government hoped to obtain 54,000 tons of rice from Kampuchea's harvest and from bilateral aid. This left 108,000 tons of rice, 8,500 tons of oil, 6,500 tons of sugar, 18,000 tons of dried beans, 4,250 tons of fish to be provided by the joint program. This would make a daily ration of at least 1,320 calories and 36 grams of protein per person—assuming, of course, that it was distributed among all those said to be at risk.

A further 10,500 tons of milk, sugar and enriched food would be provided for supplementary feeding of 400,000 schoolchildren and 100,000 teachers and families. A similar program would be established for orphanages and hospitals. Altogether almost exactly 160,000 tons of food would be provided to Cambodia over the next six months.

At the same time, the U.N.'s Food and Agriculture Organization (FAO) would help rehabilitate Cambodia's agricultural system. Tools and vegetable seeds would be provided to enable schools, hospitals and orphanages to grow their own produce. FAO would send an expert to advise on rebuilding the all-important fisheries on the rivers and Great Lake. FAO would also send experts on rice production if requested.

Since all children desperately needed clothes, 600,000 meters of fabric and 200 sewing machines would be sent to clothe about 400,000 children. Further, 20,000 mosquito nets, 20,000 cotton blankets, 20,000 sheets and 20,000 mats would be provided for hospital beds, and 40,000 reels of cotton thread would be sent to restart the weaving industry. All these goods would either be air-freighted or sent by ship to Kompong Som or to Phnom Penh via the Mekong. Forklift trucks and unloading equipment for the ports would be provided. So would trucks and fuel for transporting everything around the country. It was hoped at that stage that Vietnam would provide trucks as well as barges, and so the original program reckoned on the import of only about 150 vehicles. In the event, the Vietnamese did not produce much transport and so the Joint Mission eventually imported over 1,000 trucks.

The proposed budget at this stage was $104,300,000. Logistics would cost $13 million, vehicles $10 million, health and social action $15 million. The fisheries and rice-field rehabilitation would be funded separately.

By far the largest component was food, at $52 million. The Joint Mission hoped to deliver 10,000 tons of food during the rest of October, 20,000 tons in November and 30,000 tons every month thereafter. These figures are worth remembering. They are what the Joint Mission reckoned essential to save the 2.25 to 3 million people who the government was claiming—in private rather than in public— were threatened by famine. In the event, the amounts of food that were actually imported and distributed in the next few months did not approach those totals.*

Even as agreement was finally being reached between ICRC and UNICEF and the Heng Samrin government, so Brian Walker of Oxfam was setting the seal on a consortium of twenty nongovernmental European organizations intended to mount a large emergency operation inside Cambodia. On his return from Phnom Penh, Walker held a press conference in which he confirmed the visions of apocalypse. He spoke of Cambodia as peopled by "emaciated Belsen-type

* In part this was because the authorities never allowed the Joint Mission to have its radio link to the outside world. To reach the target of importing 1,000 tons of food a day, very careful coordination of air and sea transport would be needed. In order to persuade the authorities to allow the radio, Bugnion proposed that an identical receiver be given to the government so that it could monitor all Joint Mission communications, that a government official be present day and night in the radio room, that that room be in the Foreign Ministry or wherever else the government wished, and that the Joint Mission prepare and give the government transcripts of all transmissions. Even so, the government never agreed. Instead, all messages had to be sent in and out of the country by pouch on the daily relief flight, a far longer and more cumbersome procedure, which made effective coordination almost impossible. Partly as a result, the 1,000-tons-a-day target was never reached, and many specific programs that required a continuous exchange of information between headquarters and the field—such as the provision of specialized equipment for certain hospitals or of scientific books for the faculty of medicine—had to be either abandoned or postponed for many months.

walking skeletons." He also said that, as far as he was concerned, the Pol Pot regime "exceeds in immorality the wickedness of that of the Nazi regime against the Jews in Germany." He quoted Hun Sen as saying that they would not accept aid from anyone helping the border and announced that he was hoping to raise £25 million from a consortium of voluntary agencies and would ship at least 60,000 tons of food to Cambodia in the next five months. (Oxfam's own annual budget is about £15 million.) As a first step, the consortium agreed to dispatch $12 million worth of food, seed and drugs to Cambodia by the end of the year. Oxfam headquarters began what it called a "home-front campaign" to raise funds in Britain—"Oxfam is now engaged in the largest single operation in its history. Fasting is to be used as major means of reaching fund-raising target of one million pounds sterling in U.K."

In fact, however, much had changed since Walker signed his agreement with Phnom Penh only two weeks previously. Then he had expected Oxfam to supplant the international goliaths of the ICRC and UNICEF. Now the Joint Mission's program was under way. In Phnom Penh Guy Stringer realized this and seemed to UNICEF and ICRC officials to be rather embarrassed by the unilateral role that Oxfam had played in early October. Knowing that François Bugnion of the ICRC was enraged by Brian Walker's actions, Stringer strode into his room at the Samaki declaring, "Guy Stringer of Oxfam. I've come to apologize for any misunderstandings between us." Bugnion accepted the apology; subsequently Oxfam presented to the Joint Mission a Land Rover, by way of a peace offering.

On October 20 Stringer asked Foreign Minister Hun Sen what was happening. Hun Sen made it clear to him, amid rhetorical assertions of independence, that UNICEF-ICRC food was indeed to be accepted, even though they had refused to stop working along the Thai border. "We need and are grateful for food from them," he said, "but although we are accepting it, there are still many misunderstandings between us and them. We will continue to accept their aid, but will also maintain our independence and integrity." Echoing Cambodians' historic fears of being carved up between Siam and Vietnam, Hun Sen said, "We will do our best to cooperate but would rather die than accept help that aims to divide our country into two parts."

It was obvious to Stringer that the categorical position conveyed to Brian Walker had been quietly forgotten by officials in Phnom Penh. When he asked whether Oxfam could and should now collaborate with ICRC/UNICEF, Hun Sen replied "By all means cooperate in planning with them, but your aid should come direct from you."

In these circumstances Stringer thought that the consortium should move away from relief and concentrate instead on the more traditional Oxfam role—development. He thought it would be absurd for Oxfam to try to duplicate the Joint Mission's feeding program. He suggested that they should still bring in more trucks—50 at once—since transport was such an obvious priority; emphasize agricultural production, particularly seeds and irrigation; set up supplementary feeding programs for orphans, pregnant women and others at special risk; undertake a major immunization program with a cold-storage system; restart specific industrial concerns like the Rusey Keo textile factory and the fishing-net factory, and help restore the Phnom Penh water supply and improve the port facilities. The Foreign Minister agreed.

Stringer cabled his proposals home to Oxford, where some officials, including Walker, were reluctant to abandon their original plans for massive food shipments. Stringer had to send increasingly impatient telegrams—"You do not seem to have understood the radically changed situation here since Walker left. Consortium plans must take note that staple food and medical covered by UNICEF/ICRC." Eventually, Oxford accepted that it was so, but from now on there were considerable divisions of opinion in the Oxfam hierarchy about the wisdom with which Oxfam had become committed in Cambodia.

Walker's critics in ICRC and UNICEF argued that he refused to cooperate with the Joint Mission at a moment of crisis and instead involved Oxfam in an attempt by one side of a civil war to prevent relief agencies from helping the people on the other side. It had not happened in Biafra or Bangladesh, why should it happen here? Jean Pierre Hocke, ICRC's Director of Operations, said later that he thought Walker's unilateral agreement with the Heng Samrin authorities was a "catastrophic breach of a vital principle"; he also said it undercut the Joint Mission's bargaining power, it further delayed an agreement with Phnom Penh, and it meant that the eventual agreement was less effective in making sure that aid reached the people who needed it. Such was the ICRC view.*

On the other hand, in early October 1979, Oxfam was under growing, though not always well-informed, public pressure in Britain to act at once in Cambodia—unilaterally if necessary. Moreover, Walker was put under extraordinary pressure by the Vietnamese and the Heng Samrin regime. They placed him in a difficult situation. The country's needs appeared vast and he was told that UNICEF and ICRC would have to leave and that Oxfam and its consortium might be the only lifeline into the country. He said later that Jacques Beaumont of UNICEF had himself "pleaded" with him not to jeopardize Oxfam's own position if Oxfam "were left as the only thin thread between Cambodia and the outside world." Walker pointed out that he agreed only not to give aid to "the Pol Pot forces"—and there was nothing to prevent Oxfam from helping other Cambodians along the border. In the event, Oxfam did give money to UNHCR for Cambodians inside Thailand. But it never operated on the border.

Walker said also that he accepted the government's conditions because "I think all agencies that are guests in any country must accept what is laid down by the government of that country or get out. You can't have it both ways." By contrast, UNICEF and ICRC officials point out that the doctrine of impartiality demanded that the Joint Mission must try to "have it both ways" and that their attempts

* On October 21, 1979, François Bugnion cabled ICRC headquarters on the whole saga of relations with Oxfam. He said, "Relations excellent up to departure James Howard, who proposed common relief agency position and continued close contact with Joint Mission. Relations deteriorated during Walker's visit, apparently for following reasons: (A) Oxfam's desire for totally independent action as leader of all non-governmental organizations. (B) Choice of interlocutors and very little pressure on government. Walker's attitude would have led government to consider Oxfam as valid alternative to Joint Mission. (C) Attitude based on assumption that Joint Mission would be defeated because it was imposing requirements which were too great for the government and because of the frontier operations. Consequently Walker sought to dissociate Oxfam from Joint Mission. Relations have improved since October 12. We are keeping contacts and exchanging useful information with Oxfam representatives Phnom Penh, who are now seeking to define new objectives which would be complementary to Joint Mission and not a substitute for it."

were ultimately successful: they called the bluff of the Phnom Penh authorities and were able to work both in Phnom Penh and along the border.

When Stringer left Phnom Penh, he hitched a lift on a rickety old DC-3 that had flown in supplies purchased by the unlikely figure of Stan Mooneyham, the president of the fiercely anti-Communist American-based evangelist group, World Vision. The agency had been active in medical care and supplementary feeding of refugee children during the Lon Nol period. Now, by chance, one of its former wartime employees was a senior official in the Foreign Ministry; he had arranged visas for the group. Just before the Khmer Rouge had captured Phnom Penh in 1975, World Vision had completed a one-million-dollar children's hospital. Since then the hospital had been destroyed, and now Mooneyham wanted to rebuild it as part of a large World Vision relief operation in Cambodia. As with Oxfam, the Phnom Penh authorities tried to insist that World Vision could not operate on the border if it was in Phnom Penh. Mooneyham categorically rejected this, declaring, "There is no way politics can stop us helping people anywhere. I won't violate your borders, but I *will* help your people in Thailand." He had his way; World Vision was able to operate both inside Cambodia and along the border.

The old DC-3 reminded Stringer of the days when he had flown across "the hump" from Burma to China. It was piloted "by a slightly dotty Englishman who had been in the Korean war at the same time as me." As it lumbered down the runway the daily Royal Air Force Hercules, with its Red Cross patches on its emblems, was unloading drums of edible oil and a truck. "Just beyond," wrote Stringer, "was the most enormous Russian jet surrounded by Vietnamese soldiers with every sort of small arm and radio communication, while from its belly emerged large box after large box. The Soviet ambassador himself was in attendance—what a commentary on the society in which we dwell."

10 ❦ Sa Kaeo

Now, in October 1979, the border erupted to produce for the rest of the world a vision of misery and despair worse even than that inside Cambodia.

Pushed by a renewed Vietnamese offensive in Western Cambodia, propelled by a desperate search for food or anxious to seek new lives elsewhere, thousands, tens of thousands, and then, indeed, hundreds of thousands of desperate Cambodians staggered toward the Thai frontier in search of some salvation.

Through the first half of October there was still no institutionalized feeding program along the border. The U.S. Embassy had provided the American voluntary agency Catholic Relief Services (which had often had close links with the U.S. government in Indochina) with a grant to purchase food, and the World Food Program had delivered considerable quantities of supplies. But, because of the pressure they were under in Phnom Penh—directly from the government, indirectly from Oxfam's conduct—UNICEF and ICRC were still delaying involvement in a full-scale and formal border operation. They would not be able to do so much longer.

An important point about this disaster is that it was easily accessible. As Bernard Melunsky, the Reuters man in Bangkok, wrote, "Catastrophe is a few hours' drive in an air-conditioned car from Bangkok to the Thai-Kampuchean border." After the collapse of the American-backed Indochinese regimes in April 1975, many correspondents had moved to Bangkok. Thailand, which has excellent communications, an easy life style for foreigners and the freest press between Hong Kong and Calcutta, became the logical place from which to cover Indochina and much of Southeast Asia. Now the resident press corps was being daily supplemented by scores of reporters and camera crews from around the Western world. Their ease of access first to Thailand and then to the refugees themselves was unusual in a disaster of this sort. It was one of the reasons why it became such a widespread matter of concern. Covering famines in the Sahel, for example, is much more difficult and for many people, it should be said, less attractive than taking short trips out of Bangkok.

The most terrible sights were to be seen south of Aranyaprathet, the Khmer Rouge-held areas where the UNICEF-ICRC survey mission had been appalled in mid-September. It was there that most journalists went and from there that, at this stage, most stories came. Daily, awful spindly creatures, with no flesh and with wide vacant eyes stumbled out of the forests and the mountains into which the Khmer Rouge had corralled them. They had malaria, they had tuberculosis, they had dysentery, they were dehydrated, they were famished, they were dying.

In many cases, they were so badly starved that their bodies were consuming themselves. Many were so weak they could hardly move; the lassitude of death had taken over. They just collapsed on the ground, exhausted, waiting without a sound, their silence a terrible reproach.

For most of the foreigners who went there, whether relief workers, diplomats or journalists, the spectacle was the most horrible they had ever seen. Roland Pierre Paringaux of *Le Monde,* Claas Bratt, a Swedish cameraman working for UPITN, and Steve Heder, an American scholar, arrived at a place called Ban Laem on the border, where no relief supplies had yet been delivered. There were about one thousand people there "in horrific conditions." They spent hours carrying water to dying children: "there was nothing else to do," said Paringaux later. Bratt reported to UNHCR, "In an atmosphere of eerie silence the only sounds heard were groans and moans of people in pain, cries and whimpers of children and continuous coughs. . . . The flat field of some 3,000 meters in area was nearly motionless, with only a few individuals walking slowly with greatest effort. . . . He saw hollow-eyed children whose skin and flesh were stretched over their tiny ribs. A few were rolling on the ground quietly moaning in pain, others lay motionless, curled up in fetus position. . . .''

A ten-year-old girl was lying alone on the ground, doubled up with pain, occasionally shifting and letting out agonized groans. No one was taking any notice of her. A Thai marine officer pointed out her mother a few meters away. She was "also shifting and turning on the bare ground. The officer told the film crew that both were suffering from stomach disease. He said there were many severe cases of malaria and that no medical aid was available. The officer asked Mr. Bratt to contact the Red Cross and international organizations to send immediate help."

These were some of the people to whom UNICEF and ICRC had delayed sending help, because they were so concerned lest it would jeopardize securing an agreement to start their program in Phnom Penh. Others were found at a place called Klong Wah by Robert Ashe of the Christian Outreach agency. On October 12 he asked ICRC and UNICEF to send supplies; there was more delay.

Bratt's film was shown throughout Europe. It was one of many such sights. Similarly, Marsh Clark wrote in a *Time* Magazine cover story, "Never have I seen people in such despair and deprivation. Not in India, Vietnam, the Middle East or Northern Ireland. Not even in Bangladesh."

Time's story, entitled "Deathwatch in Cambodia," was reported entirely from the border. The only photograph from inside the country was of skulls from a mass grave. The report began, "It is a country soaked in blood, devastated by war, and its people are starving to death. . . . Relief agencies believe that as many as 2.25 million Cambodians could die of starvation in the next few months unless a vast amount is provided soon."*

* *Time*'s eight-page story included a dramatic summary of what happens to a starving body. "There is nothing ennobling about death by starvation. . . . Soon after food is cut off, the body switches to burning fuel reserves in the liver and fatty tissues. After fat is exhausted, the body accelerates the breakdown of protein in the muscles, including the heart, which saps strength. At the same time, the body attempts to husband its resources by cutting energy requirements to the minimum. Pulse rate and blood pressure fall and body temperature drops. Men become impotent; women stop menstruating and nursing mothers fail to produce milk; children stop growing. . . . Death comes in many ways. The intestinal walls become damaged; severe and constant diarrhea may develop. . . ."

Scores of other newspaper and television reports expressed similar fears. A form of terror, similar to that which had arisen during the crises of Biafra and Bangladesh, gripped people across the world. We took these Cambodians as typical of the whole nation. The Vietnamese had earlier said that 2.25 million people were threatened by famine and the reports of those few foreigners who had been allowed into Phnom Penh seemed to confirm that. Now, in muddy clearings and in corpses, in fields and on river banks on the rim of Thailand lay the barely living witness of the horror that lay within. The whole country, it appeared, must be a charnel house, where the barely living picked their way gingerly through hundreds of thousands of dead.

On October 17, 1979, the Thai Prime Minister, General Kriangsak Chamanand, visited the border area with the military, who estimated that there were now 155,000 Cambodians there. He too was visibly shocked by the suffering—one boy died horribly in front of him.

At the same time, his military emphasized that the Vietnamese offensive might push the fighting over the border, and they warned, as had recent articles in the Bangkok press, that although the Khmer Rouge could survive military attack they might not survive starvation. If they collapsed, the Vietnamese would face no effective military opposition inside Cambodia at all and Thailand's hopes of forcing Hanoi to reconsider its assertion that the situation in Cambodia was "irreversible" would be accordingly diminished. In order that the Khmer Rouge be allowed to restore themselves as a fighting force, the military recommended that they be allowed sanctuary in Thailand. It later became known that the Khmer Rouge leadership were divided on the wisdom of this course from their own point of view. They feared losing control of the people they had seized once they were inside Thailand. But the threat of imminent defeat by starvation was worse.

Kriangsak returned from the border on October 18 to dine in Bangkok with the Swedish, Danish and Canadian ambassadors. He said that his visit had changed his views "one hundred percent." From now on any Cambodian or Lao refugee would be allowed in without the precondition of a resettlement place. Thailand would not repatriate anyone.

The Danish ambassador thanked him and said that the new policy would improve Thailand's image abroad and make it easier to obtain financial support for the relief operation. The ambassador immediately recommended to his government that it make funds available specifically for relief work in Thailand.

Next day Kriangsak summoned ambassadors and international organizations to another meeting to announce his new policy. From now on, Thailand would have an "open door" and no Cambodians would be turned away. Refugees arriving at the border would be moved "within two days"—into holding centers that the government intended to construct with UNHCR finance and assistance.

Later that same day, October 19, Kurt Waldheim finally launched a public international appeal for Cambodia. At a press conference which he held in New York with Henry Labouisse of UNICEF, the U.N. Secretary General declared:

> The world community is witnessing a national tragedy, the proportion of which may have no parallel in history. I am referring, of course, to the fate of the population of Kampuchea. This is a country which, according to most counts, has lost up to one half of its entire population. The Kampuchean people are suffering misery and deprivation on massive scale. They face shortages of food, medical supplies, shelter and transport. There is appalling malnutrition, particularly among children, of whom up to 90 percent are severely malnourished.

Waldheim explained that the appeal had not been launched before because he had wanted to be certain that it would be possible to mount a major relief program "on acceptable terms." Asked by the press what these might be, Waldheim replied, "We have to organize this relief operation in such a way that the food, medicine and other relief reach . . . the people concerned, the suffering population of the country. In this regard we must make sure that we have the possibilities to get this done."

"So you want to make certain that warring factions do not get the relief supplies?" he was asked. "Obviously if I speak of the 'suffering population,' I mean the civilian population," Waldheim replied.

Waldheim made no mention at all of the border operation in his statement, and when Labouisse was asked about contacts with "the Pol Pot people" he ignored the still-secret meetings in Bangkok, especially those with Ieng Sary, and he replied merely that UNICEF had "had talks with some officials of the government of Democratic Kampuchea here in New York, including its Permanent Representative."

At this, Kurt Waldheim interrupted to say, "I should like just to clarify one aspect of this question. These are purely humanitarian contacts, practical contacts based on purely humanitarian considerations; they have no political implications."

In Bangkok, Kriangsak's new "open-door policy" threw the United Nations High Commissioner for Refugees (UNHCR) into crisis. Although some such move had been anticipated—the Supreme Command had given hints of it to the American Embassy as early as August, and the Embassy had passed these along to UNHCR and the ICRC—almost no preparation had been made. Only the day before, the ICRC, UNHCR and the voluntary agencies had met for the first time to see how their resources could be coordinated. UNHCR's staff was already fully extended on processing the resettlement of refugees already in Thailand.

Throughout the summer, the Thai government had excluded the organization from the developing border crisis (despite its complacency over the forced repatriation of the 45,000 refugees at Preah Vihear in June) because of UNHCR's theoretical duty to protect refugees from just such forcible repatriation. Some middle-level officials in UNHCR's Bangkok office had begun to feel that the only way in which they could get involved in the developing refugee crisis was by giving money directly to the Thai government without conditions. In the middle of September UNHCR had offered to fund a three-million-dollar program to establish "holding centers" for the "illegal immigrants soon to arrive from Kampuchea." In response Thai officials asked UNHCR to confirm that any help would be "unconditional," since the government might eventually want to "let them [the Cambodians] go back." UNHCR agreed and handed over a first installment of $500,000.

Soon after, Michel Moussalli, UNHCR's Director of Protection, came from Geneva to Bangkok. His report betrayed a tension between his general function and his particular mission. "It was clearly understood that I should take particular care during my discussions with the Thai authorities not to irritate them by pressing too hard on the various protection problems prevailing in Thailand."

Moussalli reported that he was "astonished to see the recovery of the ICRC" despite its condemnation of Thailand's forced repatriation at Preah Vihear. He had not expected that it would now be "playing a leading role." This meant, he considered, that, "in spite of UNHCR's restraint before and after the forced repatriation of the 40,000," other agencies now had much larger parts in the crisis than the High Commissioner.

Air Vice-Marshal Siddhi told Moussalli that the Thai government did not want to deal with several agencies and that the World Food Program and the ICRC were already involved with "the illegal immigrants from Kampuchea." Moussalli offered more money to secure UNHCR's participation.

There were some within UNHCR who believed that this was imprudent because it meant that if the Thais later decided to repatriate forcibly those "illegal immigrants," UNHCR would hardly be able to protest, despite its mandate. But those who made the decisions argued, philosophically, that in an imperfect world compromises have to be made, that money is often the best means of access and that the important thing was to get UNHCR involved at all. The defense of its principles could come later.

Siddhi accepted Moussalli's offer. Moussalli reported back to the High Commissioner in Geneva that he had regained some of the "initiative" from other agencies. "Furthermore, WFP [World Food Program] on whose performance both the Thai and the U.S. Embassy seem to rely highly, may not be able to cope alone with the complex and considerable logistical problems. UNHCR should therefore be ready to play its role when requested." It was not.

On Monday, October 22 Colonel Sanan Kachornkram, one of the Supreme Command officers most closely involved in the border crisis, called UNHCR in Bangkok to announce that the military would be handing over 90,000 "illegal immigrants" to UNHCR, starting in forty-eight hours.

This was the first such direct operational authority that the Thai government had ever given UNHCR. Until now, everything had been handled by the Ministry of the Interior, with UNHCR merely paying the bills. This was not unusual; UNHCR is not normally an operational agency; instead, it funds other bodies to implement agreed programs. So, Colonel Sanan's telephone call came as a shock; such is the explanation that UNHCR staff tend to give of their unpreparedness in October 1979.

On the same day, one of UNHCR's few recent recruits, Mark Malloch Brown—an English journalist who had been David Taylor's eventual replacement as field officer for the Aranyaprathet area—was taken by Thai officers to an empty bog of a field near a small town called Sa Kaeo, about forty miles from the Cambodian border. He was told he had to build a camp; 60,000 "illegal immigrants" would be arriving en masse, between Wednesday, the twenty-fourth, and Saturday, October 27. He did a fine job.

Brown, together with his Thai assistant, Kasidis Rochanakorn, and another UNHCR field officer, Ted Schweitzer, obtained a bulldozer and started carving roads in the mud. They contracted for a warehouse to be built. They rented a back hoe to dig latrines. They looked for water. There was none on the site; some was found six kilometers away. Brown hired eight trucks to transport it. ICRC hired another ten.

An American evangelist group, Christian and Missionary Alliance (CAMA) agreed to buy water tanks. ICRC bought more. Brown hired a company to purify water. Christian Aid and Missionary Alliance ordered some 100,000 pieces of bamboo and thatch to build a clinic and some huts. UNHCR paid Catholic Relief Services for delivery of plastic rope, straw mats and baby bottles. The World Food Program agreed to start delivering food for up to 90,000 people; UNHCR paid them $500,000. Brown hired 200 local Thais at $2 a day for construction work. Many other people, Thais and foreigners, came from Bangkok to volunteer their services.

Eight thousand Cambodians were sent by bus and truck into Sa

Kaeo on the first day, October 24. They all came from the Khmer Rouge areas south of Aranyaprathet; some of them were Khmer Rouge soldiers and their families, some were civilians unwillingly caught in the Khmer Rouge embrace. Their condition was dreadful, and their arrival was a shambles. It was raining heavily most of the day, and bulldozers were still trying to flatten the slush.

The next day the military moved about 7,000 more people, both soldiers and civilians, from the border. A medical crisis developed. The Thais had allowed very few medical teams to the border sites from which these people were being brought. Many of the worst cases were abandoned to die on the border. Others died on the trip to Sa Kaeo; their bodies had to be hauled out when the buses and trucks arrived. Now there were mass graves in Thailand as well as in Cambodia.

At the beginning there were only three doctors and nurses in all Sa Kaeo. The Thais had given the ICRC responsibility for coordinating all medical relief; ICRC had failed to arrange adequate medical teams or facilities. The one tent that served as a clinic collapsed in the monsoon downpour. Patients in the "hospital" were lying on straw mats in the deep mud; some, too weak to move their heads, were drowned. French doctors from the group Médecins sans Frontières were there; but they did not always have enough equipment. The Le Monde correspondent, Roland Pierre Paringaux, recalls that they had to sew up one woman's bowels with the needle and thread from a journalist's travel kit. She survived. Teams from the Thailand Baptist Mission and the large American agency International Rescue Committee were there promptly, but the Thai Red Cross was late. The nearby Thai District Hospital was efficient. Its resources were very poor, but it made them all available with no complaint and saved a few of the worst cases.

Thirty people were dying every day at Sa Kaeo, yet ICRC rejected offers of help from doctors and nurses around the world, including Thailand itself. It was only on October 25 that Geneva appealed to national Red Cross societies for volunteers, and even then only fifty-three nurses were requested.

ICRC was unable to lay on proper blood supplies at Sa Kaeo; at the height of the crisis, only 30 pints were available. Lionel Rosenblatt, a senior refugee official of the U.S. Embassy, advised ICRC to build a 2,000-bed hospital. He was told that 500 beds were enough. In the end 3,000 beds were needed. At one point, Martin Barber of UNHCR wrote to the ICRC delegation, saying "I would be most grateful if you could let me have a written indication of your contingency planning to meet the needs."

Nor was UNHCR very efficient. The Bangkok regional office sent no one to help Mark Brown. There was no one to send; the staff there, both Thais and foreigners, were working astonishingly long hours. Requests to Geneva for permission to take on extra staff had not yet been granted. It was not until December that UNHCR provided Sa Kaeo with an engineer. Without a man on loan from the American Embassy, Brown would have had no one. This American engineer, Rod MacDonald, was, said Brown later, "our salvation." He and two other engineers seconded from the Embassy put together a team of young Peace Corps engineers whom UNHCR then contracted directly.

For weeks conditions at Sa Kaeo remained execrable. Drainage was almost impossible. Latrines, mere trenches, were hard to build, harder still to keep clean; they flooded during every rainstorm. A month after Sa Kaeo opened, one relief official there reported in a letter to Martin Barber: "I have not seen, in many years of . . . camp experience, a situation as humanly degrading as exists in Sa Kaeo. There isn't the remotest vestige of privacy as men, women and children defecate in full view of and within feet of the camp living areas. . . . UNHCR cannot continue to be associated with situations like this and continue to command respect."

In the face of such problems the American Ambassador in Bangkok Morton Abramowitz and his staff became increasingly angry and began to play an ever larger and more controversial part in the crisis.

Abramowitz is an unusual diplomat. Like his friend Richard Holbrooke, who was then the Assistant Secretary of State for East Asia and the Pacific, he spurns elegant diplomatic dress and formal diplomatic manners. He is far more accessible than most ambassadors both to journalists and to his own staff, even junior staff. He is remarkably candid, he has extraordinary energy, is perpetually restless and rarely suffers foolishness, inefficiency or contrariness gladly. Once, when a journalist asked him what questions might be interesting to put to the Thai Prime Minister General Kriangsak, Abramowitz shouted, "Give him hell for not doing enough for the border."

Abramowitz, forty-six in 1979, had served in the Foreign Service since 1960. He had been stationed in Taiwan and Hong Kong, and he had had several assignments with the Pentagon. In the four years before coming to Thailand in 1978, he was on loan to the Pentagon's Office of International Security Affairs.

This Pentagon connection led some people on the left to see Abramowitz as a hard-line hawk. But, within the government, conservatives tended to view him as a dangerous liberal; they noted, for example, his friendship with Holbrooke, the principal architect of the 1977–78 plans to restore United States diplomatic relations with Vietnam, and concluded that Abramowitz too was "soft on Hanoi." Richard Moose, a fierce critic of America's Indochina involvement on Senator Fulbright's staff and, later, President Carter's Assistant Secretary of State for Africa, says of Abramowitz. "His problem is that he is so intellectually honest and so straightforward that he offends everybody at some time or other."

In fact, throughout the 1979–80 Cambodia emergency, Abramowitz was neither neatly "hard-line" nor "liberal." He strongly supported the relief program to Phnom Penh, and prodded others in the Carter administration, particularly those around Zbigniew Brzezinski who were less concerned with Indochina problems and were interested principally in forging a closer link with China at Hanoi's expense. At the same time Abramowitz was always trying to build up the operation on the border and was fiercely critical of the Vietnamese, arguing both that they had no right to be in Cambodia and should withdraw, and that since they were in control they must be held responsible for many of the country's present travails. He associated United States political aims with those of ASEAN.

At the end of 1979 Abramowitz and his wife, Sheppie, genuinely feared, like many other people, that the extinction of the Cambodian people was at hand. They immersed themselves totally in the crisis. Abramowitz, a Jew, was conscious of how little the world outside had done to save his own people trapped in Nazi Europe; he was determined to do his own best to prevent any new holocaust. Unlike many other U.S. officials, he believed that Americans had considerable responsibility for what had happened to Cambodia. He had been predicting famine in Cambodia since April and, until recently, had been largely ignored by the State Department. In June he had arranged a grant of $300,000 for Catholic Relief Services to start trucking food to the border. Now he was constantly arguing with his own government for increased resettlement of refugees and was trying to bully both Thai and international officials into doing more and more. To that end he set up a special new section in the Embassy.

With a staff of over four hundred, the Bangkok embassy is one of the largest U.S. missions in Asia. Since the American defeat in Indochina, it has also been one of the most important. It contains a large contingent of Defense Attachés as liaison with the Thai military, many of whose officers have been trained at one time or another in the United States. Much of its third floor is given over to the CIA. At this time the CIA station chief was a man named Dan Arnold, who was close to Prime Minister Kriangsak and apparently felt that Abramowitz was not close enough. (In 1980 Arnold resigned from the CIA and joined the campaign staff of George Bush. After President Reagan's inauguration in 1981, Arnold was one of those right-wingers within the administration who attempted, with considerable success, to deny Abramowitz any further appointment with the State Department. They accused him of having tried to withdraw U.S. troops from Korea during the Carter administration and of dovishness on Vietnam. They helped destroy his nomination as ambassador to Djakarta, and for over a year after he left Bangkok in 1981, Abramowitz was given no job whatsoever. Eventually George Shultz managed to overcome right-wing objections and in 1983 Abramowitz was placed in charge of the Mutual Balanced Force Reduction talks in Vienna.)

In 1979 the Bangkok embassy contained a number of "old Indochina hands" in its various sections, though Abramowitz's deputy, Burt Levin, rejoiced in the fact that he had never been posted to the area. The CIA station held at least one man who had been inside Cambodia until after the collapse of the Lon Nol regime in 1975 and was now working along the border.

One of the senior political officers was Timothy Carney, who had served in both Vietnam and Cambodia. A fluent Khmer speaker, he had been in Phnom Penh until the Khmer Rouge victory. In 1977, while on sabbatical at Cornell University, he had produced one of the first and most authoritative studies of the origins of the Khmer Rouge. In 1982 he was to win the coveted State Department Inspector General's Prize as the best reporter in the Department, for his work on Cambodia during the emergency. Perhaps even more remarkable is that he is also recognized outside the U.S. government as one of the most careful and honest scholars of recent Cambodian history.

One of the embassy's senior refugee officers was Lionel Rosenblatt, who had served as a district officer in Vietnam in the sixties. During the fall of Saigon he was stationed in Washington but had taken special leave in order to fly, on his own initiative, back to South Vietnam to evacuate many "high-risk" Vietnamese who had worked for the U.S. government and who, he feared, would be left behind by the government's ponderous evacuation program. Since then he had had a passionate commitment to the cause of Indochinese refugees. Like Abramowitz, he felt and said that the United States had a responsibility for what had befallen Cambodia. He thought that that responsibility should be discharged in active, if not aggressive participation in the relief program.

Although the State Department, the CIA and the Defense Intelligence Agency were all active along the border in the fall of 1979, Abramowitz decided that the scale of the Cambodian crisis was such that a special unit was needed within the embassy. He set up the Kampuchea Emergency Group, known as KEG. It had a branch in Aranyaprathet, known as "Taphouse." KEG contained both refugee and aid personnel; it was led by Lionel Rosenblatt and was also to include Colonel Michael Eiland, a former Special Forces Officer in Vietnam. In the late sixties Eiland had taken part in the secret, illegal intelligence-gathering missions into Cambodia from Vietnam. More recently he had served for three years in the State Department's East Asia Bureau, where he had been involved in the unsuccessful talks proposing the normalizing of relations with Vietnam. Inevitably, his Special Forces work made some journalists and relief officials suspicious of his new task on Cambodia's western flank. Others found him a diligent and effective official concerned above all with the efficacy of the relief operation. Eiland himself later said that his work and his views during the 1979–80 Cambodia crisis were dominated not by memories of Vietnam but by his first posting in the U.S. Army— to a base near Dachau. In 1983 he returned to the Pentagon to work in the Defense Intelligence Agency.

KEG's principal task was to monitor the border and to watch, from a distance, the relief operation in Phnom Penh itself. Along the border, it was intended by Abramowitz to identify needs and problems and then to cajole the humanitarian organizations, both international and private, into meeting them. Its staff were constantly in the border camps and in the holding centers interviewing refugees on their present state and on conditions inside Cambodia. Like other sections of the U.S. Embassy, KEG had far better communications than the relief agencies. It was constantly providing them with reports and demanding action. Abramowitz in turn bombarded the State Department and the Geneva Mission with complaints about the chaos that the International Committee of the Red Cross and UNHCR had allowed to develop.

In one such cable, the Embassy declared: "ICRC's record on contingency planning at Sa Kaeo leaves much to be desired. . . . We therefore see strong need for United States contingency planning that would enable us to deploy from Clark (Air Force Base, in the Philippines) to here within 12 hours 10 doctors and 30 medics/ nurses . . ." This offer was refused by ICRC, which was anxious to protect its neutrality.

Abramowitz acknowledged in another cable that it was not only the fault of the organizations. "Everyone shares a bit of the blame." The crisis had developed very quickly, changed constantly, and in many places refugees had been difficult to reach. Moreover, "The Thais have contributed a generous share of the difficulties. Their indifference, preoccupation with the Vietnamese threat, callousness, and lack of attention to planning and detail create enormous problems for us all. No crisis can occur on Saturday or Sunday in Thailand, because no one is around to deal with it."

In conclusion, Abramowitz thought that more rapid response

and better planning was essential. It was the task of the international organizations rather than the embassy, and his staff was exhausted. "But if they cannot do it, and I am in serious doubt, we will have to do more and more under their fig leaf."*

Abramowitz was much harder on the international organizations than many of his colleagues. United States officials at the mission to the U.N. or in Geneva, for example, tended to be more tolerant of their problems. As for the organizations themselves, some officials recognized that the performance of their agencies often merited serious criticism. But others deeply resented what they saw as both unwarranted interference and political pressure from the most powerful donor of them all. Many believed that Abramowitz was exploiting the humanitarian crisis for the purposes of America's anti-Vietnamese policy. They also argued that the prominent role of the embassy on the border was bound to increase the suspicions of the Vietnamese and Heng Samrin governments that the entire operation was being controlled by the United States.

More credulous people decided that the crisis at the border had been invented by the United States with the sole aim of rescuing the Khmer Rouge. The point needs to be repeated that although the Khmer Rouge and other resistance groups did indeed benefit from the operation, border relief was essential in saving hundreds of thousands of people. Lionel Rosenblatt, of KEG, acknowledged on one occasion that KEG had three purposes: to increase food deliveries and improve medical care along the border; to explore the ways in which Cambodian resistance to the Vietnamese could be helped; and to lobby for resettlement of Cambodian refugees in the United

---

* In this cable, Abramowitz also complained that "we have tried, sometimes successfully, sometimes not, both with the international agencies and Thais, to push, cajole and plead for the necessary things to be done. I am increasingly unimpressed with the ability of the international organizations to handle crisis problems, to plan adequately and to move rapidly. If a crisis can develop over six months, they can probably respond well, but in a matter of days the record so far is uninspiring. Even ICRC, which I have had the most respect for, has been slow in meeting Khmer problems and clearly remiss in anticipating needs at Sa Kaeo holding center. UNHCR has played its usual belated-catch-up role."

States. As so often in such emergencies, the humanitarian and political aspects of the crisis were almost impossible to disentangle.*

On October 24, several prominent American church and relief-agency officials led by the Reverend Theodore Hesburgh, President of Notre Dame University, and Terence Cardinal Cooke of New York, assembled in Washington to appeal for substantial American help to Cambodia. In a prepared statement, they said they were about to deliver a letter to the President asking that Carter pledge additional resources through the U.S. Food for Peace Program; order United States government agencies to give Cambodia the highest possible priority; demand prompt action on aid bills not yet passed by Congress; call on the Pope, Chairman Hua and Secretary Brezhnev to exert their influence on behalf of the Cambodians; promise to respond positively to Kurt Waldheim's appeal for Cambodia; and issue a public appeal for Americans to give generously.

Their letter concluded with an appeal to remember the Holocaust—"Many of us stood by then, excused ourselves later on the ground that we did not know the extent of what was going on, and vowed that we would never again concur passively in the attempt to destroy a nation. But what has taken place in Cambodia is a mass assault on the basic human right to life. We cannot say that we do not know this, and we cannot permit political, financial or technical difficulties to bring about another holocaust."

Simultaneously, Senator Edward M. Kennedy, as yet Carter's undeclared challenger for the 1980 Democratic nomination for the Presidency, charged that the United States government had done nothing since Secretary of State Cyrus Vance had acknowledged the

---

* In a background briefing for journalists in Bangkok early in 1980, Michael Armacost, Deputy Assistant Secretary of Defense for East Asian Affairs, said, "The U.S. shares common interests with China on Indochina. That is to dilute the Soviet influence in Indochina and get the Vietnamese out of Cambodia. China's objective is to ensure maximum Khmer resistance, not necessarily only through the Khmer Rouge. They are looking for a lifespan of three to five years. It is in U.S. interests to see a neutral and independent Cambodia." But he added that the United States understood that "any political settlement would have to take into account Vietnamese interests. That is, that a government in Cambodia should not be hostile to Vietnam."

crisis in July. "Three months have passed with no action by the government. Incredibly, the only movement was the heroic effort of the Red Cross and UNICEF to do the job alone." Kennedy urged "an immediate, massive airlift of food and medicine" and advocated the use of U.S. Air Force planes from the Philippines.

President Carter, apparently aware that Cambodia was by now an issue of enormous public concern, responded at once. When Father Hesburgh's group presented him with their appeal he said, "This is the fastest answer you ever got to a letter," and ushered them straight into the White House press room. Carter held an immediate press conference, with Hesburgh and Cooke standing beside him—a striking picture for the camera crews and photographers. Flanked by Protestant and Catholic leaders, the President too called upon the past suffering of the Jews to dramatize the present.

"Thirty-seven years ago, a holocaust began which was to take the lives of more than six million human beings. The world stood by silently in a moral lapse whose enormity still numbs the human mind. We now face once again the threat of avoidable death and avoidable suffering for literally millions of people, and this time we must act swiftly to save the men, women and children who are our brothers and sisters in God's family." Carter announced that he was increasing the United States government's pledge to Cambodian relief from $7 million to $70 million in order to help avert "a tragedy of genocidal proportions."

Of this, $30 million was in direct response to Waldheim's appeal made five days before. Nine million dollars were for refugees in Thailand, and $30 million had actually already been approved that day by the House Foreign Affairs Committee. In a sense, therefore, Carter's new pledge was for rather less than the $70 million he claimed. Nonetheless, his warning of a tragedy "of genocidal proportions" made the lead story in papers and broadcasts all around the nation. When Carter came to write his memoirs in 1982 he made absolutely no mention whatsoever of the Cambodian relief operation or of his dramatic evocation of the Holocaust.

By the end of October, the international organizations in Thailand had begun to respond to criticisms from the U.S. Embassy in Bangkok and others. ICRC replaced a medical coordinator in Thailand, and Jean Pierre Hocke agreed with donors in New York that ICRC had been slow to respond. Now, he said, twenty doctors and eighty nurses were en route to Thailand. In Geneva UNHCR decided to send out to Bangkok a high-level team led by Zia Rizvi.

Rizvi, a Pakistani, has neither the appearance nor the manner of a bureaucrat. An intelligent, self-confident and elegant man, he has flair. A junior official at the time of Bangladesh, he brought himself to the attention of the then High Commissioner, Prince Sadruddin Aga Khan, by producing at very short notice a clever scheme for helping solve the Bengali refugee crisis. Sadruddin, who was no bureaucrat himself, had found this young man attractive and, to the fury of many more senior officials in the organization, had promoted Rizvi to be his personal assistant.

His elders had their revenge when Poul Hartling replaced Sadruddin in 1978. Rizvi was banished to Rome. There he was stabbed in the stomach by a Somali refugee with a grievance against UNHCR. The wound was serious and he was hospitalized for several months.

By the fall of 1979, many officials in UNHCR's Bangkok office had become convinced that only Rizvi had the originality and the skill to pull UNHCR out of its quagmire in Thailand. With reluctance the senior staff around Hartling in Geneva—sometimes known to their disrespectful subordinates as "the Danish mafia"—had agreed, and Rizvi was dispatched to Bangkok.

With characteristic showmanship, he drove straight from the airport to an audience with the Prime Minister, to whom he handed another check, for one million dollars. "Thailand," declared Rizvi, "will not carry the burden alone."

Later that day, October 29, Rizvi, together with the man he was in effect replacing, Leslie Goodyear, went to see Ambassador Abramowitz. According to Abramowitz's own cable to the State Department, he "severely lectured" Rizvi and Goodyear on UNHCR's wretched performance at Sa Kaeo. "While Thai shortcomings contributed importantly to the mess, the UNHCR had no contingency plans for holding camps, which everyone knew would be needed, and failed to make productive use of the 48 hours' advance notice the Thais provided on the move." Abramowitz insisted this must not happen again and that HCR must immediately begin to build another camp on a site the Thais had already selected. He also "expressed his amazement" that HCR had failed completely to fill the vacancies on its staff, let alone "beef it up." Still today staff had not been augmented. Why not?

In response Rizvi, according to Abramowitz's cable, "made all the right noises"; he admitted that there had been shortcomings, he promised that new camp construction would begin at once, and he agreed to increase the staff.

The next day Rizvi and other UNHCR officials met with Air Vice-Marshal Siddhi, who suggested that UNHCR start coordinating the reception of up to 300,000 refugees. Rizvi agreed with this, but said that the government would formally have to give UNHCR the coordinating role, for the agency needed "a solid base" on which to build. Siddhi said that he understood, but that back in September he had authorized ICRC and UNICEF to work on the border and WFP to coordinate food. He could not go back on this.

Rizvi returned to the U.S. Embassy. "While still vowing that this time the UNHCR would not be caught flatfooted as with Sa Kaeo, he then proceeded to confound, disappoint and frustrate us with an account of the U.N. bureaucratic hurdles that seemingly have to be cleared," Burt Levin, the Deputy Chief of Mission, cabled Washington. He said UNHCR "did not have the funds in hand for camp construction." Money would have to be diverted from other, less pressing projects; this might take time. The American reaction was incredulity. "We expressed amazement over funding problems since we were told two weeks ago that UNHCR had ten million and possibly eighteen million dollars available for construction and operation of holding camps. We urged that UNHCR line up contractors today and offered facilitative assistance as well as full-time services of aid engineer. He left aware of our disappointment and promised to keep in touch."

In his cable to Washington, Levin insisted: "We cannot waste more time on this." He requested that, at the U.N., the United States mission at once contact Waldheim's staff and in Geneva it speak personally to Hartling, "to forcefully request that UNHCR here be immediately instructed to commence building the camps. UNHCR personnel should be on the earliest plane to provide needed assistance in this effort. We will continue to do our best on the Thai side but clearly something has to be done to get the UNHCR to move quickly on an issue where countless lives may be at stake." While this cable was being completed, Zia Rizvi called Levin at the Embassy to say that he had been in touch with Geneva and had been assured that the necessary funds would be available, and that there had been further meetings with Air Vice-Marshal Siddhi and Supreme Command. "We feel that we may have pumped some life into them but still recommend strong approach at N.Y. and Geneva to help get this urgent task done."

A week or so later, President Jimmy Carter announced that he was sending his wife, Rosalynn, to visit the refugee camps in Thailand and to report to him on what further action the United States might take to help the Cambodians. The trip was announced and prepared almost literally overnight. Jean Pierre Hocke of the ICRC and Charles Egger of UNICEF briefed Mrs. Carter at the White House before her departure. They were both concerned lest her visit become part of the rising American campaign against Vietnam. (In fact, it probably had more to do with Carter's reelection campaign— it was arranged in such haste in order to preempt a visit to the border by Senator Edward Kennedy.) They stressed to her the need to maintain absolutely the international character of the program and insisted that it could not succeed unless the aid organizations discussed everything with the Cambodian authorities "in order to obtain their concurrence." They thought it was essential to "show more trust in their desire to help their own people." (They were amused by the fact that although Abramowitz was constantly criticizing their inefficiency, the Embassy came rushing around to ICRC in search of a gift for Mrs. Carter to present to the refugees.)

The Thai government was still strictly limiting access to most of the hundreds of thousands of Cambodians who had come to the Thai border north of Aranyaprathet, and security there was very bad. The only large group of refugees who were easily accessible for the First Lady were those at Sa Kaeo—that is, the starving wreckage plucked from death in the areas controlled by the Khmer Rouge. They consisted of both genuine civilian refugees and Khmer Rouge troops and cadres, who had till now been the civilians' captors and were striving within the camp to remain so. One might have thought that the United States government would hesitate to have the President's wife walk among the Khmer Rouge. But the precise Khmer Rouge connection with the people at Sa Kaeo was not something that was then widely advertised or understood in the West. The dreadful images were all that had really been registered.

The trip started badly. The night before Mrs. Carter arrived the Thai military commander along the border, Colonel Prachak Sawaengchit, ordered his troops to shell a Cambodian border encampment, in retaliation for the fact that a Thai soldier had been killed after raping a Cambodian woman. About a hundred refugees were killed. The Presidential party was embarrassed; Richard Holbrooke, the Assistant Secretary, announced lamely that it proved how dangerous the border was.

On arriving at Sa Kaeo, Mrs. Carter seemed stunned by both jet lag and the horror of the place. The misery of the refugees was compounded by the accompanying herd of about 150 reporters, photographers and camera crews, pushing and kicking each other and even refugees to get closer to the President's wife, who was surrounded by Thai soldiers toting M-16 rifles and by her own Secret Service agents. An overweight, sweating British cameraman kept trying to thrust himself past a Thai soldier to get a better shot; he failed and roundly cursed the soldier—the Thai Minister of Defense and future Prime Minister, General Prem.

As for the refugees themselves, hardly any one of the civilians could have the slightest idea who this person in the white dress was, nor what this fantastic new invasion could mean. The Khmer Rouge soldiers just watched sullenly. "Our leaders ordered us to come out and watch," said one middle-aged man with a shrapnel scar on his cheek.

One of Mrs. Carter's aides kept screaming at Mark Malloch Brown, the UNHCR man in charge of the camp, "Create a photo opportunity. Create a photo opportunity." Exasperated at his failure to do so, the aide dragged a priest from Catholic Relief Services away from a dying child. The First Lady was then alone with the helpless infant, and she and the press had their chance.

The scene was an extraordinary symbol of the relationship between the West and Cambodia—a strange blend of pathos, politics, ignorance and concern, dominated now (though not before and not later) by the fickle and vulgar demands of Western communications. For Mrs. Carter and her husband the visit was presumably of some political use. And by tying Presidential politics into the Cambodian crisis, her trip undoubtedly drew wider American attention and more money toward Cambodia. But it was also very bizarre. In 1978, Jimmy Carter had denounced the Khmer Rouge as "the world's worst violators of human rights." Now he sent his wife to walk among them and the people whom they had brought so close to death.*

* The U.S. Embassy used Mrs. Carter's visit to put further pressure on the international organizations in Thailand, particularly the U.N. High Commissioner for Refugees. She wrote to Poul Hartling: "I urge you to direct your staff be augmented rapidly by the best top-level expertise that can be found." She also described the conditions at the Lumpini transit center, where refugees accepted for resettlement awaited flights out of Thailand, as "intolerable." "I cannot understand how such a situation has been permitted to continue. Management of this transit center, as well as the conditions of the center itself, seems to me to be unacceptable by any standards of criteria. I would urge you to deal with the problem as a matter of high urgency . . ." Mrs. Carter's demands had some effect: a new transit camp was opened within a few days. UNHCR set up a new unit called "Regional Office Kampuchea Unit" under Martin Barber.

11 &⋈ Pledges

And so, in the fall of 1979, nearly ten whole years after its acute suffering began, Cambodia was at last receiving concerted Western attention. Finally the crisis, which had hovered only at the rim of Western consciousness for so long, had shuddered, sickeningly, toward the fore.

By October 1979 there had been so many firsthand reports from journalists, from Catholics, from Quakers, from Communists, and from nondenominational aid groups who traveled into Cambodia or to the border that all over the United States and many other countries, voluntary agencies, churches, synagogues, schools, factories, universities, businesses, clubs and associations started to mobilize their resources and to demand that their governments do likewise in an effort to prevent the new catastrophe of "two million dead by Christmas."

In Britain, for example, BBC Television's children's program *Blue Peter* began to receive letters from children all over the country. One Anglo-Thai child wrote, "dear Plue Peter, LASt YeAr I came from Thailand. NoW our neighbours The Khmers are Starving. Would Blue Peter help Oxfam noW. AYe Davies." *Blue Peter* launched a bring-and-buy sale through all of Oxfam's 584 shops throughout the country. The response was staggering. Tens of thousands of children and their parents swamped the shops with toys, clothes and money. *Blue Peter* had originally set a target of $220,000—

enough to buy one truck and 70 tons of rice, 42 tons of seed, 10,000 hoes and 1,000 fishing nets. The target was reached within forty-eight hours. Eventually the *Blue Peter* appeal fetched almost $8 million for Oxfam. The film *Cambodia, Year Zero,* by John Pilger, which was shown at the end of October, also had a fantastic response and raised over $2 million.

In good part because of such public pressure, the United States government and other Western governments now began to direct their resources—for the first time in this decade of destruction—toward publicizing what was happening in Cambodia. During the Lon Nol period, the White House had conducted its Cambodian policy as covertly as it was able. During the Khmer Rouge rule, neither Washington nor its Western allies had concentrated their energies on exposing Khmer Rouge atrocities—partly because their Thai partner was seeking its own rapprochement with the regime in Phnom Penh. Now, for the first time, the United States and other Western governments were making an international issue of Cambodia.

Popular humanitarianism coincided with political and strategic considerations. There was the conviction within at least sections of the Carter administration (it is often difficult to speak of any United States administration as monolithic) and other Western governments that any famine in Cambodia could now be blamed upon the Vietnamese; thus the diplomatic isolation of Hanoi, which had been reinforced by the terrible drama of the boat people, could be extended still further. There was also a determination by the Western allies to engender international support for the policies of Thailand (both overt and covert) now that the crisis in Cambodia and along the border was in danger of becoming unmanageable.

At the same time there was, at least in the United States, a certain sense of responsibility, if not guilt, among some officials, many journalists, and part of the public for the travails that had beset Cambodia. (The coincidental publication of Henry Kissinger's memoirs, *The White House Years,* provoked a fairly vigorous public debate over the extent of American involvement in the suffering that Cambodia had endured.)

Finally, there was the constant evocation of the Holocaust, in the face of which no one could be complacent.

. . .

The high point of Western rhetoric for Cambodia was reached on November 5, when Kurt Waldheim opened a pledging conference in the U.N. General Assembly. The near-death of the country was considered important enough for many Western countries to send their foreign ministers.

The tone of Western outrage was set by the first speaker, French Foreign Minister Jean François Poncet, who made an impassioned plea to "all those who have authority and conscience to save the Cambodian people . . . who are on the edge of extinction." The sight of dying children "who have only ever known a life of suffering" should mobilize members. Political considerations must be set aside, there must be no delay, "we must save an entire people." By taking exceptional action over Cambodia, the United Nations had the chance to prove that "it can contribute to building a more humane and brotherly world."

Cyrus Vance, the U.S. Secretary of State, called Cambodia today "a human tragedy of almost unfathomable proportions. . . . An entire generation of Kampucheans may have been lost." He declared that "the reality of Kampuchea . . . of a people on the verge of extinction . . . is most powerfully conveyed by the images of suffering carried in our daily newspapers. The silent grief of a young Khmer mother cradling her dead baby in her arms . . . or the vacant gaze of an infant beyond help and hope in a makeshift orphanage in Phnom Penh."

Canada's Foreign Minister Flora Macdonald had thrown out the speech prepared for her by her department's officials; it was not dramatic enough. She spoke instead from a text written by her personal assistant and declared that "the entire Khmer people of Cambodia are faced with annihilation through famine and warfare." She too thought that "at the very least a full generation of Kampucheans will be lost." Like other Western delegates, she paid fulsome tribute to Thailand. (No one now remembered the expulsion of the 45,000 Cambodian refugees down the cliffs at Preah Vihear in June.) "Even greater tragedy would have happened had it not been for the selfless response of the noble Thais. Their open asylum policy . . . and their generous aid to the starving stand out as a beacon of light in a

dark sea of inhumanity. . . ." Even Thai officials were rather astonished by this extraordinary tribute.

By contrast, Macdonald thought Vietnamese restrictions on food
deliveries "must forever condemn them in the eyes of the world."

Britain's delegate—only a junior minister—asserted that, had the
United Nations reacted more decisively to the reports of Khmer
Rouge violations of human rights, thousands of lives might have
been saved. (He chose not to mention the reluctance of all members,
including Britain, even to raise the matter in the U.N. before 1978.)
"We must not fail the people of Kampuchea a second time. We must
act and act fast. History will rightly condemn us if we fail." The
German representative agreed that immediate action was needed, the
Belgian felt that the humiliation of man had reached a vile new low.

Singapore's permanent representative, Tommy Koh, said he
could not understand the recent assertions from Hanoi and Phnom
Penh that the famine was an invention of "Western imperialists and
Chinese expansionists." Singapore would help the international organizations.

For Thailand, Air Vice-Marshal Siddhi declared that "massive
human catastrophe, almost beyond words to describe, is unfolding today in Indochina." Three hundred thousand people were about to enter Thailand. But Thailand was "not unduly worried about the burden. . . . No one will be turned back. The Khmer people must be
allowed to survive." At the same time, however, Western aid to
Thailand must be increased. So must the rate of resettlement of Cambodians abroad.

The Australian Foreign Minister Andrew Peacock said that "the
disaster which has befallen the Khmer people and their culture is
possibly without parallel in modern times . . . the extent of man's
inhumanity to man seems to have known no limits. This modern holocaust threatens to destroy the uniqueness of the Cambodian civilization, indeed, the very identity of the Khmer race itself."

The Israeli intervention obviously had especial pathos. The Israeli delegate declared that "the people of Israel, who have known
what it is to suffer and be refugees, could not remain unmoved by
this human drama." Indeed, the fate of Cambodia was a very real issue both in Israel and among Jewish communities in the diaspora at
this time. Many Jews accepted, with generosity, the holocaust anal-

ogy and were determined that the Cambodians should be rescued as their people were not. Jewish groups were to the fore in demanding that governments respond with speed to the Cambodian crisis.

I have quoted here almost no Third World country except those from ASEAN. This is because a high level of concern was expressed almost exclusively by the Western powers. This was a Western, not an international, crisis of conscience.

The nations of the socialist bloc denounced the "libels" against Hanoi and Phnom Penh, and said that they had been helping "the legal government" of Cambodia since January 1979 and would continue to do so. Vietnam said that the socialist bloc had already delivered 200,000 tons of food. (Similarly, S.P.K., the news agency that the Vietnamese had set up in Phnom Penh, had just declared that 570,000 hectares of rice fields had been planted during the current season. "Such results obtained in a completely disrupted country and by a bleeding people who has lost three million of its citizens and is rebuilding its native land with empty hands constitutes a great victory for the People's Republic of Kampuchea.")

From Latin America only Argentina—apart from Cuba—spoke. No OPEC country had anything at all to say about Cambodia. Africa's silence was conspicuous; only Uganda and South Africa spoke.

African countries were, in fact, already becoming restless with the attention that the Western world was devoting to Southeast Asian refugee problems. There were at that time about four million refugees in Africa as against well under a million in Southeast Asia. In most African countries refugees are allowed to cross borders without immediate danger of forced repatriation. This does not mean that their other needs or suffering are the less, but their plight has rarely attracted the same sort of Western attention as that which first the boat people and then the Cambodians were given in the West in 1979. African representatives at the U.N. were by now beginning to put pressure on Kurt Waldheim to give their problems equal attention. Under that pressure, as well as that from the Soviet Union, Waldheim was beginning to back away from his own rhetorical exhortations on behalf of Cambodia; his statement at the pledging conference was much less passionate than the visions of apocalypse that he had invoked only a few weeks before.

Most of the pledges came from North America, Western Europe, Japan and Australia. They were considerable, but despite the extraordinary rhetoric, they did not amount to the $350 million that Waldheim had requested. Instead, just under $210 million was pledged. Of this, $31 million was at once allocated to the Joint Mission in Phnom Penh, $44 million was earmarked for the purchase of food by the World Food Program for both Phnom Penh and the border, and $47 million was given to the UNHCR for use in Thailand. Not all the pledges were honored promptly, and within weeks the program was in financial chaos. But in the end the Joint Mission would be given and would spend over $600 million over the next two years.*

By now a new crisis was developing in Phnom Penh. Food and other relief supplies were finally arriving in considerable quantities, but they were not being distributed with any of the urgency that many relief officials considered commensurate with the scale of the impending disaster. Instead they were piling up in warehouses in Kompong Som and in government stores in Phnom Penh. At the same time Joint Mission officials, particularly those from the ICRC, were beginning to realize the self-limiting nature of the proposals they had made to the authorities in mid-October. Indeed, the Heng Samrin regime had still not made any formal response to the detailed program submitted by the Joint Mission on October 20; there was still no agreement on just how food aid should be distributed, and there was actual disagreement on the way in which vehicles being imported by the Joint Mission were being used.

On November 5, Henry Labouisse, UNICEF's Executive Director, met in Phnom Penh with President Heng Samrin. François Bugnion of ICRC, and Jean de Courten of ICRC, who accompanied Labouisse, felt that Labouisse ought to make a strong *démarche* on these issues. Bugnion, for example, had been outraged to see two of

---

* At the November 5, 1979, Conference, the United States pledged $69 million; Japan, $37 million; Canada, $13 million; Australia, almost $8 million; West Germany, $9 million; France, $5 million; Britain, over $6 million; Norway, $3.5 million; Sweden, almost $6 million; Switzerland, almost $2 million. From Pakistan came $836,000; from Italy, $544,000; from the Common Market, $42 million; from the Netherlands, $5.5 million; from Finland, $526,000; and from Belgium, $588,000.

the Land Rovers imported by the Joint Mission filled with armed soldiers and being used as military escorts. He had cabled Geneva to say that he thought it was impossible for ICRC to continue supplying vehicles in such circumstances.

Labouisse, however, was determined to be conciliatory. In this he reflected the preferences of the UNICEF team in Phnom Penh and, indeed, a basic difference between the styles and mandates of UNICEF and ICRC respectively. UNICEF is primarily a development agency, used to working closely with governments. ICRC is much more attuned to emergencies and is also more used to confronting governments—even if only on a confidential basis. In Phnom Penh the difference in approach was fairly fundamental: ICRC officials constantly felt that their partners were too weak with the authorities, while UNICEF people often complained that ICRC impatience might upset the whole operation.

In this case, Henry Labouisse did not ask Heng Samrin whether the authorities had actually approved the Joint Mission's October 20 plan. Nor did he confront Heng Samrin with the problems of vehicles or the poor rate of distribution. But he asked Heng Samrin whether the Joint Mission's program was "in line with what the government wants."

Heng Samrin did not give a direct answer. He replied that three out of the four million remaining Cambodians had been threatened by famine and the other million were very sick. Bilateral aid from Vietnam and the USSR had been very important. As for the Joint Mission, he referred again to the three conditions laid out in the *aide mémoire* of September 28. "We are not happy that aid is being distributed to both sides," he stated.

Stretching a point, Labouisse said that "the assistance you are referring to, Mr. President, is assistance going to children on the Thailand border. . . . We have a duty to prevent children dying. . . ."

Heng Samrin was obviously not convinced, but the meeting was cordial—precisely because Labouisse raised no difficult problems and made no attempt to extract any concessions from the government to improve either the distribution of supplies or the Joint Mission's ability to monitor them. Afterward he cabled New York, "Although I am not fully satisfied with visit and know there is much yet to be done to expedite aid to those in need, I believe things are in fact improving and that we should continue our efforts, including shipments of all supplies and vehicles . . ."

By contrast, François Bugnion of the ICRC was dismayed by the fact that Labouisse had not taken a far tougher line; he cabled Geneva to say that he had missed an important opportunity. After his departure Joint Mission officials in Phnom Penh made their own further *démarches* to the authorities. Eventually, on November 17, four months after Beaumont and Bugnion had first arrived in Phnom Penh, the Foreign Minister formally approved their relief program.

From Phnom Penh, Labouisse traveled to Hanoi, where UNICEF had been active since 1973. Prime Minister Pham Van Dong and Foreign Minister Nguyen Co Thach praised UNICEF's work in Cambodia. They also allayed some of Labouisse's concerns by making several specific promises. They agreed to allow UNICEF to open an office in Ho Chi Minh City and said that they were prepared to allow internal relief flights within Cambodia to alleviate the transport problems. Labouisse cabled Waldheim, "I am glad to say that my talks with these and other ministers confirmed the esteem in which UNICEF and its representatives are held in Vietnam . . ." Despite that esteem, the Vietnamese kept none of the promises they made to Labouisse.

Through November and December 1979, Western government and editorial attacks upon the Vietnamese and the Heng Samrin regime became ever harsher. They were accused of failing to distribute the food shipped in by the international organizations, of diverting it to their own armed forces, and even of preventing the peasants from harvesting what little rice might have been planted. In short, they were held responsible for aggravating the famine which they themselves had advertised in July and in the face of which they had sought Western assistance. In many ways this hardly seemed logical conduct. Nonetheless, the belief that it was happening grew more and more widespread throughout the Western world before Christmas 1979. It was encouraged by the United States government.

The issue of the "land bridge" was seized upon.

If the logistics inside the country were so terrible—so few trucks and such bad roads—and if the shortage of food was so acute, then how in conscience could the Vietnamese and the Heng Samrin regime refuse to allow supplies to be trucked or taken by train across the border at Aranyaprathet? This would clearly be a far more efficient way of getting food to the large numbers of people thought to be dying of hunger in western Cambodia than shipping it to Kompong Som, several hundred kilometers away.

The idea was formally proposed at the end of October by three United States Senators (Danforth, Sasser and Baucus) who flew for a few hours into Phnom Penh. Foreign Minister Hun Sen gave them no firm answer, saying the matter would be considered. But soon afterward Phnom Penh rejected the proposal on the grounds that it was another device to feed the Khmer Rouge. (In fact it would have reduced the border population and the border-relief operation.) Obviously the fact that the proposal came from American politicians and was being pressed by the United States government made it difficult for the Phnom Penh authorities to accept. But the refusal made it much easier for Vietnam's critics to charge that it was not concerned to deliver food as quickly as possible to the 2.25 million people who, it had said, badly needed it.

Senator Danforth, a former P.O.W. in Vietnam, said, "If a Government is determined to murder its own people, I don't know how to stop it." (There were echoes here of the anguish that George McGovern had expressed in 1978, when he speculated on the idea of an international invasion of Cambodia to stop the Khmer Rouge massacres.)

Similarly, Leo Cherne, a supporter of the American war in Indochina and the head of one of the largest private American relief agencies, International Rescue Committee, which has a long social-democrat, anti-communist tradition, and was at this time very active on the border, declared that "one million, probably more, will soon die if help of sufficient magnitude is not rapidly organized and implemented." He urged that food be pushed into Cambodia from all possible points, including over the bridge at Aranyaprathet, and by the use of provincial airstrips within the country. How was this to be achieved? "We will place the heaviest focus of our efforts in stimulating the formation of an outcry of the human conscience aimed at

Hanoi, which determines what happens in Phnom Penh. . . ." That outcry was orchestrated by the United States government by the skillful use of information.

There were two sources of information—the border and Phnom Penh. There was still only a handful of relief officials in Phnom Penh; their movements were being strictly controlled, and their communications with the world outside were very poor. Far more information was coming from the border. And much of that news came through the United States government. The process demonstrates the extent of its reach and influence.

It began with interviews of refugees along the border by officials of the Kampuchea Emergency Group and others from the Embassy. These were written up as "situation reports" by political officers in Bangkok and were sent to Washington, where they were used to brief journalists and relief officials. They were also cabled to other United States missions around the world, and the Embassy in Bangkok distributed copies of them to "friendly" embassies in the city, and sometimes also to Western journalists. (The contrast with embassy reticence during the Khmer Rouge period from 1975 to 1978 was very marked.)

Thus a series of interviews along the border had an extraordinary snowball effect. They would reach, say, Australia, in briefings given by the embassy in Bangkok to Australian embassy staff and Australian journalists, in talks between Australian diplomats in Washington and State Department officials, in talks between American and Australian diplomats in Canberra, and in columns of journalists who had been allowed to see either the complete reports or their gist.

The United States also used NATO to spread its views. Thus, for example, on November 5, the United States ambassador to NATO urged his colleagues to press for all possible routes into Cambodia to be opened, particularly a formal land bridge at Aranyaprathet.* On

---

* In one three-page report to NATO just before the U.N. pledging conference, the United States said, "As we have already reported to NATO, as many as 3 million of the 4 to 6 million surviving Khmers may die of starvation and disease unless massive humanitarian relief is forthcoming immediately." The report was relatively favorable to the Heng Samrin regime, noting that their cooperation was vital and that they did seem to be cooperating

November 21, United States officials told NATO representatives in Washington that fighting between the Vietnamese and the Khmer Rouge was spreading and that the Khmer Rouge would survive because the Vietnamese army had supply problems. As for Khmer Rouge supplies, Chinese weapons were flowing fast through Thailand. Indeed, one official compared the scale of Chinese assistance to the Khmer Rouge to Thai support of the Americans during the previous Indochina war.

Washington was also telling its allies that the Vietnamese were taking villagers' scanty food stocks to feed themselves and were looting the countryside. Fish nets, tools, pumps, tires, almost everything that could be moved had been stolen and taken to Vietnam—particularly in the first months after the invasion. Why had these reports not surfaced before now? Because Cambodians who had been refugees in Vietnam's Ha Thien province till mid-1979 had just arrived at the Thai border. They had seen the movement. (In August a reporter from the *Washington Post,* Elizabeth Becker, had reported from Saigon the evidence of looting that she had seen in the markets there.) The State Department suggested to United States allies, "If Vietnamese actions took place nationwide, these reports may explain how the famine spread so quickly following Hanoi's full-scale invasion last January. They may also explain why Cambodia's ability to unload and distribute relief supplies at Kompong Som remains so limited."

"despite their objection to aid going to areas under the control of Pol Pot." It pointed out that ICRC and UNICEF had promised to see that their relief "in no way contributes to the war effort of either belligerent" and said that "on the basis of these assurances and given the desperate need of the Khmer people, we believe there is no humane alternative to going ahead with an international relief program notwithstanding the risk of some possible diversion of relief supplies to improper channels."

The Americans claimed that the Vietnamese had deliberately prevented Cambodian villagers from cultivating fields and had destroyed food stocks rather than have them fall into hands of the Khmer Rouge. According to Washington, the Vietnamese were constructing "showcase distributions" around Phnom Penh to please the international organizations, but food was actually being diverted to the Vietnamese army. Of one shipload of 700 tons coming up the Mekong, only 100 tons had arrived in Phnom Penh and one could only suppose the rest had been diverted to Vietnamese troops en route.

The Canadian Embassy in Washington reported that it was Washington's view "that deliberate and willful Vietnamese actions and not merely disruptions resulting from the fighting exacerbated or perhaps even directly caused the serious famine in Cambodia."

In Bangkok, Mort Abramowitz was becoming more and more outraged. His views are illustrated by a cable he sent at the end of November, accompanying a report on conditions in Cambodia written by an embassy political officer, Desaix Anderson. "The picture it paints not surprisingly is very grim indeed," wrote Abramowitz. "While refugee sources must of course always be handled with caution, I think the record of reports from Cambodian refugees since the advent of the Pol Pot regime have been on the mark, and we may not have paid sufficient attention to them. . . . The simple fact is that for a number of months large numbers of Cambodians have been without food. The international effort to bring them food has been minuscule. . . ."

Abramowitz dismissed the Soviet claims of massive socialist aid and said:

> What the international organizations are doing is very necessary and to be applauded, but it has not prevented half a million refugees on the Thai border and many more on the way. Their efforts are speeding up and they are doing their best to get more food in. But it is clear that while there are real logistical constraints, distribution is the principal stumbling block and that politics is a major element in that distribution. . . .
>
> What to do? I am bereft of any bright ideas. The international relief agencies are doing what they can to increase the supply of food. Every effort should be made to increase the airlift to Phnom Penh, to open up provincial airports and to expand the cargo unloading capabilities of Kompong Som. But all that will not assure adequate distribution within Cambodia. I have pondered over the notions of an airdrop: it strikes me as delusory since there are no significant refugee concentrations, the problem is countrywide and there is a major Vietnamese anti-air capability. I fall back on two notions: One, we must step up the international campaign against Moscow and Hanoi for permitting this scene to continue. In the past few years Hanoi for the first time has lost most of its diplomatic

and international support. We must maximize their isolation on humanitarian grounds much as we did on the boat refugees.

Second, and it will be enormously difficult for Thailand, we must encourage people to come to the Thai border. We are doing this already; the presence of food on the Thai border is already getting well known all over Cambodia. VOA broadcasts will further contribute to it. We are setting ourselves up for a very difficult long-term problem but unless someone can show me a better way of getting food into Cambodia, and distributing it, I see no other way to go.

Abramowitz's cable and, in particular, his proposed remedies, raised a number of issues. It might be true that very little food was being distributed in the Cambodian countryside. But what would be the effect of using the specter of famine to complete the diplomatic isolation of Hanoi? One might argue that if the Cambodians were threatened with extinction, the only proper course was the closest cooperation with the de facto authorities, whatever one thought of them. American pressure had rarely induced Hanoi to change its policies before.

More problematic was the idea of using the Thai border as a magnet. There were thought to be only four million Cambodians alive now. If almost half a million were already on the border and more were to be attracted, very soon perhaps a quarter of the country would be along the border. This would clearly destabilize the government the Vietnamese had installed in Phnom Penh and would increase the recruiting base for any resistance movements along the border, the Khmer Rouge among them.

There were people in the relief agencies and some journalists who believed, now and through the succeeding months, that this was Abramowitz's principal aim. Obviously America's strategic goals were well served by a buildup of the border operation. ASEAN's resolution calling for the withdrawal of all foreign troops from Cambodia, an international conference and free elections to decide the country's future had just been passed overwhelmingly by the General Assembly. It was supported by the United States and rejected out of hand by the Vietnamese and their allies. But whatever the politics of the border, Abramowitz always insisted that getting food and care to

Cambodians was his overriding ambition. One needs to recall once again the sense of panic, even terror, that was then infecting many of those people concerned with Cambodia. "Two million dead by Christmas" was still the predominant fear. If food could not be got to the starving through Phnom Penh, then it was vital that every other route should be tried.

Nor was it just Abramowitz and his colleagues who were criticizing Vietnamese conduct in Cambodia. In Paris the organizers of the boat *Ile de Lumière* (which had previously been rescuing Vietnamese boat people in the South China Sea) announced that they had sent one shipload of supplies up the Mekong to Phnom Penh, but would send no more. They declared that the Vietnamese were perpetrating a gigantic fraud and were using food not to feed but to subjugate the Cambodian people. Even Oxfam officials in Britain acknowledged that the first two reports on distribution that the government had given them were "useless." Along the border, journalists heard the same stories that embassy officials heard. So did French priests. Father François Ponchaud, the author of *Cambodia Year Zero*, the first account of life under the Khmer Rouge, circulated many refugee reports that seemed to show that the Vietnamese were indeed using food as a weapon to control the population.*

Passions—and advertising—became very inflamed. Oxfam published posters directly linking Cambodia to the Nazi death camps, a World Vision advertisement declared, "If we don't act by Tuesday—come Friday they won't be starving—they'll be dead," "A million children dying of starvation," said the British Committee for UNICEF. "Some children in Kampuchea look like this," announced the British Red Cross over a picture of a barely living creature, "the rest are dead. Millions of Kampucheans, adults and children alike, have died. The survivors face imminent death through starvation and disease." From huge posters on newsstands and hoardings all over Paris a

---

* Denis Gray of the Associated Press reported that refugees said some fields had been mined "and some farmers have been shot by Vietnamese soldiers for entering the fields. The Kampucheans were told that rice would be harvested by proper authorities to insure future stocks and seeds." Refugees also reported that the Vietnamese often confiscated at night food they had handed out during the day. They said that the Vietnamese were giving out rations of red corn (from the USSR) rather than rice.

starving yellow child stared, puzzled and accusing, across the rain-swept streets. It was an enlarged cover of the current issue of the newsweekly *Le Point;* the legend read "Cambodge: Holocauste." Another magazine, *Le Nouvel Observateur,* carried a long debate between the philosopher André Glucksmann and Bernard Kouchner, leader of the French paramedical group, Medecins sans Frontières, which was trying in vain to work in Cambodia. "Today," declared Kouchner, "we are taking part, thanks to satellite television, in the extinction of Cambodian children. Genocide is happening every evening, over supper."

Like so many others, Kouchner was drawn to the Jewish precedent. "When the ICRC failed to denounce the Nazi camps, Auschwitz or Buchenwald, it did a great service to clear consciences. Because no one would have lifted a finger to pull the Jews out of the ovens . . . Jews are being killed? It's normal. Cambodians being assassinated? That's life. What are the Jews doing today to prevent genocide in Cambodia? History has no memory. No one can count on anyone."

I took part in a two-hour debate over Cambodia on French television. With emotions at such a pitch, it was perhaps inevitable that it should generate much more heat than light. Prince Sihanouk was there, and so was Pin Yathay, a Cambodian who had survived the Khmer Rouge and written a book, *L'Utopie meurtrière,* on the horror of their regime. The rest of the panel consisted largely of French politicians, journalists and doctors of strong political views. Those of the rightist persuasion appeared to detest Vietnam and all its works, while those of a leftist point of view seemed to feel that Vietnam could do little wrong. Neither of the Cambodians, Prince or refugee, was able to say much—the Frenchmen spent most of the two-hour program denouncing each other for underwriting the most monstrous crimes against the Cambodian people. Sihanouk is not used to being upstaged in this way, but he seemed to find a certain humor in the situation.

One French Communist doctor who had been in Phnom Penh in the summer declared over and over that the Vietnamese were doing all they could for the Cambodians, while François Ponchaud declared that they were committing a "subtle genocide" in Cambodia.

My own view then was extremely gloomy. Like Abramowitz I thought that Cambodian refugees had a record of telling the truth. On the basis of the reports from Phnom Penh, the visions on the border, and the stories of refugees, I believed the worst case analysis of millions on the edge of death. Back in September, on the basis of Oxfam reports, I had written of the danger of "two million dead by Christmas" unless massive aid was given. I did not now see how the tiny amounts of food being distributed from Phnom Penh could prevent it.* After the debate Sihanouk invited me back to his suite at the George V Hotel. We talked of the ten last terrible years in Cambodia. He feared that Chinese and Vietnamese intransigence was such that no compromise settlement was possible for Cambodia. He himself had sent three letters to the Vietnamese, offering a compromise. He had had no reply. So he thought he would have to lead the resistance against Heng Samrin. "Yes, it is a vicious circle, a terrible dilemma. I acknowledge that. But what to do?"

* In a long article for the *New York Review of Books* entitled "The End of Cambodia?" I repeated François Ponchaud's charge of "subtle genocide," and many of the stories that refugees were bringing to the border about starvation and the harassment of Vietnamese troops.

12 ❧ Confusions

The view from Phnom Penh was not the same.

By now there were about thirty foreign relief officials living at the Hotel Samaki. Twelve of these were in the UNICEF-ICRC Joint Mission. The rest were from voluntary agencies such as Oxfam, World Vision, the World Council of Churches, the American Friends Service Committee, and the French Comité de l'Aide Médicale et Sanitaire.

At the head of the Joint Mission were François Bugnion of the ICRC and John Saunders, an Assistant Secretary General of the United Nations. Saunders had replaced Knud Christensen, who had arrived to take over from Jacques Beaumont in October but had been injured in a car accident on the road to Kompong Som and had been flown back to Bangkok. Saunders, a British Quaker, had been involved in international relief work since the Second World War. He had been with UNRRA in China and had then spent most of his life with the U.N. Development Program, in Yugoslavia, Iran, the Congo, Addis Ababa and Beirut. He had been involved with the emergency in Biafra and that in Lebanon. He had, in other words, considerable experience. He was brought out of retirement to go to Phnom Penh.

One of Saunders' principal aides was Ian Hopwood, a Welshman who was the UNICEF program officer. A young man, he had worked with UNICEF in both Cameroon and Hanoi; he spoke fluent French and some Vietnamese. His principal interest was education; he worked zealously and, as a result, a good deal of UNICEF's resources went into schools. (Some thought too much.) There was also a man from the World Food Program who tried to follow what was happening with food shipments. The Food and Agriculture Organization had supplied a young German named Hans Page. His task was to help in the agricultural reconstruction of the country. It was a job that he performed for well over a year with extreme efficiency.

The American Friends Service Committee had sent an Englishman named Paul Quinn Judge, who spoke fluent Vietnamese. He was probably closer than any other Western official to Mr. Bui Huu Nhan, the principal Vietnamese adviser to the Foreign Ministry. The World Council of Churches had a French Protestant priest, Jean Clavaud, in Phnom Penh. Clavaud had lived in Cambodia throughout the sixties and early seventies. He loved the country and, alone among the relief officials in Phnom Penh, he spoke the language of Cambodia fluently. He was able to learn far more about what was actually happening in the country and what the people felt about it than any other aid official. He became increasingly disillusioned with what the Vietnamese were doing in Cambodia. As a result, the Phnom Penh authorities treated him with an ever-growing suspicion.*

The Oxfam team was now being run by a diligent English Protestant named Malcolm Harper, who had been with Oxfam for sixteen years. He was utterly committed to the cause of the Heng Samrin government, and he was working closely with UNICEF and ICRC in Phnom Penh. Like other Oxfam officials, he was greatly relieved that the agreement "not to cooperate" with the Joint Mission had been torn up; he was embarrassed by the episode.

Probably all the foreign relief officials in the Samaki were overwhelmed by what they could see of the destruction of the Pol Pot years and were determined to do their best to help the Heng Samrin regime rebuild Cambodia. They did not accept Washington's analysis of what was going on inside the country. And they tended to see the border operation as a device to rebuild "Pol Pot"; indeed, some of the UNICEF people in Phnom Penh were appalled that their colleagues were there at all. Unwisely, perhaps, UNICEF did not re-

---

* Clavaud was able to remain in the country until May 1982. Then his visa was not renewed, his appeal against this was refused, he was arrested at the Hotel Samaki and bundled on the ICRC plane wearing only his sarong.

quire that people working on one side go see what their colleagues were doing on the other. It would have been simple enough for those in Phnom Penh to visit the border when on one of their trips to Bangkok. They would have seen that hundreds of thousands of innocent people there had real needs.

Some life seemed to be returning to the streets of Phnom Penh. People had set up stalls selling sugar cane, coarse bread, dried fish. The Heng Samrin regime had still not introduced a currency. Rice was the currency with which anyone who worked for the government was paid—16 kilos a month and 8 kilos per dependent by December 1979—and at this stage the government was the only employer in Cambodia. This had enormous and obvious consequences for the relief program. In a very direct sense the Joint Mission and the other agencies were importing money as well as food. In the markets rice was the medium of exchange.

By late 1979 one kilo of fish was worth 300 grams of rice, one kilo of pork fetched 3 kilos of rice. The government said that there were now about 170,000 people living in and around the city, about 70,000 of them in the center. Families had moved into the looted houses, camping sometimes in their old homes, most often in others. The government was already trying to assign housing, and there were now checkpoints on every road leading into town.

The government was still tiny. There were ministries in name, but few of them consisted of more than a dozen people with only a few pens and pieces of paper between them. No typewriters, no transport, no real infrastructure at all.

Three schools had been reopened in Phnom Penh by mid-November 1979. The Ministry of Education, one of the more effective ministries, claimed that there were already 700,000 children in primary school throughout the country—almost double the 400,000 which the UNICEF-ICRC program of October 20 had envisaged. There were said to be 12,000 teachers working in these schools, but three quarters of them had no training whatsoever. They were simply people who had completed secondary or even just primary school. The ministry was anxious to recruit and train more teachers. By emphasizing education, the regime hoped to be able to give a glue to the new society. At the same time, there was a real hunger among people for education, after four years in which it had been so systematically denied.

Less easy to comprehend was the lack of urgency that the regime seemed to feel about health care. The atrocious state of the hospitals and orphanages had deeply shocked the first relief officials and journalists to come to Phnom Penh in the summer. Since then, doctors and nurses all around the world had been volunteering to go to Cambodia, both with voluntary organizations and for national Red Cross societies. The Joint Mission had been offering since July to send medical teams. The Soviet, Polish and East German Red Cross societies had also asked to send teams. But although several agencies had been allowed to send in individual doctors, as advisers, not as practitioners, no teams—except a few from Vietnam itself—had been allowed into Cambodia. Since the authorities claimed that only fifty or so doctors had survived the Khmer Rouge, this seemed to many relief officials unconscionable.

At the Seventh of January Hospital in Phnom Penh there were at this stage 700 patients in 577 beds, and just 8 doctors. This was hardly better than when Beaumont and Bugnion first came to Phnom Penh in July. Both Oxfam and the Joint Mission had imported the supplies needed to start a supplementary feeding program in schools, hospitals and orphanages, but they were still lying idle. Oxfam's Marcus Thompson found to his dismay that the official responsible for setting up any such program (Ang Sarung) was too busy meeting delegations from the socialist bloc to do any actual work. Moreover, the Minister of Trade, M. Taing Sarim, simply refused to release food.

Their principal concern was the same as that felt in the world to the west—the lack of distribution. But, whereas from the outside it seemed that supplies were being deliberately withheld, inside, logistics appeared to be the problem. As more and more ships came from Bangkok and Singapore to Kompong Som, the delays were becoming worse and worse. The port had only four berths. It had no cargo-handling equipment. The dockers were being fed from the boats that docked, but they were still a weak, untrained and unskilled force, able to unload only about 300 tons a day. By November, ships were backing up outside the harbor. Only the arrival of a crew of efficient Soviet dockers relieved the situation.

At the end of November, Marcus Thompson of Oxfam drove down to Kompong Som. He found that two of the warehouses were full of food and one was empty save for some heavy guns. To his dismay he came across almost all of the 400 tons of wheat flour that Guy Stringer had brought on the first barge in early October. Rice, sugar, soap and medical equipment dispatched by the World Council of Churches were also there. He was disappointed that the Ministry of Health "have made no journeys to Kompong Som to collect cargoes consigned to them, and don't seem to have made much effort to get these to Phnom Penh."

Unloading at Kompong Som was bound to be difficult. The railway to Phnom Penh was barely working yet; its capacity was no more than 900 tons a week. The Joint Mission had underestimated the need for trucks. Originally only 100 had been thought adequate. In the end, the Joint Mission would bring in 1,041 trucks in all, together with Oxfam's 300 and another 300 or so from the Soviet Union.

As in many such situations it proved impossible to standardize what was acquired. The Joint Mission wanted to buy Japanese trucks—partly because they were efficient, partly because they were more quickly available than others, and partly also because, as is often the way with aid programs, the Japanese government insisted that its contribution be spent, as far as possible, on Japanese products. Oxfam was asked to buy the same Japanese trucks so as to reduce the problems of servicing and spare parts. That was sensible. But even the Japanese could not at once provide the large numbers of trucks needed. And Oxfam was under pressure from both the British government and British public opinion to buy trucks made by British Leyland, the principal British auto manufacturer, which was then in serious financial difficulties. Oxfam bought the Leyland trucks—but almost all of them were made under license in Turkey, not in the U.K. Many arrived with Turkish manuals but proved efficient.

On top of these formidable logistical problems, bureaucratic and political rivalries were developing between ministries, as they do everywhere. The Ministry of Economy was trying to insist that everything, including medical supplies that had previously gone to the Ministry of Health, should go first to Economy. The Minister of Commerce was saying much the same. In the event, no ministry seemed to have any clear idea of what was going where. For example, Oxfam lost five and a half tons of rice seed. Marcus Thompson searched for it in Kompong Som, to no avail. He was told that it had already been distributed in Kompong Som, Kampot and Takeo provinces. Later, Oxfam asked the Minister of Commerce where the seed had gone; he said he had no idea. Then the Ministry of Agriculture was told to search in all of the Ministry of Economy's warehouses. It was never found. Similarly, Thompson reported, "They have lost the clothes and sewing machines from Barge 1, and I do not know who the clothes from Barge 2 will actually reach."

It would have been absurd to expect efficiency from the fledgling government. Some of its officials were coping extraordinarily well with the vast problems involved in constructing an entirely new administration. Others were having difficulties. The aid officials' principal contact at the Foreign Ministry, Mr. Borith, a former medical student, had at first no paper, no typewriters, no files, no bicycle—and absolutely no experience.

Whatever the reasons, it was clear in Phnom Penh by November 1979 that the authorities were either unable or unwilling to provide the agencies with detailed or reliable information as to how their supplies were being used. But at the same time the donors were becoming more and more insistent that these supplies were being misused. Thus the conflicting pressures upon the handful of relief officials in Phnom Penh and on their superiors in the West became, at times, almost unbearable.

Paradoxically, their position was rendered more, not less, difficult after their knowledge of conditions in the countryside increased. The early visitors to Cambodia had been allowed only very limited tours. Throughout October and early November the teams pleaded with the government and its Vietnamese advisers to be allowed to visit the provinces. In the middle of November the requests were finally answered: several of them were allowed to travel around the Great Lake (the Tonle Sap)—around the heart of the country. They were surprised by what they saw.

Malcolm Harper and Hans Page went on one trip together. "We were looking everywhere for the famine," said Malcolm Harper later. "And yet we found no trace of it. People were poor, they were malnourished, they were badly clothed. But they were not dying of hunger." Harper recalls that outside Battambang their car passed a cyclist. The cloth blew off his pannier and Harper saw that it was filled not with food but with brand-new transistor radios, which evidently came from the Thai border. When Harper and Page returned to the Hotel Samaki, their colleagues were incredulous. "But I have been sent from Geneva to stop a famine," said François Bugnion of the ICRC. A few days later Bugnion himself went around the lake. To his astonishment he came to much the same conclusion; his detailed report of what he saw makes no mention of famine.

It was, to say the least, perplexing to the aid officials inside Cambodia. To the world outside it would be almost incomprehensible. Harper was not encouraged by Oxfam officials in Oxford to repeat to journalists what he had found.

In that outside world, the prevailing images were still from the border, and the prevailing fear was still of "two million dead by Christmas." Indeed, the Heng Samrin regime itself had once again reinforced such fears. Despite their public propaganda that there was no famine at all, in November officials had privately told the Joint Mission in Phnom Penh that the situation was even worse than they had previously stated. In July they had asked for supplies for 2.25 million people "threatened by famine." Now they actually increased this number to 3 million. In other words, three quarters of the 4 million Cambodians who they said had survived Pol Pot were now, according to their own account, threatened by famine. To aid officials in Phnom Penh this was hard to reconcile with what they had seen around the Lake. But on the outside it made the failures of distribution seem even more grotesque and indefensible.

On December 5, the White House declared that "the flow of aid is deliberately blocked by the Vietnamese and Heng Samrin authorities." It claimed that the holdups in Kompong Som were due to Vietnamese interference with schedules, that food was being diverted to troops or, at best, given to officials of the regime, and that rice fields were being mined. "In the face of widespread human anguish, this delay and diversion of humanitarian efforts is unconscionable." The White House called upon Vietnam "not to feed the flames of war, but use aircraft and airfields to ferry food to feed the people of

Kampuchea." A few days later James Reston wrote in *The New York Times* that the latest intelligence report to the President said that Moscow was actually blocking the distribution of food from other countries. He quoted Jimmy Carter as asking, "Is there no pity?"

In the face of such charges, UNICEF New York was constantly cabling John Saunders to ask, for instance, for "any real exposition" of what was actually going on. Labouisse and Egger reminded him that such allegations were seriously disturbing the donors at a time when the Joint Mission really needed to raise more money from them.

Saunders replied to such cables by repeating that the main problem was indeed shifting supplies from Kompong Som to Phnom Penh. Until that was solved there would be no large-scale distribution. He declared "here is no evidence of Vietnam using food as weapon to manipulate population or taking rice . . ." and repeated that the government's inexperience and the country's recent emergence "from a staggering ordeal" explained a great many of the problems.

Labouisse appreciated those problems, but in another cable he warned Saunders that UNICEF could not indefinitely blame the poor distribution on the inexperience of the government and the lack of transport, when offers of expert Western advice "and other assistance to improve rail, road and air shipments within the country are not acted upon."

On December 5, Saunders and François Bugnion of ICRC (who was much more critical of the government's performance than Saunders) wrote to Foreign Minister Hun Sen about the buildup of supplies in Kompong Som. "As friends of Kampuchea, we are obliged to draw the personal attention of your excellency to the extreme gravity of the crisis. The governments that have announced generous contributions of food assistance for the population of Kampuchea would not be able to understand why important quantities are still in the warehouses. . . . This situation will not fail to prejudice the image of Kampuchea in the eyes of the world. . . ." They urged immediate steps to improve distribution.

The next day Jean Pierre Hocke, the Operations Director of

ICRC, flew into Phnom Penh on the daily ICRC flight to voice his own concerns. Foreign Ministry officials were most helpful; they assured Hocke, Saunders and Bugnion that everything would be done to improve the unloading from Kompong Som and the river port at Phnom Penh. They said they were quite happy for the Joint Mission to hire Vietnamese trucks, to hire a Lao airplane for internal flights within Cambodia, and even for a United States C-5A Galaxy to land cranes for the docks at Phnom Penh. They also promised that the flight path of the ICRC plane from Bangkok could be shortened so that it no longer had to loop over Vietnam.

In a separate meeting, the Minister of Health told Hocke that they hoped that a Soviet medical team would soon arrive. Hocke asked for permission for a Swedish medical team; the Minister said he would be in favor of it. Later in the week Hun Sen confirmed what his officials had already agreed. He said he would look into the idea of a Swedish medical team.

The international officials were delighted. François Bugnion cabled Geneva to say that internal flights "would finally give the Joint Mission and relevant ministries the chance of mobility which is essential to be able to evaluate the situation and develop action better. It would equally permit faster distribution of medicine and food straight to the provinces."

It was another illusion. Despite the Foreign Minister's imprimatur, these promises were soon withdrawn by the Phnom Penh authorities. No internal flight would be allowed, the flight path of the daily ICRC plane could not be changed, and—perhaps because of an impolitic premature announcement by United States officials—the Galaxy was refused permission to deliver the cranes. (They were flown to Singapore and eventually arrived by ship.) No non-Communist medical team was allowed in until the fall of 1980.

All of this time the aid officials were giving very different accounts to their donors of what was happening inside Cambodia. Oxfam was the most bullish. On December 14, Brian Walker addressed a meeting of its consortium of voluntary agencies. He did not repeat Malcolm Harper's view that there was no famine, but said that "reports of misuse of aid and failure of distribution emanate from sources who had not visited the stabilized areas of Kampuchea." This concept of a "stabilized" area was original—what could have "stabilized" them? Walker also declared that the Oxfam team in Phnom Penh was able to move freely and had seen no misuse of aid. Later in the month Malcolm Harper came back from Phnom Penh; in London he gave a press conference in which he carefully praised the honesty and dedication of officials in the Heng Samrin regime.

In New York, Henry Labouisse said that the United States intelligence allegations of deliberate diversion of supplies "may give a false impression of what the facts are." He said that Soviet trucks had just arrived at Kompong Som and so had the Soviet dockers. Nonetheless, he said, "there may be some truth" in the charges. By contrast, Jacques Danois, UNICEF's information officer in Bangkok, a longtime supporter of Hanoi, was at pains to emphasize the most positive aspects of Vietnamese rule in Cambodia.

This was not Jean Pierre Hocke's view. When he came out of Phnom Penh to Bangkok he was quoted in *The New York Times* as saying that food was not being properly distributed inside Cambodia; he warned that the Joint Mission could not continue shipping it indefinitely unless distribution was improved. The *Times* ran an editorial declaring that "Phnom Penh and its friends keep saying the hunger isn't disastrous. Cambodia's refugees in Thailand say it is, and their bodies show plain evidence. Whatever one calls it, the lack of food has killed many people, food remains in short supply, and Phnom Penh and Hanoi refuse to give full support to those most able to help. . . . Phnom Penh, Hanoi and Moscow are making any civilized arrangement more difficult with their cynical tolerance of starvation when there is food at hand. They must be doing something very, very wrong when they drive professional feeders of the hungry to start talking about withholding food."

In Phnom Penh, Saunders was alarmed by Hocke's criticisms of the government. He wrote to New York, "Since ICRC has some tendency to be less patient and flexible than we are in dealing with nonstop run of problems, it is very important we speak in public with a common approach." Later Hocke said that he had been misquoted, but at a donors meeting in New York, where ICRC and UNICEF were appealing for more money, he agreed that only between 10 and 20 percent of the supplies delivered had been distributed.

All this reflected not only the incoherence of Western perceptions of Cambodia, but also the incoherence of the actual relief effort itself. Within the U.N. system Waldheim had appointed UNICEF the lead agency, but he had never properly defined just what that involved. Many U.N. officials were skeptical—wrongly, as it happened—about UNICEF's ability to coordinate a program as vast as the Cambodia operation. Within UNICEF, there was considerable concern that the lead-agency role was diverting too much of its manpower resources from other essential programs throughout the world.

In UNICEF's New York headquarters, the operation was under the daily control of Robert Walker. Charles Egger, the deputy executive director, devoted much of his time to Cambodia in the second half of 1979. So did Henry Labouisse until his retirement at the end of the year. The Geneva office concentrated on fund raising, particularly from the EEC. Throughout, the EEC was one of the operation's principal backers, and the Commissioner Claude Cheysson one of its most consistent advocates. But UNICEF had no control over those funds that the donors had actually allocated (rather than just pledged) and therefore no real authority over its partners in the operation. The program lurched from one financial crisis to another as expenditures overran actual income. As often as not, it was UNICEF that had to bail out the other U.N. organizations. That it was able to do so often reflected Charles Egger's experience of where money was to be found in which government treasuries, and the organization's own flexibility.

Coherence might have been imposed by a Secretary General willing to take risks. But by the end of 1979 Kurt Waldheim appeared to many U.N. diplomats and officials to be so preoccupied with his own reelection campaign that he was more than usually cautious. He was especially anxious not to alienate the Soviet Union or its allies. The donors found this increasingly irritating.

The Western allies, Japan and their ASEAN partners considered that Waldheim should be doing far more to implement the ASEAN resolution on Cambodia that the General Assembly had passed overwhelmingly in November. Why was he not working for an international conference, U.N.-supervised elections and the withdrawal of foreign troops, as the resolution required? Thailand had also been asking him to declare the border a "safe haven" and station U.N. observers along it.

But it was clear that Waldheim had no intention of pressing any of these issues. Take, for example, a report to Canberra from Australia's Permanent Representative in December. He said that Waldheim had told him that the Vietnamese had continually rejected the idea of a safe haven along the border. The Vietnamese had also said that they would not attack refugee encampments along the border, but had reserved the right to attack any resistance forces and to exercise hot pursuit into Thailand. He said flatly that he saw no prospects for any international conference such as the ASEAN resolution required. Asked how he intended, then, to implement the resolution, Waldheim replied, rather defensively, that he was already carrying out its humanitarian aspects and intended to visit Bangkok and Hanoi next month. "The Vietnamese were, however, extremely difficult people, and they were receiving strong political support from the USSR."

Summing up, the Ambassador concluded:

> Conversation yielded little that was new. Call probably had its uses, however, as a further expression of international concern at present situation and hence a further point of pressure on the Secretary General who, without always bearing the imprint of his latest visitor, is usually sensitive and responsive to pressures from most quarters. In the last analysis Waldheim will not take action which will offend or be opposed by the USSR. His margin for manoeuvre is limited by his office, by his hopes for re-election and by his temperamental circumspection. But in most cases, the more pressure that can be brought to bear upon him, the better the prospect that some action will be taken.

But there was at least one significant action that Waldheim had been prepared to take. He had invited one of the United Nations' most redoubtable servants, Sir Robert Jackson, to become (as of January 1, 1980) his "special representative with responsibility for co-ordinating on his behalf, in close co-operation with all the U.N. organisations concerned, the recent humanitarian programmes resulting from the developments in Kampuchea." In other words, Jackson was to try to impose some order on an operation that now involved some five international organizations, sixty voluntary organizations and the interest of at least sixty governments.

Robert Jackson, Under Secretary General, KCVO, OBE, CMG, knight bachelor, invariably known within the U.N. as "Jacko," has spent his life as an international civil servant. Born in 1911, he has both Australian and British nationality, and his biography is a roll call of international action. Chief Staff Officer, Malta, 1939–40; Director General Middle East Supply Centre, Cairo, 1941–44; Senior Deputy Director General, U.N. Relief and Rehabilitation Agency, 1945–47; Planning Commission, India and Pakistan, 1952–53; Commissioner Volta River Project, Gold Coast/Ghana, 1957–60, and so on. In the last thirty years he has worked for the United Nations in a large number of developing countries, including India, Pakistan, Ghana and Liberia, as well as in New York.

In 1969 Jackson produced "The Capacity Study," an examination of how best the U.N. system could be coordinated in the interests of the developing world. Unlike most U.N. documents, the "Capacity Study" was well written. In it Jackson argued that the U.N.'s thirty-or-so specialized agencies had developed into independent principalities. They needed a central coordinator—which, he suggested, should be the U.N. Development Program.*

* Jackson wrote the foreword to the "Capacity Study" in the form of an open letter to the head of state of a developing country he knew well. He said he was convinced that the United Nations was the best instrument for assisting developing countries to achieve social change, and there was now an unprecedented opportunity to revitalize the U.N. Development system, if inertia did not prevent it.

The problem was that the system had about thirty separate and uncoordinated parts, which failed to work well together. "At the headquarters level, there is no real 'Headpiece'—no central coordinating organization—which could exercise effective control. Below headquarters the administrative tentacles thrust downward into an extraordinary complex of regional and sub-regional offices and finally extend into field offices in over ninety developing countries."

He thought this "Machine" now had an identity of its own and was neither controlled by governments nor capable of intelligently controlling itself. "This is not because it lacks intelligent and capable officials, but be-

He knew that such recommendations would be resisted. The specialized agencies wanted to surrender no independence, UNDP did not want the burden of coordinating them and, after the experience of Dag Hammarskjöld's activism, many governments had shied away from allowing the United Nations to have a strong, centralized and effective managerial system. In the ten years that followed the publication of "The Capacity Study," the problems of underdevelopment which it was supposed to address became more serious, but the U.N.'s principalities grew, if anything, more independent and less well coordinated, as was to become clear during the Cambodian crisis.

Characteristically, Waldheim never gave Jackson a precise written definition of his job. After accepting, Jackson said later, "I tried to find out what the actual needs of the Cambodians were. Then those needs had to be fitted in with what the Thai Government saw as its requirements." He flew down to Washington to try to persuade

---

cause it is so organized that managerial direction is impossible." As a result, the machine was "becoming slower and more unwieldy like some prehistoric monster."

Jackson saw that consolidating all the components of the machine into a single organization was impossible. But he thought that greater development cooperation could be achieved by restructuring the U.N. Development Program so that it provided strong central coordination of the specialized agencies. However, he knew that many of the agencies would resist any coordination. "Supported by governments, most of them have now become the equivalent of principalities, free from any centralized control. Over the years, like all such institutions, they have learned to safeguard and increase their powers, to preserve their independence, and to resist change. . . ." The core of Jackson's proposals was to provide UNDP with the power of the purse. By controlling the bulk of the funds provided for international development, UNDP would be able to exercise sufficient authority over the specialized agencies to ensure that the U.N. system's programs of development at the national level would be reasonably well coordinated. Such a scheme worked well in Bangladesh.

There was now an unprecedented opportunity for the world to review its policies toward its own poor, "yet, tragically, too many people—including too many leaders of the affluent states—now appear to believe that the plight of two thirds of mankind can be safely swept under the political rug and left there." He concluded by ruminating on "the ultimate folly of nuclear weapons" and declared that "the Twentieth Century, on its record so far, could well be called the 'Century of Destruction.' Never before has Mankind destroyed so much of its inheritance so quickly. We still have time to do the most constructive job in the history of the world."

the United States government to agree to give him centralized control over at least some of the funds for the operation. If Washington would make its own contribution (which worked out eventually at about a third of the entire program) directly to the Secretary General—as it had done in the Bangladesh operation—some co-ordination would be possible. It would not. Jackson failed. "The agencies all have very effective lobbies in Washington," he said later. "None of them wanted to surrender any financial independence." Nor, apparently, did the White House wish to surrender its own power of the purse to Jackson. Even so, Jackson's work was to be essential.

Jackson has a meticulous memory and loves to reminisce—hardly a meeting goes by when he will not recall *en passant* how he overcame supply problems in Malta, Bengal, the USSR, or Bangladesh. Such experience, and the joy of repeating it, was often irritating to younger bureaucrats and place men within the U.N. system. Inevitably, in a lifetime at the U.N., a place more obsessed than most with polishing protocol, Jackson had made enemies as well as many friends in various principalities. He had clashed in particular with senior officials of the Food and Agriculture Organization and of the High Commissioner for Refugees.

During December 1979 Jackson made a preliminary tour of some of those principalities and went to Bangkok. (He did not go to Phnom Penh for another five months, for fear that this would be taken by the Thais and other governments as giving the Secretary General's imprimatur to the Heng Samrin regime.)

He was dismayed by the fact that the agencies were embarked on programs that expired at the end of March 1980. Yet, in Cambodia food production is governed by the monsoon, which begins in May; the main rice crop is not harvested until the end of the year. Jackson felt that the emergency program should continue until at least the end of 1980. He also felt that it was essential that the agencies "speak with one voice." Now no one had a clue as to what everyone else was doing.*

* This view was shared by John Saunders in Phnom Penh. In one message in response to New York's criticism that information was not being properly coordinated among agencies, Saunders said:

"You have to take into account:

. . .

Christmas 1979 was a rather mixed feast in the Samaki hotel. The promises given to Jean Pierre Hocke were quite clearly not being fulfilled. Two French engineers who had come at the request of the Ministry of Transport to help with the repair of railway engines were allowed to do absolutely nothing and were then asked to leave. And when a UNICEF official went down to Ho Chi Minh City to finalize the arrangements—agreed to by Prime Minister Pham Van Dong and Labouisse, as well as by Hun Sen and Hocke—for the hire of Vietnamese trucks and barges, he was told that none was available after all.

John Saunders and Jean Hoefliger, who was replacing François Bugnion for ICRC, had written another letter to the government complaining about poor distribution of food. Like the first, it led to no clear improvement. Saunders sent a message to Labouisse saying that "this program is at the same time the most difficult and the most vital of any I have ever known." He urged Labouisse, who was about to retire, to write to President Heng Samrin, to point out that the Joint Mission had already had to cut back shipments and might have to do so again unless distribution improved. Labouisse did so.

The authorities were reacting with obvious impatience to criticism. John Saunders informed the UNICEF office in Bangkok, "We

"A. Discrepancy in the approach of the various agencies in Phnom Penh.
"B. Discrepancy between the actual situation observed by everybody in Kampuchea and its image sent to the outside.
"C. Discrepancies between the agencies here and the over-all policy of their HQs.
"D. Discrepancy between operational informations and their dispatch to the medias.
"E. The tremendous discrepancy between reports and coverage of Thailand's operations and ours, which still remains, though not officially, one of the main problems here."

In another cable Saunders offered other explanations for the "gap in mutual understanding." He thought that even though all the agencies in Phnom Penh lived together in the Samaki and shared information, their understanding of what was really happening in the countryside was very scanty. And their communications with the world outside were so poor that they were in fact isolated in Phnom Penh. There was no way they could keep up with the various Western arguments about what exactly was taking place in Cambodia.

have been subjected to an endless series of harassments at the airport (visas, customs, security searches of aircraft, diplomatic pouches) all in a spirit of making life difficult rather than showing co-operation.''

By contrast, Guy Stringer, who had come back for Oxfam for a spell, was heartened by the progress made since his first trip in October. He thought that his decision to have the consortium invest in industrial reconstruction was clearly paying off. Jim Howard's proposal that Oxfam help restore Phnom Penh waterworks appeared to be well justified.

On Christmas night Stringer went to the Phnom Penh port, which had finally been opened for shipping.* One of Oxfam's barges was being unloaded there. The Filipino crew, reported Stringer, "are devout men and had rigged up a loudspeaker on which were played the old traditional hymns of Christendom: it was strange to sit beside the brown waters of the Mekong hearing these ancient melodies—to my infinite regret the last tune on the cassette was 'Rudolf The Red-Nosed Reindeer.' "

Other celebrations were less enjoyable. John Saunders and some of his colleagues were invited to a formal meal with the Cambodian managers of the Samaki hotel and their Vietnamese advisers. Saunders was acutely embarrassed by the contempt which the Vietnamese displayed for the Cambodians. Other aid officials, including Jean Clavaud of the World Council of Churches, Paul Jones of World Vision and Ebel Dykstra of the Oxfam consortium, were invited to the house of a Cambodian Christian, Ung Sophal, a former Sunday-school teacher. But the Vietnamese were not encouraging religious freedom, and soon afterward Sophal was arrested, accused of working for the CIA and thrown into prison. He was locked in a windowless cell in solitary confinement and fed almost nothing. Eventually he became very sick and was removed to a hospital. He finally escaped and made his way to the Thai border in 1981.

Over-all still hung the crisis of food distribution. Concern was

---

* Vietnam had caused much unfavorable Western comment by imposing fees of about $9,000 for any relief ship transiting Vietnam by the Mekong. In Oxfam's case these had been reduced by $1,200, thanks to the intervention of Mr. Bui Huu Nhan, the Vietnamese adviser to the Foreign Ministry in Phnom Penh.

increased—at least among ICRC and UNICEF staff in Thailand—by the arrival on the Thai border of a defector from the Heng Samrin regime. He was Hieng Mea Nuont, and he had been Chef du Cabinet of the Minister of Commerce for the last four months. He was President of the "Reception Committee for Humanitarian Aid." Now, interviewed by ICRC delegates in Thailand, he said that he had not been able to talk freely to aid officials in Phnom Penh because so many people were "agents." He said the Vietnamese did not like the foreign-aid officials, but the Cambodian people did. He said that much of the food was being shipped to Vietnam and only a tiny portion was being distributed to ordinary people in Cambodia. He claimed that much of the food distributed in front of aid officials was collected again after their departure. The bulk was being stored and would be sold to people after a currency had been reintroduced. He said that he had fled after learning that he was to be arrested for suggesting better distribution to the people. ICRC and UNICEF did what they could to keep his story completely secret.

13 ❧ On the Border

Thousands of small huts were crammed higgledy-piggledy together. Piles of melon skins, chicken bones, beer bottles, empty tin cans, plastic bags lay over the ground. A stream running through them, low because it was the dry season now, contained only a foul-smelling slick of sewage. A little girl squatting to defecate was at once covered in a cloud of flies—flies were like a film over the camp. There was no running water; when the tanks filled daily by the ICRC ran dry, early, people bathed and washed their clothes in the dank stream. Arrogant young soldiers, some with ancient weapons, some with new, prowled around the camp overseeing food distribution, arresting newcomers, sometimes shooting those who tried to leave.

Mak Moun—a rural slum, the largest of the Cambodian encampments along the Thai-Cambodian border, an unsettling limbo of poverty, extortion and menace, where murders were rife and the threat of artillery attack, by Vietnamese or Thai troops, was constant—was controlled until spring 1980 by a man named Van Saren.

Van Saren walked around the camp in a pork-pie hat, with a large crucifix around his neck, surrounded by a troupe of young men armed with automatic rifles. He said he used to be a captain in Lon Nol's army. In fact he was at best a lieutenant, and there was some doubt about even that. He called himself "Marshal," and he claimed to be the most honorable of the Khmer Serei, or "Free Khmers," who sought to liberate Cambodia from both the Vietnamese and the Khmer Rouge. In fact, he was a teak smuggler during the Pol Pot period, a man with close links to corrupt Thai officials, and he apparently had a rather comfortable house a few miles back from the border inside Thailand. Those links were perhaps just too close; in April 1980 Van Saren and his closest lieutenants were murdered, apparently by Thai soldiers.

Van Saren was leader of what he called "The National Liberation Movement of Cambodia." The absurdity of his rule was compounded by the fact that his self-styled "Minister of Defense" was an unbalanced American freebooter named Gary Ferguson, who wore a Colt-45 stuck in his paunch and shouted instead of talking. Ferguson claimed that Van Saren was his "father" as well as the father and savior of all Cambodia, and he threatened to blow out the brains of anyone who demurred. Almost every day he got into fights with the ICRC doctors who came to the camp for a few hours to try to run a hospital. The ICRC staff left their patients every afternoon—they said that the constant shooting on the border rendered it too dangerous for them to stay after dark. There was no way in which the ICRC was able to carry out its protection function under the Geneva Conventions here.

Van Saren's real strength did not lie in his so-called "Minister of Defense" or just in his troupes of young bandits. It was provided to him by UNICEF and the ICRC—in large sacks. Food was power along the border, just as it was inside Cambodia. Part of the history of the border was to be of Thailand's attempts first to build up the different resistance groups and then to coerce them into an anti-Vietnamese alliance. Food and the organizations that supplied it were important parts of the struggle.

The border was divided, both by geography and to suit the political and military imperatives of the Thai government, into three sectors. There was the northern sector, where Thailand curves east toward the Mekong around Cambodia's northern border; here the frontier was guarded by the Dangrek mountains. There was the southern sector, where the thickly wooded Phnom Malai mountain range performed the same function. And there was the central sector, known confusingly as the "northwest sector," a sparsely wooded plain, the only possible invasion route from the east. Mak Moun was here, just north of Aranyaprathet. It was to this sector that most refugees came. It was this sector that Thailand was most anxious to defend. And it was this sector to which, for both those reasons, foreign relief agencies were allowed most access.

After the victory of the Khmer Rouge in 1975, various small groups of Free Khmers had been formed, in the shadowy no man's land along the border. It was not Thai government policy to seek an open confrontation with the Khmer Rouge, but many such groups had been tolerated by local Thai army officers or the Thai border police. Some had links with the intelligence or special-operations branches of the army. Others had support from exile groups in France or the United States. But none was impressive; for the most part they smuggled teak, gems, small amounts of gold and occasional statues out of Kampuchea. It was the massive 1979 exodus from Cambodia that gave them both aspirations and power.

Refugees had begun to gather in huge numbers in the early fall, as the fighting between Vietnamese and Khmer Rouge spread, as it became clear that the harvest would be very poor, as concern about Vietnamese intentions grew, and as the rumors spread throughout the country that there was food available at the border. There were moments of great joy and reconciliation there, as people feared lost under the Khmer Rouge emerged from the four-year horror and sent word to their friends or relatives that they had survived.*

By the end of 1979 there were said to be about 600,000, or even 750,000, people along the border. No one knew. But there were obvious emotional (as well as political) reasons for assuming that vast numbers of Cambodians must be trying to flee the "holocaust" that was thought to be threatening Cambodia at that time.

* One of the best-known such reconciliations was between Sidney Schanberg, the *New York Times* reporter who covered the fall of Phnom Penh, and Dith Pran, his Cambodian colleague. Pran had been compelled, like other Cambodians, to leave the sanctuary of the French Embassy in Phnom Penh in April 1975 and had been marched into the countryside. For the next four years, Schanberg feared that he must have been killed. Then in spring 1979, a message arrived in New York, via an East German correspondent who had visited Cambodia, that "Dith Pran, survivor" was still alive. A few months later he made his way to the border. The story will be told in David Puttnam's 1984 film, *The Killing Fields*.

The largest war lord was Van Saren at Mak Moun. He claimed that there were 400,000 Cambodians in his camp and for some time this was not disputed, though there were probably fewer than half that number. A few miles away from Mak Moun, the camp of Nong Samet was presided over by a thinner, slightly more serious-looking Khmer named In Sakhan who, with a number of other former soldiers from the Lon Nol army, had promulgated the "Khmer Angkor Movement." In Sakhan was marginally less vicious than Van Saren. The camp was better organized, civilians had more chance of being freely fed, there was a sense of community—schools, cafés, temples— but armed soldiers still dominated the place.

The third principal non-Communist camp north of Aranyaprathet was called Nong Chan. It was run by a former officer in the Cambodian navy named Kong Sileah, who was loyal to Sihanouk. He called his movement Moulinaka (*"Mouvement National de Libération de Kampuchea"*). Kong Sileah insisted that his troops stay separate from the civilians in Nong Chan; his camp was much the most honest and the least terrorized of the Khmer Serei border sites.

There was one Khmer Rouge camp, named Phnom Chat, north of Aranyaprathet. The leaders there claimed that they were not hardline Khmer Rouge, but were "born again." The principal Khmer Rouge camps in the "northwest" sector were two small enclaves just south of Aranyaprathet, Nong Pru and Ta Prik. These were the places to which the dying skeletons had stumbled in September and October 1979, the people whose photographs had helped invoke Western visions of a new holocaust. By the end of 1979 there were perhaps 30,000 people here.

All these camps in the central "northwest" sector were the responsibility of the Joint Mission of ICRC and UNICEF, who were by the end of 1979 delivering about 600,000 rations to them. They were relatively accessible to both relief workers and journalists. There were other parts of the border where almost no foreigners were ever allowed.

Thai Supreme Command claimed that there were about 70,000 refugees in the mountainous northern and southern sectors, but no one was allowed to check whether they were real refugees, whether they were Khmer Rouge soldiers or whether they were "phantom refugees," like the "phantom soldiers" who had padded the payrolls of corrupt commanders in the Lon Nol army and had helped march their brave comrades to defeat. There was also a small camp belonging to the "Khmer People's National Liberation Front." This was the most serious of the non-Communist resistance groups and was led by a distinguished former Prime Minister of Cambodia from the Sihanouk era, Son Sann.

UNICEF and ICRC were not involved at all in these sections of the border. Instead, the Royal Thai Army had a discreet relationship with the World Food Program, which simply delivered food to army warehouses for disposal as the army wished. Internal World Food Program memoranda show that U.N. officials were well aware that the food was used by the Thai army to feed either the Khmer Rouge and other resistance groups, or for other purposes than aiding starving Cambodian refugees. But WFP did not make even a pretense at monitoring or questioning what was going on.*

Similarly the World Food Program delivered considerable quantities of food to the Thai army for the express purpose of feeding "displaced Thai villagers." These were people along the border whose lives had been disrupted by the influx of refugees. There were undoubtedly tens of thousands of such people—some had had to flee their homes; some had had their water table disrupted by the massive influx of refugees; some had had their fields destroyed—but once again no one knew just how many. An American Embassy estimate was that there were about 70,000; the Thai government's estimate was 200,000. On average, 85,000 daily rations were supplied over 1979–83.

Thus, by the end of 1979, food was being delivered to many different groups under widely differing conditions. The largest amount was going to the Heng Samrin regime in Phnom Penh—and was, for the most part, still in warehouses.

In Thailand, it was being delivered to the holding centers like

---

* Among other bizarre WFP deliveries were those to 30,000 or even sometimes 50,000 people supposedly living on Khong Island off the coast of Thailand close to the Cambodian border. No one knew who these people were or even whether, as seemed quite likely, they were fictional. In any case, rations were delivered to the Thai army for them, regardless of reality.

Sa Kaeo and Khao I Dang set up by the High Commissioner for Refugees inside the country. Here it was well monitored.

Food was being delivered by UNICEF-ICRC to border camps like Mak Moun and Nong Samet, where massive diversions were taking place, but where civilians were being fed. Similarly in the Khmer Rouge camps in the "northwest" sector.

Food was being handed over by the World Food Program to the Royal Thai Army for its own uses in the northern and southern sectors and for displaced Thai villagers.

Finally, food was being put across the border into Cambodia on the human "land bridge."

It was a fantastic sight. In clouds of dust over tracks from the west came a daily convoy of trucks each laden with thirteen tons of rice. Moving much more slowly over trails from the east came a far longer convoy of hundreds upon hundreds of old but often beautifully crafted oxcarts, rickety bicycles strapped together with bamboo, and thousands upon thousands of Cambodians. Perhaps nowhere in the world were so many oxcarts with their oxen and their drivers gathered together at one time.

The two convoys would meet at the border camp of Nong Chan. Their heads covered in their checkered scarves, or *kramars,* the Cambodians waited with extraordinary patience in the full heat of the dry-season sun. The trucks were unloaded, and one by one, or family by family, the Cambodians were given rice—twenty kilos per person or forty kilos per oxcart. They then turned around and set off back down the trails, back home into Cambodia. Such was "the land bridge."

In December 1979, after the Heng Samrin regime refused to open the road or the railroad from Aranyaprathet into Cambodia— which would undoubtedly have been the most effective way of shipping a large amount of food into the country for the regime's own distribution—an informal system was begun beyond its control. It was devised by Kong Sileah, the former Cambodian naval officer, and Robert Ashe, the British relief worker who had tried, back in 1977, to interest Jimmy Carter and the British government in Khmer Rouge atrocities. In a relief operation that was filled with extraordinary programs, it was one of the most remarkable.

Ashe was now working for the ICRC. In October and November he had helped to rescue the debris of humanity who struggled to the border in the Khmer Rouge camps south of Aranyaprathet. Then at Nong Chan he met with Kong Sileah who, unlike the other border warlords, was attempting to run an uncorrupt camp where civilians were fed. Kong Sileah suggested that food should be distributed at Nong Chan for Cambodians to take home to the interior. On condition that armed soldiers keep out of the camp, Ashe agreed to try the idea and UNICEF agreed to provide the food. The United States Embassy was enthusiastic. On December 12, 1979, two UNICEF trucks, each carrying 135 sacks of rice, drew up in Nong Chan. The sacks were handed over to Cambodians.

News of the operation spread much faster than Ashe had expected. By Christmas 1979 twelve trucks of rice a day were being distributed at Nong Chan. Encouraged by the good order of the site, the ICRC built a hospital.

The success of Nong Chan threatened the profits of Van Saren at Mak Moun and of his Thai military patrons. At the end of December 1979 Van Saren's troops attacked; the hospital was burned down, and the land bridge was cut. But Ashe and the Cambodians rebuilt the camp, and ICRC agreed to run a new hospital. By early 1980 well over one hundred thousand people were coming each week from the interior to pick up rice. Most of them were from Cambodia's western provinces, but a few came much greater distances; some said they had walked for fifteen or twenty days. They were nearly all peasants and they usually reported, predictably perhaps, that little or no food was being distributed to them by the government in Phnom Penh. They said also that the Vietnamese army did not stop them from coming to the border, but that, on their return, Vietnamese troops often took a toll of their supplies.

The land bridge was interrupted several times during 1980, but by the end of that year about 148,500 tons of rice had been distributed over it. There was no way that its end use could be monitored, of course. Certainly some of it was sold in other camps along the border or made its way back into Thailand. But there was no reason to doubt that most of it was going back into Cambodia, not under the control of officials but on the backs, on the bicycles and in the carts, of the ordinary people of the country.

. . .

In some ways the operation mounted in the "northwest" sector of the border by UNICEF and the ICRC was a logistic miracle. The feeding had begun on a vast scale in November 1979, in the same atmosphere of panic that informed the delivery of supplies to Cambodia itself. Conditions along the border were chaotic. Months of monsoon rain had turned tracks into muddy streams. Few if any of the foreign-aid workers knew where Thailand ended and Cambodia began. (There were irregular concrete markers placed at the time of the Franco-Thai border treaty in 1907, but this delineation was fiercely disputed.)

UNICEF brought in an energetic and combative middle-thirties Swede named Ulf Kristofferson to organize the border operation. Kristofferson knew Indochina well; he had a Lao wife, and he had worked for UNICEF in both Laos and Cambodia; he was in Phnom Penh until the Khmer Rouge victory in 1975. When the border crisis broke, he was summoned from Bangladesh. Originally it was a short-term appointment, but the crisis lingered and so Kristofferson stayed almost three years in Aranyaprathet, becoming in many senses the baron of the border.

Food for the border, as for the UNHCR holding centers inside Thailand and as for Phnom Penh, was procured by the World Food Program. For the sake of convenience and cheapness—and at Thai insistence—most of it was purchased inside Thailand, a rice-exporting country. Kristofferson organized a sophisticated warehouse near Aranyaprathet. By the end of 1979 convoys of between ninety and a hundred trucks were driving 2,500 tons of rice for the resident population along the border every week. Fleets of tankers took 650,000 liters of chlorinated water there daily. Quite apart from the drivers, UNICEF was employing 200 Thais to help in the operation. But UNICEF managed to keep its expatriate staff on the border to fewer than ten.

Kristofferson prided himself on the fact that there were almost no losses or thefts from UNICEF's warehouses. It was at the border that the trouble began. In the early days it was virtually impossible to do anything more than guess—to the nearest ten thousand—how many people were in different sites. And the aid officials decided that it was impossible to do anything but dump food at the feet of those who appeared to be in charge in both the Khmer Rouge and the Khmer Serei camps. This was a fateful decision; it meant that the organizations had no better control of food along the border than they did inside Cambodia itself.

A lot of rice was freely distributed to the ordinary people for whom it was intended. But a lot was also being sold to them by corrupt warlords. Some found its way back into the Thai wholesale market, and a part of this was even sold a second time around to the World Food Program, which had just purchased it. In this regard, some camps were worse than others, and Mak Moun was probably worst of all. One UNICEF report suggested that fully 84 percent of the food delivered there was being diverted away from the hungry civilians for whom it was intended. A United States government paper acknowledged that it was "not possible to say to what extent food may be diverted to military as opposed to civilian refugees, but under the border circumstances, there is probably little that could be done about it. While the reports are not uniform, the impression is that food is reaching and sustaining the civilian refugees while also going to the military."

With the profits they made from sales of the U.N.-donated food, some camp commanders were able to amass fortunes and to purchase more arms and thereby increase their control over the populations they exploited. It was for this reason that they disliked so intensely the experiment with honesty being conducted by Kong Sileah at Nong Chan, and why they tried, unsuccessfully, to destroy the camp and the land bridge at the end of 1979.

Many of the activities along the border were controlled by Colonel Prachak Sawaengchit, the commander of the Royal Thai Army's Second Infantry Regiment, a close ally of Prime Minister Kriangsak Chamanand, a Senator, and a man eager for even more power. His career and methods bear some examination; they help to show the conditions under which international organizations were operating along the border.

Prachak was keen on the idea of "charisma." He dressed smartly and used to carry a flask of brandy. He had fought with Thai troops in South Vietnam, where he attempted to distinguish himself by achieving high body counts of dead Communists. On his return to Thailand he was sent to combat Communist insurgents in the north, a task he performed with vigor. By the time he was promoted to lieutenant colonel in 1974 he was recognized as a high flyer among a group of young officers who were known as the "Young Turks." This group played a part in the bloody military coup which overthrew Thailand's democratic government in 1976; Prachak was rewarded with a Senate seat and a command along the Cambodian border at Aranyaprathet.

After the Khmer Rouge murdered Thai civilians along the border in January 1977, Prachak ordered a retaliatory shelling of the Khmer town of Poipet across the stream from Aranyaprathet. But his government did not seek a military confrontation with the Khmer Rouge regime and he was ordered to desist. He then actually fired upon the helicopter of the Interior Minister. He was relieved of his command and sent off to pasture in a military academy. But after the Young Turks helped Kriangsak Chamanand into power in October 1977 he was restored to favor. Early in 1979 he was reassigned to the border.

In the fall of 1979 Kriangsak made him a member of Thailand's delegation to the U.N. General Assembly—one of "the noble Thais" praised by Canada's Foreign Minister Flora Macdonald, at the pledging conference—and then, after a six-week world tour, he was appointed commander of the Second Infantry Regiment at Aranyaprathet at the height of the border crisis. He used to take a helicopter ride to Bangkok at least once a week for late-night drinking and consultations at the Prime Minister's house near the airport. With such connections and with his avowed political ambitions, the international agency officials found Prachak a formidable interlocutor, if not adversary, at times.

Mark Brown, the young British journalist who ran first Sa Kaeo and then Khao I Dang holding centers for UNHCR, found Prachak easy to deal with. The two men shared a certain elegance and a taste for brandy. The relationship evidently contributed to the ease and efficiency with which Brown and UNHCR built and then ran Khao I Dang. Other agencies had more problems. Ulf Kristofferson, UNICEF's border coordinator, met Prachak for the first time when soldiers stopped a UNICEF convoy of trucks en route to the border and demanded one truckload for themselves. Kristofferson began to argue. Then he saw the stylish figure of Prachak sauntering over.

The Colonel was fairly explicit. Either his men had a truck now or the entire border feeding program would be ended. Kristofferson stood his ground, but rather than prolong the confrontation he said, "Let me take the whole convoy through now and if I get permission from my office in Bangkok to give you a truck, you can have it tomorrow." Eventually Prachak agreed. Subsequently UNICEF decided that since the World Food Program was already handing over so much to the Thai Army, it should provide a truckload of supplies to please the Colonel.

This was certainly prudent, for Prachak did not like to be contradicted. Once when an American embassy official challenged him over some problem, Prachak's reply was to take his pistol out and place the end of the barrel on the man's temple. In February 1980, Prachak unilaterally closed down the land bridge in protest against a decision by Supreme Command to set up another military unit, named Task Force 80, to oversee the border relief operation instead of Prachak. (This decision reflected one of the many tensions in what the Vietnamese like to call "Thai ruling circles." Supreme Command objected to Prachak's use of the frontier as his personal fiefdom. On many occasions Supreme Command, the National Security Council, the Foreign Ministry, and the army had different views as to how border policy should be made.) It took considerable pressure from the United States government on Prime Minister Kriangsak to have the land bridge reopened. In May 1980, Prachak ordered a suspension of all food and water to the residents at Nong Chan. By subterfuge, and with the help of Colonel Kitti of Task Force 80, Prachak's rival, Ulf Kristofferson, got provisions to the camp. Fearing Prachak's revenge, Kristofferson then drove straight to Bangkok to hide for a few days till the Colonel's temper cooled.

Prachak also considered that it was the duty of UNICEF and ICRC to pay for the building of new roads from the main road into the border camps at Mak Moun and Nong Samet. Before the organizations had a chance to agree he went ahead, built the roads, and then presented them with a bill for $125,000 for construction costs.

These accounts were presented on little scraps of paper, like receipts in an inexpensive restaurant—"Bill for one road."

Ulf Kristofferson sent him a gentle letter to remind him, "Under UNICEF price procedures, we have to request you to provide a detailed specification of the costs involved, and upon receipt of the said detailed specification, we will then be in a position to pay our share of the costs." Eventually UNICEF paid for the road—with a check made out directly to Prachak.*

No one knows how much Prachak was able to make out of the food delivered by World Food Program or UNICEF-ICRC to their respective sectors of the border. But out of the whole border he made a fortune. He also controlled much of the commerce in and around Aranyaprathet. This was on a truly fabulous scale.

It was not just rice that Cambodians wanted at the end of 1979. In the preceding ten years an incalculable amount of their national and personal wealth had been destroyed. Every Cambodian family had lost what much of the world takes as essentials. Now the nation began to restock itself—in a unique, open-air bazaar along the Thai border at places like Mak Moun and Nong Samet. It must have been the greatest open-air market in the world. Almost everything you can imagine was available there.

Every day thousands of Thai traders set off in brand-new pickup trucks from Aranyaprathet and Tapraya, a town just to the north, laden with goods for sale. They had to pass through dozens of Colonel Prachak's checkpoints; at each a few baht would be paid for the privilege. Cloth, plates, knives and forks, cups, bottles, sandals, fishhooks, string, flashlights, batteries, candles, matches, whisky, beer, drugs, lipsticks, radios, firearms, cigarettes, cassettes of prerevolutionary pop music, perfume, car tires and spare parts, cameras, soap, shampoo, canned food, ribbons, tools, teapots, rope, toothpaste, chains, hypodermics, stereos—everything necessary for everyday life

* Subsequently, Prachak sent Ulf Kristofferson another bill for 375,000 baht ($18,500) for another road into Nong Chan. This time there had been no prior discussion at all. Kristofferson wrote to his office in Bangkok: "No commitments whatsoever have been made from this office for the construction of this road, however, we are informed that ICRC have already paid a 50% share of the expenses." At the very least, Kristofferson felt, UNICEF should not pay for the "land compensation" itemized on the bill. It did not.

and a lot that was not could soon be had for sale in the fields along the frontier.

The sums of money that changed hands were staggering, almost unbelievable. On some days up to $500,000 worth of gold poured out of Cambodia across the border. For the last four years it had been desperately hidden from the Khmer Rouge—possession of wealth could easily be a capital offense—and now it flooded in a torrent out of the country. The ingenuity with which it had been hidden and the excitement with which it had been refound (often, of course, by new owners) and was now exchanged on the border was astounding. Moneychangers and merchants had scales on which to weigh the precious metal. Rings, necklaces, bracelets, brooches, chains, ingots—the Cambodian gold kept coming and coming. It was often sold not by the ounce but by the kilo. One of the few kind ways in which the international system had treated Cambodians lay in the rise of the gold price during 1979. This had almost doubled the purchasing power of those Cambodians who had survived and who held the metal, though few Thai merchants gave them the correct price for it. Indeed, it was not unknown for gold to be exchanged on the border at $200 below world market price.

The trade had several stages. Thais sold to Cambodians, who either resold to other people on the border or took the goods back into Cambodia itself. There were, of course, markups at every stage. A packet of Thai cigarettes which cost forty cents in Aran sold for sixty cents to a Cambodian trader on the border, for seventy-five cents to ordinary Cambodians there and for at least ninety cents in the interior. A bicycle went from $50 in Aran, to $75 to $100 to $150 by the time it reached Phnom Penh. By early 1980 goods from the border could be seen through much of Cambodia.

The Cambodian crisis transformed Aranyaprathet into one of the greatest boom towns in Asia, perhaps in the world. The little place had been virtually forgotten after the Khmer Rouge closed the border and cut Cambodia off from Thailand in 1975. Apart from smuggling, commercial life came almost to a halt; the town was asleep by 8 P.M. In 1978, there had been only about twenty foreigners living in "Aran," most of them doctors and nurses working for such groups as Medecins sans Frontières, International Rescue Committee, and Christian Outreach, with those few refugees who did manage to escape the Khmer Rouge. Journalists sometimes visited the town to interview those refugees, but few of them stayed long: it was not very gay, not very comfortable—and their editors were not very interested.

By December 1979, all that had changed with the inflation of the refugee business. Now shops stayed open till after midnight as owners arranged the stock that had careered dangerously in overloaded trucks down the main road from Bangkok that day. (Thai drivers are always fast, but no truck driver would want to arrive at Aran after sundown—in the open countryside west of the town, bandits ambushed the trucks after dusk, and drivers were occasionally killed.)

The other foreigners—those who had flocked to the border from the west rather than from the east—were also very profitable for Thai traders. Prevented by the Heng Samrin from working inside Cambodia, the vast energies and emotions unleashed in the west by the Cambodia crisis were directed toward the border. In Aranyaprathet the alms bazaar was often impressive, was sometimes absurd or distasteful, but was always colorful.

By early 1980 there were, quite apart from all the U.N. agencies and ICRC—which had twenty different nationalities among its family in Thailand—ninety-five voluntary agencies flush with funds, enthusiasm and varying amounts of experience, working on the Cambodian crisis in Thailand. The non-Khmer foreign population of Aranyaprathet and the area around it had swollen close to one thousand. Rents for small houses soared from $50 a month to over $1,000. Scores of Thai families sensibly moved out of their homes into sheds to take advantage of this bonanza. Rich merchants threw up new houses almost overnight to seize the windfall profits. The price of maids rose too, from $20 a month to $200. (But Thai doctors in the local hospital were still paid only $150.)

One of the biggest spenders was the ICRC, which by early 1980 had about four hundred people working in medical and other teams along the border. They took over the whole of the local hotel, paying double the room rent previously charged. (The German Red Cross donated to ICRC an entirely new housing and administration complex, which was not completed until the initial emergency in Aran was almost over. It was destined eventually for the Thai Red Cross.)

Restaurants in Aranyaprathet flourished. The Café Aran, a haunt of soldiers and black-marketeers, had a live Thai band and was undoubtedly the first night club on the Cambodian border. Another served late-night fast food; it was known to the doctors and nurses and other refugee workers, as Maxim's.

Most of the foreign-aid workers were responding fervently to the holocaust visions and were sincerely anxious to help Cambodians. And most of their organizations were competent. To take just one example: a young woman named Susan Walker, moved by *Time* Magazine's November 1979 cover story "Deathwatch in Cambodia," flew out from Minnesota in December 1979 with a new group called The American Refugee Committee. She remained in Thailand for four years, administering medical teams from the Middle West in one of the most effective of the health programs in the holding centers and later on the border.

But, inevitably, there was a MASH-type atmosphere in Aran; some doctors and nurses strolled nonchalantly into Maxim's in full medical regalia, even though the hospitals in which they worked were over twenty miles away. As in many such humanitarian emergencies, rivalry between some agencies was intense. Some doctors competed for bodies the way the gospelers fought for souls. At Maxim's there were constant stories about how a German anesthetist refused to help an American doctor, how the Japanese would not cooperate with the Italians, how a French medical team was expelled from the surgery, and so on. The one thing that united many of the groups was impatience with the ICRC. This reflected in part irritation at the aloof pomposity and expensive life style of some Swiss delegates, but was more a result of the ICRC's attempt to impose some order and limits on the delivery of medical care to the refugees.

The Thai government had entrusted ICRC with the task of medical coordination along the border; ICRC interpreted this as requiring that it keep almost all other medical groups away from it. ICRC delegates argued that their own teams were adequate—they had fifty-one by the end of 1979—that the border was too dangerous for a mass of foreigners to be there, that many of the organizations were longer on zeal than on local knowledge or general experience, that they often arrived unannounced, that their personnel often stayed for only a few weeks (perhaps the Christmas holidays), and that they were therefore impossible to coordinate.

There was much truth in all of these assertions. Despite the sincerity and competence of most aid workers and their groups, some were ghoulish, incompetent or otherwise outlandish. There were Western doctors (a minority) who arrived at Bangkok's international airport with stethoscopes already dangling from their necks, as if Thai officials should for some reason therefore fawn upon them. Planeloads of outdated drugs arrived—some of them from a small American agency that had distinguished itself by sending water beds to Vietnamese boat people in Malaysia. An American organization called Food for the Hungry came to the border with a large stock of woolen underpants. A French agency called Enfants sans Frontières sent a consignment of foam mattresses—it is difficult to imagine anything more disgusting in a rain-sodden refugee camp. A Japanese organization chartered a boat (costing $500,000) bearing 500 Japanese youths who came to Thailand and spent four days instructing refugee children on the harmonica and *joie de vivre*. Countless foreign agencies tried to ship Cambodian babies out of Thailand; among the most successful was the French government— President Giscard d'Estaing demanded and received dozens of them for Christmas 1979.

There was another problem with some of the best-run and most experienced agencies; they were American, they had United States government funds and they often identified themselves with United States government policy. Catholic Relief Services, for example, had had United States grants to ship food to the border since June 1979. Leo Cherne, the head of one of the biggest agencies, International Rescue Committee, was leading a campaign to criticize the Vietnamese for not opening a formal land bridge. In February 1980 he, together with Joan Baez, Bayard Rustin and several French *nouvelles philosophes,* conducted a well publicized "March for Survival" to the bridge at Aranyaprathet. None of this detracted from the International Rescue Committee's efficiency in medical work on the border.

But for the ICRC, the Phnom Penh operation and the far greater number of Cambodians who could, in theory, be reached from there were the priority; ICRC did not wish to provoke Vietnamese displeasure by turning the border into a United States government-sponsored enclave. Like many U.N. officials, ICRC delegates resented the constant pressures from the American Embassy. Men from the Embassy's Kampuchea Emergency Group, KEG, were always on the border and in the holding centers. They had far better communications, more local knowledge and more experience of both Thailand and Cambodia than many of the relief personnel. Their help and advice were often invaluable in specific crises. But the ICRC and other groups frequently interpreted their information and recommendations as politically inspired. Sometimes this was true; sometimes it was not.

Some of the voluntary agencies who were excluded from the border argued that ICRC itself was playing its own politics with the lives of people there. They pointed out, for example, that in early December 1979 there were at Nong Samet a total of just seven doctors and ten nurses attempting to provide daily care to an estimated 100,000 people living in grossly unsanitary conditions. Medical outreach was minimal, even though there were four clinics in different parts of the camp. Mak Moun was even less well serviced. But much that ICRC did was well considered and impressive.

The ICRC presented very clear guidelines for medical policy:

Give priority to basic public health, sanitation, nutrition and hygiene (teaching and training).
Support the existing Khmer medical infrastructure.
Give autonomy in as many medical fields as possible and as soon as possible, utilizing every talent.
Provide medical aid with what is normally provided by the government to Thai population.
Thai Red Cross has a tremendous role.
Avoid creating dependency on sophisticated Western medicine.
Pay special attention to psychological needs and related sufferings.
Learn and respect Khmer culture, traditional medicine and existing local medical systems and levels.
Avoid overmedication.
Maintain professional standards at all times (no amateurism).

Avoid creating professional refugees who would become everlastingly dependent on our self-gratifying charity.
Share information with (all) medical personnel so as to facilitate coordination.
Promote full coordination while remaining flexible in the medical aspects of the program.

One of the basic problems that ICRC faced at first related to food donations. Masses of surplus or unsuitable foods had been sent from Europe and the United States. Hundreds of different kinds of milk, dried and canned, had arrived in bags as large as 25 kilos and cans as small as half a kilo. ICRC and UNHCR had decided not to use much milk, except in Supplementary Feeding Programs—for one reason, they wanted to encourage mothers to breast-feed. Similarly, ICRC reported,

> huge donations of the Western type of baby foods in glass jars or bottles have arrived here and great problems have arisen regarding their use. The fruit-and-vegetable varieties contain almost only carbohydrates and have lost most of the original vitamins during processing. . . . The logic of sending, at great expense for transport, banana drinks in glass bottles from Europe to a banana-producing country is difficult to understand. . . . The savory varieties of baby foods are composed according to Western tastes and habits and do not fit the Khmer diet.

Actual medical disagreements between the ICRC and some voluntary agencies were most noticeable in the holding center that UNHCR built at Khao I Dang, where there were about 120,000 "illegal immigrants" by early 1980. None of these people were Khmer Rouge. They came from the encampments like Mak Moun and Nong Samet, north of Aran. This was the place in which most voluntary agencies preferred to work. It had a much higher proportion of middle-class Cambodians, who were more oriented to Western values than were those of the other holding centers. It was close to Aranyaprathet and was the one holding center on the tourist route for any visiting foreign politician or journalist—important for fund raising. At this stage, thirty-seven foreign agencies were working in Khao I Dang. There was a surgery run by the ICRC, a feeding and rehabilitation ward run by Catholic Relief Services, an Adult Medicine ward run by the American Refugee Committee, another in the hands of a German group called Maltheiser Hilfendienst, an obstetrics and gynecological ward run by Médecins sans Frontières, a pediatric ward set up by the International Rescue Committee and World Relief, and a team of holistic healers from Marin County, California—to mention just some. Indeed, the level of medical care offered there in early 1980 was probably higher than that which could be obtained by any ordinary peasant or city dweller anywhere in Southeast Asia or most of the Third World. (One ICRC delegate worked out that there were more medical teams on the border than in four African countries combined.)

Thousands of lives were saved in Khao I Dang. But many of the voluntary agencies were anxious to concentrate on prestigious intensive-care projects rather than more basic public-health, sanitation and health-education programs, which, to donors back home, were less attractive. ICRC delegates tried to change this emphasis. They had the support of the medical coordinator of the voluntary agencies, Dr. John Naponick, who was constantly urging groups to abandon high-powered surgical techniques for public-health programs and the training of public-health workers in the camps. "As the fate of this population remains unknown I believe it better to make them self sufficient in health care even at a low level, than to give them sophisticated care for a short time," he told one meeting. One problem, as Naponick and the ICRC pointed out, was that some of the doctors who came out from Western Europe and the United States, their consciences inflamed by the suffering shown in their papers and television screens, had little experience of the Third World, let alone refugee emergencies. "They know only intensive individual care, which I believe not to be in the best interests of the refugee population." He urged the agencies, "Don't turn Khao I Dang into the Mayo Clinic."

As well as pressing for more public-health and sanitation programs, the ICRC was encouraging the use of traditional Khmer medicine, as practiced by village healers known as "Krou Khmers." Traditional medicine had been the only sort allowed by the Khmer Rouge, and for that reason, many middle-class Cambodians were disdainful or fearful of it. Nonetheless, ICRC encouraged Krou

Khmers to set themselves up in the outpatient departments in the holding centers. One ICRC doctor and analyst, Jean Pierre Hiegel, immersed himself in the Krou Khmer methods, and concluded that the herbal potions and incantations could be an essential complement to Western drugs. He argued (against fierce opposition from some American evangelical doctors, who said that only their medicine, working through Jesus Christ, could be seen to save) that the traditional methods were especially helpful in cases of psychological distress.*

* Hiegel pointed out that the Krou Khmers believed that some diseases—malaria, flu, cholera, scabies, typhoid—have rational causes. But "some diseases are due to black magic or the spirits: spirits of the ancestors, spirit of the village, or another spirit to which the promise of an offering would not have been fulfilled. These beliefs are shared by the patients themselves, so they cannot feel better unless they are convinced that the appropriate practice to calm the spirit and to take it away is being applied. Human being is an entity soma and psyche and we must keep this in mind . . ." Hiegel urged collaboration between Western and Khmer medicine. Of the Baptist complaints that only Jesus could fight the devil, he noted, "This attitude, without taking into account ethical considerations of the psychological power of the one who is helping people in straitened circumstances, is worrying because there may be just sufficient time to induce doubts about Buddhism and about traditional belief but not long enough to enable the Khmers to cope with the present and, especially, future difficulties of everyday life." He warned against Western takeovers: "You will see a mother who does not take care of her newly born child and just leaves him beside her, without looking at him and feeding him. In this case, it could be very easy for a nurse to think that this woman is an awfully bad mother, lacking human feelings and that she herself would be a good one, because she is ready to love this child and take care of him. In fact, this mother is not bad; she just cannot afford to love her child, but she is not responsible for it. These women have seen so many babies, and so many children, sometimes their own, dying, and they are so exhausted from a psychological point of view that they cannot anticipate another issue for their newborn babies; they have to protect themselves because they feel they could not stand another mourning. They cannot consider their babies as living creatures in connection with them. Some other reasons may motivate this attitude, but whatever they are, we must keep in mind that one day we shall leave the place whereas the child will stay with his mother; so, treating the relational trouble between her and the baby is a priority. It is very easy to yield to the temptation to play the part of the mother by keeping her aside. But if we really care for the future of the child and not only for our immediate gratifications, we shall, from the very beginning, associate her to all we do for the baby, even if she is not very co-operative."

Hiegel himself found that the Krous had managed to relieve him of great pain from a hernia—by massaging his toes and making ritual chants.

Some groups agreed to change their emphasis. Others, like Catholic Relief Services and the International Rescue Committee, were locked in constant battle with the ICRC over their methods. The International Rescue Committee's pediatric ward was very sophisticated, and the medical teams tried to give critical care to seriously ill children. It was extraordinary to witness the intense emotional relationship that, say, a nurse or doctor from Milwaukee developed with an individual dying child. I watched one doctor spend most of a morning attempting to pump the lungs of a boy for whom an oxygen mask was not enough. The effort failed. The International Rescue Committee tried to send such gravely ill patients to Bangkok. This the ICRC sought to prevent, arguing that triage was a more appropriate method. This infuriated some doctors, who claimed that it was grossly immoral not to give refugees the benefits of the best available methods.

That sort of problem was agonizing. It was made more so, as ICRC constantly pointed out, by the fact that the level of care being given to the Cambodian refugees was far higher than anything that the Thai people could hope for. Was this either just or politically wise? This is a dilemma that occurs again and again in refugee situations throughout the world. Refugees often flee from one poor country to another; there is often a danger that, even with far less assistance than was being given to the Cambodians in Thailand, they will become more privileged than the local population and thereby arouse great resentments.

By early 1980 there were frequent complaints in Thai newspapers and from some Thai politicians that the Cambodian "illegal immigrants" were being absurdly cosseted. The Joint Mission's programs for "Affected Thai Villagers" were essential in helping to offset understandable envy.* Nonetheless, Thai newspapers were also be-

* Thus, for example, Ulf Kristofferson, UNICEF's border coordinator, reported that he had been asked by Colonel Kitti, the Thai officer in charge of Task Force 80, the military unit along the border, for educational supplies for Thai children in affected villages in the south. Colonel Kitti asked for 5 kilos of rice, 1 liter of oil, 1 tin of condensed milk, 1 kilo of milk powder,

ginning to demand that the Khmers do something useful for Thailand—like building roads—while they were enjoying Thai hospitality.

Such were some of the conditions and problems on the border and in the holding centers when James Grant succeeded Henry Labouisse as UNICEF's Executive Director, on January 1, 1980.

Grant is an attractive personality. Born into a missionary family in China, he had worked, like Robert Jackson, for the U.N. Relief and Rehabilitation Administration after World War II. He had spent most of the fifties and sixties working with U.S. AID programs in India, Ceylon and Turkey; in 1967 he became Assistant Administrator of AID in Vietnam. He is an exuberant man who wears his enthusiasms on his sleeve; in Vietnam he was one of those officials who remained determinedly bullish about the American cause. After he returned to the States, he was made President of the Overseas Development Council—a post he held until, as the candidate of the United States government, he took over UNICEF.

Before he formally succeeded Labouisse at the beginning of 1980, he was appalled by the extent to which UNICEF's slender resources appeared to have been sucked into the Cambodia operation. (UNICEF offices from all over the world were complaining either that their staff had been whisked off to Cambodia or that headquarters officials no longer had enough time for their more mundane, everyday problems.) Grant was especially disturbed by what he learned of the border. He asked Robert Jackson, who was himself just assuming his role as Waldheim's coordinator, to have some other agency to take over. The obvious agency for the task was the U.N. High Commissioner for Refugees.

By now the border population was said to be about 600,000. Back on November 5, UNICEF had appealed for funds to feed a border population of only 250,000. It was, therefore, considerably

---

one blanket, and biscuits for each child. Kristofferson agreed and went with Kitti to distribute the supplies. "The goods were warmly received by all concerned. I personally believe that this action had further encouraged the feeling of good will, and further strengthened the cooperation between the Thai authorities and UNICEF. Therefore, I feel we should, in the future, be flexible enough to be prepared to accommodate further requests of this kind."

overspent. UNICEF was also advancing funds to the World Food Program—which had a cash-flow crisis—to buy 2,500 tons of food a week for the border and was itself supervising the distribution of much of this food, by truck. By the end of December, 36,494 tons of food had been distributed—deposited, perhaps—along the border; the cost had been $11.2 million.

Charles Egger, UNICEF's deputy director, who had been closely immersed in the entire operation, confirmed that the border "goes considerably beyond UNICEF's mandate. We never included in our budget the financial provisions for such a large operation." Moreover, many governments had apparently assumed that the High Commissioner (UNHCR) was responsible for all refugees in Thailand and so contributed to him rather than to UNICEF. "It does seem, therefore, imperative for UNICEF to seek in principle an early transfer of its present responsibilities in the border area to HCR."

In one sense UNICEF's reticence was unusual, almost refreshing. The natural tendency among U.N. bureaucracies, as among any others, is to increase, rather than to diminish, empires. Both the World Food Program and the High Commissioner for Refugees said they were happy, under certain conditions, to expand their area of authority in Thailand and to take the central, "northwest," sector of the border over from UNICEF.

Both the Thai government and the U.S. Embassy also sought to have UNHCR on the border. In early December, Prime Minister Kriangsak had written to Kurt Waldheim asking the Secretary General to create some kind of "demilitarized zone," or "safe haven," along the border. For a U.N. peace-keeping force to be deployed there would require a Security Council vote—which would inevitably be vetoed by the Soviets. What the Thais wanted was an extension of the U.N.'s civilian presence along the border, and the most obvious way of doing this was to have UNHCR be there as well as in the holding centers inside Thailand.

Mort Abramowitz, the United States ambassador to Bangkok, was pushing the idea—partly because it was what the Thais wanted, partly because he thought it would give better protection to the people on the border, and partly because he was impressed with Zia Rizvi, UNHCR's new representative in the area. In one cable to

Washington he described him as "light-years ahead of most of the assorted U.N. personnel here." Rizvi himself told Abramowitz on December 14 that he thought it would be much more sensible for UNHCR to take over the border and for UNICEF and ICRC to be responsible only for Phnom Penh. Washington agreed. One cable from State to Bangkok pointed out that "the psychological advantages of establishing a UNHCR permanent presence among noncombatants along the border would be great and could lead eventually to internationally recognized safe-haven areas. We hope that UNHCR would not be put off by the fact that a portion of each of the areas concerned is inside Kampuchea. Another fact is that they extend also into Thai territory. These are extraordinary circumstances which certainly justify extraordinary measures."

Nonetheless, UNHCR did begin to use the imprecision of the border as an excuse not to go there. Whatever UNHCR officials were saying to American diplomats at the time, they had decided by end-December to try to stay away from the border. They said, privately at this stage, that the feeding there was acting as a magnet, that nearly all the Cambodians there and in the holding centers would be best off if they were encouraged to return home, and that the border was so volatile that it would present for UNHCR serious problems. HCR officials began to insist that, since the border was so poorly defined and since some camps certainly straddled it, the people there could not be considered to come under UNHCR's mandate; they had not properly left their own country.

The issue had not been formally decided when Robert Jackson left New York for rounds of talks in Geneva and Bangkok. As he set off, fierce fighting broke out once again among the different Cambodian resistance groups of bandits, and self-professed "freedom fighters" in the Nong Samet camp north of Aranyaprathet. UNICEF and the ICRC felt compelled to suspend their operations and pull their personnel out of the camp. Thousands of refugees fled in terror—some to Khao I Dang, some to other encampments along the border. The Thai army was either unable or unwilling to restore order for days. The affair gave urgent emphasis to Jackson's meetings.

In Geneva, Jackson saw Alexander Hay, the President of the ICRC, and assured him, as Kurt Waldheim had already done, that his appointment would not mean that ICRC was even further embroiled in the United Nations. Jackson promised him that ICRC would be regarded as independent in accordance with the Geneva Conventions, but interdependent when it wished to be.

Over the course of his meetings in Geneva and Bangkok, Jackson heard many different, sometimes conflicting, complaints from each of the international organizations. One of his own principal complaints was that the agencies were not "speaking with one voice." So many different things were being said that the public could have no real idea of what was going on.

Jean Pierre Hocke of the ICRC complained bitterly about the Thai government's failure to "live up to its part of the deal" and improve security along the border if the organizations stationed more personnel there. The international presence had been increased, yet security was still terrible. The political problems had not been overcome by humanitarian action. ICRC wanted to withdraw from the border.

Charles Egger of UNICEF complained that there was no monitoring, let alone any control, of distribution in the border camps. Numbers had been inflated and supplies diverted from the start. Armed elements were being helped. UNICEF was involved far beyond its mandate (children under five and pregnant and lactating mothers) in a mass feeding program for the population at large. (So it was, of course, inside Cambodia itself.) Yet, he complained that UNICEF had not had a "fair share" of the funds pledged at the November 5 conference—because governments seemed to believe that UNHCR was in charge of the border as well as the holding centers.

This sort of argument did not impress UNHCR. Many promises made to it by governments that had made emotional and dramatic pledges in November had still not been met. Belgium, Cyprus, Denmark, Greece, Israel, Italy, Japan, Lebanon, Malaysia, Philippines, Qatar, Singapore, Switzerland—all of these promised contributions (some token, but some large) were still outstanding. UNHCR attacked ICRC for compelling all the medical teams that had flocked to Thailand to work in the holding centers and not allowing them on to the border. Sa Kaeo holding center was "a zoo," said Zia Rizvi, "choked with doctors and nurses." ICRC repeated that, like UNICEF, it wanted to get out of the border.

Only the World Food Program representatives spoke up for the border operation, pointing out that "both Kampuchean governments had requested food," that very little had so far been distributed through Phnom Penh, and that the people on the border obviously needed to be fed.

The meetings agreed—as Zia Rizvi, who had now been made the Regional Coordinator of the High Commissioner for Refugees, had written in a cable to his headquarters—that the border "must be seen as interdependent part of overall problem requiring humanitarian aid to Kampucheans inside and outside their country of origin. This aid must be solution-oriented. The common objective of agencies represented is voluntary return for vast majority of Kampucheans now in Thailand or straddling border. Efforts must be made to discourage exodus which now constituted essentially of masses seeking food." (Not spelled out was that the only real solution to that was the better distribution of food inside Cambodia.) "Situation at border constitutes a significant source of tension which should not be perpetuated. Humanitarian assistance provided in the area should consequently not have durable character. Absence of reasonable security conditions is fundamental problem which falls under Royal Thai Government responsibility. Only if reasonable security conditions exist can agencies concerned provide humanitarian aid effectively."

At a final meeting under Jackson's chairmanship held in the UNICEF office in Bangkok on the morning of Friday, January 19, the agencies agreed to meet again in Geneva on February 7 and 8 with final accounts of what had already been spent and detailed budgets for the next period. They agreed also to make another financial appeal to the donors in March.

After this session Jackson drove across Bangkok's traffic to address the ambassadors of the major Western donor countries, meeting, as they often did, at the Canadian Embassy. He said that aid would be needed in Cambodia at least until the end of 1980; the agencies realized that they could not keep on going back to the donors, but he hoped "the system might bear one more appeal." Like others concerned with Cambodia, Jackson was well aware that the Secretary General, Washington and other Western governments were now consumed with two new international crises—the hostages in Iran and the Soviet invasion of Afghanistan. The "holocaust" in Cambodia no longer commanded much attention.

To Jackson's plea, the Canadian Ambassador Fred Bild complained that the donors had not yet been given proper accounts of current operations, particularly not by UNHCR. Jackson agreed. He said he had insisted that the international organizations put their books in order, placing more emphasis on short-term cash flow and actual expenditures in order to give the donors the financial information they needed. He had found duplication of disbursements and instances of no records at all in Thailand.

Two weeks later, at another meeting with donor ambassadors at the residence of the American ambassador in Geneva, Jackson repeated such criticisms but said that nonetheless money was a serious problem now. He felt that after informal talks with the donors, the Secretary General should call a new pledging conference as soon as possible. This would give time for any changes in the area to become clearer. In particular, was the Heng Samrin regime really prepared to work with the relief organizations? The crunch in aid was very close now. If the situation turned sour in the next month, Western governments might be forced to decide collectively on some unprecedented way of helping a population whose government was demonstrably unable to deal with its suffering.

Giving the ambassadors character sketches of the agencies, Jackson said he thought the UNICEF staff in Thailand was good; but the office in Bangkok needed strengthening. ICRC was "professional," he thought, despite all the complaints about it. It had good relations with the older voluntary agencies, but would not get involved with the new ones for which it could not vouch. He was not impressed by the office of the High Commissioner for Refugees; the staff seemed inadequate, though they clearly had done well at Khao I Dang. He said he would not recommend that UNHCR take over the border; indeed, he doubted whether UNHCR was capable of doing so. One problem was that UNHCR would need to call upon the help of voluntary agencies and many of the most efficient were American. Like the ICRC, Jackson did not wish to provoke the Vietnamese by having a large American presence on the border.

This judgment coincided with UNHCR's own reluctance to take over the border. But the conclusive factor was Thai policy. In February 1980, Thailand quietly but abruptly closed the "open-door" that Kriangsak had opened with such fanfare in October 1979. From now on, people coming to the border could no longer ask to be bused to a holding center inside Thailand. They would have to try to make the passage covertly and at risk of being shot. Indeed, the Thais began to encourage people to move back from the holding centers to the border, to enlarge the population buffer there. At the same time, the government was determined that there should be no change of U.N. personnel at the border unless this had the effect of increasing their over-all number. On February 4, 1980, Air Marshal Siddhi made this clear to Jim Grant.

UNICEF's Executive Director had just returned from his first visit to Phnom Penh. Like many other Westerners before and after him, he had fallen in love with the country and was now fired with his characteristic enthusiasm for UNICEF's role in the Phnom Penh operation. Siddhi made it clear to him that UNICEF must definitely stay on the border, as they were leading the operation in Phnom Penh. He said that UNHCR could join them there, but they must not leave. He was still asking Kurt Waldheim to increase the over-all U.N. presence along the border as a deterrent against Vietnamese attack.

UNHCR never did agree to go to the border. Its refusal to do so undoubtedly reduced its own concerns. But it also reduced the protection that was offered to the people on the border, many of whom certainly qualified as genuine refugees under the terms of UNHCR's mandate. (ICRC attempted to fulfill some of the protection functions that UNHCR had abdicated.) Over the next three years, tens of thousands of people drifted home to Cambodia. But by 1983 there were still over 200,000 people on the border. Some were soldiers and their families, but others were genuine civilians, pitifully caught in the continuing international deadlock over Cambodia.

14 ❦ Samaki

In the spring of 1980 the international aid effort in Cambodia reached a major crisis, caught between the differing priorities and perceptions of the donor and the recipient governments. It was the first of many such cyclical events.

The number of foreign relief officials and organizations in Phnom Penh was still growing. A group of Catholic organizations, under the umbrella of International Council for Economic and Social Development (CIDSE), sent an Italian woman named Honesta Carpene, who was to become one of the longest-serving, most energetic and devoted foreign relief workers in the country. (She stayed until 1983.) The American Friends Service Committee (AFSC), which had been a constant critic of United States policy in Indochina, had a grant of over $500,000 from the U.S. government and was concentrating on agricultural rehabilitation. That was also the priority of another American church group called the Consortium for Agricultural Relief and Rehabilitation in Kampuchea (ARRK); it had a grant of $1,250,000 from the United States government. The group of French doctors, Comité de l'Aide Médicale et Sanitaire, was continuing its work in Phnom Penh hospitals. Oxfam's program was still being run by Malcolm Harper and included agricultural rehabilitation, nutritional surveillance, industrial reconstruction and trucks.

The evangelical group World Vision sent a slow-speaking Christian named Ben Boyd to Phnom Penh. He was unusual in that he was a West Pointer. He had been an officer in South Vietnam in the sixties and, in common with other American soldiers, had frequently been frustrated by the sanctuary that Cambodia offered the Vietnamese Communists. Now he was enrolled in an army of God, and his principal mission was to rebuild the children's hospital, which World Vision had completed just before the Khmer Rouge victory in 1975. It was used as a prison under Pol Pot and a barracks for the first few months of the Heng Samrin regime; it was completely wrecked. In January 1980 World Vision's messianic leader, Stan Mooneyham, had returned to Phnom Penh to make an impassioned plea to Foreign Minister Hun Sen for permission to rebuild the hospital. "Don't look at my face," he cried, "you will only see an American, an enemy. Look instead at my blood." And with that Mooneyham drew his penknife across his wrist and began to bleed. Hun Sen gave permission.

World Vision, which had a grant of over $3 million from the United States government, was intent on creating the finest children's hospital in Southeast Asia. When finished, it was indeed very splendid.

The Joint Mission's staff had expanded. The ICRC had finally managed to get a medical team—from the Soviet Red Cross—into Cambodia. UNICEF had sent an experienced transport officer, Horst Ruttinger, from West Germany. He had four East German mechanics, hired by UNICEF, and together with Oxfam's mechanic they attempted to organize the fleets of new trucks. By the end of April 1980, the Joint Mission had imported about 500 trucks, Oxfam 90, bilateral donors (the USSR and Eastern Europe and Vietnam) were said to have given 670, and there were now thought to be 230 old Cambodian trucks on the road.

Cooperation among all the different agencies was improving. They held regular Friday-night meetings to discuss what they had learned during the week and what they were each trying to do. Relations between Malcolm Harper of Oxfam and John Saunders, the leader of the Joint Mission, were excellent, though Saunders was irritated by the Oxfam publicity machine back in Britain, which claimed, wrongly, that Oxfam had far better access to the countryside than any other agency. Saunders was also frustrated by the secrecy of some of his partners in the Joint Mission. The men from the Food and Agriculture Organization and the World Food Program often sent information on agriculture and food supplies back to Rome without telling him what they knew. ICRC he also found secretive.

For many, not all, foreign relief officials, coming to work in Phnom Penh was a moving privilege and an awesome responsibility. Cambodia, after the Khmer Rouge, aroused intense emotions and engendered great passion—a tiny country with a people who seemed, despite all they had suffered from without and from themselves, to exude an extraordinary warmth, struggling, now under foreign occupation, to rescue some traces of distant life from the horrors of more recent death. Many of the foreigners in Phnom Penh brought a zeal to this particular mission that they had rarely felt elsewhere.

But by early 1980 it seemed to some—not all—of them that their zeal was no longer being matched by the local authorities. As well as being subjected to constant criticism and skepticism from the Western donors, relief officials were also meeting more and more difficulties raised by the Heng Samrin regime. As the regime consolidated itself with the assistance that the agencies were delivering, it did not make life easier for the foreigners in Phnom Penh; on the contrary, it imposed restrictions on them that seemed the more onerous because of the unusual conditions under which they were living.

The ICRC radio had never been allowed out of the pound. The only daily contact with the outside world was the ICRC flight from Bangkok. Communication with the world to the west was therefore very slow. The most urgent problems could sometimes be answered within thirty-six hours by dint of saturation use of the telephone out of Bangkok, where colleagues relayed to New York, Geneva or Rome messages that had come by the flight from Phnom Penh.

The government had refused requests from different U.N. and voluntary agencies that they be allowed to set themselves up in any of the thousands of deserted villas in Phnom Penh. (UNICEF, World Vision and others had had offices in Phnom Penh before 1975.) Instead, everyone was confined to the Samaki hotel, where the gloom of the atmosphere and the monotony of some people's conversation was matched only by the gloom and monotony of the food. Trips into the countryside became more, not less, difficult to arrange. Contacts with Cambodian officials became rarer. More and more of them were away, undergoing political education in either Vietnam or Eastern Europe, and the regime was demanding ever longer political "study sessions" in work places in Cambodia. The authorities tried to stop Western officials (not those from the Soviet bloc) from driving their own vehicles. They attempted to subject them to an all-night curfew. They even told them they were forbidden to speak to anyone in the street. At the same time, government propaganda, spread by word of mouth and by loudspeaker broadcasts in the towns, denounced the aid officials as imperialist spies with whom no one must make contact.

One reason, no doubt, was that the regime and its Vietnamese supporters had failed to win the General Assembly's recognition as the government of Cambodia. Even though the regime had celebrated the first anniversary of the "liberation" on January 7, 1980, it was still recognized by only Vietnam and its Soviet-bloc allies. Some Cambodian officials genuinely did not understand, and others chose to ignore, the difference between the U.N.'s specialized agencies and the decisions of the General Assembly or the Security Council. At one level the Joint Mission became the focus of Vietnamese and Heng Samrin frustration with the unfriendly world outside—despite the paradoxical generosity of that world expressed by the presence and work of the Joint Mission.

Malcolm Harper of Oxfam thought that another reason for the increasing difficulties might have been the growing involvement of Vietnamese cadres in the administration of Cambodia. He noticed more and more tensions between Cambodian officials and their Vietnamese "advisers." When he had arrived, in October 1979, Cambodians would speak of the Vietnamese only with gratitude for their "liberation." Now he never heard any such expressions. "Indeed, the reverse is true," he reported to Oxford. "Some of my closer friends speak to me about Vietnamese imperialism with a real hint of bitterness in their voice. It is widely believed, certainly among educated Khmers and probably in the countryside too, that the Vietnamese are here to stay as the masters of Kampuchea and that there is no real future for the Khmer people any more." By way of confirmation, some Vietnamese officials began to hint, to a few foreigners in the Samaki (and to those visiting journalists whom they trusted), of their own dissatisfaction with the Heng Samrin regime. They suggested that the Cambodians were congenitally incompetent, and that many officials of the regime could not be trusted; they also acknowledged that many of them were, until very recently, Khmer Rouge.*

Yet the Vietnamese and the Heng Samrin regime were allowing no Cambodians back from the diaspora. Quite apart from the border, there were tens of thousands of Cambodians in the west whose skills would have been useful to the regime. Few of them showed any sign of wishing to return—a remarkable testament to their distrust of Vietnamese Communism—but the regime made it clear that they would not be permitted anyway. All the movement was the other way. Even some officials of the Heng Samrin regime were now making for the border and, they hoped, resettlement in the West. Like other aid groups, the Oxfam team had several Cambodians asking their help to escape to Thailand and then the West. In a few cases, where they thought their friends risked real persecution if they stayed in Phnom Penh, the Oxfam people did give them dollars with which to get to the border. The Heng Samrin authorities learned of it and made their anger very evident; Oxford ordered its team to desist from such acts, on the grounds that they could lead to the consortium's expulsion.

There were other symptoms of unhappiness. Cargo handlers tried to stow away on the ICRC plane. When the plane was being reloaded in Bangkok, desperate letters to lost relations were often found hidden in the frame. The authorities had refused to allow any attempt by the ICRC to fulfill its tracing mandate and thus reunite families. Eventually, a restricted postal system was begun, but the ICRC was never allowed to do any tracing. Nor was it ever permitted to visit prisoners of war. In Thailand it was able to do both.

At the heart of the crisis between the relief officials—particularly those of the Joint Mission—and the regime, was still food distribution. No one had seen evidence of massive diversion to the Vietnamese, as the U.S. government had alleged, but by now even Oxfam of-

* An exception was often made of Penn Sovann who had abandoned the Khmer Rouge cause as early as 1973 and had lived in Hanoi until the Vietnamese invasion. He was now Minister of Defense and leader of the reformed Communist party. At the end of 1981 Penn Sovann was purged and disappeared from sight, apparently because he was attempting to assert some independence from Hanoi.

ficials in Phnom Penh (though not in Oxford) agreed that the authorities had failed to distribute much of what was landed and had also failed to keep their promise to report on such distribution as was carried out and to allow at least some of it to be effectively monitored.*

The World Food Program's figures showed that by the end of February 1980 it had dispatched 59,000 tons of food to Kompong Som and Phnom Penh. UNICEF and World Food Program people in Cambodia knew, on the basis of their visits to the warehouses, that of this less than half, only 27,000 tons, had left the ports.

And what had happened to that which did actually leave the warehouses? In reality, very little of it was being eaten by the peasants whose starvation to death it was originally intended to prevent. Instead, it was being consumed first by people working for the government and secondly by other townspeople.

Was this so wrong? Cambodia needed a government, its workers had to be paid, and food was the only currency in the first few months after the aid programs began; all that was undeniable. If the imported food had all been distributed to the peasants, then the countryside would also have had to be taxed to feed the towns. When Jim Grant of UNICEF visited Cambodia in February 1980, he was especially impressed that the government had allowed the peasants to keep whatever they had managed to harvest. Without imported food that would have been impossible.

The trouble was that underwriting the Heng Samrin regime was not the stated purpose for which the relief operation had been mounted. That purpose was to save a people from extinction.

The predicament of the aid agencies was unenviable. Their relations with the Heng Samrin regime were deteriorating. At the same time they had to convince the donor governments that genuine progress was being made inside Cambodia, and that further funds not only were essential but also would be well spent. Unless the donors were persuaded, their generosity might well evaporate—especially now that the hostage crisis in Iran and the invasion of Afghanistan were helping everyone to forget Cambodia.

* An American television-network correspondent, Jim Laurie, made a long trip around Cambodia and reported that there was no evidence of diversion to the Vietnamese army.

By early March, funds were almost exhausted. In one report to the donors, the Joint Mission warned that "even if governments meet all the pledges so far made to the individual international organizations, there will be a deficit at the end of March 1980. The flow of essential supplies will, therefore, cease within the next few weeks unless new substantial, financial support is forthcoming immediately." About $262 million was needed till the end of the year.

The picture that the Joint Mission then gave of Cambodia was conflicting. In this report it was hopeful. "For the moment the disaster feared in August and September 1979, when the survival of the Khmer people seemed to be at stake, has been averted. Since early winter a substantial majority of the population appear to have been receiving at least minimally adequate food supplies."

On distribution and monitoring the report noted that "it has been alleged that military authorities have, to some extent, diverted the shipment of food supplies and prevented the cultivation of crops. Certainly, there have been faults of distribution. However, independent observers moving around Kampuchea have seen no evidence to support the more extreme allegations. There is, in fact, general agreement on the part of the international representatives now in Kampuchea that the great bulk of relief supplies has gone to those civilians most in need of them."

The last sentence was underlined in the original document. It did not in any way reflect the views coming from most aid officials in Phnom Penh. It might be true that there was no evidence of "the more extreme allegations"—for example, that food was being taken by the Vietnamese army—but many of the other allegations—that food was not reaching ordinary people, and even that Heng Samrin troops were being fed—were accepted by aid officials in Phnom Penh.*

* John Saunders' internal cables and memos from Phnom Penh reflected deepening gloom. In one such, he wrote: "Total volume getting into nationwide system of distribution . . . is still so small that when priority groups such as officials, heavy workers, etc. have received rations, it appears that the amount reaching average adult consumer is of order of one or two kilograms monthly and sometimes less and occasionally none at all." In response, Ron Ockwell, an astute analyst in UNICEF's Bangkok office, who was maintaining liaison between Phnom Penh and New York-Geneva, agreed with his assessment that "the situation is now more serious than at any previous time."

Equally surprising was a briefing given by Bernardo Brito of the World Food Program to Australian Embassy officials in Rome. He assured them that the Heng Samrin government had offered WFP carte blanche on personnel, that WFP now had more people in Kampuchea than in India or Bangladesh, that access was unfettered throughout the country, and that WFP was "fully satisfied with its accounting and monitoring capability." This was, to say the least, an optimistic interpretation of what was going on inside Cambodia. Moreover, Brito somewhat surprised the Australians by admitting that the Heng Samrin army received three times as much food as civilians. This was exactly the sort of diversion of which the donors had complained. Brito did not make it any better by assuring them that there were only 50,000 soldiers in the army.

By contrast, in March 1980 some of the growing concern—about both distribution and funding—was translated into predictions of another famine by relief officials. Sir Robert Jackson, who was embarked on his constant circumnavigations, trying to maintain concern and encourage pledges, told a meeting of the donor embassies in Bangkok that a miracle would be needed to avert critical shortages of food in the next few months. The dry-season harvest had been worse than predicted, the Joint Mission had now revised upward its estimates of the country's food deficit. He was very worried about money; he knew that it would be "like getting blood out of a stone" the second time around. He told the voluntary agencies in Bangkok that he "remained doubtful whether disaster in [the] coming months could be averted."

Further gloom was added by the collapse of one of the jetties in Phnom Penh's port—the ancient wharf could no longer take the strain of the shipments. Now even fewer supplies could be unloaded. Jean Pierre Hocke of ICRC told the donor embassies in Bangkok that he thought that a "very grave" food situation was developing in Cambodia. The Oxfam representative in Singapore, Geoffrey Busby, went so far as to tell the press that one million tons of food had to be

---

Ockwell thought—as so many people then did—that the best way of getting food quickly into the country would be to have a formal land bridge by road from Thailand, and perhaps also from Laos. Failing that, the informal land bridge at Nong Chan would have to be expanded.

shipped into and distributed through Cambodia in the next eight months if a disastrous famine was to be avoided. He was critical of the way food had so far been distributed. (His statement caused alarm in Oxford, where officials were still at pains to avoid criticizing any aspect of the Heng Samrin regime. But Oxfam officials in Phnom Penh shared many of his views, though not his calculation of a one-million-ton shortfall.)

In New York, Bernard Nossiter, United Nations correspondent of *The New York Times,* published an article based on leaked cables from John Saunders and Berndt d'Avis, of the World Food Program in Phnom Penh. He cited d'Avis's gloomy conclusions after a trip around Cambodia's Great Lake that the food needs were even greater than anticipated. He also quoted Jim Grant as now saying that the danger of a new famine was "the equivalent of a holocaust in Kampuchea." Nossiter pointed out that only a month ago, after his own tour of Cambodia, Grant had declared "there is no mass hunger or malnutrition" and "disaster has been averted." I, myself, wrote a series in the *Washington Post* based on a trip to Thailand, in early March 1980. It concluded that a catastrophic famine had only narrowly been averted in 1979 and now once again loomed. The *Post* asserted in an editorial that, despite the diversion of food, both on the border and inside Cambodia, "The United States should stay in the forefront of the relief mission. To back off in frustration is to doom additional hundreds of thousands of poor Cambodians who otherwise, however miserably, might survive."

One reason for these dire predictions was the failure of the dry-season harvest. Another was that it now appeared to the relief officials in Phnom Penh that the population was far higher than the 4.5 million the government had originally claimed. Some estimates put it at 5.5, even 6, million. Later the estimate would rise to 6.5 million. (Even allowing for the baby boom that was taking place, this called into question the real toll of the Khmer Rouge years.) A third was that it seemed impossible that the country's wretched logistics could cope with the import and distribution of both adequate food and the 30,000 tons of seed that FAO planned to get to farmers for the monsoon crop, whose planting began in April.

Throughout March, the chancelleries of many donor countries—

the United States, Canada, Australia, West Germany, the United Kingdom, Norway and then Denmark—continued to complain privately that the Joint Mission had not provided enough information on distribution and monitoring inside Cambodia to justify further contributions. (Few donor officials expressed similar concern about monitoring at the border.) They also pointed out—and it was a cogent point—that the previous fall the Joint Mission had said that 30,000 tons of rice a month were needed to stave off disaster inside Kampuchea. Yet only about 57,000 tons had been delivered and by no means all of that had been distributed. Now the Joint Mission was claiming that "the primary objective of averting famine and preserving life of Kampucheans inside and outside their country have been achieved." Where had the 1979 disaster gone? How had the earlier specter of famine been banished? This was a question that was posed more and more frequently.

On March 24, two days before the donors were supposed to meet formally in New York to pledge more funds, Jim Grant, Jean Pierre Hocke and Robert Jackson met with representatives of the major donors at the Australian mission to the United Nations; the donors insisted that they did not have enough information and so the March 26 meeting must be downgraded. It would not be considered a normal pledging conference but rather an information meeting at which pledges could be made if anyone wished.

This was not only a rebuff to the Joint Mission but also a disappointment to the Thais. They were fearful that the world was losing interest in their problems and were urging the Secretary General actually to convene a full-scale international conference on Kampuchea as required by the 1979 ASEAN resolution passed by the General Assembly. Waldheim, by contrast, was trying to back away from any such commitment; the Soviet Union and its allies were utterly opposed to it.

The March 26 confrontation between donors and organizations took place in the rather formal setting of the Trusteeship Council at the United Nations—a hall hardly conducive to intimate discussion. Robert Jackson had hoped to raise another $262 million on top of the $210 million pledged in November 1979. He and the organizations outlined the way in which they intended to spend this sum.

Some of the donor ambassadors were constructive, others were fiercely critical. The Belgian ambassador, an odd character, was abusive. UNICEF and ICRC apologized that their figures on distribution were imperfect; they agreed that their plans were ambitious, but they thought the situation called for ambition. They said that they believed that on the whole the situation inside Cambodia was improving, and they repeated boilerplate assurances—there was no evidence of diversion; monitoring was getting easier; more medical teams would surely soon be allowed in; and so on.

None of it was very successful in the short run. The United States offered $8 million—compared with the $80 million it had pledged in November. The United States ambassador said that any further American contribution would depend on the extent to which Washington could verify that ordinary Cambodians were really getting what they needed. Sweden offered $3.8 million, Australia $3.3 million, West Germany and Switzerland each $3 million, Holland $2.5 million and Italy 200,000 tons of rice. In all, less than $30 million was pledged toward the target of $262 million.

Back in Bangkok, Jackson stressed to officials of the U.N. organizations and ICRC that it was imperative that they "convince donors of the capacity of the infrastructure in Kampuchea to deliver the supplies that are needed." First of all, they would need to convince themselves of that.

Phnom Penh street life in the spring of 1980 seemed to be ever more active. The Vietnamese were still allowing considerable freedom of movement and a market economy. Indeed, the vigor with which capitalism was thrusting itself from under the ground in which the Khmer Rouge had tried to inter it was quite extraordinary. Scales, protected in glass cases, were set up in stalls all over the town for weighing and exchanging gold. In the Phnom Penh market you could now find many of the goods being traded over the Thai border—beer, digital watches, cigarette lighters and vast cassette players, as well as basic necessities.

Little restaurants were opening in old shops and houses, particularly in Monorom Avenue near the Samaki hotel. One which the foreign-aid workers often patronized was run by a woman called

Chung Tu, who had arrived back in Phnom Penh with her daughter in July 1979. She began by exchanging clothes for soft drinks and bartered the drinks along the roadside. She then moved into cigarette sales, and by October she had managed to save 1,000 dongs. (This was about $71 at the black-market rate, and $400 at the official Vietnamese rate of exchange.) With these she bought some crockery, cooking utensils, a table and chairs, and set up a food stall in the market. This did well, and she soon moved to her restaurant. By April 1980, she had six tables, a real kitchen and a bar, and was making between 2,000 and 3,000 dongs a day. She paid her cook 60 dongs a day and her waitresses 40 dongs. By contrast, a Vietnamese official in Cambodia earned about 80 dongs a month, and someone working for the Heng Samrin regime could expect 16 to 20 kilos of rice for himself and somewhat less for each of his close dependents.

But not everyone could work for the government or become a part of the new bourgeoisie. By spring, 1980, there were thousands of people in Phnom Penh with no visible means of support, many of them sleeping in the streets, some of them begging. Many were ill clothed. Malnutrition was beginning to increase, especially among children. When Dr. Nick Maurice of Oxfam started a nutritional survey in March he found that fully 22 percent of the children in Phnom Penh were suffering from malnutrition and 35 percent were on the border line. It was getting worse weekly.

The plight of people outside the tiny new economic system worsened when the government reintroduced a currency at the end of March. This was a fairly momentous occasion—the country had been without money for almost five years, and its restoration was an important symbol of a return to normality. The unit of exchange was, as before, a riel. In the Lon Nol era notes had been the size of a small flag, but the new notes were tiny, like the Vietnamese dong.

The market rate, which established itself during April, was one riel to one dong to one kilo of rice. But in early May the government announced that people must turn in their dong immediately; they were paid only one riel for three dong. Government workers, paid now twenty riels a month instead of twenty kilos of rice, could still buy one kilo of rice for one riel, but for everyone else the price of rice rose to between two and three riels. And since it was only government workers who were paid in money, it was really only they who could participate in the monetary system. Peasants could get riels only by selling their low-priced produce—and the devaluation further reduced the value of that produce by a factor of three, while making such consumer goods as cloth three times more expensive for them.

By the spring of 1980, part of industry was working again.

Among the first plants repaired were the fishing-net factory that Oxfam had helped, a factory making bicycles and watering cans, and a textile mill. Phnom Penh was also producing such essentials as cigarettes, soft drinks and a rice whisky named Angkor Wat. This last was rumored (perhaps mischievously) to be distilled from rice provided by the World Food Program. It was rather delicious.

The Rusey Keo textile factory had somehow escaped major damage during and at the end of the Pol Pot years. After the Vietnamese occupation its prewar technical director, Tiv Chhiv Ky, who had managed to survive the Khmer Rouge years by posing as a peasant, returned to Phnom Penh, identified himself and was given back his old job. Many of the old workers followed him, and they began to restore the looms and other machinery. Unfortunately, much of the plant had been manufactured in Japan and, because of Tokyo's hostile attitude toward the Heng Samrin regime, spare parts or even manuals were hard to obtain.

Nonetheless, by April 1980 Ky had managed to get 200 of the 325 looms working again—at least so long as cranks, pistons and levers forged in the fifties and sixties did not give way. Once Chinese yarn left by the Khmer Rouge was used up, the factory began to produce cloth with yarn provided by Oxfam. Instead of Khmer Rouge black it was brightly colored and checkered. It was sold in government stores at a slightly cheaper price than that brought over the border from Thailand. Mr. Ky disarmingly acknowledged to foreign journalists that the quality of the Thai cloth was higher.

The aid officials had very different relations with different ministries. One of the best of the ministries was Agriculture, where the Vice-Minister Kom Som Ol, who had been educated in the United States, was absolutely and efficiently dedicated to restoring Cambodia's once munificent agricultural system.

By contrast, the Ministry of Health was a shambles, and the

delivery of health care largely nonexistent. Large sections of the population were suffering from tuberculosis, malaria, ankilostomiasis, respiratory and infectious diseases—all of which were compounded by malnutrition. Supplementary feeding was isolated and random; no vaccine cold chain had been established. UNICEF had provided personal kits for health workers and initial supplies for nurses training, while ICRC was providing the basic equipment for restoring hospitals and infirmaries throughout the country. At the local level, Cambodians were attempting to create a health system. But they were not getting any help from Phnom Penh. The Ministry of Health showed no concern over Nick Maurice's malnutrition figures.*

Relief officials were further depressed by a prolonged hiatus that occurred in April, when most of the senior staff of the Ministry of Health, together with one of the best doctors at the Seventh of January Hospital, Dr. Nouth Savoeun, were carried off to Laos for a prolonged tour to demonstrate medical solidarity. By this time, the Director of Maternal and Child Health Services had been away in Moscow for seven weeks, and there was no sign of her return.

Despite the critical lack of medical personnel in the country and the surfeit of doctors and nurses in Thailand who were eager to come to Phnom Penh, the International Committee of the Red Cross was still forbidden to bring any Western medical teams into Cambodia. Only under urging from Kurt Waldheim and pressure from Moscow had teams from the socialist bloc been allowed in. By April 1980 there were about thirty-three doctors and nurses in East European Red Cross teams, supplementing the fifty Khmer doctors who, the regime claimed, had survived the Khmer Rouge, and the two hundred or so Vietnamese medical personnel in the country. By no conceivable standard could this be described as adequate for a population that had suffered such deprivation in recent years.

---

* Maurice was very gloomy about the future of curative services. "The hospitals are places to die, they are dirty and war-torn, ill-equipped, they lack food for the patients and above all they lack motivated personnel." The Ministry of Health was incapable of drawing up any comprehensive plan. All that it wanted was drugs and equipment. In the middle of a discussion on nutrition surveillance, the Director of Public Health produced a list of things which the provincial hospitals badly needed. Included on it were *"televisions et radios pour la distraction des malades."*

Moreover some (not all) of the socialist teams were quite in-competent. Few of the personnel had volunteered—they had been or-dered to Cambodia. Hardly any of them spoke French. Their knowl-edge of tropical medicine was scant; most of them had never been out of the USSR or Eastern Europe before. They hated the country's heat and its food; ICRC spent a good deal of money flying in their national foods (as it did for itself). Many were terrified that every other Cambodian was a Khmer Rouge bent on killing them; perhaps for this reason they had constant rows with Cambodians.

At the same time they were required, like all Cambodian gov-ernment employees, to take part in constant political study sessions; two Hungarian nurses went home early complaining that their work was so controlled there was nothing useful they could do. One Polish doctor actually admitted to Maurice that their presence was just a public-relations exercise. For many of them the only good thing was that they were paid by the ICRC in dollars; this was tax-free back home—but only if they were abroad less than three months. They all, therefore, insisted that their tours be short. I once spent a few days staying with the East German medical team in Kompong Thom. They were friendly people but were terribly unhappy. They did about two hours' work in the hospital every day and spent the rest of the time lying on their beds waiting for the next canned meal and their repatriation. The Swiss ICRC nurse assigned to Kompong Thom spent much more of her time looking after them than after sick Cambodians.

Socialist medical aid reached its nadir with the arrival of an in-ternational fraternal immunization team on a one-week tour. The team had eight members and included a Mongolian, a Russian, a Pole, a Czech, an East German and a Vietnamese. The Czech, who was in fact a gynecologist, proudly declared that they would be erad-icating cholera, smallpox and yellow fever in Cambodia. Fine, ex-cept that one injection gives only very short protection against chol-era, there is no longer any smallpox in Southeast Asia, and yellow fever has never been known there.

The team arrived in Phnom Penh, but their vaccines did not. These were finally found on the simmering tarmac at Hanoi airport by an Indian ear, nose and throat specialist sent by his government to join the team, as a gesture of Indian good will. After a great deal of argument, he managed to persuade the Vietnamese customs officials to load the consignment on the Air Vietnam plane that he was taking to Phnom Penh. But then the Soviet ambassador to Hanoi intervened; he insisted that the vaccines could be transported only on a Soviet aircraft. So the Indian flew off without them. This was perhaps just as well, since they had undoubtedly been ruined by the heat of the sun.

Not all Soviet-bloc personnel were inappropriate. A team of Soviet dockers at Kompong Som was quite indispensable; without them the unloading rate would have been far lower. Equally effective were the East German mechanics contracted by UNICEF to work under its West German Transport Officer Horst Ruttinger; together they provided the government with guidance on driving standards and training, fleet utilization, repair shops, and so on. Several of the Soviet-bloc ambassadors were helpful to the Joint Mission—in particular the Soviet ambassador himself, a suave diplomat named Oleg Bostorine, who spoke excellent English and had considerable Asian experience. He had now set up a smart embassy in the house that had been the Australian embassy in the Lon Nol years.

All through this period, aid officials became more and more concerned about the lack of food distribution to ordinary people in the countryside. It was now also becoming clear, at least to John Saunders and Jean Hoefliger, that the Americans and other donors were probably right in alleging that food was going to the Cambodian military. Saunders wrote to the government to complain of this. (It was never admitted to the public.)

During April and May they had arguments over these matters with the government, which brought relations close to breaking point. The government had failed to carry out the promise it had made to Jim Grant in February to set up interministerial meetings to resolve common problems. Even meetings with their principal interlocutor, Hor Nam Hong, the Foreign Vice-Minister, became more irregular, and to their chagrin Hoefliger and Saunders even had their personal interpreter removed.

At the end of March, Hoefliger wrote to the Foreign Ministry to ask that the flight path of the daily ICRC plane be shortened. He did not ask for a direct flight path from Bangkok, merely that the arc out over the South China Sea be reduced. Even this could save between 40 and 50 percent of flying time and the same percentage of fuel, thus enabling the plane to carry more supplies on each trip and releasing funds for extra flights. The request was never granted.

Hoefliger also asked the Foreign Ministry to authorize internal flights inside Cambodia to meet the food crisis that seemed to be developing in some provinces. The ICRC would provide the planes—which they might hire in Vietnam or Laos—they could be checked by customs at Pochentong, and flights to provincial airports could be supervised and accompanied by government officials. In short, they would be under the complete control of the Heng Samrin regime. Despite the fact that Vietnamese Prime Minister Pham Van Dong had agreed to such a request from Henry Labouisse, UNICEF's Executive Director, in November 1979, the Foreign Ministry responded with a public denunciation of all aid given by "imperialists and international reactionaries," to "pirates and other Khmer reactionaries" along the border.

Similarly, Saunders complained of the fact that most people were receiving at most one or two kilos of rice a month and often nothing at all. He protested also at the information, which Hor Nam Hong himself had given, that there was no way of knowing whether some of the food had been distributed to the army. In the same vein, Malcolm Harper of Oxfam reported home:

> There now seems to be little doubt that the ordinary people of Kampuchea are not getting adequate food supplies. Nor are they receiving even inadequate quantities in any form on a regular basis . . . [Instead] distribution is being made to the cadres of central and provincial government workers down to rock level. . . . In other words, Phnom Penh bureaucrats are doing well, others adequately, and the broad mass of the people disastrously.

Such inequities were becoming increasingly public as more Western journalists were allowed to tour Cambodia. Henry Kamm reported in *The New York Times* in early April that civilians were receiving only one or two kilograms of rice per month. A few days later Denis Gray of the Associated Press wrote a similar story. So, then, did John Burgess of the *Washington Post.* "Despite the enormous volume of international aid being sent to the Heng Samrin Government here, only tiny quantities are reaching famine ravaged Cambodian villages. In contrast, civil servants and some private citizens in towns and cities seem to be getting adequate rations," wrote Burgess in a rather devastating report.

Almost everywhere that foreign aid workers or journalists were able to go, the story was the same. Some food had been received by villagers in late 1979, but usually rather less had been distributed in 1980, even though there were far more trucks available. There had been virtually no distribution of rice or other foodstuffs over the last few months in Prey Veng, Kompong Speu, Takeo, Kampot, Battambang, Siem Reap, Kompong Thom, Kompong Cham or Svey Rieng. Where distributions were now taking place at all, they seemed rarely to include rice.

Different parts of the countryside were, of course, faring differently. Kandal province, just south of Phnom Penh, had one of the most efficient departments of agriculture. Land was carefully and cleverly used, and in April 1980 the main road was lined with fields of beans, cabbages, lotus and water hyacinths, onions, cassava, herbs, and so on. The rice fields were already being tilled.

In Svey Rieng, a poor province close to the Vietnamese border, provincial officials told Pete Davis of Oxfam that very little food had been received from Phnom Penh. A special government distribution had been carefully arranged for Davis and other members of the Oxfam consortium. The peasants in the village to which they were taken gazed amazed as the seven trucks arrived; they said they had never seen so many before. The village midwife said they had received just two kilograms of maize per head each month this year. The trouble with the maize, apart from the taste, was that it took over an hour to cook and the village was in a flat bare plain with almost no trees and hence no firewood.

While the supplies were being unloaded, scores of children grabbed at the bales of dried fish in the trucks, stuffing the fish into their mouths while dancing, laughing, out of the way of the adults. It was a pleasant scene, but Davis was shocked to discover that on seven trucks there were only five tons of rice, the staple food of the Cambodians. He reported that a Vietnamese soldier supervising the scene said, in Vietnamese, to a Cambodian soldier, "They really should give these people more rice," to which the Cambodian replied, "Yes, I'm O.K. I receive 21 kilograms a month, but they receive very little."

Davis reported back to Oxfam that only tiny amounts of rice had been distributed to ordinary peasants and that, despite all its promises, the government still refused to allow any monitoring of what was going on. "A policy is in force which prevents rice, and adequate quantities of other foodstuffs from reaching the rural population as a whole. Rice and other items are only directed in the main to official salaried staff, that is, official government employees and their families." He thought it was imperative that the agencies induce the government to alter its policy. Otherwise food aid must be stopped and a public announcement be made of the reasons why.

Davis was not alone in his concerns. John Saunders frequently asked his colleagues, "What of the woman with three children who works in the fields? What is she getting from all this help?" An informed guess had to be "Very little."

All of this time, the fear was growing in the world to the West that a new famine was about to engulf Cambodia. Officials from the Joint Mission and other agencies reiterated it. So did Sir Robert Jackson. So did the United States government. Assistant Secretary of State Richard Holbrooke told the Council on Foreign Relations in New York in April that more international attention must be directed toward Cambodia. "Its need is justified by the uniqueness of the situation: An entire nation and its people are threatened with destruction. Without Cambodians there will be no Cambodia. Even in these difficult times, there is no other nation facing extinction." Holbrooke urged Waldheim to respond to the General Assembly's 1980 resolution that called for an international conference on Cambodia.*

---

* Holbrooke made his call after consultations with the U.S. Ambassador Mort Abramowitz, who, at Thai request, was urging such a conference. However, he had not informed the United States mission to the United Nations. The permanent representative, Don McHenry, was far less passionate about

At the end of April almost all the agencies in Cambodia launched an effort to change government policy. They were becoming increasingly worried about logistics. Seed for the main 1980 harvest was being rushed into the country. (The detail of this remarkable operation is included in the next chapter.) It was vital that it should be distributed at once in time for the season's planting. Yet the hundreds of trucks which had been imported were still being used utterly inefficiently. Half the time they were idle, their turnaround time was always slow, and they took far longer to make journeys than even Cambodia's appalling roads dictated. It was also clear that government officials had sold many trucks to individuals who were using them not to transport food to those who most needed it, but as a profitable bus service. As a result, offtake from the ports was still very slow. One Soviet ship waited two months off Kompong Som to be unloaded. There seemed to be a real danger of the government being totally unable to distribute anything like the quantities of food and seed that the country needed over the next few weeks.

The Joint Mission's leaders in Phnom Penh bluntly told the Foreign Ministry that the present logistics arrangements were "catastrophic." In New York, UNICEF prepared a logistics report urging new ports of entry, like Vung Tau and Ho Chi Minh City in Vietnam, the more efficient use of trucks and railroads, internal flights, and the old, politically contentious idea of opening a formal land bridge from Thailand so that convoys of trucks or trains could come straight into the heart of the country. ICRC and UNICEF jointly submitted a strongly worded *aide mémoire* to the government, pointing out that the donors were reluctant to provide more money partly because of the needs of other parts of the world, like Africa, but partly because of the problems of distribution within Cambodia.

The *aide mémoire* requested that the government take fourteen different steps. These included: respect for ICRC and UNICEF's mandates in deciding to whom food and medical relief be given;

Cambodia than Holbrooke or Abramowitz; he and his officials disliked the pressure that both men had tried to put on U.N. organizations and the Secretary General. He sympathized with those African nations that complained that far too little attention had been paid to their refugee problems. He reacted with anger to Holbrooke's speech.

proper monitoring; restoring the medical infrastructure and allowing more medical teams into the country; permitting the ICRC and the Kampuchean Red Cross to trace the missing and reunite families; carrying out the assurances given to Grant and Hocke that there would be regular ministerial coordination with the Joint Mission; establishing a direct radio link with ICRC and UNICEF headquarters; authorizing a more direct flight path to Bangkok—so far $3.3 million had been wasted on fuel on the long flight path.

To underline the severity of the crisis, Jim Grant and Jean Pierre Hocke flew to Phnom Penh again. Foreign Minister Hun Sen said that the government might allow internal flights of Soviet or Vietnamese aircraft—he hoped that Sir Robert Jackson would be able to acquire Soviet planes when he went to Moscow. He gave some assurances about allowing aid personnel greater freedom to travel around the country and to meet with government officials. But the frequency of trains from Kompong Som to Phnom Penh could not be improved. Nor could trucks make the round trip in two instead of three days—Hun Sen said that the journey was just too dangerous unless they were in large convoys and such convoys took a long time to form. A more direct flight from Bangkok was unlikely "because Kampuchea has no means of defending its airspace," and a radio link was still out of the question. So was the idea of a formal land bridge—unless the Thais were prepared to sit down and discuss it with his government. Hun Sen knew that this was something Thailand would not and could never do so long as it did not recognize the regime.

The visit did not achieve very much. Afterward, at a joint press conference in New York, Grant was asked by a reporter about distribution problems. He declared that there was no diversion to Vietnamese or to the Kampuchean military or other "nonessential civilian purposes."

By this time, Malcolm Harper, once one of the most enthusiastic partisans of the Heng Samrin regime, believed that Oxfam might have to reconsider its entire operation inside Cambodia. He had come to the conclusion, shared by many others, including some of the better medical personnel from Eastern Europe and the East German engineers, that the authorities really only tolerated them because of the supplies they brought. Visas were more and more difficult to obtain; so was permission to travel within the country. Oxfam's drivers and interpreters were being increasingly harassed by the secret police for their friendship with the foreigners. Some old friends were now too frightened to talk to them at all. Recently almost an entire consignment of Oxfam-consortium shoes from Australia had disappeared from a ship even before it was unloaded; only the boxes were left when Harper got to Phnom Penh port. There were now reliable reports that in some provinces, like Prey Veng, the government was making peasants buy international supplies. Oxfam sugar was on sale in the market. Since food was not getting out, malnutrition was getting worse and worse. One Oxfam nutritional survey now showed that 50 percent of Phnom Penh children and 60 percent of those in the provinces were now malnourished or at risk.

Harper saw that the Vietnamese were increasingly unpopular and that the regime was "disliked by the broad mass of the people, distrusted by them and has little idea of how to rule effectively. Peace is as far away from Kampuchea as ever. Sporadic fighting, increasing government enforcement of a political ideology which nobody but they wants, violence, corruption and hunger stalk the lives of the Khmer people."

Harper and the other members of the Oxfam team in Phnom Penh asked themselves how much longer the Oxfam consortium could honestly continue its work in Cambodia. In early May, Harper wrote a long, intensely gloomy letter back to Oxford listing these and other problems. He reminded Oxford that the team had been given no proper reports on what had been done with the aid the consortium had delivered despite the promises to Brian Walker in October 1979.

"I do not honestly believe that this Government any longer cares greatly about the ordinary people of Kampuchea. They are now engaged in a programme of political indoctrination which is, in the view of many of us, doomed to failure, but which they will try to impose, through the use of fear and favouritism." Harper thought that the presence of the Western aid officials was vital in that it proved to ordinary Cambodians that there was concern for them in the world outside. Even so, there must come a point where the authorities made life so difficult and monitoring of the program so impossible "that we decide that the time has come to pull out and to consider spilling the beans. We are not there yet but we should not allow any woolly idealism to prevent us from reading the signs properly for the future."

This letter caused alarm in Oxford. Brian Walker, Oxfam's director general, sent by open telegram to Harper in the Hotel Samaki the text of a cable he was proposing to dispatch to the Foreign Minister. This message complained, very starkly, that despite the large amount of supplies shipped by the Oxfam consortium, "we have received no reports from our team in Phnom Penh confirming the effective distribution of this programme to village people, repeat to village people." Walker pointed out that this was contrary to the agreement he had made with Hun Sen and, moreover, "increasing independent reports of journalists and other visitors to Kampuchea cast doubt on the distribution of seed and food supplies to village people. This unacceptable to the consortium members and to our donating public. Consequently regretfully we are suspending all aid puts [sic] to Kampuchea with immediate effect." He said he would come to Phnom Penh in early June to resolve matters.

Malcolm Harper was somewhat shocked by this cable (which he knew the Foreign Ministry would have read before it reached him) and hurriedly replied asking Walker to do nothing till he came in June. In the meantime Oxfam sent its own protest, together with the ICRC and most other agencies except UNICEF in Phnom Penh, to the government.*

Instead of the telegram, Walker sent an *aide mémoire* to Hun

---

* John Saunders of UNICEF did not sign this protest; he held that he had already protested enough. The letter enclosed a copy of Oxfam's new nutritional survey supervised by Dr. Nick Maurice. It stated: "We in the international organisations have discussed these findings and view them with considerable alarm. . . . The agencies are unanimous sharing the view that these findings reflect an increasingly serious situation." They complained once again about the inadequate distribution and inefficiency of transport and pointed out that if, after all that had been imported, the Cambodian people were becoming even more hungry this would "seriously damage our ability to raise further funds for our programmes in Kampuchea. May we once again urge the government to consider most urgently what measures can be taken, even at this late stage, to improve the distribution of food to the people of Kampuchea . . ."

Sen in which he complained of "the failure of distribution to village people of food aid" and asked the government to "honour its side" of the agreement he had made with it in October 1979. He also asserted, "There is no doubt, however, that in cooperation with the Revolutionary Council, a land-bridge operation from Thailand and from Vietnam would be more efficient, less costly and a common-sense approach to easing the burden of the people of Kampuchea." He asked that Oxfam be allowed to bring five hundred draft buffaloes and oxcarts full of seed and rice across the Thai border and that it be allowed to drive trucks across the Thai border. Until now some Oxfam officials had tended to dismiss the border as principally an American ploy to rebuild the Khmer Rouge.

When Walker arrived in Phnom Penh in June, he was treated as a most honored guest; he was much encouraged by what he saw and by the assurances he was given. His own report states that he told the Foreign Minister that the thefts by drivers and dockers were "not an issue between us." Other aid officials believed that this wastage now reached epidemic proportions. After returning to Britain, he wrote an article for the *Observer* in which he declared that the gloom of Western commentators about what had been done originated "largely, I suspect, because they rely for their source material on stories and rumours circulating out of Bangkok and along the Thai border, liberally laced with propaganda. Inside Kampuchea it looks different."

Relations between the government and the agencies deteriorated further at the end of May, when John Saunders, Hans Page of FAO and Malcolm Harper of Oxfam refused, at a "Solidarity Conference," to stand with everyone else to acclaim a resolution denouncing Thailand, the United States, China together with Pol Pot and Ieng Sary, and demanding that the United Nations seat the Heng Samrin regime forthwith. Saunders explained to the Foreign Ministry afterward that as nonpolitical aid personnel they could not officially support any such resolution. But to some members of the Heng Samrin regime and to some Vietnamese the incident was undoubtedly further confirmation of their belief that the aid agencies represented the hostile world outside, which still recognized the Khmer Rouge government seventeen months after its overthrow.

The regime was further irritated by criticism expressed at the U.N. Conference on Cambodia, which, under pressure from ASEAN and the United States, Kurt Waldheim finally opened in Geneva at the end of May. It was described as a humanitarian not a political conference. After an unenthusiastic welcome from Waldheim, the chair was taken by Michael Peacock, the Australian Foreign Minister—about the fourth choice after several European foreign ministers had turned down the ASEAN invitation to chair the session.

The fear of famine—a second famine—was reiterated by many delegates, and the American and other delegates called for more foreign aid workers inside Cambodia, improved monitoring, more medical teams and greater distribution in areas of provincial need. Much of the criticism was based on much more pessimistic and critical reports which the Joint Mission in Phnom Penh had recently been supplying to the donors.* It was not, in other words, mere Western propaganda. That, however, made it no more palatable to the Phnom Penh authorities.†

However, from their point of view, the conference was useful, even essential. After the hiatus at the March donors meeting, it reaffirmed the commitment of the donors to the entire Cambodia relief operation. This was partly a tribute to Robert Jackson's powers of persuasion. It reflected also the fact that the donors now felt that they

* Thus, for example, a report of May 1, 1980, to the donors had acknowledged that "The bulk of the relief food available appears to have been distributed in Phnom Penh and to the consumers in the provinces, who had priority under the government's allocation system—such as government employees, and manual workers, for whom it has been the only remuneration. It appears that little so far has been distributed to the ordinary consumer, especially in rural areas where local stocks might have been presumed to be available. . . ."

† Mr. Bui Huu Nhan, the Vietnamese adviser to the Foreign Ministry, complained to UNICEF's public-relations officer, Jacques Danois, who had never hidden his friendship for Hanoi, about such criticisms. According to Danois, he said that "the increasing number of high-ranking visitors imposed on the Kampuchean authorities by those agencies gives the impression that their government is under permanent surveillance; traditional Khmer hospitality is 'used' for the agencies to control and check on the work achieved with the government; no patience is shown by the visitors." Mr. Nhan also declared that it was well known that "international agency members are working closely with agents of foreign powers in trying to undermine the Kampuchean effort to reconstruct the country. We know how close is the contact between responsibles of so-called 'operation' and very aggressive embassies in Bangkok."

were getting more truthful reports from the Joint Mission. On the American side a lot of the pressure came from Richard Holbrooke and Mort Abramowitz. Each of them wished to continue to support Thai policy, but each was also determined that the over-all relief effort should continue—even if only at a lower level than the rhetoric of the fall of 1979 had presaged. The conference raised pledges of about $116 million.

It was also now clear that the donors wanted UNICEF to remain as the lead agency. With considerable misgivings, especially about the border, Jim Grant agreed.

In early June, John Saunders left Phnom Penh. Despite the fact that he had run the program since December 1979, not a single Cambodian official came to the airport to say goodbye, let alone to give him any thanks. Offsetting this extraordinary, hurtful rebuke, was the rather surprising fact that the Soviet ambassador did come to bid him farewell.

Saunders returned to New York to take charge of UNICEF's Cambodia operation there. He was replaced in Phnom Penh by Kurt Jansson, a calm Finn who had spent his career in the U.N. Development Program and other posts. Jansson had been brought out of retirement by Sir Robert Jackson; he came to Phnom Penh in June 1980 without the burden of disappointed hopes and frustrations felt by many of those officials who had been there since the early, heady days of the operation in 1979.

Throughout the summer of 1980 relations between the Joint Mission and the authorities in Phnom Penh improved. This was not because the program in Cambodia suddenly started to work smoothly; it was rather that Jansson considered that complaint was now counterproductive. There were still serious problems with the rate of unloading at the ports, with the use of trucks, with the methods of distribution. And the extent to which the Soviets and the Vietnamese really wished to cooperate with the Joint Mission remained a matter of doubt. For example, despite Vietnamese promises—initially those of Pham Van Dong himself to Labouisse, back in November 1979— the Joint Mission was not able to make use of the port of Vung Tau in southern Vietnam for shipping supplies into eastern Cambodia. It turned out that the Vietnamese would allow it only if the Joint Mission paid road haulage fees across Vietnam which were quite prohibitive.

More disappointing was the affair of the Soviet aircraft. Robert Jackson had flown to Moscow in May convinced that, *inter alia,* he could persuade the Soviet Red Cross to provide planes or helicopters and crews for internal flights delivering emergency supplies within Cambodia. The Soviets agreed to send another team of dockers to Kompong Som, but it transpired that the only Soviet interest in the aircraft was to make money. Charles Egger of UNICEF went to Moscow in June to follow up Jackson's request. He was directed not to the Soviet Red Cross but to Aeroflot and was told that the cost of five helicopters for three months would be $4 million. This included the crew, but fuel and insurance would be extra. Egger's cable to New York reflected his frustration. "Civil Aviation from the beginning considered it entirely a commercial proposition to be paid in dollars. . . . Aircraft would become available only during November. Aeroflot had no answer concerning how jet fuel could be obtained and made available to landing places. Flying time per day would be a maximum of four hours. Aeroflot would also not accept ruble payment in the unlikely case of (Soviet) government grant. Government never considered even possibility of granting aircrafts to international organizations."

Despite these external setbacks, Kurt Jansson felt that by mid-July many of the internal recommendations of UNICEF's Logistics Report—which he had actually written—had been quietly implemented. There was indeed some improvement in offtake—thanks in good part to the efforts of the UNICEF transport officer, Horst Ruttinger and his East German team. More trucks had been assigned to the Phnom Penh–Kompong Som route and the turn-around time had been reduced. There was now one train a day, and its capacity had been increased to 15,000 tons. The Russian dockers at Kompong Som were working very hard.

Unfortunately, before this improvement, the World Food Program had unilaterally—and to the consternation of its partners—decided to cut back on its rate of food shipment to Cambodia. By the end of June just 110,600 tons of food had been delivered since the beginning of the program. This was a far cry from the 30,000 tons a month that the organizations had envisaged back in October 1979—that would have brought in about 240,000 tons of food by now. Yet WFP slowed the shipments even further.

The row about the rate of shipments continued throughout the summer. WFP's principal argument was the cost of demurrage—up to $4,000 a day. But UNICEF and Jackson had always taken the view that "large deliveries [of food assistance were] essential to provide a continuity of supply." Jackson was one of the most experienced transport organizers in the U.N. system; he had been decorated twice for a superb supply operation in support of the Allied base in Malta during the Second World War and subsequently for a much larger operation in the Middle East theater. More recently he had masterminded the vast U.N. relief operation to Bangladesh. He argued that only the visible pressure of waiting ships would improve the rate of unloading and that in terms of the over-all cost of the relief operation, the demurrage was quite insignificant. (Moreover, the World Food Program rarely paid its own costs; its fund-raising and management system was so poor that it frequently had to be bailed out by UNICEF or other organizations.)

Throughout the summer, in his tireless but exhausting voyages around the world's capitals, Jackson repeated a single slogan to WFP and other international officials: "Ship. Ship. Ship. Ship. Ship." To ministers of the Heng Samrin regime he insisted that if they really wanted to be recognized as the legitimate government, they must show that they could govern. Among other things, they must produce good discharge figures. This was a rather original criterion for membership in the U.N.

WFP refused to do as Jackson asked until Jackson persuaded Waldheim himself to agree to send a strongly worded telegram to Rome:

> Secretary General fully shares Jackson's deep concern that unless WFP, in partnership with UNICEF and ICRC, can deliver the approximately 120,000 tons of rice required by mid-October, the humanitarian assistance programme as a whole will be regarded as a failure with grave implications for human beings concerned and, although less important, credibility of U.N. system . . . Sec. Gen.

and Jackson dismayed at preoccupation of Rome with offloading and offtake capacities, which best left to Jansson to assure through information and means at his disposal, and with demurrage costs, which we have made clear are the responsibility of the joint programme [UNICEF, ICRC]. It absolutely essential in our judgement that KPS [Kompong Som] and PNP [Phnom Penh] ports be pressed to capacity. . . . Risk of some quote unnecessary waste of resources on demurrage unquote far less important than possible waste of human resources. U.N. will be placed in intolerable position if there is repetition of recent situation where offtake dwindles as result low volume of supplies delivered to ports.

Such pressure finally compelled WFP to increase its shipping rates once more. But by the end of August 1980 it still had managed to deliver, in the last year, only 141,882 tons of food. In defense of the World Food Program, it has to be said that by the end of August 1980 the Heng Samrin regime had distributed less than 100,000 tons of the food that had been delivered (or 99,356 tons, to be precise). This meant that over 41,000 tons of food were still in the warehouses at the ports.

One explanation that the authorities gave for this—which Jackson and Jansson accepted—was that they were building up stocks in anticipation of the country's indigenous food supplies becoming completely exhausted by the end of the year, when the need for imported foods would be even greater than now. At the same time they insisted, with some plausibility, that it was more important to use the trucks for shipping seed to the farmers while there was still time for it to be planted.

15 ❧ Seed

Water has fashioned Cambodia, and rice, together with water, gives its people life. The massive shipments of food and trucks on which the international community embarked in late 1979 could only be a short-term response to immediate crisis. What was needed was the restoration of agriculture in order to return the countryside to the abundance that it had enjoyed before war and revolution began to destroy it. In this process the provision of seed was a vital part. The story of how the world tried to resow Cambodia was, perhaps because of the symbolism of seed, one of the most contentious of the whole operation.

There are two Cambodian rice crops every year; they are planted around the monsoon. The main crop is planted in May, June, July and August as the rains inundate and soften the land. It is harvested as those waters recede toward the end of the year. In the areas around the Great Lake, which bursts its banks every monsoon, the peasants plant floating rice every April and May. This is harvested nine months later, when the stems may have grown to a height of three or four meters in response to the peak of the flood. In November the smaller dry-season crop is planted, and it too is harvested in January or February. The rituals of rice cultivation, together with fishing, could easily be adequate to occupy the peasants throughout the cycles of the year.

Before 1970, 90 percent of the people lived off the land, and Cambodia was more than self-sufficient in rice production; rice was also the country's principal export. In 1969–70, 3.8 million tons of paddy had been harvested off 2.4 million hectares of land, most of it in the provinces around the Great Lake and the Mekong river—Battambang, Siem Reap, Kompong Cham, Takeo and Prey Veng.

The bombing, the fighting and the flight of peasants from their land between 1970 and 1975 almost destroyed Cambodia's riziculture; by 1975 the country was dependent on United States food handouts. After their victory, the Khmer Rouge attempted to construct a completely new agricultural system based more on theories of collectivism and economies of scale than on local conditions. It is still unclear just what the rice production was by the time they were overthrown by the Vietnamese in January 1979. Rather astonishingly, rice was being exported again, but the Cambodian people themselves were being deprived of adequate rations throughout much of the country. Afterward, peasants claimed that the vast new fields, dams and canals that they had been ordered to build rarely worked. Instead they upset the ecological balance of the countryside.

Once, I was in a boat steaming up a narrow river, just off the Great Lake. I was being taken to see a fishery in one of the richest of the fishing areas. Along with rice, fish is a staple food in Cambodia and the most important source of protein. Long before our old boat came around the bend of the river, an extraordinary smell came wafting out to greet us. The river was jammed with hundreds of thousands of dead fish, packed tight as ice floes. What had happened? I asked. "Pol Pot" came the reply.

It turned out that the Khmer Rouge had built a huge dam just upstream from here and the water in this ancient fishing village was now far shallower than it had ever been before. In the heat of the dry-season sun the fish had, quite simply, cooked. Such dramatic problems apart, there was a great lack of fish nets, hooks and boats. The government claimed that fish production in 1979 was only about 15,000 metric tons. Ten years before it had been 200,000 tons.

The size of the 1979 rice crop was impossible to judge accurately. According to the Ministry of Agriculture, between 600,000 and 700,000 hectares of rice were harvested at the end of the year. The total paddy production in the 1979–80 crops was said to be 637,000 tons. Kom Som Ol, the Vice-Minister, was making plans which were specifically intended to double the production during 1980 to over 1.2 million hectares. This was a necessarily ambitious target. The government was trying, with some success, to organize the peasantry into communal groups known as Krom Samaki ("Solidarity Groups") for the cultivation of the land. But the constraints were enormous. Large numbers of draft animals had died under the Khmer Rouge; there were constant stories of people having to pull plows themselves. In 1979 there were said to be only 850,000 draft animals, compared with 2.5 million before the war. There was also a shortage of men to till the fields, which were in many places quite derelict, and a dearth of plows, plow tips and hoes, quite apart from seed and fertilizer.

For the Ministry's plan some 80,000 tons of seed would be needed in 1980. Kom Som Ol thought that less than half of it would be available as paddy from the 1979 harvest. This meant that up to 50,000 tons of seed would have to come from abroad.

Vietnam promised to provide 10,000 tons. (It was never possible to verify whether it actually did so.) Oxfam offered to buy 10,000 tons. And the Food and Agriculture Organization (FAO) drew up an Agricultural Rehabilitation Program under which it would provide 30,000 tons.*

With the FAO seed, which was expected to cost about $14 million, were to go 1,600 pumps, 4,400 tons of fertilizer, 125 tons of insecticides, 1,500 sprayers and 5,000 tons of urea. It was hoped that this would be enough to rehabilitate 370,000 hectares of farmland in several of the main rice-growing provinces. How much food would all this provide? FAO calculated that with luck, and assuming a basic ration of 400 grams a day, it should produce enough to feed the three million inhabitants of those provinces for 150 days.†

---

* Unlike UNICEF, the FAO could not legally operate on its own in Cambodia, since the Heng Samrin regime was not a member of the United Nations. It was able to do so only under the umbrella of UNICEF. In order to unfreeze old U.N. Development Program funds, the plan was put forward under the device of continuing an agricultural-development project started under the Lon Nol regime in 1972.

† It was impossible to say just how much food the country would need in 1980. It depended on whether one accepted the government's propaganda claim that only 4.5 million Khmers had survived Pol Pot, or the Ministry of Agriculture's assessment that there were now 6 million Khmers alive and to be fed.

. . .

The United Nations world is often accused, by those outside it, of inefficiency, of complacency, of overstaffed headquarters, of overpaid, pompous and protocol-conscious officials, of lack of cooperation and coordination with other agencies, of sweetheart relationshps with governments, and more besides. Perhaps no other agency has been so widely criticized in recent years as the Food and Agriculture Organization, and its director, Edouard Saouma.

FAO was created at the end of 1945, with responsibilities for agricultural rehabilitation and development. At first it was also involved in emergency food relief to starving civilians. As the wounds of war were healed and as the food emergency receded with the war itself, FAO began to concentrate on agricultural development in what later became known as the "Third World." It was not until the 1960s, when it became clear that agricultural development often could not be separated from the problems of starvation and overpopulation, that FAO again became involved in relief work. In 1962 the General Assembly and FAO itself set up its subsidiary, the World Food Program (WFP). WFP was supposed to be a clearing house between food-deficit and food-surplus nations and to channel food aid in emergencies—as in the case of Cambodia.

In 1983 a Rome-based English-language paper, the *Daily American,* published two long dossiers documenting the follies of FAO. It accused the organization of becoming an "arrogant, over-budgeted, and rarely effective bureaucracy incapable of attending to a problem that is grave enough to change the course of civilization as we know it today." FAO was accused of being more concerned to protect its own image than to feed the hungry and of refusing to accept any sort of outside accountability.

Much of the blame for the organization's problems has been laid at the door of FAO's Director General Edouard Saouma, a Lebanese Christian official who has become one of the most regal of the U.N.'s princes. In 1977 Saouma engineered a change in FAO's constitution to enable him to be reelected for a second term, as he was in 1981; he was to be paid $750,000 for his services over the six-year period.

FAO is a highly centralized agency, with a staff of over four thousand in Rome. One of its most serious organizational problems is that Saouma has allowed almost no delegation. Its few men and women in the field have to refer almost all decisions back to Rome. They are also enjoined, even more than other agencies, to secrecy. The leaders of the Joint Mission in Phnom Penh frequently found that the FAO representative there would not give them statistics on agricultural matters that he had acquired or worked out—because Rome insisted that the other agencies obtain them only through FAO headquarters.

FAO's plan was accepted in principle by the Joint Mission at the meetings in Bangkok in January 1980. But FAO did not take adequate account of the urgency with which the seed had to be acquired. Some of it, particularly the floating-rice seed, had to be found, purchased, shipped, unloaded and distributed among Cambodia's rice-growing provinces by the end of April—that is, within three months. The congestion at Cambodia's ports alone would have rendered that a formidable challenge. Additional procurement problems, especially in Thailand, made it even more difficult to overcome.

FAO decided to procure almost half of the 30,000 tons of seed— and all of the 2,500 tons of floating-rice seed—from Thailand. There was a good reason: Thai seed matches the varieties needed in Cambodia more nearly than seed available elsewhere. The rest of the seed was to be bought in Vietnam and the Philippines.

However, in Thailand—unlike in the Philippines—rice seed is considered a strategic commodity, which can be exported only under license. As a result, there is no commercial rice seed industry with experience of procuring, processing, testing and exporting rice seed. It is not clear that FAO understood this; certainly it did not concentrate resources on solving the problem early in 1980. Licenses were not granted, and it soon became clear to other organizations, if not to FAO, that there was a real danger of the seed being shipped to Phnom Penh too late to be planted. To some relief officials in Thailand and to some diplomats an alternative route began to seem attractive—the land bridge.

In logistic terms the idea made a lot of sense. Over 20,000 Cambodians were coming three times a week to the land bridge for rice. It led straight into Battambang, Cambodia's largest rice-growing province, for which the FAO plan had earmarked 11,000 tons of seed, but which could take much more. In theory, seed could be got to farmers and into the ground far quicker across the border than if it were shipped to Kompong Som and then had to make its way painfully and slowly hundreds of miles overland to the west.

There was also a political catch in favor of the land bridge; since the Thai government favored the land bridge and the distribution point was technically on Thai soil, there would be no problem about export licenses.

The idea of putting seed as well as food across the land bridge came from UNICEF's border office, from CARE, one of the larger American voluntary agencies in Thailand, and from the Kampuchea Emergency Group (KEG) in the U.S. Embassy. The real impetus came from the Embassy. Michael Eiland of KEG encouraged Rudi von Bernuth, CARE's director, to submit a formal proposal; within thirty-six hours, Morton Abramowitz had guaranteed von Bernuth an initial $100,000 from his Ambassador's Discretionary Fund. It was an extraordinary demonstration of the United States government's ability to harness voluntary agencies to its policies.

As in so many of its initiatives on Cambodia, the United States motives were mixed. Most Embassy officials dealing with Cambodia were genuinely, even passionately, concerned about the country. Some felt great guilt about the United States history there. They were predicting, as were some relief officials, a new famine in Cambodia. They were castigating the failures of distribution within the country. They were genuinely anxious that the 1980 harvest be as large as possible. And they saw no way in which the country's frail logistics could cope with the import of adequate seed as well as food. At the same time, most of them intensely disliked the Vietnamese rule of Cambodia, and the idea of putting seed over the land bridge was politically very attractive. It would show Cambodian farmers once again that the West was able and willing to hand over crucial supplies directly to them, without the layer of officialdom that the Vietnamese and the Heng Samrin regime interposed. Obviously it would offer Cambodian farmers a compelling contrast to Vietnamese rule. By the end of the 1980 rice-seed program, the United States government had provided about $5 million to the voluntary agencies with which to purchase seed for the border operation. Most of this was provided through the Food Management Grant under which the United States was giving money to the U.N.'s World Food Program for the use of voluntary agencies cooperating with WFP. In 1981 it provided another $4 million for seed across the land bridge.

In February 1980, Knud Christensen, the director of UNICEF's "Kampuchea Emergency Unit" in Bangkok, had doubts about the operation, but he soon became almost as enthusiastic about the idea as the American Embassy and proposed that UNICEF should try a pilot distribution of 400 tons. But his partners in the ICRC were much less keen, largely because they feared it would further damage their standing with the authorities in Phnom Penh.

This was the fear of both UNICEF and ICRC officials in Phnom Penh. John Saunders told Bangkok that such an American-financed expansion of the land bridge might strain the agencies' relations with the Heng Samrin regime. And he noted with exasperation that, while the donors made a great fuss about monitoring the supplies distributed through Phnom Penh, there was no attempt to monitor anything that went over the land bridge.

FAO headquarters in Rome also disliked the land-bridge idea and wanted the seed to go formally through Phnom Penh. FAO officials argued that their energetic and efficient man in Phnom Penh, Hans Page had, after a lot of work, drawn up a detailed plan with the Ministry of Agriculture and that this should be respected. They said also that seed was not just any relief commodity, and that its distribution must be organized within the context of a careful plan. But by the middle of March 1980, FAO had managed to ship only 620 tons of its promised 30,000 tons of seed to Cambodia—all from the Philippines. None of the floating rice, which needed to be planted in April, had even been procured, let alone shipped. At a gloomy meeting of U.N. and CARE officials in Bangkok on March 19 the FAO official, Mr. Vira, acknowledged that "Delivery of sufficient seed to the planting areas in time is clearly going to be a major problem and could well prove to be impossible."

UNICEF agreed to the pilot distribution. Two days later, on March 21, the first 200 tons of seed purchased by CARE was distributed at Nong Chan. Twenty thousand people from the interior were given about ten kilos of seed per person. Knud Christensen of UNICEF cabled New York to say "Khmer farmers received seeds with unconcealed delight." But ten kilos does not plant much; they wanted more. CARE immediately applied for more money from the U.S. Embassy. At this stage the U.N. agencies and even ICRC delegates in Thailand agreed.

That same day UNICEF, ICRC and WFP in Bangkok sent a statement to their respective HQs saying that the present discharge rate of Phnom Penh and Kompong Som ports was so low that other methods of delivery had to be explored. If every family coming to the border were given forty to fifty kilograms of seed that would be enough to plant 125,000 hectares. They recommended that efforts should be made "at highest level" to persuade the Thai and Phnom Penh authorities to open a formal land bridge and take seed across the border at Aranyaprathet, straight to the Battambang rice fields only 35 kilometers away. They dismissed the possibility of an airlift to Phnom Penh, as able to provide only a "costly and an insignificant contribution."

But within a week, the Joint Mission decided to launch an airlift. Thailand finally granted some export licenses. A DC-10 was chartered to fly at least the floating-rice seed into Phnom Penh in time for its planting deadline at the end of April. In the middle of April a second DC-10 was hired. At the same time, to the anger of aid officials in Phnom Penh, who believed that, despite its poor distribution of food, the Heng Samrin regime would make every effort to push seed urgently into the provinces, the land bridge was expanded.

First UNICEF and ICRC agreed that 3,000 tons could be sent across. Then UNICEF received a call from an American official named George Warner. Warner, who was on loan from U.S. AID, had been installed by the Embassy in the World Food Program office to oversee the United States Food Management Grant. It was an odd position and revealed the extent of United States influence over the World Food Program. On March 28 he informed UNICEF that the Embassy now thought that at least 10,000 tons of seed should go across the border, and the United States was prepared to provide $3 million toward its purchase. He invited UNICEF to a meeting not at the U.N. headquarters but at the United States Embassy to discuss the proposal. Unhappy with the choice of venue, UNICEF agreed only when ICRC was also invited.

To their shock the UNICEF and ICRC representatives found themselves in a very mixed group. It included not only several American voluntary agencies, which were critical of Phnom Penh and anxious to build up the border, but also Bangkok seed dealers eager to sell as much as they could.

Knud Christensen refused to have any discussion of policy in front of the dealers. They were therefore asked to leave. It then became clear that the United States government was offering funding to four American voluntary agencies—CARE, World Relief, Food for the Hungry, and Catholic Relief Services—to purchase not ten thousand but fifteen thousand tons of seed. Furthermore, one of the voluntary agencies, World Relief, announced that it intended to buy seed with its own funds as well.

The purpose of the meeting was clearly to pressure UNICEF and ICRC into allowing such an amount to be pushed across the land bridges they managed at the border. Christensen cabled New York to express his resentment at such United States maneuvers—but unlike ICRC he was not opposed in principle to increasing the scale of the project.* He thought Battambang alone could easily absorb at least 16,000 tons of seed.

While UNICEF and ICRC were deciding what to do about the massive expansion proposed, World Relief and CARE each provided 2,000 tons of seed to be put across the border in early April. This initial distribution was marred by the fact that some of the seed provided by World Relief was of very poor quality—indeed, it had been

* Christensen would have been even more alarmed had he known of Warner's personal interest in the seed program. He was later charged with having demanded a kickback of seven dollars for every ton of seed that the World Food Program purchased through the Bangkok-based company, Suisindo, with which it and many of the other international organizations were dealing. Suisindo informed Ambassador Abramowitz of the extortion demand from a member of his staff. Abramowitz asked the company to make the payoffs as Warner demanded until the United States government had enough evidence to arrest him. In September 1980 Warner was arrested in Washington and charged with having illegally accepted $138,562. After a complicated bargaining process he pleaded guilty to a lesser charge and was fined $40,000.

mixed with chaff by unscrupulous Thai merchants. When this was discovered, the agencies imposed stricter quality controls and the rest of the seed pushed across the border was almost all of high quality. It was difficult to determine just how much of the rice seed was actually being taken back into Cambodia instead of being kept at the border by residents to be eaten or sold, but since large quantities of food were also being distributed there, this loss may not have been serious. As for Phnom Penh's attitude, farmers from the interior said that Vietnamese officials and soldiers had encouraged them to come to pick up seed now, but had said that they would close the border during May to make sure that everyone was at home during the planting season. That was sensible.

One must remember that throughout this period, spring and early summer 1980, constant predictions of a new famine were being made—by some aid officials, by the United States government, and by some reporters on the basis of those two sources. This put further pressure upon the organizations to expand the land bridge.

On April 8, 1980, during a worldwide telephone conference between the New York, Rome, Geneva and Bangkok offices of UNICEF, WFP and ICRC, the organizations agreed to purchase 7,500 tons of seed offered under the U.S. Food Management Grant. ICRC was still backtracking and insisted that distribution be limited to 150 tons a day. This restriction was bitterly denounced by Reg Reimer, World Relief's Asia Director, who was taking a very aggressive attitude toward the ICRC. He said that World Relief would refuse to take a grant of just under one million dollars if the 150-ton-per-day restriction was imposed.

World Relief, which had no operation in Phnom Penh and therefore no reason to be concerned about the attitude of the authorities there, became more and more strident in its denunciations of ICRC. Words like "short-sighted," "immoral," and "criminal" were frequently bandied about, even in public. As a result ICRC delegates became increasingly disenchanted with the entire border operation and what they saw as American bullying. The whole dispute received critical press attention. *Newsweek* ran an article entitled "Seeds of Sorrow," and the *Far Eastern Economic Review* one called "Seeds of Survival." Each was critical of the international organizations, arguing that the airlift was terribly wasteful and that far more seed could be got into Cambodia far more quickly and far more cheaply by expanding the land bridge. By contrast, the Bangkok *Post* carried an article by Jacques Danois, UNICEF's public-relations officer in Bangkok, who, rather remarkably, attacked his own organization's border program. The land bridge was, he said, diverting farmers from their homes and the task of sowing. He suggested that it be ended. On the border UNICEF's representative Ulf Kristoffersen was outraged by his colleague's piece—it was "a stab in the back," he wrote to Knud Christensen.

Meanwhile, the FAO's formal shipments to Phnom Penh were finally getting under way. FAO's first boatload left Bangkok on April 19. The airlift was behind schedule because of breakdowns in one aircraft, but by the last week of April about 2,000 tons of floating-rice seed had been flown into Phnom Penh. As the Joint Mission in Phnom Penh had predicted, the government was shipping the seed with unprecedented efficiency to the provinces. FAO now hoped to deliver 20,000 tons to Phnom Penh and Kompong Som by the middle of May.

In Bangkok rows about whether to expand the seed land bridge further continued, with ICRC always resisting it, on the grounds that it was becoming disproportionate to the Phnom Penh operation and could be a magnet attracting people away from their fields. At the end of April Knud Christensen actually threatened to resign as a mark of his frustration at not being able to hand out more than 150 tons of seed a day. Under this and other pressures ICRC relented and agreed that during May 200 tons a day would be allowed across. But ICRC delegates in Aranyaprathet demanded that they be allowed to check UNICEF convoys; if they carried more, they must be turned back. UNICEF often just ignored their partner's anxieties.

Many farmers who picked up seed at Nong Chan were complaining that they did not have the tools, let alone the oxen, with which to carry out their planting. So, World Relief proposed supplying hoe heads, plow tips, rope, fish nets and fishhooks, and even oxen and oxcarts at the border. The oxcarts proposal was also taken up by Oxfam-America, which, independently of Oxfam-U.K., had become involved in the border.

World Relief also proposed sending sickles over the land bridge. This idea appalled many of the U.N. and ICRC personnel, including Jackson, Christensen and Hocke. "We cannot be accused of arming the peasantry," said Christensen, who recalled how, in the Danish resistance, he had used sickles against the Germans, before he was imprisoned in Sachsenhausen. Eventually, however, World Relief obtained permission direct from Thai Supreme Command to send sickles, hoe heads and other agricultural supplies across the border. UNICEF and ICRC insisted that it be done on a different day, quite separately from the seed distribution. "This is your country, you can do what you like," Jean Pierre Hocke of ICRC said to Thai officials. "But not with us."

Throughout this period Abramowitz was continually attempting to force the ICRC to send more and more seed across the border. On May 9 officials from the United States, British, Australian, West German, Japanese, Swedish and Canadian embassies met in Bangkok to discuss how to overcome what they considered ICRC's continued "obstructionism" on the seed land bridge. They agreed to ask their embassies in Geneva to put pressure on Alexander Hay, the president of the ICRC, to raise the 200-ton daily limit.

In Geneva Alexander Hay told officials of the donor countries that ICRC would continue to be "flexible" and would respond to changes in circumstances. But ICRC could not compromise its world-wide humanitarian mandate by appearing to take sides in a political dispute. It had already gone far enough. "If the Americans insist on having it their way in Cambodia," he told one Western ambassador, "they would have to use someone else, not ICRC."

In Washington, Jean Pierre Hocke met with two senior State Department officials, John Negroponte and Frank Loy, on May 13. Hocke attempted to convince them that FAO's own shipments to Phnom Penh and Kompong Som were proceeding satisfactorily. He argued that FAO intended to deliver 16,000 tons from Phnom Penh to Battambang, that 13,000 tons had already been sent across the land bridge and that this would, on present funding, be increased to 19,000 tons. He thought this was more than enough. Moreover, there was no way FAO officials could advise farmers how to plant rice delivered at the border. (No more could they inside Cambodia, of course.) Finally, he argued, the oxen should now be used for plowing rather than traveling to the border.

Hocke impressed his interlocutors; they cabled a summary of his to the Embassy in Bangkok with the comment that "Hocke presents a cogent argument." This was not the view of the Embassy, and the Embassy view won the day.* Throughout May and early June the United States and other Western governments continued to put pressure on the ICRC and, to a lesser extent, UNICEF. At the Geneva Conference at the end of May, delegates poured scorn on ICRC for declaring that there was now "seed saturation" within the country. Under such assaults, ICRC finally agreed to increase the distribution of seed to 600 tons a day. But by now the rains were beginning to make the trails to the border impassable, and it was true that the farmers and oxen were now needed to work the fields.

Robert Ashe, who was working for ICRC at Nong Chan, wrote a weekly field report, which was distributed to other agencies before ICRC realized its content. It complained, *inter alia,* that "we should have been doing much larger distributions in the dry weather and be tapering off the operation now. As it is, we face a whole series of problems at this stage . . . shortage of trucks . . . shortage of rice . . . break-up of the road . . . rice and seed sacks lying in pools of water . . . break-up of the trails leading back into Cambodia. . . . When will ICRC start to think ahead? Where is the planning? Is it our intention that ICRC become known as the too-little, too-late

---

* In the Kampuchea Emergency Group office, Colonel Michael Eiland drafted a reply that Abramowitz then sent to Washington. This declared that Hocke's arguments were neither "cogent" nor new, and they were based on "limited observation and inadequate data." "It is almost irrelevant to speak of the needs of the country or any province given the dearth of reliable data and the number of variables involved. . . . It is perverse to argue that provision of seed should be limited because FAO officials are not on hand to give technical advice. Khmer farmers have been at this game rather a long time and are proficient at the basics of growing rice. . . . Our aim is to get the maximum amount of seed and food in before the rains—no limits. We too want the draft oxen to be used for ploughing. The quicker the ox carts can be loaded now, the quicker the oxen and farmers can return to the fields. Once the rains come we should see the border reduced and perhaps we should move to reduce it. That will in part be the test of food deliveries through Phnom Penh . . . If it has been passed, we can all relax a little more and we will tip our hat to ICRC and get off this seedy subject. Abramowitz."

agency? . . . It is time to throw away the 'getting out' mentality that many in ICRC are suffering from and to throw ourselves more wholeheartedly into the business of saving lives. . . . It is time, also, to begin making decisions on assistance less for political reasons and more on a humanitarian basis, so that the people of Cambodia can begin to rebuild their own lives instead of continuing to suffer." Ashe was told by ICRC delegates that, while ICRC welcomed criticism, such comments should in future be made only internally.

By the time the seed land bridge finally ended on June 20, some 23,521 tons of seed had been distributed at the border. During the same period only a little more than half of the 30,000 tons of seed that FAO had planned to ship to Phnom Penh had arrived. All of Oxfam's 10,000 tons had arrived and some seed had come from Vietnam, though no one knew just how much. It had been distributed efficiently by the regime, along with fertilizer and tools—but it was still not enough.

In Phnom Penh, government officials now said that it was possible to plant in some areas as late as August. So FAO continued to try to purchase and ship more seed out of Thailand. The problems became more, not less difficult.

The Thai government now decided that seed was not only a "strategic commodity" requiring an export license, but also an extremely profitable commodity in which the government should have a greater share. At the end of June, FAO was informed that for any future purchase it would have to deal exclusively through the official Marketing Organization of Farmers and pay whatever premium they required.

The inflation in the price of seed was considerable. At the beginning of the year it had started at around $150 a ton. In June, FAO contracted with private suppliers to buy another 7,000 tons at $237 a ton plus $25 a ton export premium. But the Marketing Organization of Farmers intervened, demanding that FAO pay another $110 for each ton, bringing the price to $347 a ton plus premium.

It is understandable that FAO might object to this; however, it is worth remembering that prices outside Thailand were far higher. Oxfam was paying $625 a ton for rice from China for Phnom Penh.

Throughout July, FAO refused to pay the new Thai charges; officials in Rome decided that they would have no dealings with the Marketing Organization. Unfortunately they did not tell their partners in the Joint Mission of their decision.

When Jean Pierre Hocke of ICRC and Jim Grant of UNICEF visited Cambodia again at the end of July they realized that there was still time to plant and decided that, whatever the cost, 15,000 tons more rice seed must be got into the soil before the end of August. If FAO could not meet its obligations alone, UNICEF and ICRC would have to play a more direct role. ICRC would charter another plane to restart the airlift and, even more to the point, they would pay the "procurement and handling fee" that the Thai Marketing Organization of Farmers was demanding of FAO. The organizations agreed to airlift 1,500 tons of seed and to send the rest by sea. ICRC chartered a DC-10—the contract inevitably had a heavy penalty clause in event of cancellation.

Negotiation that can fairly be described as "Byzantine" proceeded among ICRC, UNICEF, FAO and the Thai Marketing Organization of Farmers through early August. The one success was that the Marketing Organization agreed to reduce the surcharge from $110 to $55 a ton. UNICEF and ICRC agreed to pay this fee but stressed that the seed must be shipped "within a matter of a few days."

But FAO had not checked whether the supplier with whom they had been negotiating for months actually had an export license. They now discovered that he did not. Their contract was worthless; those months had been wasted.

On the evening of July 25, Sir Robert Jackson called an emergency meeting in his room at the Hotel Erawan. Kani P. Wagner, the head of FAO's Office of Special Relief Operation, who had been sent out from Rome to deal with the crisis, declared that FAO would have absolutely nothing to do with the Marketing Organization. UNICEF and ICRC would have to make any purchase entirely on their own.

This announcement caused some anger among Wagner's colleagues. According to UNICEF's minutes of the meeting, both Hocke and Jackson rebuked him sharply, pointing out that the Food and

Agriculture Organization had committed itself months ago to deliver 30,000 tons of seed to Cambodia. They warned that the consequences of failure would be very damaging to Mr. Saouma, FAO's Director General.

Wagner apparently was shaken by the tirade and understood what might happen. He called Rome at once. Jackson was not surprised when Saouma told Wagner to go ahead and deal with the Marketing Organization after all and to accept the UNICEF and ICRC offers to pay the procurement fee.

Then a new crisis intervened. The next day it became clear that the Marketing Organization was not actually capable of producing the 15,000 tons it had promised to procure for FAO. The organization had been, at best, bluffing.

Robert Jackson went straight off to see the Thai Foreign Minister and said that in these circumstances FAO really must be allowed to purchase the seed on the commercial market after all. Air Marshal Siddhi asked for a written request from FAO. This was produced and was passed on to the National Security Council, which acceded to it.

But then the Ministry of Agriculture, which had been locked in a constant battle with other departments over the whole issue, refused to accept the National Security Council's decision. At this, Jackson wrote to the Prime Minister and then, although the days before the mid-August planting deadline were whirring away, he decided to wait until Secretary General Waldheim's visit on August 4 before making another *démarche* to the government.

Waldheim's visit—to see whether there was any possibility of compromise between Vietnam and Thailand over Cambodia—was not a great success with the Thais. They had always thought him biased toward Hanoi. Nonetheless he did raise the matter of seed, and on August 5 the cabinet overrode the Ministry of Agriculture and authorized commercial suppliers to sell directly to FAO. FAO was told to expect a letter from the Ministry of Agriculture confirming this within twenty-four hours. It did not come.

The Ministry had not liked the decision and so, as often happens in bureaucracies, it simply delayed implementing it. Day after day FAO officials went along to the Ministry hoping to collect the letter; for almost a week it was held up. To the fury of his colleagues in Bangkok, Wagner returned to Rome while the matter was still unresolved. He was warned by Jackson's office that he and FAO would be held directly responsible if the seed did not arrive in Cambodia in time to be planted at all.

Eventually the letter was handed over. But the Ministry would agree to FAO's having only 7,000 tons, not the 15,000 tons requested and promised. The reason given was domestic shortage.

There was now no point in chartering the DC-10. At a cost of $300,000—the equivalent of about a thousand tons of seed—it was canceled. UNICEF searched to see what other seed might be available at once. Officials learned that Oxfam had just shipped 2,500 tons of seed from Hong Kong to Phnom Penh, and that it had an option on another 2,000 tons, which it had not taken up. So UNICEF encouraged FAO to purchase and ship it at once. The price was very high—over $600 a ton. FAO refused, and UNICEF then bought this seed itself. (As it happened, the urgency was misplaced. The seed was not used by the Phnom Penh authorities until three months later for the dry-season crop.)

On and on it went. Summing it up, Jay Long, a senior U.N. official who was at that time running Jackson's office in Bangkok, cabled the Secretary General's office:

> Unfortunately whole episode became political and bureaucratic football, not helped by some sensational local press treatment. . . . Attainment of full target of 15,000 tons should have been achieved at time of much earlier Thai approval and could have been had there been better co-ordination and co-operation among agencies and with Jackson. Failure of FAO reps to keep Jackson informed and especially to signal problem areas not only wasted valuable and irreplaceable time, but also created unnecessary confusion, embarrassment and irritation especially unwelcome in context of Sec. Gen's visit. The chief losers are of course the Kampuchean farmers and people but also the U.N. system and the programme, whose competence and credibility are being questioned.

What in the end did the seed achieve? As usual, figures were both hard to obtain and contradictory. By the end of the summer, FAO had shipped only about 4,500 tons of seed through Phnom Penh to Battambang, the country's main rice-growing province. This was less than half of what it had planned to send there and only about a quarter of the 16,000 tons that everyone agreed Battambang could absorb. This seed would have planted just over 60,000 hectares.

Yet, in August 1980 the Battambang provincial authorities told Kurt Jansson, the head of the Joint Mission in Phnom Penh, that they had planted 150,000 hectares, out of a goal of 220,000 hectares. An FAO mission that traveled to Cambodia in October 1980 was told that the target of 220,000 hectares had actually been reached in Battambang. This was improbable, but whichever was true, the bulk of the seed must have come from the 23,000 tons put across the border. In other words, on this issue the U.S. Embassy in Bangkok and the voluntary agencies based there had been absolutely correct in stressing how vital the land bridge would be.

With the help of this and the many other aid programs that were operating by 1980–81, the Cambodian peasants apparently managed to more than double the amount of paddy that they had produced in the 1979–80 crops. The total was said by the Heng Samrin authorities to have increased from 637,000 tons to 1,470,700 tons. It was still a long way from the prewar figure of 3,800,000 tons, but, if correct, the improvement was substantial. For it, credit must go first of all to the farmers themselves; to the Ministry of Agriculture in Phnom Penh; to Hans Page, the FAO man there who devised the planting program that his own agency helped to disrupt; and to all those who insisted that Battambang be "saturated" with seed across the land bridge.

During 1981 the Joint Mission mounted another seed-import program. An FAO food-assessment mission recommended that 23,000 tons be imported, but in the event 37,000 tons were sent into the country.* Unfortunately, the 1981–82 crop did not represent another great leap forward. Indeed, the amount of rice eventually harvested actually fell from the previous year.† This was largely because of a very erratic monsoon.

* Thirteen thousand tons were supplied by FAO, 18,385 tons by voluntary agencies, 3,000 tons by Vietnam, and 2,950 tons went over the land bridge.

† Once again, it must be stressed that no figures can really be relied

In some ways 1981 was depressingly repetitive of the 1980 history. Once again FAO failed to master the intricacies of Thai bureaucratic politics and to acquire all the necessary seed in time. Once again the land bridge was used; this year, however, distribution from Phnom Penh was less efficient than in 1980. Once again, the U.S. Embassy attempted to goad the agencies into further action. The principal difference was that ICRC had retired from all food distribution along the border and UNICEF raised far fewer objections to the Embassy's role and views. Instead, now that Ronald Reagan was President and Richard Holbrooke was no longer Assistant Secretary of State, Abramowitz encountered much more bureaucratic opposition within his own government.

His suggestion that the United States finance a much larger seed program than FAO recommended met with an angry response from the Embassy in Rome. There, American officials had more sympathy for FAO and, perhaps more tellingly, felt more involved with other of the world's crises. One cable from the United States Ambassador to Rome, Robert Paganelli, in February 1981, indicates the way in which those further from Cambodia saw the problem. He suggested that demands for more seed simply reflected the acquisitiveness of Cambodian ministers and their Vietnamese allies who wanted all the aid the donors were willing to give. And he concluded:

---

upon. Some of the figures which were given by officials of the Heng Samrin regime to the Food and Agriculture Organization and accepted by the FAO were as follows:

Area planted for monsoon-season rice crops:

Year	Hectares.
1979	700,000.
1980	1,317,000.
1981	1,226,900.

Total paddy production for monsoon and dry-season crops:

Year	Metric tons.
1979/80	637,000.
1980/81	1,470,700.
1981/82	1,453,000.

There are emergencies besides Cambodia. Some of them are even worse. The people of Somalia, Pakistan and in the countries of Southern Africa also lay claim to our largess. In the months ahead we shall be under tremendous pressure in the fora of the international food agencies to do more at a time when our ability to respond will be less. Against this backdrop, it seems to me that U.S. policy must be aimed at maximizing the use of every dollar spent. We owe it to the people we help as well as to ourselves to do good well.

16 &❖& Refuge

The United Nations High Commissioner for Refugees has a series of dramatic and emotive fund-raising posters. In one a well-known face surrounded by its shock of gray hair gazes intently at the onlooker. The legend reads "Einstein was a refugee."

The image of Einstein fits the traditional definition of refugee as someone who, "owing to well-founded fear of being persecuted for reasons of race, religion, nationality, or political opinion," has left his country and does not wish to return. It does not necessarily describe most of the estimated ten, twelve or eighteen million people (there is no more accurate figure) who, for reasons of war, want or persecution have left their homelands today.

The United Nations High Commissioner for Refugees has three principal duties toward the people under his care. He has to offer them protection (against attack or forcible repatriation, for example); he must offer them material assistance (food, shelter, clothing, medical care); and he has to try to find them what UNHCR calls "a long-term durable solution." This can be voluntary repatriation, permanent settlement in the country of first asylum, or resettlement in a third country.

With the help of donor funds and all the voluntary agencies—at one time there were thirty-seven working in Khao I Dang—UNHCR managed to provide Cambodian refugees in Thailand a high level of material assistance. Indeed, so keen were the Western donors to provide money for UNHCR's work in Thailand, that refugees there had more dollars per head spent on them than refugees anywhere else in the world. They also had much more than Cambodians on the Thai border, who in turn had far more aid per head than those who remained behind in Cambodia. And Cambodian refugees in Vietnam and Laos received even less than the others. This did not reflect any rigorous assessment of need, but rather the priorities, political and otherwise, of the donors.*

Protection was much more difficult. It was needed both from other refugees and from Thai guards, who frequently robbed, raped and sometimes even killed refugees. The protection files at UNHCR offices in Bangkok quickly became filled with "incident reports" in which field officers in the camps logged countless attacks upon the person and meager property of the refugees.

The policies of the Royal Thai Government did not always help. It must be stressed that it is difficult to imagine many European countries that would have taken in several hundred thousand foreigners as Thailand had done by the end of the seventies. But the compassion that Prime Minister Kriangsak had expressed in October 1979 when he announced his "open door" policy became less evident after Thailand quietly closed that door. As I have noted, some Thai newspapers began to inveigh against the "comfort" in which the "illegal immigrants" lived and to demand that they be put to useful work—like building roads. They also complained about the birth rate in the holding centers. This complaint afforded a bizarre clash of interests and perceptions.

Thailand has a highly developed and successful national birth-control program and it has reduced the birth rate from 3 to 2 percent. By contrast, in obvious natural compensation for the losses of the last decade, Cambodians were procreating as fast as they could by 1980—there was a baby boom at home, on the border and in Thailand. About 30 percent of the women in the holding centers were pregnant. This threatened to increase the population there, and

* Similarly, UNHCR officials in a camp for Afghan refugees in Pakistan were once asked by a Scandinavian ambassador what help they needed. "Drainage," they replied. "I think we would prefer to give you blankets," said the ambassador. "Well they will just be taken straight across the border into Afghanistan by the guerrillas," said UNHCR. "Perfect," said the ambassador.

so Thai newspapers began to demand that the national birth-control program be applied to the "illegal immigrants" as well. Thai relief workers began to offer the controversial drug Depo-Provera, which was banned by the U.S. Food and Drug Administration in the United States in 1978 but is widely used in Thailand.

Some of the Western relief workers tried to discourage women from agreeing to the injections, and then in some camps the military actually began to give them by force. This led to an extraordinary situation—an instruction by the committee coordinating the voluntary agencies to its members that they must cooperate with a rigorous birth-control program in the holding centers. "We must use every means available to come closer to Zero Population Growth of the Khmer Illegal Immigrant population while they are on Thai soil. Their very security here, as well as the longevity of the VOLAGS [voluntary agencies] in the relief effort here, might well depend upon success in this endeavor." So wrote Dr. Daniel Susott, the American Medical Coordinator of the voluntary agencies. And this of a race that the world, especially the Western world, had thought was "on the edge of extinction" only a few weeks before, and which those same voluntary agencies had come to succor.

Many families had been separated in the chaos that obtained at the end of 1979. Along the border ICRC and the International Rescue Committee ran effective tracing programs seeking to reunite families. There were boards at the border carrying photographs of all the lost children ("unaccompanied minors") who were in the holding centers or the border agglomerations. Parents came from all over Cambodia to search for pictures of their children. Many families were restored in this way. Records show that 1,953 out of 2,600 registered unaccompanied minors found relatives in the holding centers or on the border. Another 265 children were sent abroad to foster homes. Throughout, UNHCR absolutely opposed any large-scale adoption of Khmer children by Western families. By mid-1981 there were 779 registered unaccompanied minors. The Heng Samrin regime refused to allow the ICRC to fulfill its tracing mandate inside Cambodia, and this seriously limited the number of reconciliations that could be effected.

After the "open door" was closed, there were still thousands of

Cambodians on the border who wanted to go to Khao I Dang. Scores of them still tried every night to make their way through the open scrubland that covered the eight miles between the border and the holding center. If caught by Thai military or police, the best they could expect was to be bused right back to the border. Sometimes refugees who tried to evade arrest were shot.

At the same time the Thai military started both to encourage and to coerce people in the holding centers to return to the border to strengthen the anti-Vietnamese resistance groups there, both the Khmer and the anti-Communist Khmer Serei. Such movements were almost always carried out at night, when UNHCR personnel had returned to the safety of Aranyaprathet or other towns. Come morning it was impossible to tell whether such departures had been voluntary or not.

The reactions to this were very different in Khao I Dang and in Sa Kaeo. At Khao I Dang were gathered many of the survivors of Cambodia's middle class. (At the time it seemed as if all of them might be there, but that was an exaggeration.) Interviews with them showed that one of their main reasons for fleeing was that, for a variety of reasons, they saw no future for themselves under the Vietnamese administration. Almost all of them had initially welcomed the Vietnamese invasion. But for some the risks of remaining after what had happened under the Khmer Rouge, would have been too great in any circumstances. Others, who had been prepared to try to work with the Vietnamese, were disheartened when they found that their new rulers often gave preferment to former Khmer Rouge cadres rather than to middle-class survivors. Many people disliked having their work overseen by Vietnamese advisers. Moreover it became gradually more clear that even though Vietnamese policies were by no stretch of the imagination Khmer Rouge, they were nonetheless Communist. For many people by now any variation of that creed was understandably terrifying.

Another reason that refugees gave for flight was a literal feeling of homelessness. After the Vietnamese liberation they had attempted to make their way across country to their former homes—only to find them gone. Thousands of villagers, for example, had the greatest difficulty in finding, let alone recognizing, the hamlet in which they had spent their lives until either the war or the Khmer Rouge drove them out. During the Pol Pot period many old houses had been razed and new cooperative dormitories had been built in their place. Often the pagoda had been destroyed. Similarly, many townspeople returned home to find that their houses had been smashed. Others discovered Vietnamese soldiers, Heng Samrin officials or just other survivors who had returned to the towns earlier, in their former homes. They left for Thailand.

For many of these people the notion of repatriation to Cambodia in its present state—real or perceived—was horrifying. In early 1980 there was a great deal of tension in Khao I Dang. When a Voice of America broadcast speculated that the camp might one day close, there was panic at the rumor that forcible repatriation was imminent. Some Khmer talked openly of suicide rather than returning to Cambodia or even to the border.

In Sa Kaeo the problems were quite different. Unlike Khao I Dang, the population was almost entirely rural—much more representative of prewar Cambodia. More importantly, Sa Kaeo was controlled by the Khmer Rouge, by those who had sought to persecute and destroy the people now living in Khao I Dang.

The atmosphere (as in the border camps the Khmer Rouge controlled) was menacing. The Khmer Rouge there had been disarmed (unlike those on the border or the Afghan guerrillas in UNHCR camps in Pakistan). Nonetheless, young Khmer Rouge soldiers lounged around, regaining strength, sullenly eying foreigners and silently gazing at the ordinary civilians whom they had taken close to death in the Phnom Malai mountains and whom they intended to lead back to Kampuchea again. Their presence posed a dilemma for UNHCR—at least in theory.

Both the Statute of UNHCR and the 1951 Convention of Refugees, drawn up in the aftermath of World War II, insist that the refugee status cannot be given to anyone who is seriously suspected of having committed a crime against peace, a war crime, or a crime against humanity.

The most comprehensive definition of crimes against humanity is to be found in the 1945 London Agreement and the Charter of the International Military Tribunal. Article 6(c) states:

Crimes against humanity: Namely, murder, extermination, enslavement, deportation and other inhumane acts committed against any civilian population, before or during the war, or persecutions on political, racial, or religious grounds in execution of or in connection with any crimes within the jurisdiction of the Tribunal, whether or not in violation of the domestic law of the country where perpetrated.

Leaders, organisers, instigators, and accomplices participating in the formulation or execution of a common plan or conspiracy to commit any of the foregoing crimes are responsible for all acts performed by any persons in execution of such plan.

It was unanimously agreed by the states drawing up UNHCR's mandate that such criminals should not be protected. The crucial phrase that confers refugee status—"having a well-founded fear of persecution"—was specifically not to interfere with prosecution of war crimes or crimes against humanity. The key text in this regard was the Universal Declaration of Human Rights. Article 14 states:

1) Everyone has the right to seek and to enjoy in other countries asylum from persecution. 2) This right may not be invoked in the case of prosecutions genuinely arising from non-political crimes or from acts contrary to the purposes and principles of the United Nations.

By the end of 1979 prima facie evidence that the Khmer Rouge had committed crimes against humanity had long been overwhelming. Moreover, once they had been brought back from the threshold of death, non-Communist Cambodians in Sa Kaeo made specific accusations of murder against many of the Khmer Rouge cadres in the camp. These refugees clearly hoped at first for action by UNHCR or the Thai authorities, a hope which, given the nature of the crimes of which the Khmer Rouge had been charged by almost every Western and, lately, by every Soviet-bloc government, was hardly unreasonable. It was nonetheless vain.

One problem was that asylum is granted by nations, not by UNHCR. None of the Cambodians in UNHCR camps in Thailand had been given refugee status by Thailand; they were all still called "illegal immigrants." Moreover, the Convention is basically concerned with granting refugee status on an individual basis. Where UNHCR assists masses of people, particularly in countries that, like Thailand, have not signed the Convention, it is required to be certain that the majority of those being assisted are in a "refugee-like situation" and would be found to be refugees if an individual determination was made. Even in Sa Kaeo, that would apply to the overwhelming majority of people.

But what exactly was UNHCR's duty, under its mandate, toward those Khmer Rouge soldiers or cadres in Sa Kaeo suspected of having committed crimes against humanity? Should it merely have sought to have them quietly removed from the camp? Or, conversely, did it have a duty to point out that such people were innocent until proven guilty and should therefore be given a trial?

The answers were complicated by the fact that any crime would have been committed in their own country by a regime still recognized by most governments in the world—including, of course, the donors and Thailand—as that country's legitimate representative. The Thai authorities had no obvious interest in pursuing the possible crimes of the Khmer Rouge cadres in Sa Kaeo. Nor, therefore, did the donors who, quick to pursue perfidy or less on the Vietnamese side, were content to follow Thailand's priorities within Thailand itself.

There were about twenty Khmer Rouge men and another twenty women who tried to police Sa Kaeo. The best-known was Colonel Phak Lim, who had previously been a cadre in Battambang. Like many of his comrades, he could appear disturbingly genial and mild-mannered. It was hard for many foreigners to believe that he could be a murderer.

Indeed, to those who were ignorant of the recent history of Cambodia—and that meant many if not most of the often young and often idealistic Westerners who flew to Thailand under the wing of one or another humanitarian agency—it was often difficult to realize that the people they were attempting to succor in Sa Kaeo or in the Khmer Rouge camps along the border were really the same as those charged with terrible crimes. I remember listening with astonishment as a young American woman with UNICEF talked about one Khmer Rouge leader; he was so sad, she said, because his son had died. He had asked the whole UNICEF team to the funeral. He was such a good, kind man and she hoped they would all go along to express their sympathy for his cruel loss.

Colonel Phak Lim worked hard, he made a formal conversion to Buddhism (an act of piety that made a deep impression only on Westerners) and used his conversion to try to persuade the genuine leaders of the newly built pagoda—to which, as in the other holding centers, non-Khmer Rouge refugees were flocking in relief from the enforced atheism of the last four years—to support calls for a return to Cambodia. Meekly he assured foreign aid workers how much he now valued the precepts of a religion his regime had done so much to destroy. At the same time he ensured that his own troops were promoted within the Khmer camp administration. Among other things they controlled was the distribution of food. This, as UNHCR knew, they used as a weapon with which to force people to return.*

For example, on February 19, 1980, in full view of the Thai administration building, on the spot where food was distributed, fifteen Khmer Rouge soldiers led by Phak Lim, forced a refugee, Yan Dayt, to take off his shoes and climb into an empty water tank.

According to the UNHCR Incident Report, "After Mr. Dayt had entered the water tank, the men closed the lid and padlocked it. Then a fire was lit around the tank by the men, who pounded on the top of the tank with a hammer. Yan Dayt was heard screaming from inside the tank. Two Thai soldiers guarding the camp main gate came over to investigate. They said nothing to the men involved, but walked back to the gate without interfering." Only when Wayne Cartwright, an American engineer, at considerable personal risk, ordered the Khmer Rouge away and opened the water tank, was Yan Dayt released. His feet were by now very badly burned.

On another occasion ten days later a similar punishment—in which a refugee was stripped to his underpants and made to stand barefoot on a sheet of metal in the midday sun—was actually orga-

* In one report to Zia Rizvi, John Jensen, a UNHCR field officer in Sa Kaeo, wrote that Phak Lim and seven other cadres "have attempted to control the Khmer by physical punishments, methods of terror, intimidation and controlling all camp services and food distribution system. Colonel Lim and his men have been promoting the Khmer people in Sa Kaeo to return to Cambodia against their will."

nized by Thai officials in the camp. John Jensen protested to the deputy governor, Khun Amorn, that this sort of conduct was unacceptable to the U.N. Amorn shot back angrily, "Why don't the U.N. take themselves and the refugees somewhere else?" However, he did agree to let the man go. Colonel Lim became increasingly angry with Jensen's interventions and threatened his life. UNHCR removed Jensen from the camp.

Zia Rizvi brought up Lim's activities with the Thai government on several occasions and asked for Colonel Lim's removal from the camp. For weeks the Thai authorities did nothing. Eventually, six months after Sa Kaeo was opened, the Colonel was removed, but then he returned, and further protests had to be made to obtain his removal once more.

In early April 1980 discontented UNHCR officials assisted the diligent Melbourne *Age* correspondent, Michael Richardson, to make the scandal public. Richardson's story, datelined Sa Kaeo, was headlined, "Pol Pot men rule in refugee camp"; it pointed out:

> The Khmer Rouge hold on Sa Kaeo is a source of embarrassment to the UNHCR, which suspects that millions of dollars in international relief aid may have been spent to support a "rest and recovery" center for the Khmer Rouge. In interviews over the past few days aid officials and refugees said they feared Thai policy was to underwrite Khmer Rouge control of the camp because Khmer Rouge leaders here plan to return to Kampuchea soon with all their "followers" to fight against pro-Vietnamese forces.

Thai policy had obvious implications for the long-term future of the refugees. It seemed that they would be unlikely even to be able to remain indefinitely in the holding centers, let alone ever be integrated into Thai society. The second possible durable solution was third-country resettlement. By now resettlement programs for Lao and Vietnamese refugees were at their height—the United States was taking about 14,000 Indochinese a month. But UNHCR officials actively discouraged this on behalf of the Cambodians. Instead, Zia Rizvi's policy was informed by the dogged conviction that voluntary repatriation—to the interior of Cambodia, not just to the border—was the best possible option for almost all Cambodians in Thailand.

Rizvi aroused the anger of his partners in the relief effort and particularly of Sir Robert Jackson when he gave an interview to this effect with Roland Pierre Paringaux of *Le Monde* in February 1980. No other international organization had made such a decision, and it was contrary to both American and Thai policy, if only because it would have suggested an acceptance by Cambodians of the Heng Samrin regime.

For that very reason, of course, the Heng Samrin regime itself was keen for some sort of relationship with UNHCR. At the end of February 1980 Zia Rizvi was welcomed first in Hanoi and then in Phnom Penh, when he came to discuss the possibility of a UNHCR program inside Cambodia. Cambodian Foreign Minister Hun Sen asked for UNHCR assistance to 200,000 refugees returning principally from Vietnam but also from Thailand and Laos. He requested emergency food aid and long-term assistance to enable these people to become agriculturally self-sufficient. On March 10 Hun Sen wrote to High Commissioner Poul Hartling to repeat the request, and on April 28, his deputy Hor Nam Hong sent another letter asserting that another 50,000 refugees had recently returned and they too needed UNHCR assistance. UNHCR did not reply to either of these letters formally. But neither did it share them with its partners. In Phnom Penh, John Saunders was irritated by the secrecy of the *démarches.*

UNHCR officials claimed that their belief in the viability of repatriation was confirmed by a study that the organization had commissioned from one of the most experienced scholars of Cambodian affairs, Dr. Milton Osborne. He conducted a survey of the holding centers and found that almost two thirds of the people he interviewed "expressed an interest in returning to Kampuchea." But, in citing this figure, UNHCR officials sometimes forgot to note that Osborne's sample was only 100 people and that he himself carefully qualified his findings. Referring to the terrible traumas of the last decade he noted that no one wanted to go back unless it was to "peace"—a state of grace which Cambodia was still denied and would be denied for years.*

* Osborne also found in Khao I Dang considerable disquiet with recent Thai efforts to encourage people to return to the border camps run by troops

For its part, UNHCR became more and more vexed by the Thais' unofficial nighttime repatriation of Cambodians from the holding centers to the border. On March 19 Rizvi told the donor ambassadors, in a meeting at the Erawan Hotel in Bangkok, that even though it did not appear to be forcible, "The High Commissioner has a clear mandate to set up procedures for voluntary repatriation. He cannot ignore it for the sake of expediency in any given situation."

Talking about the possibility of a formal program of repatriation to the interior of Cambodia, he pointed out that "the conditions prevailing in the country to which the individual wishes to return are immaterial" in deciding whether his return is or is not voluntary. "UNHCR must assume that the individual requesting repatriation has given the matter due consideration. It cannot be UNHCR's role to provide information on conditions in the country of origin." He also noted that, when requested, UNHCR sometimes helped transport refugees back to their country of origin and provided assistance for them at home. He stated that "no such requests have at this time been received" from the government in Phnom Penh.

By this time the covert nighttime repatriations were beginning to receive considerable, and often unfavorable publicity. The Melbourne *Age* reported:

> Aid officials fear the repatriations may lead to mass evacuation of more than 150,000 displaced Kampucheans at present in two temporary "holding centers" in Thailand . . . Thailand has started sending refugees back into Kampuchea where they are liable to face fighting, disease and threat of famine, according to international aid officials. . . .

Thai officials complained that such articles were offensive and inaccurate and that the generosity of the open-door policy still obtained.

One method that UNHCR and other agencies employed to persuade the Thais to continue to tolerate refugees was money. Thus,

---

of Son Sann, the Khmer People's National Liberation Front. Many of those who had been persuaded by the Thais to return had been disillusioned by the poor security, the dependence on Chinese weapons (which they associated with the Khmer Rouge) and the inability to grow food. Many had already returned secretly to Khao I Dang.

for example, on April 1, Martin Barber cabled Zia Rizvi, who was in Rome, to tell him that he had just handed the Foreign Minister a letter of intent "covering estimated construction costs for [new] holding centers at Mai Rut, Kampot, Chonburi, Sakaeo 2 and Kapcherng value $20,250,000. . . . Air Chief Marshal Siddhi clearly delighted and requested us to transmit gratitude of Royal Thai Government to HICOM and SECGEN. He promised to try his best to obtain understanding of Thai people for need to continue present policy."

Money did not solve the problem of nighttime repatriations. In Sa Kaeo, Khmer Rouge leaders began to circulate forms, given them by the Thai military, on which refugees could declare that they were returning voluntarily to Cambodia. They stated, *inter alia,* "The Cambodian people who decide to return to Cambodia should have that right according to the law of humanity and should be supported by the Thai Government and the U.N." Throughout April more and more people left at night. Not all of them went voluntarily. UNHCR was told that the Thai military was preparing to arrange for thousands to leave, and from Khao I Dang as well as from Sa Kaeo.

This placed UNHCR in an obvious quandary. It has a duty to protect refugees against forced repatriation, yet it was unlikely to be able to prevent the Thais from carrying out their covert repatriation policy—especially because the donors were simply not very interested; they accepted Thailand's aim of building up the border. UNHCR's representations to Thai officials brought the reply that "these people wish to return—we should not try to prevent them." Some no doubt did, yet in his report for UNHCR Milton Osborne had emphasized "I make no apology for recording in this report my strong personal judgement that the implementation of any policy that leads to the non-Khmer Rouge population of Sa Kaeo being returned to Kampuchea under the control of the camp's Khmer Rouge leadership and its associates would be an act of the most profound immorality."

In these circumstances, Zia Rizvi said later, "I decided that if it had to take place, it had better be done under our control, in daylight. I told Siddhi that there must be a formal voluntary repatriation, which must be done like UNHCR repatriations all over the world. My main concern was not to have a repetition of the forced repatriation of June 1979, to Preah Vihear. It was quite possible. After all, the same Thai military commanders were still along the border."

Throughout May 1980, UNHCR and Thai officials conducted complicated negotiations over the precise way in which the voluntary aspects of the program would be guaranteed. The Thais hoped and expected that most of the 30,000 or so people in Sa Kaeo and a large proportion of those in Khao I Dang and other camps would want to return.

While these talks were going on, UNHCR kept the whole operation concealed not only from the press but also from its partners in the U.N. and from the ICRC. Rumors, of course, spread, but when ICRC, UNICEF and World Food Program officials asked their UNHCR colleagues at a meeting at Supreme Command on June 3, about the rumors of repatriation, Glen Dunkley of UNHCR responded, "It's still unofficial." He said that "the planned scenario [is] in response to requests by refugees to return, rather than a programmed voluntary repatriation with guarantees or assistance waiting for them on the other side à la Burma."

On June 9, UNHCR and the Thai government finally agreed on a procedure that satisfied UNHCR officials that they could ensure that people were not being coerced or forced to leave. Each individual or family group would go separately into a tent manned by UNHCR and Thai army officials and an interpreter. The interpreter would read the consent form and ask to which area of the border—Khmer Rouge or Khmer Serei—the refugee or refugees wished to go. This form stated: "I, the undersigned . . . hereby declare of my own free will and without duress or pressure of any kind, that I wish to return to Kampuchea, which is my former country of residence. I was born on . . . I am a national . . . formerly living at . . . wishing to return to Kampuchea through a safe border crossing point or at . . . which I have voluntarily chosen as the safe route for me to take, in order to return to my way of life in Kampuchea." Once the forms were signed, the refugees would wait to be taken in a bus provided by the Thai army to the border site of their choice.

As soon as the agreement on the technical arrangements was

made, Thai officials gave the story to the Bangkok *Post,* which published a front-page article on June 10 headlined "Khmers to be voluntarily repatriated." It was only now that UNHCR acknowledged to its partners the scale of the operation planned. Many of them were appalled.

The ICRC, which, unlike UNHCR, had protested the brutal Preah Vihear repatriation a year before, formally dissociated itself from the new scheme; its Bangkok delegation wrote to the Thai Foreign Minister saying that the ICRC "has reservations as to whether conditions currently prevailing within Kampuchea are such that the safety and physical integrity of those wishing voluntarily to return to their homes can be considered adequate and as to whether they will be able to reach their villages."

UNICEF's border coordinator, Ulf Kristofferson, complained angrily to his Bangkok office about the impact on the border. Vincent O'Reilley of UNICEF noted in a memo that he was shocked by "the remarkable lack of clarity and depth of planning by UNHCR as to the political and social implications of this repatriation." What, if any, agreement had been made with Phnom Penh? Was it UNHCR's expectation that these people would stay on the border? If so, why had ICRC, UNICEF and WFP—who, after all, would have to look after them—not been informed? "Rather than solving the problem of Khmer refugees in Thailand, UNHCR may only be passing the responsibility for their care to UNICEF and ICRC."

Two days later, the Thai Foreign Minister said that over 100,000 refugees might be involved. The scheme was denounced in Hanoi and by S.P.K., the Phnom Penh press agency, as "a new extremely serious aggression against Kampuchea." It warned that "the Thai authorities must bear full responsibility for all consequences of their acts."

Was Vietnam's opposition real or just a public position? On June 13, Zia Rizvi met privately with the Vietnamese Foreign Minister Nguyen Co Thach in Vientiane. Thach later claimed that he had told Rizvi that the repatriation scheme was quite unacceptable to Vietnam. But Rizvi said later that Thach's criticism to him was only *pro forma.* Sir Robert Jackson—who was angry that UNHCR had not consulted him on the planning—met Vietnamese officials in

Hanoi on June 16. He later said that they made their unhappiness very clear to him.

Others saw the possible political and military repercussions of the move. *Le Monde* correspondent Roland Pierre Paringaux pointed out that "no one can know whether the Vietnamese and their allies in Phnom Penh will tolerate the reinforcement of movements which directly threaten their supremacy. On this essential point there is not the slightest guarantee from Hanoi, though HCR is, at the last moment, trying to obtain it."

A few days before the processing was due to begin, Thai soldiers began to tour Khao I Dang in a van with a loudspeaker, distributing leaflets and urging Cambodians to return to Cambodia now that they had the opportunity. The "voluntary" aspect of the movement was rather lost in the warnings that this was far better for them than their 'dream' of being resettled abroad. "If you go there you might get separated from some of your relatives . . . some people abroad are suffering terribly. Life is difficult, they are unhappy and have little freedom. . . . If you go back to the border you will have the opportunity to regain your country. . . . It is better than living in another country. . . . Finally, we would like to tell all of you the third countries you dream of going to could not accept all of you."

In Sa Kaeo, Khmer Rouge leaders chanted a ditty to encourage their compatriots to return.

> Those who go back first will sleep on cots.
> Those who go back second will sleep on mats.
> Those who go back third will sleep in the mud.
> And those who go back last will sleep under the ground.

The camp was full of rumors that force would be used to make people go back. The rejuvenated Buddhist community diligently tried to persuade people that they did not have to return, that there was a choice. The Thai military then rounded up the Buddhist leaders and dropped them on the border before the repatriation process began. Thus the non-Khmer Rouge in the camp were deprived of their most valuable source of support.

Zia Rizvi demanded of Colonel Kitti, the Thai coordinator of

Task Force 80, who had responsibility for the border, that the Buddhists be returned to the camp. Eventually they were returned just after the process had begun.

There was no overt intimidation in Khao I Dang. Indeed the numbers who volunteered to return were very small. On the first day only about 500 people asked to go back to the border. "I want to die in the place I was born," an eighty-three-year-old woman told Paul Vogle of UPI.

From Sa Kaeo there were thousands of volunteers, but still far fewer than the Thais had hoped. Thai officials complained bitterly about what they saw as the obstacles placed by UNHCR in the way of large-scale repatriation. "UNHCR people do not want the refugees to return to their country because an empty camp would leave them jobless," said Major General Kobboon Pattanathabutr of Supreme Command. Only about seven thousand people in Sa Kaeo finally asked to return to the border.

On the night of June 22–23, 1980, the Vietnamese launched an artillery barrage and then a brief invasion of Thailand to attack refugee camps along the border. They did not assault the Khmer Rouge camps south of Aranyaprathet to which the people from Sa Kaeo had just been taken. Instead they attacked the much more lightly armed areas north of Aranyaprathet, where the anti-Communist Khmer Serei were based and where there was a far larger concentration of apolitical civilian refugees. The ICRC Hospital at Nong Chan, where the land bridge operated, was shelled. Tens of thousands of refugees fled in terror.

The attack took place when Thai military units were being rotated and the area was almost undefended. Colonel Prachak, who was responsible for the defense of that sector of the border, took all of thirty-six hours to return from Bangkok. Nonetheless, after an initial delay, Thai troops took up positions and responded in kind to the Vietnamese artillery bombardment. Thousands of refugees were caught in the crossfire; it was difficult for them to know on which side most danger lay. About 400 refugees were killed and 900 were wounded.

The repatriation provided the most obvious explanation of the

Vietnamese attack. Hun Sen, the foreign minister in the Heng Samrin regime, sent a note to Poul Hartling categorizing it as "an attempt to introduce into Kampuchean territory armed bands of the Pol Pot–Ieng Sary and Sereika clique, supplied and trained in Thailand by the Peking expansionists in collusion with the American imperialists."

In New York, Vietnam's permanent representative to the U.N., Ha Van Lau, formally protested UNHCR's involvement to Kurt Waldheim. He said the repatriation was "a deliberate act of provocation and part of an orchestrated plan of action to destabilize the region." His government thought UNHCR's action was "unworthy" of it, and he hoped Waldheim would dissociate UNHCR from it. Waldheim replied that he had always tried to keep politics out of the Cambodia relief operations. He said he had not yet been fully briefed on the latest developments.

Some aid officials dubbed the Vietnamese attack, "Mr. Rizvi's little war." Rizvi himself maintained that the repatriation and the attack were unconnected. He pointed out that he was himself able to travel to Phnom Penh shortly afterward and was very well received. He said that Penn Sovann, the Minister of Defense in the Heng Samrin government, told him that the attack had been planned long before the repatriation.

UNHCR also pointed out that its participation in the repatriation process had effectively controlled it. Only 8,700 people went back, including the 7,000 from Sa Kaeo. "Without us the Thais would have sent 20,000 people back from Sa Kaeo," said Rizvi. This was undoubtedly true; by its participation UNHCR was able to exercise effectively its duty to protect refugees against forcible repatriation under Khmer Rouge control.

But the affair raised other questions. Under international law any refugee has the right to return home when he wishes; UNHCR camps are not supposed to be prisons. However, combatants, which is what many of the returnees from Sa Kaeo were, have no such automatic right. Critics of the repatriation also argued that a neutral country, as Thailand claimed to be, does not have the right to allow combatants to rest and be watered on its soil and then return refreshed to the battle. That is a clear infringement of neutrality. These critics also asserted that if a neutral country does wish to compromise its status in this way, U.N. organizations have a duty not to assist the process. Nonetheless, UNHCR did so.

In an internal paper criticizing the operation, Hanna Sophia Greve, a UNHCR protection officer, went so far as to claim that UNHCR violated its mandate by participating in the repatriation. She went on to assert that unless the major donor countries in Western Europe, North America and Japan had been in favor of a strong Khmer Rouge to fight the Vietnamese, the repatriation would have made a considerable international row.

As for Morton Abramowitz, he said later that he deliberately refused to get involved in the episode except to satisfy himself that the principle of voluntariness was upheld. "The Thais had always insisted that it would be necessary," he said. "What could we do or say? That *we* would take the Khmer Rouge? We wouldn't. No one would."

The whole episode illustrates some of the quandaries in which humanitarian organizations are placed, and the paradoxes with which they have to deal. How does one weigh the lives of those killed in Vietnam's assault upon the border against those people in Sa Kaeo and Khao I Dang who were protected against forcible repatriation by UNHCR's participation in the action? It cannot be done. Perhaps the most that one can say of this case is that had UNHCR insisted, much earlier in 1980, that the Khmer Rouge troops and cadres be removed from its care at Sa Kaeo and placed elsewhere, then the crisis might have been avoided; it would certainly have been diminished. And had UNHCR enlisted the help of its ICRC and U.N. partners instead of deliberately excluding them from the decision making, it would have been in a stronger rather than a weaker position in negotiation with the Thai authorities.

Throughout the next three years, UNHCR's work on behalf of Khmer refugees was plagued by continuing problems regarding repatriation, protection and resettlement.

After the Vietnamese attack of June 1980, UNHCR could no longer be involved in any formal voluntary repatriation—unless it was done in arrangement with the Heng Samrin regime. This had always been Zia Rizvi's ambition, but it was a concept to which the donors and the Thais, ineluctably opposed to that regime, did not take kindly. In August 1980, Rizvi aroused their ire with a plan that, on the face of it, seemed both humane and sensible, but one that he thrust upon them without any consultation. The row illustrated once more the complex ways in which refugees are continually being caught in political disputes not of their own making.

Rizvi felt that the longer Cambodians remained on the border or in the holding centers, the less likely they were ever to be able to return to Cambodia. He was anxious to open any sort of channel to the Heng Samrin regime in order that subsequently, and while it was still to the political advantage of Phnom Penh, a safe return route could be organized. This would be by air or by sea, so that those who wished to go home would not have to pass through the border, risking capture, robbery or death from the Khmer Rouge, the Khmer Serei or the Vietnamese.

Rizvi made his proposal to the donor embassies in Bangkok on August 29—just four days before a donors' conference in New York. He asked for $14 million to help people returning to Cambodia. He revealed that he had now had four letters from the Heng Samrin authorities requesting assistance for such "returnees." The latest letter, on August 4, asked UNHCR to provide supplies to help 300,000 returnees become self-sufficient. So UNHCR wanted to deliver "subsistence packages" to Phnom Penh. These would contain items like cooking utensils, mosquito nets, farm tools, a little rice and seed. Packages would be distributed to returning families by a special government committee for the reception of refugees.

Rizvi declared that anyone returning to Cambodia empty-handed was very vulnerable. To the astonishment of his interlocutors he announced that the need was so urgent that he wanted the program to begin just two days later, on September 1. UNHCR had prepared everything. The only thing now needed was money. He urged the donors to eschew all political considerations, as he said the Heng Samrin authorities had done, and act at once so that those on the border should not be "victims of events beyond their control."

The scheme, presented more as a *fait accompli* than as a proposal, angered many of the embassy officials to whom Rizvi presented it. Despite his assurance, it seemed to them an obvious political ploy by the Heng Samrin regime to achieve greater political respectability just before the convening of the General Assembly, and the 1980 vote on Cambodia's representation within it. They asked where he had got the figure of 300,000 returnees to the Heng Samrin regime. He replied that it was based on UNHCR's own survey within Cambodia. That was the first anyone had heard of any such survey.

Rizvi said that the returnees would be identified by provincial authorities of the Heng Samrin government, but that UNHCR would have the means to monitor the distribution of the kits. He said he expected to have a staff of eighty in Phnom Penh. Since the entire Joint Mission had been continually restricted to fewer than twenty, this was, to say the least, optimistic.

It was pointed out to him that 70 percent of his proposed budget was not for tools but for food, which the Joint Mission was already supposed to be supplying to Cambodians regardless of whether they were "returnees" or not. His answers were apparently not convincing. Ambassador Abramowitz immediately dispatched to Washington, with copies to New York and Geneva, a furious denunciation of the idea. This cable, drafted by Colonel Michael Eiland in the Kampuchean Emergency Group (KEG), declared: "Rizvi's proposal is clearly unacceptable because of its profound political implications. . . . We recommend the USG decline to support it as presented and urge other donors to do likewise." The cable suggested that the timing of the request showed that the Heng Samrin regime wanted to improve its image before the opening of the next U.N. General Assembly, at which the question of Kampuchean representation would again be raised.

The cable also pointed out that the commodities in the returnees' kits were needed by almost all Khmers,

> regardless of the course of their wanderings over the years. It is specious to distinguish on the basis that some have crossed frontiers and others have not. Finally, we cannot help but recall UNHCR's adamant refusal to get involved on the border last year on grounds that the Khmer there were not refugees. Now that some of them have returned, their status has apparently changed to that of ex-refugees. We, as other embassies here, are also upset that Rizvi has dropped this proposal on us full blown only four days before it is to

be formally presented in New York. . . . Despite Rizvi's pious in-
junctions against political considerations, the timing and method of
advancing the proposal render it highly and dangerously political.

It was not only the U.S. Embassy that was irritated by Rizvi's play.
Many of his colleagues in the United Nations system were either baf-
fled or annoyed. Sir Robert Jackson, whose relations with Rizvi were
poor, had not been informed. Jackson was now in New York preparing for the donors' conference. From Bangkok Jay Long, an official from the Secretary General's office who was manning Jackson's
Bangkok office, cabled him that Rizvi's "presentation more detailed
than anything I have seen or heard before about this proposal,
having seen the budget estimates only the day before. . . . There
are disturbing questions and elements on which agreement should be
reached before any formal presentation is made to donors." Long
shared the concern of the U.S. Embassy that fully $9.5 million of
Rizvi's proposed budget was for food, which was meant to be covered already by the existing joint program. This raised the possibility of double distribution. Long said, "As you know, this is not first
time UNHCR has attempted this method [to] inflate its financial requirements." By the time the donors' meeting began in New York
on September 3 Rizvi's opposition was well prepared.

The meeting was chaired by Robert Jackson. The influence of
the United States was obvious; much of the criticism was drawn
from the Eiland cable, which the State Department had already circulated to other governments. In response to the attacks, Rizvi protested that there was not much difference between his proposal and
previous programs for the return of Ugandan, Zimbabwean and
Burmese refugees to their homelands. But the criticisms of his plan
were so widely supported that it was clear that it would have to be
revised. In the end, Rizvi agreed to a proposal by Robert Jackson
that the document should be reexamined in cooperation with other
international organizations and in the light of the donors' comments.

Eventually UNHCR was able to mount a scaled-down version
of Rizvi's "returnees' program," and over the next two years returnees kits were distributed in Cambodia. UNHCR officials in Phnom
Penh (two, rather than Rizvi's original eighty) attempted to verify
that they were given to people who had come back from the border.

As with all distributions within Cambodia, this was often impossible. For one thing, no one knew how many people had returned from the border—because no one knew how many people had been there in the first place. All that one can say is that by 1983 the population there was around 200,000. But in one sense monitoring the distribution of the returnees' kits was irrelevant, for, as Abramowitz had pointed out, those displaced within the country merited "at least as much assistance" as those returning from the border. At the very least, the kits added to the pool of goods and supplies circulating within the economy. But the returnees' kits did not achieve their political purpose; Rizvi was never able to obtain approval for a formal program of voluntary repatriation from Thailand to Cambodia. The border remained the only route.

Soon after the Vietnamese attack of June 1980, the Thai army resumed its practice of invisible, uncheckable nighttime movements from the holding centers to the border. Thai officials hinted that there were at least another 10,000 "illegal immigrants" eager to return to the border which offered more freedom to trade and move than did the holding centers. But the Thai army also attempted to force back to the border those whom they found to have come the other way, risking their lives by slipping into Khao I Dang since the "open door" was closed in January 1980. They also sent back people who had broken camp rules, such as working outside the camp.

The ICRC protested; UNHCR did not. Instead, in order to try to exert some control over the clandestine process, UNHCR hit upon a device that it called "relocation." It argued that those people who wanted to go back to the border were not being repatriated but were, in fact, only moving from one part of Thailand to another, and from the care of UNHCR to that of UNICEF. It was a specious argument, but at some levels it worked. The Thais agreed to the idea, and some movements were carried out in the daytime, after UNHCR field officers attempted to satisfy themselves that the refugees were going of their own free will. It was hardly foolproof—one UNHCR summary noted "there is an uncontrollable balance between persuasion and coercion in the camps"—but UNHCR was unable to devise a better system.

The system broke down most obviously with "unaccompanied

minors." By mid-1981 UNHCR and the voluntary agencies had located and were caring for 779 unaccompanied minors. (Down from 2,600 in 1980.) The "relocation" guidelines did not allow unaccompanied children to be taken back to the border. But in one holding center, Mai Rut, many if not all of them were young Khmer Rouge soldiers whose age had been lowered so that they could be placed in the children's centers, where they were better fed. Khmer Rouge commanders came in at night, with Thai army complicity and in defiance of the guidelines, just shipped the children back to the border. Many wanted to go, but no one can tell just how many.

Over the crises of protection and repatriation—voluntary and forced—always hung that of resettlement. The Khmers were never given the same resettlement opportunities as Vietnamese or Lao refugees. There were many reasons for this—they reflected different policies of the Thais, of UNHCR and of the principal resettlement countries, particularly the United States.

The Thais had varying views—that no Khmers should be resettled; that some resettlement would be allowed but only over and above the existing quotas for Lao and Vietnamese; that those with close family ties abroad should be permitted to go; and that all those in the holding centers should be eligible to go, because otherwise a lot of them were likely to remain in Thailand indefinitely. Thai officials often repeated that, quite apart from common humanitarianism, they wanted the Cambodian people to survive to be, as before, a buffer against the Vietnamese. And, of course, they were also specifically keen on building up the more limited and immediate buffer of the border population.

Many UNHCR officials were absolutely opposed to Khmer resettlement. Officials used to argue that many of those who had come, near death or in panic, to Sa Kaeo and Khao I Dang, had not intended to leave Cambodia forever but were merely fleeing the present chaos. They knew almost nothing of the Heng Samrin regime and its achievements, and it was wrong to make them choose between chaos and a resettlement Shangri-la of which they knew even less. Furthermore, the resettlement of large numbers of Cambodians would contribute to the destruction of the Khmer culture and identity on which Pol Pot had embarked. (Most UNHCR officials rejected the argument that such a destruction might also take place under the Vietnamese-backed Heng Samrin regime.) Finally, the situation in Cambodia was very fluid—an international conference, as called for by the U.N. General Assembly, might take place at any moment and might result in a compromise that would allow refugees' return.

UNHCR officials also began to cite what they called "the pull factor"—an idea that was becoming quite fashionable, particularly among critics of American policy, by the end of 1980. It stated, at its simplest, that the very existence of large resettlement quotas in the West encouraged Vietnamese, Cambodians and Lao to flee their homes. Some senior UNHCR officials in Thailand, Zia Rizvi among them, even speculated as to whether this was a deliberate United States government policy, aimed at undermining and destabilizing the Communist regimes of Indochina.

In fact, attitudes within the United States government were, as so often, confused. Washington had made no protest against the closing of the door (nor did UNHCR), but Mort Abramowitz and his principal refugee aide, Lionel Rosenblatt, the director of the Kampuchea Emergency Group (KEG), felt passionately that Cambodians should be allowed the same opportunity of resettlement as other Indochinese refugees. They had to battle against opposition not only from UNHCR and sections of the Thai government, but also from parts of the Washington bureaucracy. In January 1981, Abramowitz's lobbying finally managed to secure a quota of 31,000 places for Cambodians. "We dumped them on Reagan's lawn," said one official proudly. But few members of the Reagan administration had the same fervor for the Cambodian cause that many of President Carter's officials had felt.

As the passions wrought by the spectacle of Vietnamese and Cambodian misery in 1979 subsided, so the entire Indochinese resettlement program had run into increasing criticism within the United States. The numbers and cost were unprecedented. In fiscal 1980, some 230,000 Indochinese were admitted to the United States, and in fiscal 1981, some 217,000. The costs were estimated at $1.7 billion and $2 billion respectively. (In the two previous decades the United States had accepted only about 60,000 refugees from all over the world every year.) Initially these Indochinese refugees had been accepted without rigorous case-by-case screening, on the basis that anyone leaving Communist Indochina *ipso facto* met the definition of "refugee" under the U.N. Convention and Protocol. By contrast, asylum seekers from Central America were automatically classed as "economic migrants." Indeed, in 1981 the U.S. Coast Guard actually began to carry Haitian officials aboard its ships. It then intercepted Haitian boats and returned the would-be refugees at once to Port-au-Prince. One only has to imagine the American uproar if the Thais had cooperated similarly with Hanoi against Vietnamese boat people to realize the different standards that were being applied. In its treatment of Haitians, and of Salvadorans who fled to the United States, the United States was susceptible to very similar criticisms over protection as were leveled against Thailand's treatment of Cambodians. But UNHCR, which had just been awarded the 1981 Nobel Peace Prize, failed to criticize its principal donor.*

* In October and November 1981, the High Commissioner for Refugees, Poul Hartling, visited the United States. Officials in the Geneva office warned him that "the current state of international protection in the United States is not satisfactory." One internal UNHCR memorandum of October 29, 1981, noted, "The fate of Salvadoran asylum seekers has remained a constant source of preoccupation for UNHCR. . . . Only a minimal proportion of Salvadorans (in the United States) have been recognized as refugees. Between October 1980 and August 1981, *one* Salvadoran was granted asylum and 99 denied." Among 5,459 pending applications, the State Department had reviewed 1,200 and approved only twelve. "There would appear to be a discrepancy between these figures and the declared intention of the United States authorities that asylum should be granted to all bona fide Salvadoran asylum seekers."

On the interdiction of Haitian "illegal immigrants" on the high seas, the report noted, "Whether or not the measures can be challenged from a legal point of view is not certain. The newly introduced interdiction measures, of course, deprive asylum seekers at sea of access to counsel and of the appeal possibilities which they would have had had they entered the USA. . . . The new interdiction measures could certainly constitute an undesirable precedent for other areas of the world (e.g., South-East Asia, where UNHCR has sought to prevent asylum seekers being towed out to sea.)"

To the dismay of some of his protection officials, Hartling failed to take up these matters forcefully with the United States government. Asked at a press conference about the Reagan Administration's claim that the Haitians and Salvadorans were "economic migrants" not refugees, he replied that a prospective host country was the one to make the decision. Moreover, he said, he

During 1981 and 1982 the plight of those Cambodians remaining under UNHCR's protection in Thailand deteriorated. UNHCR officials maintained the public fiction of an imminent large-scale repatriation program in cooperation with the Heng Samrin regime long after they privately acknowledged that that was impossible. As the resettlement opportunities diminished, the only alternatives were existence without future in the holding centers, which the Thai government deliberately made less and less attractive, by removal of markets and everything but the barest essentials—or a return to the border which, once a sort of haven, became more and more politicized and dangerous. Only in 1983 did the opportunities for resettlement abroad improve.

---

was satisfied that the United States interviews of Haitians on the high seas "adhered to the absolutely fair and fine tradition to treat asylum seekers in a right and generous way."

17 ❦ Feeding the Khmer Rouge

In the summer of 1978, just after Jimmy Carter had characterized the Khmer Rouge as "the world's worst violators of human rights," and while the Vietnamese were publicly denouncing and preparing to attack the Pol Pot regime in full force, a young man named Korb was imprisoned in Takeo province in Democratic Kampuchea.

Korb was "a new person"—he was one of the millions who had been evacuated from the towns after the Khmer Rouge victory in 1975. As such, he risked execution for slight errors. In prison, under torture, he apparently lost his reason and used to sing a little ditty:

> O Khmers with black blood,
> Now the eight-year Buddhist prophecy is being fulfilled.
>
> Vietnam is the elder brother
> Kampuchea the younger.
> If we do not follow the Vietnamese as
> our elder brothers
> There will be nothing left of the Khmer
> this time but ashes.
> O Khmers with black blood
> Servants of the Chinese
> Killing your own nation.
>
> Now you Americans have the upper
> hand
> You must repay the Khmer quickly,

Because the Khmer have strived and
struggled for a long time.
Don't bring back the wicked B-52s to pay
us back. That's not enough.
Bring atomic bombs. That is the
repayment needed.
Because the Khmers are building one
hundred houses at a time.

O Khmers with black blood
There will be nothing left of the Khmer
this time but ashes.

O Damreay Romeas mountains
The timber is all gone now.
No forest, no rocks any more.
There can only be ashes left,
Because the Americans are paying
Kampuchea back with blood.
Only garlic remains.

The poem was found two years later, along with a thousand pages of other prison documents, by Ben Kiernan, the Australian academic, who pointed out, "It would be hard to find a more apt depiction of Kampuchea's tragic recent history." Indeed, the madness of Korb's verses seems both to symbolize and to describe the anguished vortex into which Cambodia was thrust in the 1970s. All of Cambodia's recent history is there: the fearful relationship to Vietnam, its ever-looming neighbor; Pol Pot's dependence on China as he waged his fanatic war against both the Khmers and the Vietnamese; the destruction of the country and society wrought by the invisible B-52s whose 30-ton cargoes fell faster than the speed of sound so that suddenly and unpredictably great swaths of earth erupted in a roar of annihilation; the bitterness engendered by national and personal loss; the despair and terror of life and death in the *"gulag Cambodgienne";* and the knowledge that although outside powers played an enormous part in Cambodia's destruction, it was also self-inflicted.

At about the same time as Korb and thousands of other doomed, unvictorious spirits were being driven by low-level Khmer Rouge cadres into insanity and death, the leadership in Phnom Penh was responding with contemptuous anger to Kurt Waldheim's request for comment on the allegations of human-rights abuses before the U.N. Commission on Human Rights in Geneva. Its note in reply condemned, in the ritualistic language commonly used by socialist regimes, the "colonialists" and "imperialists" who dared raise any questions. It denounced in particular Britain, which had submitted a dossier based on interviews with refugees at Aranyaprathet, and claimed that the "British-imperialists" were barbaric and cruel and had no right to speak on human rights. The whole investigation was merely an excuse for colonialist intervention and annexation.

Nonetheless, over the objections of the Rumanian and with the strenuous backing of the American and British members, the subcommission made a historic decision. For the first time ever it voted for a report on human-rights abuses in a Communist country. The task was undertaken by the Tunisian chairman of the subcommission, Abdelwahab Bouhdiba. He prepared a superb and unequivocal report enumerating the mass deportation from the towns, forced labor, restrictions on freedom of movement, torture and the "elimination" of categories of people.

But by the time he came to deliver it to the full Commission in February 1979, Vietnam had overthrown the Khmer Rouge and installed Heng Samrin in Phnom Penh. The politics were in flux. Bouhdiba was kept waiting for days. Only when he threatened to return home with the report undelivered was he allowed a hearing. He spoke brilliantly, and several Western countries proposed an immediate debate on his report. But, although the Soviet Union and its allies had now reversed themselves and were fiercely condemnatory of Khmer Rouge "genocide," the USSR opposed the motion—Soviet opposition to any investigation ("interference") into the internal affairs of member states (save South Africa, Israel and Chile) remained paramount. Eventually the Commission voted to shelve the matter for another year.

Since then the emphasis has changed. Much of the world—not just the Western world and ASEAN—has chosen to see the Khmer Rouge first as the defenders of national sovereignty rather than as the perpetrators of massive crimes against man. Any sense that there was an urgent need to investigate their behavior has faded. A former head of American Amnesty, David Hawk, has found it hard to raise any interest, let alone any funds, for a serious commission to study the Khmer Rouge phenomenon. There is not even any accurate estimate of how many people really died under their rule, though a figure of about two million has become fairly generally accepted.*

Instead, the period has seen the military rehabilitation of the Khmer Rouge and the attempt to give them a diplomatic style. The basis of this effort was set out succinctly in the January 1979 talks that are supposed to have taken place between the Chinese leaders and Ieng Sary in Peking. In these conversations (published in part by the Heng Samrin regime in 1983) Deng Xiaoping showed himself sensitive to public opinion in the West. He instructed the Khmer Rouge to form a united front with Sihanouk and exiled Cambodians not only to regain support at home, but also to improve public relations abroad. "There is now in Paris an organization called Government for the Liberation of Kampuchea. It has issued a five-point communiqué: four of those points are good; the bad point is that those people oppose the Pol Pot government, which they call a dictatorship." Nonetheless, the Khmer Rouge should work with them—"we shall gain an advantage in the international arena, for those people can act more effectively than the comrades you send abroad . . . If you act alone and refuse to unite with these people, you'll suffer losses or at best cause victory to be delayed."

Eventually, they should make Sihanouk Head of State. The

* For a disaster of such magnitude, the scholarship remains remarkably small. In 1982, an independent Finnish group produced a useful report entitled "Kampuchea in the Seventies"; this calculated that the total loss to Cambodia's population, including refugees, in the seventies, was about 2 million, or 30 percent. This was the conclusion arrived at by Steve Heder, an American academic who did more systematic interviewing along the border than anyone else. Heder concluded that half the Sino-Khmers in the population had died, about 30 percent of the "new people" from the towns and about 15 percent of the peasantry. Ben Kiernan has been steadily publishing the results of his research, which shows that conditions were different in different provinces and at different times. Khmer Rouge rule was much harsher in some areas than in others, and was worst of all in 1978—as the crisis with Vietnam began open warfare. Kiernan's longer study is anticipated.

Prince "will operate in the international arena and spend his periods of rest in Beijing." But they should not suggest this to Sihanouk now. "Don't talk to Sihanouk, because it's not sure that he'll accept; you'd better get the subject started in the international arena, and if this happens, very favorable conditions will have been created for the struggle at home. This decision assumes a highly strategic character. The broader the union, the better it will be for the struggle, especially in view of the present difficulties. Now, with regard to your requests, there is no obstacle whatsoever."

Deng promised to finance the Khmer Rouge through Thailand and to set up a radio station for them. But he pointed out: "There is one point I'd like to mention. Formerly people in the world did not like to listen to your radio broadcasts. Nor did they like to listen to the broadcasts from the Thai and Malaysian parties. They jeered at those broadcasts for they did not reflect realities. Now the spotlight is not to be on the Communist Party, but on patriotism, the nation, democracy, this banner being the most important."

In response to such advice, Ieng Sary acknowledged that "at present we've shelved the watchword 'Socialist revolution and building of socialism' and focused on democracy and patriotism and on ever broader union with the people . . ." This conversation cannot be completely verified, but it is consistent. Many of Deng Xiaoping's prescriptions have since been fulfilled; these were to be exactly the tactics that the Khmer Rouge and their supporters used with some success over the years to come.

Through most of 1979, the Khmer Rouge concentrated on sheer survival. They retained Cambodia's U.N. seat—because the rights of nations inevitably take precedence in the U.N. over the rights of man. But they were then almost swept away by the Vietnamese and by starvation and perhaps survived only with the help of the Thai army, the humanitarian organizations along the border and then the move into Sa Kaeo. By the end of the year they had managed to regroup and then the government that had locked its country away from the Western world for its three and a half years of brutal revolution embarked on the public-relations exercise that Deng advocated—a lavish and bizarre attempt to persuade the Western world to forget, or at least reconsider, the past.

While the Khmer Rouge were in power they could be reached only circuitously and tediously through Peking.* Now the Khmer Rouge had well-informed representatives in Bangkok, Geneva and New York. They always returned calls. In Bangkok a journalist simply had to telephone the United Nations headquarters and ask for Mr. Pech Bun Ret, the spokesman for Democratic Kampuchea. Mr. Pech Bun Ret, an engineer during the Lon Nol period and a peasant under Pol Pot, had a comfortable office in the vast modern building near the Royal Palace, and was happy to arrange for journalists to visit "Democratic Kampuchea." His deputy, Khay Chhieng Bunkim, had been at the London School of Economics.

At the end of 1979, Pol Pot, whose name had come to symbolize the horrors of Khmer Rouge rule both at home (by Vietnamese design) and in much of the world, was shifted out from the top leadership. That and other changes in authority were cosmetic—Pol Pot retained power in the army and party—but they were greeted with great fanfare in the Bangkok press. Then Western reporters were invited to visit the "new" Khmer Rouge leaders in their so-called headquarters, a theatrical environment just over the border of Thailand's Surin province inside northern Cambodia.

One of the first to make the trip was Henry Kamm, the *New York Times* correspondent. His stories appeared in the *Times* in early 1980 under such headlines as "Pol Pot Living in Jungle Luxury in Midst of Deprived Cambodia" and "Cambodian Communist Concedes Ousted Regime Committed Errors." They deserve to be recalled.

Kamm related how, after an all-night bus ride and a long walk, he was led into a forest clearing apparently in the territory of "Dem-

* Once, in 1977, I went to the embassy of Democratic Kampuchea in Belgrade, one of the few capitals in which they maintained representation. There was one young man there with his wife. They had been students in Moscow during the Lon Nol years, and the new government had dispatched them to Belgrade after April 1975. The man had no idea what was happening at home and made no attempt to defend the regime he was representing. He gave me a glossy magazine, which I supposed was printed in China, extolling the new life of the people of Democratic Kampuchea. I do not know what happened to him; many people like him ended in Tuol Sleng prison in Phnom Penh.

ocratic Kampuchea." He was greeted by Keat Chhon, Minister without Portfolio, formerly a nuclear physicist.

"There was a handsome vaulted roof of dried leaves over a table, at which coffee was served to refresh the visitors who had traveled all night. Pol Pot supporters, young soldiers sporting green Chinese-style uniforms and shy Cambodian smiles, were the waiters; their weapons were out of sight. Passports were collected by a polite young man who had studied in Paris. Room assignments were announced, and the soldiers picked up the visitors' baggage with kind smiles and firm insistence."

Keat Chhon then led them a mile and a half deeper into the jungle to a larger, obviously brand-new camp, which, Kamm wrote, was "the latest in jungle luxury." The delightful bungalows had beds with mattresses, blankets and pillows. There were flowers, fruit, soap and freshly laundered towels. "The knowledge of the hunger of Cambodia, so painfully visible anywhere else on the border, was crowded out by ample supplies of food brought from Bangkok. The meals were French, except for the Prime Minister's banquet, which featured an infinite variety of Cambodian, Chinese and Western dishes." There was Thai beer, American soft drinks, Johnnie Walker Black Label scotch, bottled water, soda and ice—all brought from Thailand. "The contrast between Cambodian reality and the holiday resort atmosphere created in a particularly beleaguered and deprived part of the world, by a regime previously known for having imposed a radical and destructive revolution upon its people, testified to the regime's need to make itself acceptable to the outside world."

Kamm also interviewed Ieng Sary, who denied that the regime had practiced a policy of mass extermination, but admitted that certain "abuses" and "political errors" had occurred.

"We did not want all those things to happen. But you know, after the liberation . . ." He raised his hands in a gesture suggesting that conditions had been chaotic. "We recognize that there were errors in going too far to the left," he continued. "We moved too rapidly. There were political errors. We did not think enough about the organization of the state. We emphasized the political conscience too much and had too little experience in the management of a state. We did not choose our public servants well and lost some control. Each region constituted a small kingdom. They ran their own affairs."

Ieng Sary claimed that the evacuation of the cities in 1975 was done because of fear that Vietnam would infiltrate the cities, kill Cambodia's leaders and "take us quickly, as they did Laos."

Kamm reminded him that at the time in 1975 the Khmer Rouge had used the threats of United States bombing and of famine as excuses for the evacuation. "Ieng Sary said both were correct and that the new explanation was not made earlier, because 'We did not want to affront the Vietnamese at that moment.' "

Ieng Sary claimed that he had still been in China when the decision to empty the towns was taken as victory approached in 1975; he did not arrive until April 24, a week later. "The city was already evacuated. It was a collective decision. If there had been two or three who think like I, the decision would not have been taken."

According to Ieng Sary, he had opposed Pol Pot's decision to abolish money on the grounds that it would kill incentive. Moreover, "I defended the intellectuals . . . and was accused of being a rightist who knew nothing of the country because I had lived in exile." (He had been in Peking overseeing Sihanouk in the early seventies.)

Similar excuses were offered by Ieng Sary and by Khieu Samphan and other spokesmen from 1980 onward. With their Chinese dollars, the formerly Spartan Khmer Rouge began to throw lavish parties at the United Nations and assiduously courted delegates from around the world. Their own representatives, often chosen, as the Chinese advised, for their erudition or cosmopolitanism, dressed no longer in Mao jackets but in gray suits and armed with hard briefcases, flew all over the globe to conferences of even the most obscure of the U.N.'s many organizations.

On one occasion Ieng Sary was confronted by an American reporter, Elizabeth Becker, with copies of documents from Tuol Sleng. One of them dealt with the murder of Hu Nim, the former Khmer Rouge Minister of Information. It was from a torturer to the head of the prison and read: "He said that he is an independent CIA officer who buried himself for a long time. . . . I have tortured him to write it [the confession] again . . ." Hu Nim was killed—"crushed to bits"—along with 127 other people in Tuol Sleng on July 6, 1977.

Ieng Sary acknowledged the authenticity of the document, but claimed that he had not been aware of the murders at the time. He admitted again that "mistakes" had been made, but they were not "crimes" and they were explicable. "The circumstance was proletarian dictatorship. We were in the middle of class struggle . . ." He would not apologize: "We apologize when it is premeditated. But who is responsible? I wasn't aware of this [the executions]. How can I apologize?"

Once, in Geneva, I listened to a disturbingly elegant denunciation of Vietnamese rule by a senior Khmer Rouge spokesman. His name was Thioun Mum, and he was now the "Secretary of State for Science and Technology" in the government of Democratic Kampuchea. Monsieur Thioun Mum was a member of one of Cambodia's best-known intellectual families; he and his brothers were scholars who, like most of the Khmer Rouge leaders, had been highly educated in France. They had acquired their Marxism from the French Communist party in the 1950s and '60s, and many of them had entered the Cambodian maquis, which Sihanouk called "Les Khmers Rouges," in the middle sixties. One of Thioun Mum's brothers, Thioun Prasith, had been closely associated with Pol Pot and had then fled Phnom Penh with Sihanouk in January 1979. He had been sent by the Chinese with the Prince to New York and had since been the Democratic Kampuchean Ambassador to the United Nations. There he was constantly engaged in complaining to UNICEF headquarters that they were not doing enough for the people living under his government and were doing far too much for those under the Heng Samrin regime. But he also once complained to Jacques Beaumont of UNICEF that supplementary feeding programs for women and children in the border camps created privileges inimical to Khmer socialism.

Thioun Mum had come to the Thai border at the end of 1979 claiming, at first, to be a refugee. He was then spirited away by the Thai military and surfaced again in his new ministerial role. Now, elegantly dressed, sitting in prim Swiss suburbia, he offered me tea and sweet biscuits as he took me on a historical tour of Southeast Asia since the Bronze Age, explaining the basis of the civilization of

Angkor and expounding the obsessive (and well-grounded) fear of their neighbors that the Khmers have ever since endured. Cambodia's frontiers had continually been diminished, he pointed out. He said that in the fifties Pol Pot had been in Yugoslavia, where he had studied Tito's struggle against the Soviet Union. Soviet ambitions in Eastern Europe were very similar to those of Vietnam in Indochina. Hanoi had always wished to dominate a federation of Indochina and it was that which the Khmer Rouge had sought and still sought to resist.

There was much that was accurate and even erudite in his historical exposition. His account of Khmer Rouge rule was less reliable. He acknowledged that such acts as the forcible evacuation of the Phnom Penh hospitals in 1975 had been "not correct" and that since 1975 there had been serious repression in parts of the country. But he claimed that many of the excesses had been perpetrated by Vietnamese agents trying to turn the people against the Khmer Rouge leadership. He said that he knew at the time that there were "deformations" and claimed that he had struggled against them. "I was against the idea that you could build the country without intellectuals, against the destruction of books. So I was cut off from the leadership." He claimed that through 1977 and 1978 he had lived in a garage in Phnom Penh, looking after chickens. If he had indeed criticized the leadership, he was very lucky not to have ended in Tuol Sleng.

The hatred aroused in Cambodia in the 1970s has always reminded me of J. Glenn Gray's observations in his classic study *The Warriors: Reflections on Men in Battle:*

> Anyone who has watched men on the battlefield at work with artillery or looked into the eyes of veteran killers fresh from the slaughter, or studied the description of bombardiers' feelings while smashing their targets, finds it hard to escape the conclusion that there is a delight in destruction. A walk across any battlefield shortly after the guns have fallen silent is convincing enough. A sensitive person is sure to be oppressed by a spirit of evil there, a radical evil which suddenly makes the medieval images of hell and the thousand devils of the imagination believable. This evil appears to surpass mere human malice and to demand explanation in cosmological and religious terms. Men who have lived in the combat zone long enough

to be veterans are sometimes possessed by a fury that makes them capable of anything. Blinded by the rage to destroy and supremely careless of the consequences, they storm against the enemy until they are either victorious, dead or utterly exhausted. It is as if they are seized by a demon and are no longer in control of themselves. From the Homeric account of the sacking of Troy to the conquest of Dien Bien Phu, Western literature is filled with descriptions of soldiers as berserkers and mad destroyers.

Talking to Thioun Mum, I tried to relate those observations to the elements that had gone to make the Khmer Rouge—the intellectual power and the Marxist training of their tiny, inbred elite; the isolation they had endured, some of them for thirteen years, in the mountains and jungles of Cambodia; the xenophobic distrust that they felt for their neighbors and their notional comrades, the Vietnamese Communists; the harshness of the 1970–75 war, which had destroyed Cambodian society and which alone could have created the conditions in which they came to power; the youth and the fearful inexperience of all but war of most of the army and the cadres who found themselves suddenly in control of Phnom Penh and the country in 1975. Wartime brutality, Marxist fanaticism, obsessive and threatened nationalism—these seemed to be three of the principal elements that had contributed to their totalitarianism. As I talked to Thioun Mum, I was disturbed not by the banality of evil but by the intellectual pretensions behind it.

After 1979 Pol Pot never appeared outside Cambodia—though on more than one occasion he was taken to a hospital in Bangkok for treatment of malaria and, apparently, circulatory disorders. While others conducted the public relations, he was involved in directing the military resistance on the ground.

After the Khmer Rouge, the only plausible group along the border was the anti-Communist Khmer People's National Liberation Front, led by Son Sann, a frail, sixty-eight-year-old former Cambodian prime minister who had spent the seventies in exile in Paris.*

---

* Son Sann had been seventeen times a cabinet minister under Sihanouk but, after quarreling with the Prince, had gone into exile in Paris at the end of the sixties. During the Lon Nol years he had occasionally intervened to try

. . .

Others saw Son Sann, and he saw himself, as an embodiment of the idea of a Third Force for Cambodia. The Third Force solution—neither Communist nor right-wing colonialist—has been a dream of Westerners in Indochina since at least the 1940s. It was brilliantly derided by Graham Greene in his book *The Quiet American* as long ago as the early fifties, yet it has never completely gone away. On the contrary, by the end of the seventies the struggles of Vietnam, Cambodia and Laos had been so much more horrible than Greene and other prophets foresaw, that there was a temptation to wonder whether the time for the Third Force had finally come. When Greene was writing, nationalism was pitted against colonialism in Indochina, but by now nationalism had been subsumed by totalitarianism in Vietnam, and in Cambodia it had been consumed by the Khmer Rouge.

---

to find a compromise to halt the destruction of Cambodia. In January 1974 he returned to Phnom Penh to urge the departure of the ineffective Lon Nol. He failed and remained, during the Khmer Rouge maelstrom, in his Paris apartment. In January 1979 he flew to New York to speak with Sihanouk at the United Nations. The Prince would not see him. He went to Washington; he was disappointed to find that the Carter Administration wanted nothing to do with him. Only later in 1979 did he begin to find enough support, from Thailand and elsewhere, to enable him to set up his front and be allowed to establish a tiny foothold in the Phnom Malai mountains near the Thai border in southwest Cambodia.

His cause had now been taken up by several Western voluntary agencies. An American group called Food for the Hungry International (which also had projects in Vietnam) paid some of the expenses of his foreign tours. To visit him on the border, one needed the help not of the Thai military but of American evangelicals, the Seventh-day Adventists and the Christian and Missionary Alliance. I arrived at their headquarters before dawn to be piled into a minibus with a large group of very young nurses and doctors from Monaco. Princess Grace had also adopted Son Sann, and kept dispatching inexperienced medical teams for very short stints in the mountain village of Sok Sann. When we finally arrived, after a very long drive and a steep hike through the mountains, the young people from Monaco were, not surprisingly, terrified by the remoteness and the sight of men with guns. Several had to be shipped away after a sleepless night in the rather Westernized, polythene-covered huts, which were provided by Cambodian labor for them and their rivals from the evangelical groups. Even so, there was a surfeit of often inadequate Western medics in the camp. The different groups seemed to spend a good deal of their time badgering Son Sann to give them preference.

In fact there was still no room for a genuine Third Force. By
early 1980, the Khmer Rouge were perhaps eight times as numerous
as the three thousand-or-so soldiers that Son Sann could muster and
were, obviously, far more experienced and ruthless. The Chinese
insisted that only the Khmer Rouge was a credible military resistance
and that the united-front strategy (which Deng had outlined to Ieng
Sary) be adopted. Thailand and its partners began to force all the
other Khmer Serei groups (sometimes brutally) under the Son Sann
banner and then began to pressure Son Sann himself to combine with
Sihanouk (who could claim a tiny border force professing loyalty
first to him) and with the Khmer Rouge against the Vietnamese.

The device was intended to increase the military pressure upon
Vietnamese forces on the ground and to ensure that the Khmer
Rouge "Government of Democratic Kampuchea" retained Cambodia's seat at the United Nations. It was a depressing procedure, if
only because it ensured the continuation of the Khmer Rouge by
other means. To his credit, Son Sann resisted for almost two years.
Eventually he agreed to form only a coalition, not a united front.
Sihanouk also acceded to it, after his attempts to make contact with
the Vietnamese were rebuffed in Hanoi. He too was unhappy about
the device. His relations with Son Sann were almost as bad as with
his former jailers, the Khmer Rouge.

All of this was made possible by food. The organizations most in-
timately involved in feeding the resistance forces, together with
the mass of civilians along the border, were the World Food Program, which handed over supplies to the Royal Thai Army to feed
about 70,000 people in the northern and southern sectors, and
UNICEF and the International Committee of the Red Cross, which
had responsibility for the central, or northwest, sector of the border.
Within the northwest sector only a minority were Khmer Rouge,
but they were a major cause for the increasing disillusion with the
border felt by the hierarchies of UNICEF and the ICRC.

By the spring of 1980, UNICEF's education program on the
border was proceeding well, and most medical problems had been
contained, though there was an outbreak of cholera in May. But the

organizations still had no control over the feeding; they still simply
delivered supplies to camp leaders. The Khmer Serei camps north of
Aran had continued in their anarchic state, though some of the warlords had changed. One UNICEF survey had shown that fully 87
percent of all the food being delivered to this section of the border
was in some way misappropriated by the camp leaders. As a result
there was still considerable malnutrition, particularly among children, at the border.

Despite the promises of the Thai government to impose some
security, the murder of individual refugees and the deaths of scores
of others in continuous internecine fighting had never been stopped.
At Mak Moun, ICRC staff had been constantly threatened by Van
Saren, who would brandish his pistol in their faces. When, at the
beginning of April, ICRC tried to institute a system of direct feeding
of women and children in Mak Moun, the attempt was a brutal
shambles. Finally, after Van Saren's headquarters had been burned
down—apparently by a rival group—he disappeared forever. But this
did not mean that free and fair distribution of food could immediately be carried out.

In the Khmer Rouge camps discipline was, predictably, well enforced. At the beginning of the border operation many of the Western relief officials had been grateful for this; indeed, some of them
actually found the order of the Khmer Rouge camps a welcome contrast to the shambles that obtained in the non-Communist enclaves.
In January 1980 one UNICEF report noted of the Khmer Rouge
camp at Nong Pru south of Aranyaprathet, "We strongly believe that
this is one of the few camps where distribution is taking place and
reaching the population in the most effective manner. The camp
leader, Mitr Thon, is a highly educated man who seems to be genuinely concerned with the welfare of the camp's population."

This was not the impression that I had when I visited Nong
Pru later in 1980. The place had the same air of menace as Sa Kaeo
holding center in Thailand, where Khmer Rouge troops had been
taken during the crisis of October 1979. There was none of the spon-
taneity and laughter that could be heard in non-Communist camps.
Teen-age soldiers and girls sat stolidly and stared with hostility at
visitors. Comrade Thon and I did not immediately warm to each other.

Thon's real name had been Chhorn Hay. He was a French-educated telecommunications engineer, a left-wing intellectual who had left Phnom Penh for the expanding base areas of the Khmer Rouge in 1971. Not much is known of how he served during the war or the period of Khmer Rouge rule. He said he had been a teacher. Now he was formally Secretary of State for Posts and Telecommunications in Khieu Samphan's fugitive cabinet. His principal task seemed to be to communicate with foreign aid officials. This he obviously did successfully. He wore a rather elaborate digital watch.

Mr. Thon told me that the Vietnamese had a plan to exterminate all Cambodians; I said I did not believe him. I asked him about the Khmer Rouge massacres. He replied, "We were the victims of our own innocence. We could not believe that we had Vietnamese agents in our ranks. Almost every regional party secretary was a Vietnamese agent." He said that the Khmer Rouge would now agree to free elections being held in Cambodia. "Why should anyone believe you?" I asked. "You lied last time."

"The past is the past," he replied. He became quite angry as the argument continued. He insisted on knowing my name and then ordered me out of the camp, complaining to Ulf Kristofferson of UNICEF and later to the Thai military that I was most offensive, should never have been brought there, and must never come back.

Whatever misconceptions some, not all, aid officials had about Khmer Rouge camp leaders, they were well aware, from at least early 1980, that a considerable amount of the supplies—at least 30 percent in some camps—went directly to Khmer Rouge troops. Yet it was not until well into the spring that some UNICEF officials became seriously concerned by this.

It was not just UNICEF. Many of the people working for the aid agencies, particularly the young and idealistic volunteers who had flocked to help save the Cambodians "from extinction" were either innocent or ignorant of the nature of the Khmer Rouge. By putting forward relatively well-educated spokesmen to deal with the agencies, the Khmer Rouge succeeded brilliantly in cherishing this illusion. One American evangelical group was delighted with its success in persuading the Khmer Rouge to accept hundreds of Khmer-language Bibles. The group did not know, or perhaps did not believe, that the gospels were being used as cigarette paper.

For the less naïve, there was a genuine and continuing dilemma. Along with the Khmer Rouge troops were thousands of women and children. Many of them were noncombatants, innocents. Were they to be denied food simply because they could not be separated from the troops? Many aid officials, including Sir Robert Jackson, argued that these people had to be fed, even at the price of rebuilding the Khmer Rouge.

The organization that was from the start most mistrustful of its association with the Khmer Rouge was the International Committee of the Red Cross. In fact Jean Pierre Hocke, ICRC's Director of Operations, disliked ICRC's enforced involvement over the whole length of the "northwest" sector of the border and, throughout the first few months of 1980, sought to reduce the commitment there. By the end of April many senior UNICEF officials had come to agree with him. Ulf Kristofferson reported, "As we are without doubt operating outside our mandates by providing relief to Khmer Rouge concentrations basically consisting of fighting forces, the policy of distributing relief for humanitarian reasons has to be taken up at a central level." In May 1980 Jim Grant, UNICEF's Executive Director, decided that UNICEF also should reduce its presence and activities in at least the Khmer Rouge sectors of the border. In New York, UNICEF asked the U.N. legal department for an opinion on the Khmer Rouge feeding. The reply was that it could not be justified.

Grant thought one solution was to allow the private voluntary agencies, perhaps Catholic Relief Services, to take over. Another possibility was simply to hand the Khmer Rouge camps in the northwest sector over to the World Food Program, which was already supplying food for over twice as many Khmer Rouge in the northern and southern sectors. But although WFP officials had shown far less concern about their activities along the border than either ICRC or now UNICEF, its officials balked at being the only UN agency involved in feeding the Khmer Rouge. The matter had not been resolved when, on June 23, 1980, the Vietnamese attacked the border apparently in retaliation for UNHCR's repatriation from Sa Kaeo and Khao I Dang.

The crisis caused by the attack was seized by both ICRC and UNICEF as a rationale for altering and reducing their involvement along the border. They immediately suspended the land bridge and refused to carry out the next distribution to the Khmer Rouge camps due on June 25. In New York, Charles Egger of UNICEF and Jean Pierre Hocke of the ICRC met to decide how they could further cut back their border work. Egger and Hocke cabled their views to Bangkok. Egger's cable needs to be quoted at length, because it soon became a sensation.

Egger said that they were prepared to continue their border work to the non-Communist Khmer Serei camps on a temporary basis only on condition that security in the camps was adequate; that civilian and military groups were clearly separated; that there was "elimination of any leaders that are clearly obstructive or not willing to collaborate . . . ; that proper monitoring was finally established; that any work by voluntary agencies was properly coordinated within the ICRC-UNICEF framework."

As for the program in the Khmer Rouge camps south of Aranyaprathet, "It is the clear view of the international agencies UNICEF/ ICRC that the conditions pertaining to the distribution of aid have not been met and a large part of the supplies have reached non-civilian categories, namely soldiers of all age groups. Therefore, the two agencies have decided in agreement with WFP to terminate the distribution of aid to these camps by 21/7. This period should permit RTG [Royal Thai Government] to take such alternative measures that they wish to pursue." UNICEF and ICRC would continue to aid children in these camps if it was possible to single them out.

"This decision has been reached with reference to the respective mandates of UNICEF and ICRC, etc., and in taking account of the opinion of U.N. legal division that clearly states that it is not permissible for a U.N. agency to distribute aid to military personnel."

By chance Egger's cable was incorrectly addressed. It therefore leaked quickly through the U.N. system in Bangkok, then Geneva and New York. The Thai government reacted angrily. The Vietnamese attack had convinced the Thais of the threat that Hanoi's occupation of Cambodia posed to Thailand and of the consequent importance of building up the Khmer Rouge and the Khmer Serei. Thailand had just requested the Secretary General to station U.N. observers along the border. But since such an arrangement needed

Security Council approval, the Thais knew that it would never happen. For the Thai government, therefore, the maintenance of U.N. humanitarian officials along the border was more important than ever.

In the face of the Joint Mission's proposed withdrawal, Thai officials threatened to suspend all aid from Thailand to Phnom Penh, including the daily ICRC flight and the massive rice shipments that were being sent from Thai ports. This would have undercut the entire basis of the Joint Mission's relief effort inside Cambodia. Bangkok newspapers published lurid attacks on the international organizations—the Swiss delegates of ICRC, for example, were denounced as a nest of Soviet spies who were so pro-Vietnamese that they spent their holidays in Hanoi—and demanded that they simply obey the orders of Thai Supreme Command.

The U.S. Embassy also reacted strongly. Mort Abramowitz tried to persuade the Thais not to prevent aid from being sent to Phnom Penh, and at the same time a whole series of cables marched across the ether as the weight of the U.S. government was brought to bear on the international organizations to make them resume border feeding and the land bridge. "Those cables really sizzled," said Mort Abramowitz modestly later. He and other United States government officials, like Richard Holbrooke, then the Assistant Secretary for East Asia and the Pacific, maintained that their concern was that the program to Phnom Penh could not be kept going without the cooperation of Thailand. For this reason, they argued, the international organizations must be sensitive to Thai priorities. The Americans did not use their influence to try to effect any change in Thai policy. In one cable Richard Holbrooke suggested that "Fact that 20–40,000 Pol Pot guerrillas have benefited indirectly from this [border] operation should be kept in perspective of total number Khmer fed." There was some truth to that—though he ignored the thousands of Khmer Rouge being fed without question by the World Food Program supplies in other parts of the border. But nowhere did his cable suggest that the feeding of the Khmer Rouge, direct or indirect, be cut from the program. Instead the U.S. Embassy spent a great deal of effort trying to find a compromise between the international organizations and the Thai government.

. . .

Sir Robert Jackson, the coordinator of the Joint Mission's activities in both Thailand and Cambodia, was called upon to try to resolve the crisis.

Jackson's position was, to say the least, delicate. He was the Secretary General's personal representative. In some ways he saw himself more as the spokesman for the agencies than for the donors. However, the donors often saw him as the man who should resolve their complaints against the agencies. Jackson himself invariably said that his real loyalty lay to the Cambodian people, whose lives he was trying to save.

Jackson is a skilled diplomat, and his actual views are often hard to determine. He often said to aid officials that he thought the donors had been hypocritical about the Khmer Rouge feeding and had "turned a Nelson's eye" toward the problem. But in private meetings on his own with ambassadors he was often very critical of the organizations.

On July 3, together with ICRC and UNICEF officials, he met with officials from the major donor embassies in Bangkok. Jackson warned the diplomats that the feeding program to the Khmer Rouge camps south of Aran would have to end almost at once. He said that there had been "concern about the armed elements in the camps all along." Despite Thai promises, nothing had improved.

Jackson went on to stress the importance of the opinion of the U.N.'s Legal Bureau that agencies could not simply ignore the fact that combatants were obtaining international relief—"This makes the supply of relief not only morally unjustifiable but legally untenable." He and Secretary General Waldheim had agreed that the whole issue simply had to be raised again with the Royal Thai Government. Jim Grant of UNICEF and Jean Pierre Hocke of the ICRC were on their way to Thailand to tackle this "major and delicate problem."

The representatives from the embassies were not pleased. Burt Levin, the American deputy chief of mission, who had recently been shuttling between the Thais and the international organizations in search of compromise, pointed out that there was no guarantee that food delivered to Phnom Penh was not supporting combatants on the Vietnamese side. Jackson's reply—that the international organizations could not evade the problem in Thailand simply because it might be happening elsewhere—did not satisfy Levin.

The Australian ambassador suggested that the Thai government "might not be very receptive" to arguments unless similar safeguards against aiding the military were enforced inside Cambodia.

Within a few days, Jackson seems to have decided that it was politically impossible for the agencies to withdraw from the border and yet continue in Phnom Penh. At one ambassadorial meeting he said he thought this whole border feeding problem had arisen because the World Food Program had agreed, back in 1979, to turn over food to the Thai army before any agreement on monitoring had been made. He thought ICRC and UNICEF's decision to withdraw from the border without first consulting Thailand "disastrous" and that Charles Egger's cable announcing this unilateral decision was a grave mistake.

Throughout this period the donors were attempting to persuade or pressure the organizations to resume border feeding to the same level as before June 23. Abramowitz flew back home and lobbied members of Congress to send cables to the ICRC, to UNICEF and to Kurt Waldheim, urging that the border program be continued. He was also critical of those State Department officials—the United States ambassador in Geneva, for instance—who, he thought, were not tough enough with ICRC.

For their part, Alexander Hay and Jean Pierre Hocke of the International Committee of the Red Cross, argued to their critics that the organization's worldwide credibility as a neutral force was at stake. In one conversation with Hocke, the United States ambassador in Geneva urged that ICRC and UNICEF deliver food to women and children instead of men in the Khmer Rouge areas. Hocke said it would not work—"Even if food was put into the hands of noncombatants, there was no control that would keep it from being taken by the military."

Hocke thought it much more sensible that the World Food Program take over the Khmer Rouge camps for which ICRC and UNICEF were now responsible, and just give the food straight to the Thais—as WFP already did elsewhere along the border. Or perhaps the Khmer Rouge camp commanders should just be given cash so that they could simply buy food privately on the Thai market. He thought that was already happening. In any case, the Khmer Rouge would "get food wherever it is," he said, "including taking it from, or levying taxes on, refugees."

That same day in Washington, John Negroponte, one of Holbrooke's assistants, called in diplomats from several donor countries and urged them to make parallel *démarches* to the international organizations. He said that the United States position was that:

1. The basic objective of the feeding program from the outset had been to feed all needy Cambodians regardless of political persuasion;
2. the border was needed because of deficiencies of the Phnom Penh side;
3. the U.S.A. and the international organizations were always aware that distribution would be carried out in a war situation and that diversion was possible;
4. diversion should certainly be kept to a minimum—it was happening on both sides;
5. the U.S.A., despite Hocke's assertions, had never asked ICRC to be more lenient on the border than inside Kampuchea;
6. the U.S.A. in no way supported Pol Pot's return but wanted to get food into Cambodia in the most effective way;
7. the Thai track record was not perfect, but their constraints must be recognized. After all, they had allowed Thailand to be used as a base for the entire operation and had permitted refugees to stay in Thailand.

In Bangkok, Air Vice-Marshal Siddhi, the Thai Foreign Minister, explained Thailand's official position to ambassadors. He said the open-door policy adopted in October 1979 had been a humanitarian one, though obviously it had political reasons too. "Thailand wants the Cambodian population to survive so that one day it can rebuild an independent Cambodia."

Siddhi said that, despite press reports, the Thai government had not threatened to stop all aid leaving Thailand for Phnom Penh if the border program ended; that would be only a last resort. But he was certainly compelled to take a hard line with the international organizations, and he warned that some members of the government were in favor of being very much tougher. No Thais liked the way in which the organizations were trying to dictate what Thais did in Thailand. (This is a fairly common complaint from third-world countries against advice and "interference" from humanitarian organizations dominated by "first world" personnel and philosophies.) Siddhi said he was especially angry with the ICRC; the other agencies were more flexible, he thought.

More negotiation was needed in Bangkok. On July 15 Sir Robert Jackson led Hocke, Egger and G. N. Vogel, head of the World Food Program, to a meeting with donor ambassadors at the Canadian ambassador's residence.

According to the account made by a donor embassy official, Jackson tried to shift the onus to the donors. "To satisfy you," he said to the ambassadors around the table, "we have to monitor distribution in a common-sense way." The agencies would approach the Thais "in a spirit of cooperation," but food could not just be given to armed combatants in the camps. In response, the donors made it clear that if the Thais withdrew their support for UNICEF and ICRC, they could not expect the donors to continue supporting them. It was suggested that one way out of the impasse might be for the organizations to give more assistance to "displaced Thai villagers" instead of to the Khmer Rouge. The meeting ended without decision.

On July 16, Jackson took U.N. and ICRC officials to a formal meeting with Foreign Minister Siddhi. By now Jackson had decided that the feeding of the Khmer Rouge simply had to continue—the Secretary General could not prevent ICRC from pulling out, but he could and would stop UNICEF from doing so, whatever Jim Grant's qualms.

Jackson had prepared a careful speech to be made to Siddhi. He said that much had changed since the border operation began, and perhaps it should now be reviewed. He would like to discuss "various difficulties on our side." Among these were monitoring of what happened to supplies, security in the camps and some guarantee that supplies did not go straight to combatants. He hastened to assure the Air Chief Marshal, "We have no intention of presenting to the government any decisions taken unilaterally."

Siddhi said he was glad of that. He also accepted without protest that distributions to the Khmer Rouge south of Aran would have to be suspended until ICRC and UNICEF could be assured that aid was not simply going to "camps of a predominantly military nature." There was no doubt that he was pleased by the offer of still more World Food Program food for "displaced Thai villagers." It was agreed that UNICEF, ICRC and WFP officials should start a series of meetings with Thai officials to see what sort of compromise could be reached. On July 24 and 25 François Perez, the chief ICRC delegate in Bangkok, and Knud Christensen, the head of UNICEF's Kampuchea office there, visited the Khmer Rouge camps in question ostensibly to determine how many women and children were there.

By this time the Khmer Rouge had made their villages along the border into well-functioning communities; they were not self-sufficient, but they were growing maize, beans, sweet potatoes, bananas, manioc. Women were preparing food, sewing clothes, tilling fields and transporting goods. There were few cases of malnutrition, cerebral malaria had been greatly reduced by ICRC medical attention since the previous fall. There were few men to be seen; they were said to be about 10–20 miles away fighting the Vietnamese. Altogether UNICEF reckoned the population of the three camps to be about 45,700, of whom 31,000 were women and children.

UNICEF officials in Thailand were clearly anxious to find mandated reasons to continue the feeding—the alternative would be just too complicated—and Knud Christensen reported in a "strictly confidential" memorandum: "Above any doubt there are civilians— mothers and children—who are in need of food and medical assistance, and it is this particular target group to which we recommend foods be provided."

Back in Bangkok Perez and Christensen told Squadron Leader Prasong Soonsiri that they intended to recommend that UNICEF resume feeding women only. Prasong, the new Secretary General of the National Security Council, was taking over more and more of the management of Thailand's Cambodia policy; his views on Vietnam, on the Khmer Rouge and on the role the humanitarian organizations should play were rather more uncompromising than those of Foreign Minister Siddhi. On one occasion he declared publicly that ICRC was "like a horse operating with humanitarian blinders; they do not take into consideration the security of the host country." Such complaints by Third World governments about international-aid organizations are not unusual.

Now his question was, "What about the men?" Christensen replied, "We are anxious to reach the civilian populations only. Each woman will be given two rations." One for her, one for a child.

Prasong was evidently not pleased, and Thai pressure, or the fear of it, had its effect. Perez and Christensen drafted a report in which they recommended that 20,000 women be given not two but three rations each. This was the same as was now being distributed in the anti-Communist camps along the border. Moreover, they defined a woman as any female over ten years old. Thus a lot of children would be getting a lot of food—to hand over to their fighting fathers.

By now ICRC had finally induced its partners to let it withdraw from all the border feeding—of both Khmer Rouge and Khmer Serei. Jim Grant, who had just returned from Hanoi, was not pleased that UNICEF was left alone with the responsibility of the Khmer Rouge. But he had to accept Jackson's decision. That same evening, at another late night interagency meeting at the Erawan Hotel, Grant rejected the Christensen-Perez proposal as being too generous to the Khmer Rouge. "It gives UNICEF no way to negotiate a compromise," he said. UNICEF decided instead to start off by giving 15,000 women two rations each.

On August 4, the first distribution, to about 1,000 women in Nong Pru, passed off easily with the women lining up in the disciplined manner expected of the Khmer Rouge. In Ta Prik, however, there was chaos—4,000 women had appeared; only 1,000 were given rations. A confidential UNICEF report commented laconically, "We shall have to organize distribution in a different way." At the second distribution, 3,400 women showed up for rations; at the third the total was 6,000. On each occasion, Thai officials complained that too little food was being distributed. Aid officials promised that the number would be increased. The Thais took more direct action.

On August 6, two days after the first attempt at direct distribution, three unmarked trucks delivered 220 sacks of rice, 180 cartons of fish and 100 cartons of oil to Nong Pru. It was all handed over to the camp leaders. Such deliveries were repeated throughout the month. In an unsigned Note for the Record a senior UNICEF official commented, "We have since tried to make investigations about these extra food deliveries, but it has not been possible to establish the source from where these supplies have come." It did not require much imagination.

A few days later Ulf Kristofferson in Aran was able to document that the food being sent secretly to the Khmer Rouge camps was indeed provided to the Royal Thai Army by the World Food Program. He sent a memo to Bangkok saying this completely destroyed the purpose of UNICEF's laborious attempt to feed only women and children. In Bangkok, senior U.N. officials made half-hearted protests to Squadron Leader Prasong. He not only denied any knowledge of the unscheduled deliveries but even went so far as to express considerable curiosity as to how they could possibly be taking place.

In an attempt to sort it all out, Christensen and Kristofferson made another visit to Ta Prik on September 17. They were rather discomfited to see on the wall of the hut to which they were taken an instruction chart on guerrilla warfare. They told one of the Khmer Rouge cadres that they could not continue even direct distributions unless discipline was maintained. He promised it would be, and he asked for more rations. When they asked him about the "unscheduled deliveries" of food he refused to tell them anything.

UNICEF's own direct distribution to Khmer Rouge women was also becoming farcical. (In the non-Communist camps the same system was working quite well.) As Brian Eads pointed out in the *Observer,* "The reality is one plump flushed American relief official hopelessly scurrying hither and thither as Khmer Rouge females deposited their ration at the feet of the troops, waited in the surrounding reeds, and returned for a second or third helping." On other occasions there were riots as women tore sacks of food from trucks.

At the distribution on September 22, UNICEF took rations for 4,000 women to Nong Pru. Only 400 showed up. The Khmer Rouge camp leaders nonetheless began unloading the food at once and insisted that distribution begin immediately to avoid a Vietnamese attack. Khmer Rouge women ran up to the trucks, took off the food, dumped it in the camp a few yards away and came back for more. Khmer Rouge leaders refused to allow UNICEF men into the camp.

UNICEF stopped the distribution. They asked the Khmer Rouge leaders to reload the trucks so that the food could be taken back to Aranyaprathet. The Khmer Rouge refused. So a vast pile of food—two rations each for 4,000 people—was left on the ground and the UNICEF trucks drove away.

At Ta Prik things were no better that day. The UNICEF report notes: "We found many women walked several meters into the thick grass, handed their rice and fish to waiting soldiers and then returned for more food. During a walk through the resident area with a camp official, I saw several dozen armed Khmer Rouge soldiers carrying rice and rations. When I returned to the distribution site, men and women were running off with boxes of fish and oil and what remained of the extra supplies." In that one day alone eight times too much food was delivered to Nong Pru and twice too much to Ta Prik.

And so it went on. When Knud Christensen and Ulf Kristofferson made another visit to the Khmer Rouge camp at Nong Pru on October 16, 1980, Mitr Thon told them that because of the severe monsoon flooding, women could not get to the camp to pick up their 4,000 rations. He asked that they simply leave the rations for him and his men to distribute to the women later. They agreed.

Gradually UNICEF abandoned the attempt to give supplies only to women and children. U.N. food and Chinese arms continued to flow to the border camps through the rest of 1980, through 1981 and through 1982. In 1982, UNICEF was finally able to relinquish its role; the feeding of the central "northwest" sector of the border around Aranyaprathet was taken over by a new entity called the United Nations Border Relief Operation (UNBRO). At its heart was the World Food Program, which was still providing the Thai army with thousands of rations a day for use in the northern and southern sectors, and which had rarely displayed those qualms about either the legalities or the moralities of the process that had so troubled many officials of first ICRC and then UNICEF. To be fair, though, by 1983 UNBRO was monitoring the food it distributed to all areas of the border considerably more effectively than ICRC or UNICEF had ever managed to do. On the other hand, the border became an ever more dangerous place to be in.

In feeding the Khmer Rouge troops, UNICEF was compelled to flout its own mandate and to ignore the opinion of the United Nations Legal Bureau. For many international officials the program was undoubtedly the most painful and the least acceptable aspect of the whole relief effort. Their principal justification was that they simply could not abandon the innocent women and children who were inextricably mingled with the Khmer Rouge troops.

Partly as a result of the sustenance offered them, the armed strength of the Khmer Rouge seems to have remained fairly constant throughout the period at about 25,000 men; that of the Khmer Serei was about 10,000. As a result of the support they obtained from across the Thai border, the resistance groups were able to mount continued guerrilla attacks upon the Vietnamese main-force units occupying Cambodia, thus continually raising the military costs of their occupation to the Vietnamese. They also attacked Cambodian civilians; the crowded Battambang—Phnom Penh train was fairly frequently ambushed, and on occasion hundreds of people were killed.

The diplomatic costs to Vietnam were raised as well. In 1982 Sihanouk and Son Sann were finally induced to cooperate with each other and then to form a coalition with their mutual enemies the Khmer Rouge. A new government, with Sihanouk once more at its head, was announced. It was a depressing reprieve. Sihanouk had been the titular leader of a united front containing the Khmer Rouge during the 1970–75 war and they had, exactly as he had predicted in 1973, "spat him out like a cherry pit" after they had won victory and his usefulness was ended. Despite that experience, he was once again allowing his name to be used as their figurehead. For Son Sann too, it meant the end of any attempt to represent a "third" or any other way forward. Only the Khmer Rouge gained from the new coalition. As an actual government it was only a fantasy, but of such are the myths of diplomacy often woven, and in 1982 the General Assembly voted by a larger majority than before to accept the credentials of Democratic Kampuchea and to deny the Heng Samrin regime the Cambodian seat. In 1983 it did so again.

It is hard to assess where the primary responsibility for the continuation of the Khmer Rouge lay. Some commentators on the left have chosen to attach most blame to the United States. (Interestingly, many of those who have been most critical of Washington's policies in this regard were precisely those who, during the Khmer Rouge period in power, accused the United States of leading a vicious propaganda campaign against the regime. They included academics and some voluntary agencies, such as the American Friends' Service Committee.) This interpretation of United States policy suggests that after 1979 Washington cynically helped rebuild the Khmer Rouge, at Chinese and Thai insistence, as a further means of revenge against Hanoi for America's humiliating defeat in Indochina in 1975.

Another interpretation of United States policy is that it was weak or directionless, that China had to a large extent filled the vacuum left in Southeast Asia by the American collapse in 1975, and that Washington felt it was in no position to reject the policy of its longtime ASEAN partners and its new Chinese partner in 1979. This analysis points out further that the Khmer Rouge claim to represent Cambodia in the United Nations was upheld continuously by a very large majority of the General Assembly, not merely by the principal protagonists in the region. The majority's determination was reinforced by the Soviet invasion of Afghanistan.

Asked in 1980 how he could justify American policy toward the Khmer Rouge after 1979, Mort Abramowitz replied, "The real question is whether the United States should have bullied the Thais and Peking not to help the Khmer Rouge but to intern them. We never considered this a serious option because (1) we thought the Vietnamese were wrong in Cambodia; (2) the Thais and the Chinese were our friends; (3) they had greater interests in Southeast Asia than we; and (4) we might not have succeeded.

"What would have happened if we had said to the Thais 'Take the Khmer Rouge weapons away' and then the Khmer Rouge had resisted? Still, I have asked myself a thousand times whether that is what we should have done." It always seemed to me that Abramowitz understood and was troubled by the moral ambiguities of the problems.

After the Reagan Administration took office in January 1981, United States policy hardened. In July that year, over eighty nations attended a U.N. conference on the future of Cambodia in New York.

Ieng Sary was at this conference and made a cloying speech about Khmer Rouge love of democracy. It was also the first occasion on which the then Secretary of State, Alexander Haig, had spoken at the United Nations. Ten years before, as a colonel assisting Henry Kissinger, Haig had directed the bombing of Khmer Rouge and their Vietnamese allies in Cambodia. Now he and Ieng Sary were united in their condemnation of the Vietnamese.

The irony of the relationship was further demonstrated at a diplomatic reception given by the Austrians. Haig was there. So was the new Assistant Secretary of State for East Asia, John Holdridge, and America's ambassador to the U.N., Jeane Kirkpatrick. So was Ieng Sary. Apart from his Chinese allies, not many people wished to drink and swap jokes with the Khmer Rouge's foreign minister. He kept his eyes fixed on Haig and his colleagues and prowled around the room after them. His intentions were, of course, peaceable. He merely wanted to thank them in public for their diplomatic support; behind him followed a diminutive Khmer Rouge with a camera. The Americans, who had walked out of the Assembly during Ieng Sary's speech, dodged and weaved before Ieng Sary's advance, until finally he left with the Chinese. Then John Holdridge relaxed and proudly related how he had skipped past the canapes to avoid Ieng Sary's attack. The gesture was meaningless. ASEAN delegates had wanted the conference's final resolution to call for the disarming of the Khmer Rouge in the context of a political settlement. This the Chinese rejected in favor of weaker language that favored the Khmer Rouge; Washington sided with China.

The continuation of the Khmer Rouge undoubtedly represents a dreadful failure of political imagination and a denial of memory. But it is hard to attach sole responsibility for it to Vietnam's opponents. Vietnam itself bore considerable responsibility. Leaving aside the support that Hanoi had given the Khmer Rouge before 1978 (and the extent to which its spokesmen had undercut the refugee stories about Khmer Rouge conduct, thus adding to disbelief in them, particularly on the Western left), Vietnam's conduct since its invasion of Cambodia rarely suggested that it wished to see a compromise in which the Khmer Rouge were removed as a viable force in Cambodia—which was what the ASEAN countries and their Western partners insisted was their aim.

After its occupation of Phnom Penh in January 1979, Hanoi might have signaled a serious desire to reach a compromise satisfactory to its neighbors. It is impossible to predict whether any such suggestion would have been accepted by the Chinese or by the ASEAN countries, but the point is that it was never made. Time and again in the months after their invasion, the Vietnamese reiterated that the situation in Cambodia was "irreversible" despite the fact that so many other nations found it intolerable. In this context it was inevitable that those other nations would seek to apply all possible forms of pressure upon Hanoi to change its mind. The Vietnamese could have predicted that such pressures would include support for the Khmer Rouge.

When I traveled around Cambodia, it seemed that this was remarkably convenient for the Vietnamese. The only legitimacy they could hope to have among a people who traditionally distrusted them was that their occupation was the lesser of two evils, that it prevented the return of the Khmer Rouge. While Thailand and the Chinese were rebuilding Khmer Rouge strength along the Thai border, few if any Cambodians would have wanted the Vietnamese to leave. Within Cambodia, Vietnam's constant propaganda was designed both to instill the fear that was inevitable were Vietnamese protection withdrawn and to concentrate responsibility for Khmer Rouge crimes on "the Pol Pot-Ieng Sary clique" alone. It is worth repeating that in this way Hanoi had avoided any "de-Nazification" or "de-Stalinization" campaign and was able, on the contrary, to fill the Heng Samrin administration with cadres who had previously worked, with varying degrees of diligence, for "Pol Pot." Heng Samrin himself, Hun Sen, the foreign minister, even the Minister of Justice, Ouk Boun Chheoun, were all Khmer Rouge officials through most of the three years of Khmer Rouge rule. They were only three of thousands of former Khmer Rouge whom the Vietnamese had "turned."

Pol Pot and Ieng Sary were indeed condemned to death in the trial that the Vietnamese had staged in Phnom Penh in August 1979. But over the next four years almost no other Khmer Rouge officials were charged with any offense. Since 1975, Vietnam had imprisoned 200,000 of its own people without trial and for indefinite periods in harsh "reeducation" camps. Former Khmer Rouge officers were often deemed to be more reliable than former officials or soldiers of the Thieu or Lon Nol regimes. For the Khmer Rouge, "reeducation" might consist of a short course in Hanoi's interpretation of Marxist-Leninism. For non-Communists it could mean indefinite incarceration.*

Many of the fruits of "liberation" by Vietnam had been sweet, but it must have been bitter for many hundreds of thousands of ordinary non-Communist Cambodians to realize that their liberators placed more confidence in the torturers than in their victims, that many of those people were actually being promoted by the new order into positions of new authority over them. As I have men-

---

* Amnesty International stated in its 1983 report that it was "concerned about reports of detention without trial of people suspected of antigovernment activities" in Cambodia. "More than 200 prisoners suspected of supporting the KPNLF were reportedly held in the former *Prison centrale,* central prison, in Phnom Penh. Other prisons in Phnom Penh believed to hold political prisoners were those of the municipal police, the Ministry of the Interior and the army. Political prisoners were reportedly also held in provincial and district prisons. People arrested near the border with Thailand and suspected of connections with the anti-communist resistance were said to be sent to a labour camp at Trapeaing Phlong in the eastern part of Kompong Cham province. *Khmer rouge* deserters were reportedly sent to separate prisons and mostly released after three to six months' re-education.

"Most political detainees were held without trial. . . . Amnesty International investigated the arrest in late 1982 in Kompong Thom of two people accused of stealing rice for armed opposition groups; Amnesty International received reports that the reason for their detention may have been their participation in unauthorized Christian gatherings. Amnesty International was also concerned about reports that they were tortured to force them to confess. Amnesty International also received details of several cases of people detained without trial for up to two years on suspicion of anti-government activities; some were released after admitting the charges and pledging loyalty to the government."

tioned, in one fishing village on a tributary of the Mekong, I met an old woman who described with great passion how the Khmer Rouge murderer of her son was living, unpunished, in the neighboring village. I did not know whether any of the officials with me on that day had also previously worked for Pol Pot, but Elizabeth Becker noted in the *Washington Post* the awful discrepancy between the legacy of the Khmer Rouge rule and the propaganda purposes to which it was put.

"Few official gatherings are complete without a speaker who details how he or she saw children, parents and friends murdered by Pol Pot's henchmen, and other atrocities. It is not unusual for some of the people who carried out such orders to be seated in the audience or even on the podium with the victim recounting the story."

In a sense Vietnamese leniency toward actual Khmer Rouge cadres was rendered the more disagreeable by the fact that Hanoi's propaganda was not content with the actual crimes the Khmer Rouge committed but was determined to exaggerate them sometimes to the point of absurdity. Thus the claim that Pol Pot was a madman who, on orders from China, was depopulating Cambodia so that it could be restocked with Chinese. Such extravagant demonology enabled Khmer Rouge spokesmen like Ieng Sary and Comrade Thon to claim more plausibly that Vietnamese assertions could not be believed.*

There is a comparison to be made here with Nuremberg. At that trial defendants attempted, at various stages, to absolve themselves by directing all guilt toward the demonic Hitler. The strategy

* The propaganda declared that the Seventh of January Hospital in Phnom Penh, like almost all other hospitals, had been closed under the Khmer Rouge. But the three Western writers whom the Khmer Rouge had invited at the end of 1978—Elizabeth Becker, Richard Dudman and Malcolm Caldwell (a British academic who was murdered there)—had visited the hospital and found it filled with Cambodian soldiers wounded in fighting along the border with Vietnam.

According to the propaganda, there was virtually no industry under the Khmer Rouge. Yet the three foreign journalists were taken to several working factories in 1978; when Becker returned in 1983, she found that they were now closed and it seemed to her that there was even less industrial life than under the Khmer Rouge.

did not work, if only because of the vast body of evidence that the trial gathered and published. In Cambodia, by contrast, the Vietnamese deliberately fostered the demon theory and allowed no such exhaustive examination of the records of the Khmer Rouge. No documents from the Central Committee or from the party leadership were released by Hanoi, perhaps because they would not reflect the new version of recent history which the Vietnamese sought to teach. Indeed, the only documentation that the Vietnamese allowed to see the light of day were the confessions at Tuol Sleng. While these were a revealing testament to the fanatical brutality of the Khmer Rouge, they hardly constituted an adequate record of their years in power.

Moreover, even access to the Tuol Sleng records was increasingly restricted. I have mentioned that David Hawk, a former head of American Amnesty, found it difficult to arouse much Western interest in a detailed study of the Khmer Rouge. His problems were not just in the West. In 1983 I was told by rueful officials of the Heng Samrin regime in Phnom Penh that while they had wanted to grant his request to return to Phnom Penh to make microfiches of the records at Tuol Sleng, their Vietnamese "experts" had vetoed the proposal. They thought that now the Vietnamese did not want even that part of the real history to be fully and independently documented—though in previous years some foreign researchers had been allowed access to the files.

Thus it seems that no one was really interested in establishing or remembering what happened. Along the border the feeding of the Khmer Rouge continued. The new propaganda which Khmer Rouge spokesmen in Thailand or in the West assiduously distributed was distasteful or absurd. But inside Cambodia, under the Vietnamese, other Khmer Rouge cadres were being fed and promoted, and the deed was being done less openly, with no questions asked. And inside Cambodia, the propaganda was often equally absurd and was usually more pervasive.

The Czechoslovak historian Milan Hubl once remarked, after Soviet orthodoxy was forced again onto his country, "The first step in liquidating a people is to erase its memory. Destroy its books, its culture, its history. Then have somebody write new books, manufacture a new culture, invent a new history. Before long the nation will begin to forget what it is and what it was." Hubl's friend Milan Kundera wondered whether this was hyperbole dictated by despair, and if one thinks of applying it to Cambodia, one must repeat that Vietnamese rule was much more benign than that of the Khmer Rouge. Nonetheless, in significant ways it seemed by 1983 that propaganda threatened to bury the real and dreadful history of the recent past so deeply under new lies, new exaggerations, new ideological contraptions, that it was in danger of being obliterated and thus forgotten.

18 ❧ Feeding Heng Samrin

"Food," I told my guide. I wanted to find out what people eat. I wanted to discover how bad the famine was in 1979 and how much food had been distributed to the people since then. I asked if we could go to the port at Kompong Som to see the Soviet dockers and the loading of trucks.

The answer from the Foreign Ministry was No. Kompong Som was "not convenient." I complained about this to my guide. With considerable justification he rounded on me angrily to remind me that not everything in Cambodia was designed to please Western journalists. "Our country fell into hell under Pol Pot. Kampuchea was hell under Pol Pot," he said. "Now I can only buy sixteen kilos of rice a month for myself and eight for each of my children." By the standards of everyone else in the country he was very privileged, but after the Pol Pot years there was no reason why he should see it that way.

Like many people in the West, I had been convinced during the fall of 1979 that a terrible famine threatened to engulf those Cambodians who had survived the Khmer Rouge. Indeed, I had contributed to the widespread sense of horror by writing several gloomy articles on the prospects; I was critical of the way in which the Vietnamese seemed to be obstructing relief efforts. On my subsequent visits to Cambodia in the fall of 1980 and spring of 1981 I wanted to find out just how the aid that the international community had delivered had been used.

Everywhere I went on these two trips through the countryside I asked how much food had been distributed by the government, how many people had died during the 1979 famine and how the others had survived. Such a survey was hardly scientific. Like other journalists and most relief officials I was rarely allowed far off the main roads. But even though there were different answers from place to place, the impressions I gained were fairly consistent. Many of them I have mentioned already. Here are some of the others.

In the village of Tram Khnar, south of Phnom Penh I came across a distribution of rice donated by Japan; I was told that such distributions were sporadic, not regular. On Route 4 outside Phnom Penh we passed what looked like another rice distribution beside the road. I asked the driver to stop, and we walked back to a little thatch hut around which about one hundred people, mostly women, had gathered. The people said that they were given two sacks of 70 kilos each for twelve families; that meant about eleven kilos per family. The last previous distribution had been over a month ago. They said they were not getting enough to live on. They said also that they were expecting this year's harvest to be very bad indeed. Still, for the moment, things were better than they had been. A young woman smiled with exquisite grace as she hoisted a sack of rice onto her shoulder.

Near the town of Kompong Speu (as I mentioned in Chapter 2), I met a group of peasants carrying home U.N. fertilizer that they had just been given by local officials. Their clothes were ragged, and they were clearly very poor. They were not starving, but they said they had very little food; government distributions were rare. Sometimes they were able to exchange baskets that they made in their village for maize at the market, but they were basically living off the land. Often they ate only rice soup. Next year might be better, because they had been given some seed to plant, but it would not be enough for their village.

A few yards further along we came to another group of men, who were squatting on the ground around a large pot of rice and a bucket in which they had cooked crabs. It turned out that they were the officials in charge of the fertilizer distribution; they had been paid well in rice.

On the road to the eastern province of Kompong Cham, in the wreckage of the town of Skoun, we asked the people how much food they had received from the government; one or two kilograms a month was the reply. A kilogram can be stretched over four meals.

In the village of O Reang Au in Kompong Cham, the local officials carefully went through their rather well-kept books. Only two people had died the previous year from famine. They said they had received hardly any food from the government. They then treated us to a huge meal, while scores of children stood around the open windows, gaping and laughing. I suggested that the children be given the remains of our feast. Politely the officials said absolutely not.

In the lakeside village of Anlong Trea, in the poor province of Prey Veng, we were given another large meal of rice, many fish dishes and fruit. The villagers said that in 1979 food had been scarce, but they did not starve. They had lived off their wits and the water. This year they had received a little food from the government; life was better.

On the island of Peam Montea, whose boat races I have described, we were welcomed not only by boats but also by a banquet. As soon as we landed, we were led to a table spread with an astonishing feast—several different kinds of chicken, noodles, vegetable soup, fish, sticky rice wrapped in leaves, bananas and very intoxicating rice wine poured from an old kettle. It was embarrassingly lavish, and hundreds of people stood around to watch us and our escort and the village officials eat. When we had finished, small boys shimmied up the trees to pick coconuts for us. With machetes they made holes in the top and we drank the milk.

Everywhere I went, on this trip and again in the spring of 1981, the answers were much the same. Some ordinary people had had enough food from the government to be able to talk of it in terms of kilograms per month. (Often it was Soviet maize rather than World Food Program rice.) Most had not. Yet there seemed to be little evidence of a nationwide famine just a few months before. People said that there were food shortages in 1979, that sometimes they were very serious, that villagers had been hungry then, and that many were still hungry now. There had been deaths from starvation. But no one to whom I talked spoke of a catastrophe such as many of us in the West had feared in the fall of 1979.

There seemed to be two possible explanations. The first was that the international aid had averted the catastrophe. The second was that the threat had been exaggerated. It seemed important to look again at the evidence.

In July 1979, the Heng Samrin regime had asked for 129,000 tons of food to feed 2.25 million people who, it said, were at risk of famine. These figures, necessarily, were accepted by Oxfam and by the Joint Mission of UNICEF and ICRC. They were the basis of the fear of one or more millions "dead by Christmas."

The program on which the Joint Mission finally agreed with the regime in October 1979 called for the delivery and distribution of 60,000 tons by the end of 1979 and 30,000 tons every month thereafter.

The crucial period in which the largest number were likely to be at risk of famine would be the end of 1979 and early 1980, just before the main rice crop, however poor it was, was harvested.

But by the end of February 1980 the Joint Mission had delivered approximately only 59,000 tons of food to the ports of Kompong Som and Phnom Penh. More importantly, according to World Food Program figures, only 27,000 tons of these supplies had been distributed. This was a tiny proportion of what was thought necessary; the Joint Mission's own program had envisaged importing 120,000 tons of food by that time. Furthermore, as I noted in earlier chapters, very little of that which was being distributed was actually reaching a wide section of the population—a fact that was causing relief officials in Phnom Penh more and more anxiety by the spring and early summer of 1980, particularly as it now seemed that the population was nearer to 6.5 million than the 4.5 million the government had claimed.

The agencies' memoranda show that they feared that a disproportionate amount of the food was being consumed by government employees. By then there were said to be about 250,000 people working for the Heng Samrin regime—either in ministries in Phnom Penh, or as drivers, road builders, village officials, teachers, and so on. They were each allowed between 12 and 20 kilos of rice a month, plus another 8 kilos for each dependent. If one says, conservatively, that each government worker was getting 30 kilos a month for himself and his family, then the government was disposing of 7,500 tons a month for its own employees. By the end of February 1980 that would have amounted to more than the 27,000 tons of the Joint Mission's food supplies that had been distributed.

By the end of August 1980 only about 100,000 tons of food had been distributed in the ten months since the program began in October 1979 (99,356 tons, to be precise). If 7,500 tons had gone to the government every month, then only 25,000 tons of the Joint Mission's food would have been left for the rest of the country.

Of course, the extent of government patronage was not so great at the beginning of the period as at the end, so it might be more accurate to suppose that the government was consuming on average only 5,000 tons a month. In that case, perhaps 50,000 tons would have been available for the rest of the country over the ten-month period.

Divided among the 2.25 million who, the government had originally said, were at risk of famine, this would have given each person 22.22 kilos of rice in ten months. At the World Health Organization's recommended minimum intake of 400 grams a day, this would have sustained them for just over fifty days. But then there is the rice imported by Oxfam (7,000 tons), by the World Council of Churches (10,000 tons) and bilateral socialist sources (an unknown quantity but certainly tens of thousands of tons). These imports obviously raise the total amount of food available for the countryside after the regime had dispensed its patronage. On the other hand, set against all that should be the large quantities of food and other aid that simply disappeared into the thriving black market. Hundreds of tons of imported rice were constantly on sale in Phnom Penh, and scores of restaurants were doing an excellent trade on the basis of it.

In other words, all figures about food distribution are arbitrary. As I talked with aid officials in Phnom Penh and elsewhere a year after the crisis began, it became clear that, despite the generalized optimism that they often felt obliged to express publicly, no one was at all certain how his or her supplies had been distributed. (Nor was there, of course, any such certainty on the border.) There was never much evidence of the donors' 1979 allegation that food was being diverted to the Vietnamese army or to Vietnam. But at least once a

Joint Mission official arrived unexpectedly in Kompong Som and found World Food Program rice being loaded into Vietnamese army trucks, and there was no way of telling how often it happened unnoticed. Perhaps more importantly, no one ever had any real idea of how much food the government was keeping to itself. "We tried to get them to give us a figure, but they never would," said Dominique Dufour, the chief ICRC delegate in Phnom Penh in 1980. "Still today they can't tell us a thing they did with our food. Before every donors' meeting we beg for figures. It's impossible." Dufour said that even government officials confessed that the figures they provided were wrong. "No one knows *anything*. For WFP it's total rape."

I went to the Phnom Penh port one day to watch World Vision rice being unloaded from barges that had come up the Mekong. It was being trucked away. When I asked the port officials where it was going, they were charmingly clear that the manifests they were filling out bore absolutely no relation to reality or to what World Vision believed; they had no idea of and not much interest in the destination of the food—it would all be eaten by someone. Werner Schleiffer, the diligent World Food Program man in Phnom Penh, agreed. He said that many of the statistics his organization had provided the donors in the early months had turned out to be absolutely wrong. Like other officials, he acknowledged that a disproportionate amount of the rice was going to Phnom Penh. (In Bangkok, the U.S. Embassy calculated that by the end of September 1980, Phnom Penh had received 32.7 percent of the international food assistance, while the city accounted for only about 7 percent of the population.)

Hans Page, the Food and Agriculture Organization's man, who had traveled more widely than any other international official in Cambodia, 15,000 kilometers in all, said there was absolutely no way of knowing accurately either how much food had been distributed or how much seed had been planted on how many hectares of land. His figures for planting differed hugely from some of those provided by provincial and central authorities.

Even after the chaos of the early 1979 deliveries, this confusion continued. One UNICEF report of an August 1980 trip to villages away from the main road in the province of Kompong Speu, south of Phnom Penh, noted that "it was very obvious that the situation of the people was much worse than those encountered at distribution points nearer to the road." Many of the people "were still wearing patched Pol Pot rags and appeared very undernourished and drawn. The excitement of the villagers when the convoy arrived also caused us to doubt whether they had received much assistance in the past. Many of them must have walked considerable distances to receive the goods and appeared utterly delighted with what they received, although judging by their appearance, more solid food would have been even more useful."

By contrast, a few weeks later, just before a donors' conference in New York, the World Food Program office, the UNICEF nutritionist and the UNICEF program officer in Phnom Penh were taken by government officials to several villages in Battambang province. There, children seemed to be in good condition. People told the relief officials that the government had regularly delivered seven or eight kilos of food a month. Kurt Jansson was much heartened, and he reported to the donors in New York that food supplies in Battambang were "sufficient."

But then again, two weeks later (after the donors' meeting), UNICEF and ICRC officials in Thailand made a survey of people coming to the land bridge at Nong Chan. Their conclusions were almost the opposite of those of their friends and colleagues a few miles across the frontier inside Cambodia. Farmers and traders alike complained that the authorities in Battambang had distributed anything from two cups of rice per family per month to two kilos per family per month and in rare instances one kilo per person per month. One possible explanation of this difference is that the Joint Mission officials inside Battambang were not taken to meet representative people.*

---

* Responding to the Battambang report, the U.S. Embassy Bangkok noted that the survey was "a welcome development in monitoring. Results argue that since the spring PRK government distribution of grain has improved and spread to rural areas. Refugee reports from the border differ with this conclusion. Refugee interviews also suggest a subsistence level diet but as a result of very small quantities of food from the authorities which supplement foraging and supply from the landbridge. In contrast UNICEF statement is that food and nutrition situation is satisfactory and that distribution by provincial

Such disparities concerned Kurt Jansson. In October 1980 he sent to Sir Robert Jackson a confidential memo in which he acknowledged that distribution "remains somewhat of a puzzlement." While his own survey of Battambang had shown adequate distribution of rice, Hans Page of FAO had recently traveled around ten provinces, and his figures had shown that "in certain provinces distribution has been negligible, sometimes as little as 200 grams per person per month." This was exactly what many villagers told me on my own trips around the countryside.

One sustained effort to research what was going on was carried out by Steve Heder, the Khmer-speaking American academic who spent 1979, 1980 and part of 1981 interviewing hundreds of people who came to the Thai border. Heder had been a protagonist of the Khmer Rouge regime after its 1975 victory. In 1979–80, his research was funded by a State Department grant. He had changed his mind about the nature of Khmer Rouge rule; his work was independent of the State Department and very thorough. He concluded in the summer of 1980 that the regime had distributed food "at frequencies varying from once every two weeks to once every three months, with the quantities of grain (originally mostly corn, now a mixture of corn and rice) distributed varying from one can (250 grams) to three kilograms per person. The average monthly distribution per villager would seem to be somewhere between one and one half kilograms." Heder calculated that the regime was probably distributing between 130 and 170 tons of grain a day throughout the country. This would mean well under 5,000 tons a month—again nowhere near the 30,000 tons a month that the Joint Mission had reckoned necessary to stave off famine at the end of 1979.

In conclusion, the best thing that one can say of the regime's record on food distribution in the countryside is that it was mixed.

---

authorities of conventional and unconventional food supplements are sufficient. As the UNICEF report authors point out, however, the scope of their sample is too limited to be definitive. . . . A breakout of the number of individuals or families interviewed at each site would establish how universal the ration distribution is. In this connection we note what journalists' experience while witnessing a mid-August distribution in Kandal. They moved into the back of the village to discover some inhabitants who had not received any food from earlier distributions."

The one thing that does seem certain is that there is no way in which the amount of international food aid that was actually distributed in Cambodia during 1979 and the early part of 1980 could have saved 2.25 million people from famine. If those people did not starve to death—and there is, fortunately, no evidence that large numbers of people did—then there seems to be only one other conclusion. The threat of famine was exaggerated in 1979. The evidence must be examined once again.

The fear of famine had first been voiced by Western journalists and diplomats in Bangkok in April 1979. At first the Vietnamese and their regime in Phnom Penh had denied the risk, while also acknowledging that Cambodia's needs were great. Then, in July 1979, had come from Hun Sen the famous letter that said that famine now threatened 2.25 million people and asked for 129,000 tons of food to feed them.

In July and August 1979, UNICEF, ICRC, Oxfam and a few other Western agencies were allowed, along with a handful of journalists, very short, restricted visits to Phnom Penh and Kompong Speu. The evidence of Khmer Rouge destruction and the evident distress of the survivors they saw in and around the towns moved them greatly. On the basis of what they were told and what they could see, they decided that a catastrophe was imminent.

A few weeks later, the view from Phnom Penh was reinforced by the spectacle of death in the Khmer Rouge areas along the border. For many people, myself included, the images from Phnom Penh and the border, together with the eyewitness accounts, seemed to prove only one thing: that a nationwide famine was underway. To question it or to deny it seemed inhuman. In the context of the holocaust rhetoric that then was prevalent, it was almost impossible.

At the same time, Western perceptions were complicated by another apparent change in attitude by the Vietnamese. Having first denied and then advertised the risk of famine, now, after Western concern became widely aroused and the border had grown, the Vietnamese altered their public position once more and declared that there was, after all, no famine, and that the whole crisis was a device of the imperialists designed merely to rescue the Khmer Rouge. Having invited UNICEF and the ICRC into Cambodia, Hanoi and its regime in Phnom Penh did not then seem prepared to offer them the facilities they thought necessary to perform their task. To many people in the West, myself included, the restrictions that Hanoi began to impose seemed bound to increase the danger of widespread deaths. The United States government used these perceptions to mount fierce polemics against the Vietnamese.

But these were not the only complications. Another was that when the aid officials actually in Phnom Penh were finally allowed to travel, they themselves changed their minds several times about the real nature of the crisis with which they were dealing. Let us consider what they saw and reported.

In the middle of September 1979, Jacques Beaumont and François Bugnion, whose reports, along with that of Jim Howard of Oxfam, had helped to sound the original alarm, were allowed to make their first real trip out of Phnom Penh to Kompong Chhnang. The impoverishment of the country was obvious, but in his report Beaumont made no mention of seeing evidence of famine. This did not diminish his or Bugnion's conviction that a large-scale aid program was essential.

In late September and early October 1979, Tim Lusty, an Oxfam doctor and nutritionist with considerable experience of famine conditions, conducted a nutritional survey in and around Phnom Penh, Kompong Som and Siem Reap near Angkor Wat. His findings were quite different from the visions of his colleague Jim Howard, who was an engineer, not a nutritionist.

In Phnom Penh and other towns Lusty thought "the nutritional status in all areas we visited was fair to good." In Orphanage Number Two, which had so horrified earlier visitors, Lusty weighed and took arm-circumference measurements of 272 children and found their condition "very good, certainly better than in an average village in Wollo Ethiopia in non famine times." In most villages, nutrition was also "fair," though all villages contained some marasmic children, and in Kompong Speu children in two places were in a serious condition. He thought this was "probably due to the large numbers of migrants and also the fact that this area is traditionally a poor agricultural region."

Lusty thought that, on the basis of the scanty figures available, it was possible that in 1980 "the rural population of Kampuchea could scrape through without food aid." But aid would be justified as a buffer to feed the towns and provide supplies to vulnerable rural areas and groups—hospitals, schools, and orphanages.

By this time Oxfam had assumed the moral high ground in its criticisms of UNICEF and ICRC, and was already embarked on a massive fund-raising effort to avert the "new holocaust." When Brian Walker, Oxfam's director general, visited Cambodia in October, he seemed to accept Lusty's findings; he cabled Oxford, "I have no visual evidence of widespread starvation or famine. Food from Vietnam has improved the situation in Phnom Penh since Jim [Howard] first arrived. We can talk of terminal starvation not of genocide through failure of the West to act on food aid." Back in England Walker spoke publicly of Cambodia as peopled by "emaciated walking-Belsen-type skeletons."

Lusty's findings did not reflect holocaust rhetoric. Indeed, they infuriated many of his colleagues and led to fierce rows between himself and Jim Howard. "I was not encouraged to talk to the press," Lusty said.

In November and December 1979 relief officials in Cambodia were allowed to make their first really substantial trips into the country. They went right around the Great Lake. What they saw seemed to confirm Lusty's conclusions.

Hans Page of the U.N.'s Food and Agriculture Organization traveled with Malcolm Harper of Oxfam. They were astonished to see a lot of cultivation, plenty of buffaloes, markets in many villages, people bringing back consumer goods from the Thai border—but no famine. When they returned to the Samaki Hotel, their colleagues would not believe them. François Bugnion of the ICRC was one of the most incredulous. "I have been sent to fight a famine," he declared. But then he too went around the Lake. He compiled a long, detailed and confidential report, province by province, for his Geneva headquarters. He spoke of malnutrition in places, but he reported no sign of famine.

Robert Mister of Oxfam made a similar trip and reported to Oxford in December 1979: "I saw no evidence of famine, starvation or serious hunger. In fact I found it hard to believe that there had ever been famine or starvation on a massive scale in the parts of

Kampuchea that I visited. It is, however, clear that there are serious food shortages."

In its confidential reports to the donors, the Joint Mission of ICRC and the U.N. agencies began to speak of conditions being better than expected. And Brian Walker of Oxfam publicly talked of "stabilised" areas of Cambodia. Some of the more alarmist fundraising advertisements were toned down. But neither the international nor the voluntary agencies really attempted to explain that perhaps the basis on which the rescue operation had been built was inaccurate.

One reason, given subsequently by Malcolm Harper of Oxfam, was that by the end of 1979 "the fundraising machinery was unstoppable." So much money had been given and pledged, so much emotion and energy had been aroused in the war against a new holocaust, that it was impossible for the agencies to turn around and say that they were reconsidering the need.

Another reason was that refugees coming to the Thai border were still talking of widespread lack of rice, the staple food. Their voices were being loudly amplified by the full resources of the United States government.

Nonetheless, even on the Thai border there was more and more evidence available—to those who sought it—that the famine could not be so widespread as had been feared. The refugees who came to the border south of Aranyaprathet under Khmer Rouge control and were taken to Sa Kaeo were, as we have seen, dying—of malaria, of tuberculosis, of starvation. There were about 30,000 of them. (Other Khmer Rouge, taken to another holding center at Kampot, were in even worse condition.) But north of Aranyaprathet, in places like Mak Moun and Nong Samet, there were perhaps 500,000 people. They came from all over Cambodia, and it is reasonable to suppose that their condition was more indicative of the state of the country than was that of those who had been locked in the deadly embrace of the Khmer Rouge.

Almost all of those taken from these border camps to Khao I Dang said that there was not enough rice available at home. Their condition was poor, often bad, sometimes terminal. But the contrast between their health and the health of those taken from the Khmer Rouge areas to Sa Kaeo–Kampot was remarkable.

One report of ICRC's Epidemiology Unit showed that there were far more children in Khao I Dang than in Sa Kaeo—44 percent of the population was under fifteen as against only 33 percent. Moreover, only 5 percent of small children in Khao I Dang were undernourished enough to need intensive feeding. In Sa Kaeo the figure was 10 percent.

Deaths in the first week of Sa Kaeo were six times higher than in the first week of Khao I Dang. (In Kampot they were thirty times higher than in Khao I Dang.)* Neonatal mortality, traditionally considered to be a sensitive measurement of a population's general health, was widely different. At Khao I Dang, 5 percent of infants were dying in mid-December 1979. In Sa Kaeo the figure was 17 percent. In Khao I Dang the mean birth weight was greater than three kilos, in Sa Kaeo it was less than two kilos. The ICRC found such figures "significantly" and "strikingly" different. In summary, the Khao I Dang statistics did not define a population on the verge of dying of starvation.

In interviews for this book, almost every relief official involved in the Cambodian operation readily agreed on what few of them have said publicly—that the threat of famine had been overestimated in 1979. François Perez, ICRC's chief delegate in Thailand, later said of Khao I Dang, "It was clear that these people were in good shape. There was very little malaria. At that time we explained this by saying that these people had been able to use the black market on the border."

Knud Christensen, who was briefly UNICEF's representative in Phnom Penh in October 1979 until a car crash sent him back to Thailand, recalled that "I saw direct signs of malnutrition in the country but not of famine. It was the border which fixed our views, especially the malaria at Nong Pru," one of the Khmer Rouge camps. Kurt Jansson pointed out that "provincial hospital records would show if there had been mass starvation. The records do *not* show that. It is clear that the needs were overestimated. But it is not clear by how much."

---

* The mortality rate in the first week of Sa Kaeo was 0.91 per thousand per day. In Khao I Dang it was 0.16 per thousand per day. In 1972 the national Cambodian mortality rate was thought to have been 15.6 per thousand per year, or 0.043 per thousand per day.

So how did the Cambodians survive? The most important factor seems to have been something that, in the fever of the holocaust rhetoric at the end of 1979, many of us outside the country either forgot or, for the most part, did not know. Cambodia is a land blessed with extraordinary fecundity and natural abundance, particularly during the monsoon period at the end of the year. Pineapples, mangoes, grapefruit, bananas, coconuts, vegetables, maize, frogs with legs the size of chickens' drumsticks, and above all a plethora of fish, shrimp, crab and lobster have always been available to supplement the basic diet of rice.

Under the Khmer Rouge this bounty had been of little use to most Cambodians because foraging for food and trade in it was forbidden and often punished by death. By contrast, through 1979 and 1980 the Vietnamese allowed not only foraging but also freedom of movement and trade. This was the second factor crucial to restoring a semblance of normal life.

In his October 1980 memorandum to Sir Robert Jackson citing government distributions of as little as 200 grams a month in some provinces, Kurt Jansson commented, "At the same time nutritional levels, even in these poorer provinces such as Prey Veng, Svey Rieng and Kandal, appear, on the basis of visual observation, to be satisfactory, although clearly lower than in the villages visited in Battambang province. The only explanation for this is the availability of local conventional foods such as maize, manioc, sweet potato, beans, palm sugar, fruits, etc., and food not cultivated but generally consumed, such as the roots of lotus flowers, young leaves of certain bushes, etc., which are mixed together with pulses. Fish represents an important source of food now that fishing can be done even in the rice paddies in some of the provinces. What is clear, however, is that the population does not get enough RICE, which of course is the staple food in Kampuchea, representing about 58% of the diet in normal times."

I am left with the belief that the threat of famine was greatly exaggerated in 1979 because we had forgotten the importance of secondary crops. Charles Egger, UNICEF's deputy executive director, who was overseeing much of the operation, agreed. Nonetheless, one must be cautious. Famines are notoriously hard to define, and the borderlines between malnutrition, starvation and famine are never clear-cut. An inadequate distribution system (which Cambodia certainly suffered in 1979, and suffers still today) can often lead to localized famine. Migration often leads to famine; the sort of population upheavals that the Cambodians had endured could easily have caused catastrophe.

The fact that millions of Cambodians managed to survive without directly receiving large amounts of international food aid from the Phnom Penh regime does not mean that aid was unnecessary. It undoubtedly helped save thousands of vulnerable people, including children and the sick. Moreover, after the mayhem and the brutality of the last ten years—a period for which many powers including the United States, China and Vietnam bore great responsibility—Cambodia desperately required a relatively stable government. This the Vietnamese, with the help of international aid, provided. Indeed, one can say that the help of the Western donors was crucial in this regard.

The aid that was sent to Phnom Penh not only allowed the creation of an administration. It also meant that the peasants were allowed to keep whatever they had been able to grow. When Western and Soviet trucks began to arrive at the end of 1979, they provided a commercial bus and transport service as well as a means of transporting the aid officially delivered to Phnom Penh and Kompong Som. The trucks helped to overcome the differences between food-surplus and food-deficit provinces.

And it was not only the supplies delivered formally to the interior that were important. The Thai border was essential. Across the land bridge between 1979 and 1981 flowed over 50,000 tons of rice and 35,000 tons of seed from the Joint Mission, as well as unofficial supplies of thousands of tons of other food and almost every consumer good that the country needed—and a good many that it did not need. A lot of it was misappropriated by various armed groups, including the Vietnamese and the Khmer Rouge and the Khmer Serei. But a lot was given straight to ordinary consumers—far quicker than that which was filtered through the Phnom Penh bureaucracy. The border was the market place for the whole country. The neighboring province of Battambang benefited most, but the trucks and the train from Battambang to Phnom Penh ensured that almost all Cambodia was involved in this trade and profited from it.

This all leaves certain paradoxes. When the Vietnamese began to declare in the fall of 1979 that there was no famine, it was assumed by many in the West that they were not telling the truth. In fact it seems that their original claim in July that 2.25 million were threatened by famine may have been inaccurate.

Vietnamese officials may or may not at first have had the information on which to make a truly accurate assessment of the country's needs. And many of them were clearly genuinely appalled by what they found in Cambodia. But one plausible explanation is that they had realized in the summer of 1979 that the scale of the destruction was such that they could not build up a viable regime without extensive supplies from outside. They had no reason to believe that their allies in the Soviet bloc could muster what was needed—the Soviet Union's record on disaster relief is not impressive. Moreover, turning to the United Nations and the ICRC and enlisting sections of the Western press would help to confer international legitimacy on the regime. At that stage, a few weeks before the opening of the 1979 U.N. General Assembly, Hanoi was striving to obtain more widespread recognition of Heng Samrin.

Perhaps what the Vietnamese had not anticipated was the extraordinary emotional outpouring in the world outside, the fact that the fate of Cambodia became, for a time a *cause célèbre.* Perhaps, too, they had not expected that the Khmer Rouge too would be fed and that persistent demands would be made for monitoring and distribution within Cambodia—but not along the border. Expected or not, none of this can have been welcome and may help to explain Hanoi's subsequent denial of the very same famine that it had announced.

A second paradox to consider is that the food, fuel and trucks supplied by the donors (principally Western nations and Japan) had a political effect precisely opposite that which was sought by those same donors and their ASEAN allies both within and without the United Nations machinery. It consolidated the Heng Samrin regime and the Vietnamese control of Cambodia that they were seeking to remove.

Yet, the U.S. Embassy in Bangkok—far better informed than any other organization and often aggressive in its denunciation of relief-agency misapprehensions and mistakes—did not question at the time whether the famine was exaggerated. On the contrary, United States spokesmen continued to warn of the threat of famine through the first half of 1980.

This is partly explained by the fact that Abramowitz and his principal staff were passionately committed to alleviating the crisis; they were determined to show that the United States, whose policies in the 1970–75 period had contributed largely to Cambodia's destruction, could now play an invaluable role in rebuilding the country. Several of them, including Abramowitz, were Jews who had the destruction of European Jewry in their minds. There is no reason to doubt the sincerity of that emotional commitment.

At the same time, on a political level it was United States policy to berate, and thus to "isolate," Vietnam for aggravating the crisis by its failure to allow adequate resources into Cambodia. And so the United States reporting of refugee stories concentrated on the allegation (which was absolutely true) that very little of the Joint Mission's food was being distributed by the Heng Samrin regime to ordinary people, rather than on the fact that the peasants seemed, nonetheless, to be surviving.

Thirdly—and some on the left would say that this was the most important factor—it was Thai and Chinese policy, supported by the United States, to build up the Khmer Rouge, the Khmer Serei and the civilian border population, as both an alternative and a resistance to Hanoi. That could be best justified and explained at home by the specter of starvation.

One might have expected journalists to point out some of the discrepancies, but in the early months not many did. (I certainly did not.) One of the exceptions was Jean Pierre Gallois, the Agence France Presse man in Hanoi, who wrote in November 1979: "The only indication of a famine situation comes from the Khmer refugees in Thailand. The good faith of these eyewitnesses cannot be questioned. But are they referring to the situation for all four million Cambodians or only to the 300,000 caught in crossfire between the Khmer Rouge resistance and the Vietnamese army?" He thought that the million or so Khmer who had settled in the towns "are in the matter of food and health no worse off than hundreds of millions of people in the Third World." Similarly, the Canadian Embassy in Bangkok warned Ottawa at the end of November that to predict the extinction of the Khmer race on the basis of the tiny sample at Sa Keo was "a gross distortion of reality."* Such unemotional analyses were rare at that time.

Since 1979 some aid organizations and some journalists have tended to describe what happened in Cambodia over 1979–80 as a miraculous recovery or rebirth for which the agencies deserve much credit. It is obvious that many relief officials and their organizations do indeed deserve praise for the way in which they coped with extraordinarily complex political and administrative problems. But perhaps, as Malcolm Harper of Oxfam and Jean Pierre Hocke of ICRC thought, an even more important contribution lay simply in being in Cambodia, considerate ambassadors from the world against which the Khmer Rouge had raised the barricades, a testament to some form of humanitarian victory over foul revolution and impoverished diplomacy. Cambodia's recovery, such as it was, probably testifies more to the resilience and the renewal of confidence among peasants in an area of abundance and to the efficiency of at least a primitive market economy than to the effectiveness of international disaster relief as such.

Alas, the early promise of recovery was not sustained. Although the 1982–83 harvest was the best in years, other sectors of the economy were by 1983 moribund. There were many reasons—the fact that the generous promises of aid originally made by the Soviet Union and its allies were not actually fulfilled; that the Vietnamese showed no real interest, or at least no real talent, in rebuilding the country they had liberated from the Khmer Rouge and which they still occupied in defiance of successive resolutions of the General Assembly; that the international, mainly Western, relief effort ran down.

The basis of U.N. emergency programs is "humanitarian relief to suffering people." Authorities which are not recognized by the

* The Embassy also warned against the West deciding that the only, or even the best, solution for the refugees lay in resettlement in third countries. "We have gained impression that most refugees want to return to Kampuchea; indeed, when one becomes involved with them, one is struck by their very strong drive to protect their future as an ethnic group. What must be conveyed to interested groups is that a sort of cultural genocide could be committed through good intentions by dividing the Khmer and scattering them around the world."

U.N., or by specific donors, are worked with as necessary to that end but programs are not supposed to strengthen their hold on the population. The Cambodian aid program had been conceived as "emergency relief" against the threat of famine; as the memory of that threat (real or apparent) receded, so the donors began to draw increasingly rigid distinctions between relief and development aid to the Heng Samrin regime, which remained excluded from the United Nations. However, they were still willing to fund both the border operation and the UNHCR holding centers within Thailand.

In justification, United States officials cited not only the rules of U.N. emergency relief, but also the constraints imposed by the U.S. Trading with the Enemy Act, introduced during the First World War, and the Export Administration Act of 1979, both of which distinguish between emergency and development aid. Indeed, to the dismay of many U.N. officials and the fury of such American voluntary agencies as the American Friends Service Committee, which had programs in Cambodia and urged the recognition of the Heng Samrin regime, the United States government began in 1980 to interpret these laws rigidly. The voluntary agencies had to obtain federal export permits for almost every commodity they sent to Cambodia, except for rice and seed. The American Friends Service Committee was denied a license for exporting a small sawmill and power woodworking tools to make school furniture in Kompong Cham. When in 1981 the Mennonite Central Committee sought to supply pencils and paper for schoolchildren, a United States export permit was at first denied on the grounds that employees of the Heng Samrin regime would be handing out the goods and this would enhance the regime's image. This was, of course, true; but it was true for almost everything that the U.N. program or the Western voluntary agencies delivered to Cambodia itself.

It is in fact impossible to draw a hard and fast line between relief and development. When the donors tried to do so, the results were inevitably arbitrary. One of the areas in which UNICEF invested heavily in 1979–80 was the rebuilding of the primary educational system. This was of obvious political value to the Heng Samrin regime; indeed, some UNICEF officials were troubled that it was too political. The United States government did not at first prevent it. But the donors prevented the organization from having a similar involvement in secondary education.*

After rice, fish is one of the most important foods in Cambodia. In the sixties the country produced over 200,000 tons of fish and exported modest amounts. The industry was, like all others, badly damaged during the 1970–75 war and appears to have suffered even more under the Khmer Rouge. In 1980 the Food and Agriculture Organization (FAO) began a program to repair weirs, fishing tackle, and boat engines. The donors made no objections at first; but, for reasons that hardly seem logical, nets and then ice-making machines were criticized as "developmental."

In the town of Kompong Chhnang I visited the ancient ice factory; it resembled the engine room of some nineteenth-century steamship wrecked in a Southeast Asian storm. The director proudly showed me how the workers had made one of the three machines function by cannibalizing the others—it was a stupendous achievement, but there was still not enough ice to preserve all the fish caught in the vast and fertile waters all around. The same was true in the rest of the country.

* The ambiguities of United States policy on relief versus development aid were set out in an internal State Department memorandum of February 2, 1981. This stated that "The humanitarian and political objective of U.S.-funded relief is to ensure the survival of the Khmer race and to provide the means for the Khmer people to live in their country, thereby reducing the pressure of Khmer refugees on neighboring Thailand. While it is accepted that the relief assistance will inadvertently assist the Vietnamese-imposed regime to develop its administration, no assistance should be given beyond the subsistence level which contributes toward consolidation of the Heng Samrin regime's control over Kampuchea.

"Rehabilitation projects are defined here as those designed to restore the situation in Kampuchea to that which existed before the Vietnamese invasion in December 1978 (e.g., spare parts for existing machinery, boats and nets to replace those lost or destroyed, supplies to enable medical facilities previously in existence to resume operations). Development projects are defined as those designed to begin new enterprises or operate old ones at previously unattained levels. It is recognized that there are not always clear-cut distinctions between relief, rehabilitation and development. Circumstances can alter, so that projects to supply seed, agricultural implements and nets could be justified during a severe shortage, but would be considered to be rehabilitation projects once a level of subsistence is close, and additional food production would lead to surpluses. . . ."

Increasing the country's domestic fish production would obviously have cut the amount of rice and other foods that needed to be imported. Nonetheless, the donors resisted many of the proposals made by FAO or voluntary organizations. FAO itself did not help when, after eventually receiving donor permission to import one ice-making plant, it failed to ship it until 1981. Then the ministry of agriculture sent it to the wrong province, and it never started working until 1982.

At the same time, the donors refused to fund major repairs to the country's irrigation system. In Cambodia monsoon rains are unpredictable and unreliable. Over the centuries a complex system of irrigation had been created to respond to local conditions throughout the country. Much of this had been destroyed by the war and by the Khmer Rouge's ambitious hydraulic projects, which upset delicate ecological balances.

Animal health programs were acceptable to the donors, but despite the depletion of stocks of draft animals such as buffaloes, animal breeding programs were not. Simple farm tools were allowed; tractors and bulldozers were discouraged. UNICEF did supply seventy-five tractors and plows in 1980, but the donors refused to allow any more. UNICEF was unable to invest in power stations, waterworks, or even the adequate maintenance or fueling of its own fleet of trucks. By 1983 UNICEF was able to provide no fuel at all. One UNICEF official calculated that the amount of fuel America consumed in one hour would meet Cambodia's fuel needs for a year.*

This whole process infuriated Sir Robert Jackson, the coordinator of the U.N. program, who continued to shuttle between New York, Geneva, Bangkok, Phnom Penh and, to a lesser extent, Hanoi and Moscow through 1983. He saw his task more and more to persuade the donors to carry on funding the relief effort inside Cambodia as well as in Thailand and on the border. In one meeting with the donors in New York in March 1981, he declared that the entire

---

* In 1979 and 1980 UNICEF had provided large quantities of fuel to Cambodia. Its distribution was even more poorly monitored than food, and one might argue that it was potentially of greater strategic use to the Vietnamese. But fuel does not have the same emotional resonance as food, and the donors never complained about its diversion.

Cambodia operation "is surrounded by political contradictions virtually at every point," but the problem was that they were now becoming more obvious and acute. He warned the donors that though some progress had been made in Cambodia, there was a danger of collapse if funds ran out. "It is always about the second year in these operations that people start to suffer from the dangers of overconfidence. Bangladesh could easily have blown up again in 1973, if we had not held on for another year—and if we had not done so, the best part of a billion and a half dollars would have gone down the drain. . . ."

As for the reluctance to supply tractors, "I do not know how many of these operations I have been mixed up with, but I have not known a relief operation without tractors. The simple reason is that after any kind of war you will end up with physical exhaustion. Almost invariably there is a great shortage of draught animals." Tractors would save the donors money in the long term because they would increase annual food production and so diminish the need for food aid. To such arguments the donors asked, with some logic, why the USSR was not being more generous in its provision of tractors.

Jackson considered that the complaint that U.N. funds were going to "development" in Cambodia was absurd; he knew of nothing in the country that could be defined as development. "Good God! . . . In my own judgement, if there is any real development in Kampuchea by 1986 it will be a lucky country. There may be reconstruction in the 1990s—if foreign exchange is available. However, so long as the present deadlock exists, I don't know where any foreign exchange will come from."

Jackson's argument had considerable coherence, and he was one of the few U.N. officials (perhaps the only one) who could get away with admonishing governments in such a way. His persistence helped to ensure that the program inside Cambodia continued through 1981 and 1982. But he was unable to overcome the donors' growing political dislike of the program and their skepticism about the way in which first food and then other supplies were being used.

And it was not just the donors. Cambodia's recovery was also seriously retarded by the priorities and methods of the Heng Samrin regime, which used aid more and more for political rather than humanitarian purposes. Thus, to take just one example, the hospital at

Kompong Chhnang was bare of beds and mosquito nets in spring 1981—but the government guesthouse a few yards down the road was luxuriously fitted with brand-new fittings. UNICEF officials became increasingly concerned at the extent to which the government was intent on increasing the number of children in orphanages. "Orphans" (many of whom seemed to have either one parent or at least extended families who had been happily looking after them) were being trained as future cadres; at the age of fifteen they were sent to Vietnam for more intensive instruction. "It's an impossible situation," said one UNICEF official in Phnom Penh. "They dump children in a house and expect us to provide the wherewithal. How can we refuse? Yet we are party to taking children out of their homes, often unnecessarily."

Perhaps as a result of its failure to obtain U.N. membership, the regime placed stricter and stricter limits on the number of Western experts allowed into the country and imposed increasingly rigid controls on the movement of those who were allowed in. By limiting their access to their Cambodian counterparts, they reduced their efficacy. Indeed, some relief officials thought that there was little evidence that the Vietnamese authorities really wanted true "development" programs in the recognized sense; this would have involved much closer contacts between Western experts and Cambodian technicians than they even now allowed.

These conflicts cast the relief agencies—especially the international organizations—into an almost impossible role, that of broker between two mutually distrustful clients, the donors and the Heng Samrin regime. They rarely felt able to voice in public their serious misgivings about the way in which their aid was being used, lest the donors cut aid back even further and the Heng Samrin regime limit even more strictly their activities. Many aid officials felt that Cambodia's needs were so great and the donors were prepared to tolerate such abuses along the border, that deficiencies in the Phnom Penh government were of minor importance. The trouble was that in attempting to please or even appease both sides, they were in the end not really able to satisfy either.

19 ❦ A Balance

When I was completing this book in the summer of 1983, the attention of the Western world had many times flickered away from Cambodia and Vietnam to later crises, fresh disasters. There had been the Soviet invasion of Afghanistan, though the millions of refugees who had then fled never engendered quite the same international emotion as those from Cambodia. Afghanistan had itself been shuttled off the stage by the vengeance of the Ayatollah in Iran. Then had come the brutality of martial law in Poland, which itself was eclipsed by the mass murders in El Salvador—until the 1982 war in Lebanon. In the summer of 1982 the Israeli bombing of civilians and the massacres of Sabra and Chatilla seared our consciences and then were consigned to the lost-luggage lockers of our minds. As I wrote one draft of this chapter, television and newspapers were yet again carrying grim pictures of starving babies; the agencies were pleading for help for the victims of another and apparently more terrible famine—across wide swathes of Africa. By the time the book came to galleys, that disaster too had been swept aside by Lebanon again.

And here I mention just some of the startling assaults upon humanity that we have recently been invited, for a moment, to contemplate. On the rim of consciousness stand also the shadows of Somalis, Haitians, Ugandans, Guatemalans, Bengalis, Chileans, Timorese, Ghanaians, Assamese and many others, including almost all those who have gone before.

One question that we must surely ask ourselves is whether the brief attention given by the international community to some peoples in distress really alleviates their condition as much as it assuages our consciences, or whether it sometimes actually reinforces the underlying causes of their despair. In this regard the case of Cambodia is not necessarily encouraging.

In the fall of 1979 the country's suffering captured international imagination and concern in an almost unprecedented fashion. Thousands of people all over the world devoted some part of themselves or their savings or their prayers to Cambodia. Much that was good was, as a result, achieved. But, despite all that energy, despite all those dollars, despite all those prayers, in 1983 the plight of the Cambodians persisted.

Inside Cambodia there was said to be again a growing food shortage, the country's medical services were still skeletal, and its economic infrastructure was still almost nonexistent. Along the border, there were still over 200,000 people trapped under a bloody banner between the Thai and Vietnamese armies, suffering a series of conditions, in particular war. In Thailand there were still tens of thousands of Cambodians in the holding centers, who were, until the middle of 1983, increasingly desperate about their chances of any sort of future.

Evaluations of humanitarian aid are not easy. One problem is institutional. Humanitarian agencies do not often publish discussions of their work. They release lists of, and sometimes accounts of, the assistance they have given, but rarely offer real analysis. Their reports seldom state what the initial objectives of their programs were and how nearly these have been met. As a result, mistakes are repeated again and again from one disaster to another.* Like all generaliza-

---

* An article in *UNICEF News* by two specialists from the International Disaster Institute, Frances d'Souza and Julius Holt, quoted three examples of this. From Biafra: "The relief was chaotic. . . . Piles of unsorted clothing arrived in Biafra when the agencies had virtually no petrol or relief food . . . The supplies sent were often unsuitable (custard powder and pickled vegetables) . . ." From the 1970 Bay of Bengal cyclone: "A relief agency has given first priority to sending heavy woolen blankets to Bangladesh, a region which is cool at night for only one month a year." From the 1970 Peruvian earthquake: " 'Vacation tents,' which blew away in Costa Rica in

tions, this one has its exceptions, but it applies both to U.N. organizations and to private agencies, large and small.

There are many reasons. One verges on sanctimony. It is, as two American disaster consultants critical of some humanitarian assistance put it, that agencies often believe that "because a program has good intentions then it will necessarily have good results. Deliberate and conscious learning from experience is not part of the nonprofit welfare tradition."* Allied to this is a fairly common belief that relief work should, in some senses, be above reproach. (Several aid officials to whom I showed the manuscript of this book complained that the criticism contained within it was unjustified and unfair because they had gone to help the Cambodians out of a sense of Christian duty.)

Relief agencies often also argue that the present job of relieving actual need is so important that scarce resources should not be diverted to analyzing ends or means. "The refrain: 'We have no time or money to evaluate our efforts—the need is too great!' is all too common among aid officials. Additionally, there is often a lurking suspicion that to attempt to evaluate degrees of suffering is, somehow, immoral."

A further reason—particularly in the case of private charities that are competing for voluntary contributions—is the desire to seem to keep administrative costs down. "Most people who drop pennies into tin cans or onto the church offering plate want to see all of their donations reach the beneficiaries without any deduction for administration." This leads many of the charities to go to extraordinary lengths to conceal their administrative costs within program budgets and often to neglect analysis—seen as an administrative cost—altogether. They seem to prefer to publish fundamentally deceptive accounts that show administrative costs at only 3 percent or so, than

---

1968, have blown away again in Peru. Helicopters have been flying powdered milk to Peruvian Indians whose crops were not affected by the earthquake. Peruvian Indians do not drink cows' milk."

* This and the following quotations are taken from an article by Alan Taylor and Frederick Cuny, American disaster consultants with a firm named Intertect, "The Evaluation of Humanitarian Assistance," *Disasters,* Volume 3, No. 1 (1979), pp. 37–42.

to save future resources by learning from past or even current errors. In the competitive world of agency fund raising it is usually thought that to admit to errors will disenchant and discourage contributors. Those contributors do not have even the minimal rights of shareholders in companies. As a result, they are not always accorded the respect they deserve.

Another problem is that in disaster relief, agencies are often required to make procurement decisions fast and on the basis of inadequate information. When it later becomes clear that such decisions were not well based, they are naturally reluctant to write off the investments already made. Furthermore, career aid officials (like any other) are understandably reluctant to examine their own mistakes. And relief-aid field officers are often on short-term contracts. They rarely see a program through from beginning to end. "Preparing a review which compares the end with the beginning remains no one's responsibility. . . . Those who do prepare unsolicited reports on problems encountered are seldom rehired for further contracts."

For international organizations the situation is different but analogous. Their principal donors—particularly for an emergency relief operation such as Cambodia—are governments. These may well submit the organizations to continuing pressure and directions while an operation is under way—as they did in the case of Cambodia. But once it is over, a great deal of donor interest usually disappears. A government's original decision to assign money to a given relief program is often political; one year later the emergency may have been relieved, it may not, the consequences of the aid may have been as expected, they may not. Either way, its political importance to donors will probably have receded, foreign ministries will be far less inquisitive, and treasuries are not likely to have any real interest in attempting to follow through the way in which the funds were actually spent.

Another problem is that relief work is a process, not a single act. Agencies do not, as a rule, suddenly leave, or seek to leave, countries in which they have programs. But a truthful analysis of their work would often be critical of the host government. At a time when governments of all political hues (but particularly those of the left) are demanding closer control over humanitarian aid, this could be terminal. For obvious reasons, agencies prefer to continue to give some help under difficult conditions rather than to risk a confrontation that could lead to their being denied the right to help at all.

All these observations apply to the case of Cambodia. Despite its size and importance, very little examination has been made of the way in which the relief operation was conducted and the effects that it had, and even less of the lessons that should be learned. Take, for example, Oxfam. Oxfam is actually quite conscientious at looking at its work; it has recently examined its record in both Zaire and Zimbabwe. Most of its staff are very helpful to inquirers. Much of its work in Cambodia was impressive. But, when I asked in early 1983 to see what review they had made of the Oxfam-Consortium's Cambodia program—which, at £21 million was the largest operation Oxfam had ever mounted—it transpired that no such analysis had even been attempted.

This is not because there was no controversy within the organization. Oxfam's headquarters was deeply divided on the merits of its Cambodian enterprise. And one contract field worker, an engineer named Anthony Casey, wrote an angry after-action report criticizing what he saw as the waste and incompetence of Oxfam's industrial program in Cambodia. He complained that "Oxfam never clearly defined exactly what it wanted to achieve, and plan accordingly, and . . . decisions to spend vast sums of public money were made by people who—at least using commercial or industrial criteria— were not qualified to do so." His report went on to set out details of specific poor decisions costing well over a million pounds, and he concluded, "It's a sorry story . . . those of us who have joined Oxfam from 'without'—from agriculture, the media, industry, medicine— . . . have been virtually unanimous in our assessment of the efficacy of the operation." Casey called for "a review of the style and methods of the operation . . . to ensure the most efficient use of public money in the future." Finally, in 1984, it was done.

Oxfam was not unique in this way. Few other organizations examined very carefully what they had done in Cambodia. An important exception was UNICEF, which did carry out a rigorous internal examination of the entire Cambodia program. Indeed, this 400-page report was so critical of the entire operation as to infuriate Sir Robert Jackson, who refused even to discuss it. And UNICEF officials were enjoined not to give a copy of it to this writer.

In looking at the program, one finds that several different levels of analysis are possible. One can try to trace where the money went; one can attempt to examine its effect; and one can hope to see whether the agencies were able to fulfill their mandates, and whether those mandates were effective.

In terms of dollars spent per head of victims, the international disaster relief program for Cambodia was one of the largest the world has ever mounted. In the Bangladesh crisis of 1971–73, about $1,300 million was spent on behalf of a population of 75 million. For Cambodia, close to $1,000 million was spent over three years on a population of between six and seven million. To be precise, by the end of 1981, the donors (mostly the Western countries) had spent $633.9 million on Cambodian relief. About one third of this was contributed by the United States. At the same time Western voluntary agencies had spent at least another $100 million. In 1982 and 1983, the U.N. agencies and ICRC (which were now separated) spent about another $160 million.*

---

* There is no real way of assessing the dollar value of the aid sent to Cambodia by Vietnam and the socialist bloc. It was considerable, but, at least in the Soviet case, it was less than promised, less than the USSR could afford, and much less than might have been expected from such a close ally. According to the Soviet Mission to the United Nations, 360 Soviet specialists were sent to Cambodia during 1980–82; these included the dockers at Kompong Som and technicians to repair Phnom Penh's power station. The Soviets also provided material for road and bridge repair, fishing equipment, telephone installations for Phnom Penh, engineering advisers, medical equipment, and more. "In 1982 the Soviet Union exported goods valued at U.S. $90,800,000 to the People's Republic of Kampuchea. The People's Republic of Kampuchea was supplied with petroleum products, automatic loaders, excavators, bulldozers, tractors, automobiles, spare parts for machinery and equipment, rolled ferrous metal products, paper, cloth, soap and other goods. At the same time, the provision, on a nonreimbursable basis, of goods valued at $16,100,100, continued. The long-term, systematic, all-round assistance provided by the Soviet Union in the reconstruction of industrial, agricultural, transport, communication, health-care, educational and other facilities is promoting the normalization of the economic situation in the People's Republic of Kampuchea, and assists the training of national specialists, improving the delivery of medi-

It is surprisingly hard to trace just how this money was spent, because neither the Joint Mission nor the voluntary agencies published very detailed accounts. Take the figures that the Joint Mission produced for the donors at the end of its formal, united program in December 1981. The entire expenditure was reduced to a single table in which the headings were very broad. (See table.)

Thus, for example, the U.N. High Commissioner for Refugees said only that it had spent $125.7 million for Cambodian refugees between 1979 and 1983. How was this broken down? Merely into $32.4 million for food in Thailand; $83.3 million for "Construction, health, water and others" in Thailand; and $10 million in other countries. Similarly the ICRC baldly claimed to have spent $16.6 million on "logistics" inside Cambodia, and $15.6 million on "operating costs" along the border.

I went to UNICEF headquarters in New York to seek further enlightenment. Officials in the financial department tried to be helpful, but it became clear that they do not usually have to deal with detailed questions, after the event, as to how money has been spent. The files had long ago been retired, largely unexamined.

Assuming the population of Cambodia to be approximately 6.5 million—that, as I have stressed, can be no more than an assumption—this means that over a two-year period the Joint Mission alone spent $97.52 on every living Cambodian.

But it is not so simple as that. Expenditure per head was very different in different places. And Thais benefited also. Take first the "Thai Affected Villagers." A total of $22.7 million was spent on their behalf. If there were 70,000 of them, as was usually claimed, the expenditure on them would have amounted to $324 per head; among 200,000, which was another figure the Thai government sometimes gave, it would have been about $113 per head.

Of the Cambodians, those who had the most spent on them

---

cal care to the population of the country and raising its general level of well being."

Sir Robert Jackson reckons that the USSR provided the equivalent of about $250 million over the 1979–83 period. But at least some of this seems to have been provided not as aid, but in return for Cambodian commitments to supply commodities to the USSR later on.

Program Financial Commitments October 1979–31 December 1981
as at 31 December 1981
(in millions of dollars)

	ICRC Oct 79–Dec 81 (Actual)	UNICEF Oct 79–Dec 81 (Actual)	UNHCR Oct 79–Dec 81 (Actual)	WFP Oct 79–Dec 81 (Actual)	FAO Oct 79–Dec 81 (Actual)	TOTAL Oct 79–Dec 81 (Actual)
KAMPUCHEA						
Food	7.0	17.5		141.9		166.4
Agriculture/fisheries		11.5	3.8		40.7	56.0
Logistics	16.6	44.3	0.6		11.4	72.9
Health	8.4	5.0				13.4
Education		6.8				6.8
Operating costs	9.2	3.2	0.5	1.4	1.7	16.0
Miscellaneous	0.4	0.5	1.4		0.8	3.1
Total	41.6	88.8	6.3	143.3	54.6	334.6
BORDER						
Rice seed		0.9		4.0		4.9
Food and water	12.1	6.4		50.3		68.8
Logistics	5.5	3.5		1.6		10.6
Health and water	17.6	1.4				19.0
Operating costs	15.6	2.9		1.3		19.8
Miscellaneous	6.9	1.7				8.6
Total	57.7	16.8		57.2		131.7
KAMPUCHEANS OUTSIDE KAMPUCHEA						
1. Thailand						
—Food	2.8		32.4	0.5		35.7
—Construction, health, water and others	15.9		83.3			99.2
2. Other countries			10.0			10.0
Total	18.7		125.7	0.5		144.9
THAI AFFECTED						
Food	0.4	0.1		19.0		19.5
Health and other	1.2	2.0				3.2
Total	1.6	2.1		19.0		22.7
GRAND TOTAL	119.6	107.7	132.0	220.0	54.6	633.9

were the smallest group—the "illegal immigrants"—in the UNHCR holding centers in Thailand. UNHCR and ICRC received $134.9 million to spend on an average of about 120,000 people—which works out at just about $1,124 a head. This remarkable sum, which was far more than UNHCR required and led to such extravagances as a helicopter for its staff at Khao I Dang, reflected the fact that the donors preferred UNHCR to all other aspects of the relief program, in part because its funds were almost entirely spent inside Thailand.*

Next best-off financially were the Cambodians who came to the border. There, $131.7 million was spent. No one knows the exact size of the border population; but Ulf Kristofferson, UNICEF's border coordinator, suggests that the average for 1979–81 should be 300,000. This gives a total of about $439 being spent per head. However, this includes the cost of the land bridge of food for the interior.

What of the Cambodians who stayed at home under the Heng Samrin regime? Just over half of the Joint Mission's funds—$334.6 million—were spent inside Cambodia. Divided among six million people, that makes about $55 a head. Among seven million it would make nearly $48 a head.

Once again, these figures are at best imprecise, at worst tendentious; they merely indicate the sort of difference in totals spent inside Cambodia, on the border, and inside Thailand. They take no account of the difference in logistics and operating costs in each of three places. It cost more to build entirely new holding centers and deliver all the necessary services to them than to provide food and education and medical services to people living in makeshift camps along the border. And providing the ships and trucks to move food from the outside world to people in Cambodian provinces was more expensive than trucking food to the Thai border.

The agencies' "operating," "logistics" and "miscellaneous" costs are enormous and almost impenetrable. Each agency calculates them

---

* The helicopter, provided by the Swedish government as part of its support for the program, cost about $250,000; it was hardly used. At a cost of $28,000 each, UNHCR installed nine water towers in Khao I Dang; they barely worked.

on a different basis. Somewhere among them are the considerable costs of personnel. ICRC treats its staff superbly. In Phnom Penh much of their food was imported from Europe; in Thailand U.N. officials constantly complained that the Swiss, with their air-conditioned cars, their weekends on the beach, lived far better than anyone else.*

But U.N. staff are also used to generous tax-free salaries and perks. One World Health Organization expert asked for a fee of $50,000, a generous per diem, and a ticket for his wife, to come for a short assignment to Phnom Penh. Eventually he compromised on $16,000, the per diem, and no wife. On one occasion the Joint Mission people in Phnom Penh complained to Jim Grant because their own per diem was being reduced from $42 to $31.

Now, it is true that conditions in Phnom Penh were in some ways difficult, but expenses there were extremely low. It puts the relief program in a slightly different perspective to note that, at either rate, U.N. officials in Phnom Penh would get more in two days' allowances than the relief program would provide for the average Cambodian over a twenty-seven-month period. By contrast, many of the voluntary-agency staff lived frugally; the dedicated American Friends Service Committee representative in Phnom Penh from 1980 to 1982, Eva Mysliwiec, worked for no salary at all. In 1983 she was finally paid a modest wage when she began to work for Oxfam in Phnom Penh. (Oxfam was fortunate to acquire Mysliwiec's services. She was the most experienced foreign-aid worker in Phnom Penh—

---

* Many agencies were also too protective of jobs for their own national staff. In 1983 the coordinator of the voluntary agencies in Thailand, Simon Cornwell, criticized their reliance on expatriate, Western staff. In the annual handbook of the Committee for Co-ordination of Services to Displaced Persons in Thailand, he wrote, "During the past two years, much lip-service has been paid to the principle that increased self-reliance should be fostered among the refugee community . . . with expensive expatriate staff increasingly phased out and their work handed over to the refugees themselves. . . ." He noted, however, that despite the reduction of funds available to them, the agencies in Thailand had cut back much more on the numbers of refugees and Thais they hired than on the expatriates. This, he argued, was foolish in many ways. "For as well as reducing the need for expensive support of expatriates (at least in terms of airfares, living costs and overseas administration, even when the people involved work without a formal salary), it is in the medium and long term clearly both politically and philosophically astute to increase as far as possible the involvement both of the local community and of the refugees themselves in the planning, administration and implementation of support programmes."

while some previous representatives of Oxfam had had no relevant experience at all. She understood the regime, knew its various personalities well, and worked with them with great good humor. Thus she was able, for example, to insist that Oxfam would no longer give the Foreign Ministry an annual $5,000 p.a. for furniture and to demand that its monthly gasoline bill be reduced to what she actually used—down from $2,500 a month to $300.)

There are many functions that are impossible to "cost." Protection is one of the most obvious. How do you assess the cost of saving one or ten thousand Cambodians from a firefight along the border? It may be quite reasonable to include in it weeks if not months of aid officials talking to and dining with Thai officers in order to persuade them of the wisdom of such a move. But there is no way in which a value, let alone a price, can be placed upon it.

Perhaps, since food was the fundamental purpose of the entire effort, it would be appropriate to look just at the amount spent on food in the different areas—Cambodia, the border and the holding centers. Food costs were close to half the costs of the entire program, $290.4 million in all—$166.4 million was spent on it inside Cambodia; $68.8 million along the border; $35.7 million in the UNHCR holding centers; and $19.5 million for the "Affected Thai villagers." A breakdown of these figures shows enormous differences—just under $28 per head among six million Cambodians at home (just under $24, taking the population at seven million); $229 per head on the border; $47 per head in the HCR holding centers; and $278 per head for 70,000 Thai Affected Villagers ($97 per head among 200,000 such villagers). The only area in which food distribution was really subject to rigorous control and where adequate diets were assured was the holding centers.*

* UNICEF officials calculated that the food handed over by the World Food Program to the Royal Thai Army for distribution to predominantly Khmer Rouge camps in the northern and southern sectors of the border cost $11,753,000 over the 1979–81 period. Similarly, they reckoned, unofficially, that less than half of the food supplied to the army on behalf of "Thai Affected Villagers" was actually eaten by such villagers. This would mean that perhaps $10 million of the food supplied under this heading would have gone elsewhere. Thus from those two operations alone, the World Food Program was in effect supplying the Royal Thai Army with almost $22 million of food.

Once again it seems that proportionately the worst off were those who remained at home under the Vietnamese administration. But the adjustments one can make to the figures are endless. About half of the food delivered to the border—about 50,000 tons of rice— was put over the land bridge. If it all went into Cambodia this would reduce the per capita expenditure for the border population to $114.66 and raise that for Cambodians at home to $33 among six million and $28 among seven million. (Not all of it did go across the border.) Then, again, if one divides the food sent to Phnom Penh instead among the 2.25 million people who the Heng Samrin regime originally said were at risk of famine and for whom the aid was requested, one gets still another result. In this case, the per capita expenditure inside the country would be almost $80. That is already much closer to the sum spent on the border. One might also argue that the cost of the trucks and the investment in agricultural rehabilitation and schools and industry were of direct benefit to ordinary Cambodians and should be included in any calculations. Close to $100 million were spent by the Joint Mission on these areas inside Cambodia. That would bring the per capita expenditure among the 2.25 million high-risk Cambodians to about $118.

The permutations are endless, and it seems to be impossible to make a really accurate breakdown of the figures. But they do show an obvious preference of the donors for spending money on programs in Thailand rather than in Cambodia. (About half of the over-all total of $634 million spent by the Joint Mission for programs in both countries was actually disbursed in Thailand itself, thus giving a considerable fillip to the wider Thai economy.) This bias was partly explained by the increasing difficulty of obtaining visas for foreigners to work in Cambodia; in any case, it became more and more pronounced every year, until by 1983 one reached a situation in which the donors were prepared to give about $70 million for the border and the holding centers and less than $2 million for all of Cambodia itself.

More important than the proportionate sums of money spent on the different parts of the program is whether the funds enabled the Joint

Mission to achieve its aims and the different agencies to fulfill their mandates.

At the time this book was completed, not much optimism was being expressed. An FAO report on nutrition inside Cambodia in early 1983 concluded gloomily that "in the seven food-deficit provinces the prevalence of moderate/severe malnutrition among the examined children below the age of 13 years is still as high as 60%. . . . The food intake of children is still highly inadequate and grossly deficient . . . It is estimated that vulnerable groups such as children with moderate/severe malnutrition, pregnant/lactating women, hospitalized patients, orphans, widows, disabled and older people with insufficient resources, represent approximately 35% of the Kampuchean population." At the same time, however, the report praised the way in which the Heng Samrin regime had handled international food aid in 1982, saying that it "was distributed on a priority basis to food-deficit provinces and within these provinces the food aid went to poor villages and vulnerable groups."

Officials of the donor countries did not readily accept this analysis. They pointed out that since 1979 FAO had continually "cried wolf." Every year serious shortfalls had been predicted, every year less food had been imported than FAO—and the Joint Mission itself—had said was essential, and yet the country had survived. They asked also why, if—as FAO claimed—the Heng Samrin regime had distributed previous food aid effectively to those who most needed it, there was now such malnutrition among the vulnerable. (Some aid officials from other agencies were also critical of this FAO report, and for similar reasons.)

Moreover, in 1982 Cambodia had exported fish to Vietnam, and Vietnam had itself exported rice elsewhere, and in 1983 there was an abundance of rice and other foods in Phnom Penh markets and restaurants. The explanation of malnutrition to which the donors tended was succinctly stated by Brian Eads, often a critic of Western policy, in the *Observer* in May 1983,

> That there is severe malnutrition among a majority of children is simply a function of official [Heng Samrin] priorities. Enough rice was acquired to sustain the loyalty of government officials and em-

ployees. The sight of ragged children picking over a hill of garbage might suggest that the "emergency" continues. But sight of policemen in a popular French restaurant, quaffing bottle after bottle of Soviet champagne, each costing four times their monthly salary, suggests a new era.

Such circumstances led many of the donors to ask how further international supplies of food to Cambodia could be justified.

Apart from maldistribution (or political distribution) of food, there is another explanation for the continued high incidence of malnutrition: the lack of adequate supplementary feeding programs inside Cambodia. Nutritional deficiencies among large populations can be overcome in a number of ways. If the usual food supply has only recently been interrupted, then the mere provision of general food aid—such as was provided by the Joint Mission over 1979–81—may well be enough. However, if large numbers of people are at great risk—pregnant or lactating women, young children, those recovering from malnutrition—then supplementary feeding will be needed. This can mean either provision of extra rations for people to take home or "on the spot" feeding of only high-risk target groups. The latter is usually the more effective system. It was carried out over a long period at the border.

Similarly, people on the border suffering from long-term malnutrition (protein-energy malnutrition) were able to benefit from intensive, therapeutic feeding programs carried out by such agencies as the Catholic Relief Services. Such programs were not available inside Cambodia, largely because of the restrictions imposed upon Western aid officials there. One can argue that the general population of Cambodia would have been much better served had less of the Joint Mission's resources been spent on general food supplies in 1979–80 and more on supplementary feeding programs over a long period. But that was not the sort of aid that the Vietnamese or the Heng Samrin regime sought, nor is there any reason to suppose that they would have allowed it.

There could be no quarrel about the state of the country's medical services by the summer of 1983. They were execrable and represented a serious failure for the ICRC and, indeed, for the other agencies that had tried to improve medical care inside the country. (An important exception was the World Vision children's hospital in Phnom Penh, which was working well.) ICRC and UNICEF had spent $13.4 million on health inside the country during the period of the Joint Mission, but, according to the FAO's March 1983 nutrition survey, the health system was "disastrous." Medical supplies were "far below acceptable standards, even for poor developing countries, and the situation is nearing a deep crisis. . . . Adequate medical treatment is not available because of a general lack of basic medicines, a severe shortage of medical doctors, and absence of basic medical supply and co-ordination."* Phnom Penh hospitals were still without adequate water supplies.

* The FAO report noted: "In the seven provinces visited there are no Kampuchean medical doctors available, except in the provincial hospital of Kandal, which also serves a part of the population of Phnom Penh and is situated in the neighborhood of Phnom Penh. In the provincial hospitals the medical care was provided by medical assistants, who received some medical education in the past few years. There were some nurses and auxiliary personnel in the hospitals. In three provincial hospitals, one foreign medical consultant was working especially for emergency cases in surgery. Each provincial hospital has between 200–400 beds, mostly occupied by only seriously ill patients. The hygienic conditions were reasonable because of the efforts of the nurses and the auxiliary personnel. Laboratory facilities for proper diagnosis, except a poor service for basic haematology, were not available. . . . The supply of medicines was far below acceptable standards. The dispensaries are almost all empty and there was a lack of all basic medicines and other supplies needed for the treatment of patients such as: oxygen, infusion liquid, plasma, blood, antibiotics, analgesics, anaesthetics, antimalaria drugs, antipyretics, antihelminthics, etc.

"The facilities for sterilization, disinfection and surgical instruments were very limited, resulting in many infections after surgery or no treatment at all. The water supply for hospitals everywhere was very bad because of lack of pumps and water. The food for the hospitalized patients consisted of rice and soup and was highly inadequate because only a very limited budget for food was available. In general it is evident that the medical services in the provinces are in an emergency situation. Most of the seriously ill patients did not receive any, or only insufficient treatment. Diagnosis of many patients was not possible because of lack of all fundamental facilities in spite of the efforts of the medical personnel.

"The general lack of medicines is disastrous and prevents any improvement of medical care. The striking suffering of patients is not acceptable and needs immediate attention and humanitarian aid. Primary health care and mother and child health care no longer exist in the provinces. The whole community health system in villages, districts and provinces does not function because of a general lack of facilities."

This reflected Vietnamese policies at least as much as mistakes or cutbacks in aid by the donors. Politics took precedence over health; those few Cambodian doctors and nurses who did exist were constantly forced to neglect their duties to go to political study sessions. There was daily indoctrination, and there were frequent longer courses. Patients died as a result. In 1982 the government announced that it would no longer accept foreign medical teams that included— as medical teams nearly always do—a general practitioner. The stated reason was that the first Khmer doctors had just completed their training; they were supposed to be employed instead. But some Western aid workers saw it as simply a way of restricting even further direct contact between non-Communist relief workers and the Cambodian people. As a result, the League of Red Cross societies, which had taken over from ICRC the responsibility of providing teams, refused to send any more. By 1983 there were several attenuated foreign Red Cross teams in the country, but over-all there were still far too few doctors—foreign or native—to meet Cambodia's health needs, and the government was still very reluctant to allow Western agencies to be involved in training health workers.

Sometimes this may also have reflected Cambodian (or, more likely, Vietnamese) impatience with the arrogance and cultural superiority that some Western relief officials displayed. Third World governments often complain that their own methods and priorities are frequently dismissed or disregarded by Western humanitarian agencies. There were inevitably some foreign-aid officials in Phnom Penh who behaved badly and this may have contributed to the authorities' restraints upon them. But it seemed that Vietnamese political priorities were the overriding consideration.

Thus, for example, by the end of 1981, Oxfam had been encouraged to spend over $400,000 (£233,270) on building eighty-three "clinics" in Takeo province, but its doctor was refused permission to train enough personnel to staff them. The "clinics" were often finely built, useful propaganda for the regime, but equally often they had no water and were inaccessible. In 1982 Oxfam dispatched another doctor, Chris Manning, to Phnom Penh, to see if any useful training program or other clinical work could be carried out. Manning's view was that Oxfam had wasted much of the money spent on clinics in Takeo—"Good buildings alone do not ensure improvements in the standard of medical care in a community . . . and it must be remembered that buildings can so easily be used purely for political purposes in Kampuchea." He was convinced that training of rural health workers was more important—competent health workers can carry out preventive medicine under a tree. After long delays, Manning was able to visit Prey Veng province and negotiate with local officials a plan for training, for supplying drugs and for a limited repair program for clinics. But then, after increasingly frustrating negotiation in Phnom Penh, it became clear that the regime would never accept these proposals and that a building program was all it would agree to. Manning rejected this and left, bitterly disappointed at the government's refusal to enable foreign doctors like himself to give help to people who desperately needed it. He reported back to Oxfam that despite the great need for training, "it is deeply regretted that with the present government of Kampuchea it just is not possible, except in a very limited way and provided that a large material input [that is, buildings] is put into the program." And so, because the project did not accord with Vietnamese political priorities, Cambodia lost a $100,000 program that could have greatly helped medical services in Prey Veng. (Similarly, an offer by the Islamic Bank of Development in Jeddah of $1 million to build a hospital for the Khmer Muslims, the Chams, who had suffered especially grievously under the Khmer Rouge, was never accepted by the authorities in Phnom Penh—apparently because of its religious connotations.)

In 1983 Cambodians still exhibited the extraordinary vibrance that had carried them through the years of atrocity. Their gaiety at times masked the underlying realities of the economy. The Vietnamese were still permitting vigorous free-market activity, and there was a greater variety of goods for sale in the streets than before.

Sir Robert Jackson and other aid officials were convinced that by early 1983 the economy inside Cambodia was declining from the plateau it had reached as a result of the first massive infusion of aid in 1979–80. Jackson tended to blame this on the donors and the fact that they were refusing to follow up their initial investment of "emergency" aid with "development" funds.

At the same time the voluntary agencies' programs were now

minute compared to what they had invested in 1979 and 1980. (In the United States the recession meant that corporations were giving much less to charities in tax write-offs.) Many of them acknowledged that they would have been able to provide a much more consistent and effective aid program had they staggered their expenditure, so as to spend less at first and more over a longer period. But they also complained that in the heat of holocaust rhetoric in 1979, they were under enormous public pressure to spend quickly. In some cases, this ignored the fact that they too had been responsible for some of that rhetoric.* But, whoever was responsible, the speed with which decisions were made was indeed sometimes disastrous. To give just one other example: In 1980–81, the World Council of Churches provided $850,000 worth of equipment to five provincial hospitals. A survey conducted for WCC in 1983 showed that almost all of this money had been wasted. Much of the original equipment had been far too sophisticated and had either broken down or never been properly set up in the first place. The explanation given was that in Geneva the WCC had wanted to be seen to act quickly back in 1980. Such errors were another reason for the poor state of the medical services in 1983.

Of the voluntary agencies, Church World Service still had effective veterinary and irrigation programs in 1983. It was helped by the fact that they had brought in Cuban technicians. Lutheran World Service had a livestock and water program; CARE

* For example, the pressure upon the Oxfam consortium to spend money as quickly as possible meant that almost £19 million of its total £21 million Cambodia fund was spent by the end of 1980. This pressure came both from public opinion and from within the consortium. Some of it was of course generated by Oxfam's own holocaust rhetoric. Whatever the reasons, Oxfam officials now acknowledge that a number of mistakes were made—sometimes because Oxfam staff in Phnom Penh changed too quickly or were inexperienced, sometimes because various Cambodian ministries pushed projects which were unsuitable. One of the worst errors was the purchase of two huge Japanese irrigation pumps at a cost of £160,000 because of faulty specifications by the team's agriculturalist. They were far too large for any known site in Cambodia and have never been installed. By the time that Oxfam had begun to take a calmer look at the development needs of the country, it had little money left and the public concern it had generated in Britain had largely disappeared. In 1983 Oxfam published a report on the continued wretched state of Cambodia; it received minimal public attention.

had provided food for a Food for Work irrigation scheme. The European Catholic group, Coopération Internationale pour le Développement et la Solidarité (CIDSE) was still run by Honesta Carpene, who had been in Phnom Penh since 1980 and was one of the most effective foreign relief officials there. She was administering a hydrology program and a program to give villages blacksmiths' equipment.

But the shortcomings of and the restrictions upon the relief programs were not just the fault of the donor politics or agency mistakes. They were also the consequence of Vietnamese policy. The Vietnamese were determined to impose a dictatorship based upon Marxist Leninism, and to that everything else was subservient. They were intent also on minimizing non-Communist involvement in Cambodian affairs. Western material was welcome, but almost all Western advice and technical involvement were refused. For the Khmer population, indoctrination was deemed more vital than training. As one Oxfam field director, David de Pury, reported in 1983,

> Political courses take precedence over all other activities (even at the expense of the critically-ill hospitals). There are courses at all levels for the masses who need re-education, for civil servants, for cadres and for Party members. Key people are sent away at short notice for months at a time with disregard for current activities or personal inconvenience. It may work in the long term as more and more people come to have a stake in preserving the system, but the short-term effect on economic and social programs is deplorable.

Among the foreign agencies, perhaps the starkest failure inside Cambodia was that of the ICRC—not because of ICRC incompetence but because, under the Geneva Conventions, ICRC has unique responsibilities, and the Heng Samrin regime was determined to prevent it from discharging them. Quite apart from the inadequate medical care it was permitted to deliver, ICRC had been forbidden to visit any prisoners of war held by the Vietnamese or Heng Samrin forces. It had not been able to visit prisoners held by the Khmer Rouge either. (In Thailand, not a party to the conflict, it had been allowed to visit Vietnamese soldiers who had either deserted or been captured.)

ICRC had also been denied the right to visit political prisoners. Many ICRC delegates consider that such visits are its most important duty. One delegate described its failure to perform them in Cambodia as "catastrophic." By the end of 1983, there were reports of several thousand political prisoners under Heng Samrin, almost all non-Communist, not Khmer Rouge. Indeed, some political prisoners who had escaped or been released testified that their jailers were former Khmer Rouge and that the conditions under which they had been held, while not like Tuol Sleng, had been execrable. One former official of the Heng Samrin regime, who had been imprisoned for quarreling with a Vietnamese adviser in his ministry, later said that there were Vietnamese officers in the prison system—this was welcome, because they exercised some restraint over the former Khmer Rouge guards. ICRC had no way of confirming these reports or of offering any comfort to the prisoners.

The ICRC had also been prevented from carrying out its tracing responsibilities. For example, delegates in Thailand identified almost one hundred children there who had been separated from their families inside Cambodia. The Kampuchean Red Cross informed the ICRC that they had found their families. But the government refused to allow photographs of the parents to be taken to the children for verification. Given such uncertainty, ICRC felt that it could not send the children from Thailand back. Thousands more people were denied reconciliation for similar reasons.

Such were some of the problems encountered by the relief agencies inside Cambodia in 1983. Along the border and in Thailand they were different but equally acute.

Thin strips of blue plastic stretched over branches and poles were the only shelter from the 110 degree sun. A water truck drew up in clouds of dust and was surrounded by women and children with buckets. Food came in plastic bags—rice, some oil and dried fish, beans—delivered, efficiently, by the successor to the Joint Mission of UNICEF and the ICRC—UNBRO, the United Nations Border Relief Operation, an ad hoc group based on the World Food Program.

This was Red Hill, in the spring of 1983, just one of many pauses along the border for Cambodian "displaced persons" (no one officially recognized them as refugees—some of their camps straddled the border) on a track which now led nowhere through a no man's land as barren as the policies that almost all governments were adopting toward Cambodia.

Back in 1979, up to half a million people, encouraged by Voice of America broadcasts, had come to the border seeking sanctuary and food. Food they had found. But for Cambodians, as for many other refugees, sanctuary had at best been elusive, had at worst been denied.

Now, in 1983, it was hard to recall the concern that Indochinese refugees had aroused in the West just four years before. Then the invocation of the holocaust had helped to throw open doors—hundreds of thousands of refugees had been resettled in the West, mainly in the United States. But this had not solved the problem. Indeed, there were some aid officials, particularly in UNHCR, who argued that resettlement was part of it. They suggested that it was a "pull factor," encouraging Indochinese people who would otherwise have endured conditions at home to leave in the hope of a better life in the West. This theory, which neatly contrived to blame the United States rather than the Vietnamese government for creating the conditions that forced people to become refugees, ignored the extraordinarily strong ties that Indochinese peasants have to their land.*

Refugees were still coming in 1983, particularly in boats from Vietnam. But for most of them, such hopes were now vain. Recession, the problems that other Indochinese were having with integration into third countries, and newer international crises had caused them to be forgotten; resettlement quotas were way down and Western interest was dissipated. Relief workers had a phrase for this; they called it "compassion fatigue." As a result of it, refugees found themselves either trapped on the border or, in the case of the boat people, imprisoned in so-called "closed camps" from which there was little hope of escape.

The boat people were no longer anything like the flood they

* Since 1975 over a million Indochinese had fled their countries and had been resettled abroad. By far the largest number of these—611,000—had gone to the United States. Another 263,000 had gone to China. But of the Indochinese refugees, the Cambodians had been the least fortunate. The United States had taken only about 78,000 Cambodians, as against over 420,000 Vietnamese and well over 100,000 Lao, and this despite the horror of the Pol Pot years and Washington's opposition to the Heng Samrin regime.

had constituted in 1979, but by any other standard their numbers were still high. In the first ten months of 1983, some 25,567 boat people arrived in other countries of the region. Most of those sailing to Hong Kong were peasants from northern Vietnam with almost no hope of resettlement. There were 13,000 boat people in Hong Kong; by the middle of the year, 3,500 of them were locked in "closed camps," where conditions were wretched. There were dormitories that were unheated in winter and unventilated in summer, holding up to 250 people, crowded into small metallic cages stacked on top of one another. Defending the policy, Hong Kong officials said that they had never denied asylum (unlike many other Southeast Asian countries), but the rate of resettlement was now so low that they must discourage further arrivals.

For those boat people sailing toward Malaysia and Thailand, the hazards of piracy were still dreadful. In some months every single boat reaching shore had been attacked by pirates at least once. Thousands of people had died, thousands more women had been raped. Yet, since 1979, only twenty-seven Thai pirates had been arrested, tried and convicted. Other boats were quietly pushed back out to sea by Thai and Malaysian officials. In 1979 such policies caused an outcry in the West. Now no one noticed. Back in 1979 the West had seen the boat people as symbols of persecution, of courage and of freedom. Now, it seemed, they had outsailed their symbolism and were discarded. In Malaysia a Club Méditérranée had made one Vietnamese boat, in which several hundred people had struggled across the South China Sea, into a trendy bar for the delectation of its clientele.

The border had become much more political, much more isolated since the coalition of Sihanouk, Son Sann and the Khmer Rouge was formed in 1982 and since the donors had cut back almost all funds to the interior. In previous years Robert Jackson had tried to persuade the Vietnamese that aid to the border was a necessary price to pay for the Joint Mission's aid to Phnom Penh; now that that aid was almost nonexistent, this argument was scarcely persuasive. Now the Vietnamese were trying to stop Cambodians from going to trade at the border, and the Thais had denied access to journalists.

There were now about 230,000 people there; about 25,000 of

them were Khmer Rouge troops and another 20,000 were soldiers in Son Sann's army. Both had their families. Many of the rest were civilians trapped between the armies of Thailand and Vietnam. The voluntary agencies were now well coordinated by UNBRO and by a former International Rescue Committee official, Simon Cornwell and, together with the ICRC medical teams, were running effective programs. ICRC's tracing service was running efficiently; it was handling about 3,000 letters and receiving about 250 inquiries a month for people at the border.

But health and sanitary conditions on the border were not—according to a World Health Organization report—now improving. People were suffering from malaria, respiratory infections, diarrhea, and a host of other complaints—especially war.

In the first four months of 1983—the dry season—the Vietnamese attacked several of the border camps. Hundreds of Cambodians were killed, thousands were wounded, and fully 90,000 of the 200,000 were uprooted and forced to move with the children and their small bags of belongings, many of them time and time again. No place on the border was safe—the Vietnamese (like the Khmer Rouge) were as likely to attack civilians as soldiers and on one occasion herded civilians into a bunker and then threw grenades among them. And almost every site had been mined by one or another of the many groups of combatants who had occupied it over recent years. One of the most pathetic sights in the ICRC hospital at Khao I Dang was the scores of people, many of them children, brought in after being smashed by mines. A voluntary organization named Operation Handicap International then fitted those who had lost a leg with artificial ones made from "appropriate technology"—wood, bamboo, a bit of iron and rubber—and then they were sent hobbling back to the minefields. There was no "appropriate technology" for children blinded by mines; they were sent back in darkness to the border.

In these circumstances, it was hard to speak of the agencies, in particular ICRC, offering protection. Indeed, ICRC's chief delegate in Thailand agreed: "I do not think any of us should be overproud of the level of protection we are able to provide to the population which remains stuck between armies, in an area interspersed with armed groups as well as armed black-marketeers, in forests riddled with mines. Every civilian casualty evacuated to the ICRC surgical hospitals represents a failure of protection."

The 20,000 people at Red Hill came from Phnom Chat, a Khmer Rouge camp that had been attacked by the Vietnamese in April. At the strenuous urging of the ICRC and UNBRO, the Thai military had allowed them to be moved away from the fighting. (On several such occasions ICRC delegates had stayed with groups of refugees while they were under fire. At the same time individual Thai officers, in particular Colonel Kitti of Task Force 80, had been helpful, and Kitti had risked his life to move refugees out of the line of fire.) But the government had insisted that all these and other border people must be returned to the border when the fighting ended. Not everyone at Red Hill was Khmer Rouge; many people there hated them. Their plight demonstrated the limits of the international organizations' ability to act independently of governments' policy.

I talked to one man who had been tricked into leaving Khao I Dang in the belief that his wife was at Phnom Chat. It was a lie, and now he was desperate to get away. "I don't want to go back. I am afraid to die," he said. "Two of my children are dead, one is not. Many of the civilians here do not want to go back. But the Khmer Rouge soldiers will make them. The Khmer Rouge have not changed. Don't believe them when they say they are different."

ICRC delegates reckoned that almost a third of the people at Red Hill were opposed to the Khmer Rouge and during April and May 1983, about two thousand people signed petitions to ICRC and UNHCR imploring protection. One group of petitioners begged that they not be sent back under "the Khmer Rouge headmasters." Others asked for resettlement in the West.

Under the Geneva Conventions, ICRC has a duty to try to protect civilians in countries that are at war. Technically, that responsibility ended when the Cambodians were brought inside Thailand; those people now came instead under the mandate of the UNHCR. ICRC passed the petitions on to UNHCR, while continuing to discuss the case with the Thai authorities.

It is almost always difficult for humanitarian agencies to know how far to push discussion toward confrontation. In one of the first of the 1983 Vietnamese attacks on the border camps, refugees had been three days under fire before the Thais agreed to allow them to move temporarily into Thailand. ICRC argued that it was because these people had been moved quickly back to the border that those from Red Hill and other sites had been allowed to escape the fighting almost at once. A confrontation with the Thai authorities now might mean that in future the Thais would not permit any Cambodians to be moved into even temporary havens from border fighting.

In UNHCR's Geneva headquarters, some officials felt that the organization had been too cowardly in the past and must now try to protect the people at Red Hill. Poul Hartling, the High Commissioner, drafted a cable to the Thai Prime Minister asking him "to consider favourably granting asylum to those Kampucheans who had reason to seek asylum in Thailand." But it was held up in Bangkok by considered objections from his own office there and from ICRC and UNBRO, who argued that such a *démarche* might mean that the Thais would never allow anyone else to be moved out of fire fights. Instead, ICRC and UNBRO agreed with the Thai authorities to give people at Red Hill a choice of where on the border they wished to be returned.

On May 24, one of the hottest days of the year, a fleet of buses drew up at Red Hill. Under the supervision of international officials and the Thai army, the people were told to embark at once for either a Khmer Rouge or a Khmer Serei border site. About 2,700 people— many less than the 6,500 whom ICRC had reckoned to be opposed to the Khmer Rouge—hastily escaped "the headmasters."

In answer to inquiries from this reporter, UNHCR formally stated "the large majority of the petitioners sought not asylum in Thailand but to be returned to the area of their choice on the border." UNHCR neglected to mention that about two hundred of those petitioners were begging to be resettled abroad—where many of them had relatives. But temporary asylum was now assured.

UNHCR had also consistently refused to be involved with the "Vietnamese Land Refugees"—people who had crossed Cambodia and were seeking sanctuary at the Thai border. Such people were at great risk from both the Vietnamese army and the Khmer Rouge. Yet the Thais for a long time refused to allow them into Thailand, for fear of the magnet effect. So they were detained in exceptionally squalid prison camps along the border.

One of UNHCR's rationales for refusing to help these people was that they had entered Cambodia, and so Cambodia not Thailand was their country of first asylum. If they were now in Thailand they could no longer fall under UNHCR's mandate. Such arguments embarrassed many of UNHCR's own officials and infuriated those in other agencies.

The ICRC, which had often taken more courageous positions than UNHCR, did act vigorously to protect the Vietnamese. ICRC delegates lived twenty-four hours a day for eighteen months with them on the border and conducted arduous negotiation, in particular with Squadron Leader Prasong Soonsiri, the director of the National Security Council, on their behalf. Eventually ICRC managed to obtain Prasong's agreement to the movement of thousands of Vietnamese off the border, on condition that they were at once resettled abroad. One group of Vietnamese presented ICRC with a flag. The text on it read, "The last 95 people to leave NW 9 camp show their profound gratitude with this flag, in the shadow of which thousands of Vietnamese refugees found the first oasis of security and human warmth, provided for them by the ICRC." More Vietnamese still kept coming overland; in 1982 another camp, NW 82, was emptied in the same way, but by the summer of 1983 there were again another eight hundred land people lingering along with the Cambodians in the half life of the border.* ICRC still gave protection.

* Many of these negotiations were conducted by Count John de Salis, who was an unusual ICRC delegate. He had Swiss, British and Italian blood and was a British army officer. In 1982 de Salis was dispatched to run ICRC's operation during the siege of Beirut. There ICRC was, as de Salis himself put it, "the only lifeline. The only supplies, whether of blood, or medicine, or food, came through ICRC, which gave us a responsibility that was overwhelming, because either we could do it, by maintaining the trust and confidence of all parties, or if we failed, nobody else could." The ICRC, together with the Palestinian Red Crescent and the Lebanese Red Cross, managed to fulfill its tasks rather effectively. Asked later about the differences between Beirut and the Thai border, de Salis commented, "Unlike at the border, where we do our work and go back home, [in Beirut] we were sharing the same conditions and the same risks as the people we were trying to help. If there was no water, we knew it because there was none in our tap either." A similarity was

As with the Cambodians, the Vietnamese chances of resettlement depended in good part on the attitude of the United States. Back in 1979–80 many aid officials had railed against Morton Abramowitz, the United States ambassador, for the passion—moral and political—that he displayed, and for his insistence on constantly intervening in their handling of the Cambodian crisis. Now some relief officials were making exactly the opposite complaint—now it was United States indifference that they blamed.

Abramowitz was gone—and his career had been undercut by the Reagan Administration for his espousal of the refugee cause and other alleged "liberalisms." His successor was John Gunther Dean, who had been United States ambassador to the Lon Nol regime until its collapse in April 1975. Dean made it clear when he arrived in Bangkok that he, unlike Abramowitz, would be "ambassador to Thailand, not to the refugees."

The effect on organizations like UNHCR, ICRC and UNBRO was considerable. They were able to go about their business with less United States interference, to be sure. But the corollary was much less support—not only from the U.S. Embassy but also from the embassies of the many other countries that tended to follow American initiatives. Back in 1979–80 the combination of pressures from agencies and the donor embassies had often infuriated the Thais (Squadron Leader Prasong detested Abramowitz), but it had often been

---

that ICRC was negotiating with everyone at once. "One had the Israeli army, one had the Falangist forces, one had the PLO, one had endless armed groups in Beirut itself. The analogy there is between our negotiations with the Royal Thai Army, the Khmer Rouge component of the Democratic Kampuchea coalition, the KPNLF component, the Sihanoukist component and so forth. In both cases we try to get agreements that will stick with all parties, who could all make the thing come unstuck if they so chose. In human terms, there were two very striking similarities: firstly, it does tend to be the poor and the underprivileged who suffer the most in situations like this. Secondly, we came across a phenomenon that we all know here, that of the 'new' emergencies. In any conflict, people rush to deal with the war-wounded. One soon finds, however, that one has a whole new category of emergencies: diabetics, heart patients, undernourished—all the people who need 'routine' care to stay alive. They are suddenly no longer on anybody's particular list of priorities because they do not have war-related injuries, and they very rapidly become dramatically under-helped." De Salis was an effective delegate.

irresistible. Now the organizations were frequently presenting their arguments alone and their concerns—particularly over protection— were much more easily disregarded.

Indifference also infected much of the Washington bureaucracy. Reagan's Refugee Coordinator, Eugene Douglas, a California businessman, seemed to many voluntary-agency officials to be quite unsuited to the task and to display inadequate concern. One might think that after the cruel war of 1970–75, after the terrible revolution of the Khmer Rouge, after the Vietnamese invasion and the consequent panic, after the traumas of the border, Cambodian refugees needed no more enemies. But now came new avenging angels in the unlikely form of immigration officers from American airports—the men and women of the U.S. Immigration and Naturalization Service.

In 1981, after strenuous lobbying by Abramowitz, the State Department and INS had reached an agreement whereby Indochinese refugees would not be subject to rigorous case-by-case interrogation to determine their eligibility for asylum under the U.S. Refugee Act. That agreement expired in 1982. Dean did not at first fight as his predecessor had done, and so INS began to apply its criteria with extraordinary vigor. Its officers, most of whom had no experience of and no knowledge of Indochina, were sent out for brief assignments to subject refugees to quick, painful and often irrelevant interrogations.

In 1982 INS officials interviewed 21,000 Cambodian "illegal immigrants" who had been already designated by the State Department as "U.S. interest cases"—that is, they had family or other connections in the United States. By the time they met the INS officers, all of these people had every reason to believe that they were finally on their way out of Khao I Dang to the United States.

The interviews that the INS officers conducted had their own macabre quality. The Cambodians were asked if they had left home because of lack of food. This was exactly what United States policy had encouraged them to do in 1979; Voice of America had constantly broadcast the promise of food along the border, and hundreds of thousands of people had come. But now that was all long forgotten; probably many of the INS officers had never learned it. Now, instead, those Cambodians who answered, "Yes, we came because we were hungry," were defined by INS as economic migrants, not real refugees at all and were rejected. Even those who said they lost their family under Pol Pot did little better—INS officials insisted, with a perverse logic, that this did not amount to a "well-founded fear of persecution" under Heng Samrin. To the horror of State Department officials and people from the relief agencies, INS cast back seven thousand Cambodians, a third of those they interviewed. Weeping or bewildered—"Why did America say No to me?"—these people climbed into the buses for the trip back to Khao I Dang and to fear of forced repatriation to Cambodia.

One Cambodian refugee leader at the Nong Samet border camp expressed their predicament powerfully. "Our people," he said, "are like swimmers drowning in the sea. When they see an oar outstretched to them, they try to catch it, they don't ask whose boat it is from. Before, the oar was [resettlement in] third countries, now it is the coalition of Prince Sihanouk. Our people are still trying to catch those oars, but until now nobody comes to pull us out, and we are still in the sea, the large sea."

By early 1983 it seemed that more of them would be rescued. Ambassador Dean, himself a refugee from Nazi Germany, protested the conduct of INS officers. At a dinner in Bangkok for Refugee Coordinator Eugene Douglas, Dean argued for the reunification of Cambodian refugees with their families in America. Douglas muttered that there was a danger of Dean becoming "Abramowitz Mark Two." Nonetheless, within the bureaucracy and the lobby of voluntary agencies in Washington, protests mounted. They were encouraged by such middle-level officials as Michael Eiland, who was still handling refugee affairs in the Bangkok embassy, and his predecessor Lionel Rosenblatt, who was back in Washington, both of whom had retained a strong commitment to the Cambodian refugee cause, and by such voluntary groups as the International Rescue Committee.

In May 1983 President Reagan signed National Security Decision Directive Number 93, which instructed the Attorney General to "determine whether there are categories of persons who, under the Refugee Act of 1980, share common characteristics that identify them as targets of persecution in a particular country. This review should focus initially on the following categories of refugees: those who fled Cambodia because of occurrences during the Pol Pot regime, former members of the military, those with close relatives in the United States, and persons who refuse to work with the new regime in Cambodia. Other categories should also be reviewed, such as unaccompanied minors and those deserting from or evading military service with the forces of the Socialist Republic of Vietnam." Such people "will not have to present independent evidence regarding persecution."

By the end of 1983 it was clear that the directive was being effectively implemented. INS approval rates were up to 85 percent and the population of Khao I Dang had, as a result, fallen to less than 40,000.

Humanitarian aid is often required because of abject political failure. It is neither intended, nor is it able, to resolve political crises that governments have created or at least failed to address. But in the case of Cambodia one of the effects of humanitarian aid was actually to reinforce the political stalemate. In 1979, the Vietnamese had sought and gained from the humanitarian agencies the wherewithal to build what the international community saw as an illegal administration in Phnom Penh; the Thais and the Chinese had sought to bolster a resistance based upon the Khmer Rouge; and the donors had sought, for a complex variety of reasons—some to do with politics, some to do with passion—to help both sides. As a result both the infant Heng Samrin regime and the defeated Khmer Rouge had been made viable.

A lot of the aid delivered had also helped millions of ordinary Cambodians, both directly and indirectly. After the destruction wrought in the 1970s, aid was vital, and without it the Cambodians' predicament would have been even worse in 1983. But over-all its results were not a cause for great rejoicing. Asked in the summer of 1983 to summarize its effects, Sir Robert Jackson, the Secretary General's personal representative, was not sanguine. "I am left with a feeling of sadness and despair," he said. "The fundamental objective of preserving the lives of the people has been achieved, but much more could have been achieved if the humanitarian operations had not been subjected continuously to conflicting political pressures. Like the victims of Yalta, the Cambodians are victims of international politics beyond their control. Inside the country, the aid has been far less than the scale of destruction—the dreadful bombing and the murderous civil war—warranted. As for the refugees, one can take only partial satisfaction in resettlement—repatriation to a peaceful Cambodia would have been far better. As for the border, it's sheer, unending, bloody tragedy."

Jackson tended to place the principal blame on the superpower confrontation to which the Cambodians were prey. Some aid officials and journalists blamed the donor nations, particularly the United States. It is true that their casual acceptance of what was a fundamentally Chinese strategy to rebuild and support the Khmer Rouge exhibited at best a loss of memory and lack of imagination, at worst a cynicism that will have long and disturbing repercussions on international consciousness. But it is surely also the case that throughout this stage of Cambodia's agony, Vietnam, not the United States, was the leading actor in Indochina and that Vietnam therefore bears the principal, though not the exclusive, responsibility for the continued crisis today.

Cambodia is a dismal drama, the playing of which began years ago. During this act nearly all the players used humanitarianism as a fig leaf for either the poverty or the ruthlessness of their politics. The humanitarian instincts of people around the world, and the mandates of the organizations that are supposed to protect and to implement our collective conscience, were exploited by almost all sides to serve political ends. Thousands of ordinary people of many nationalities, including Thais and Vietnamese, were moved by their perceptions of the Cambodian crisis to try to alleviate—with their time, their money or their prayers—the suffering of a people who had endured endless wrongs. That is a cause for rejoicing. Their concern was not all in vain. But neither did it achieve nearly as much as Cambodia deserved. For, as Jean Pierre Hocke of the ICRC put it, "In Cambodia, humanitarianism was used to prolong an agonising political deadlock."

20 &&& Out of Phnom Penh

At the end of my first trip to Cambodia in 1980, I drove out to Phnom Penh's shabby, attractive little airport to wait the arrival of the ICRC cargo plane from Bangkok. I was sorry to be leaving; I have never been to any place that aroused such passionate and conflicting emotions as Cambodia. The resilience of the people and the humor with which they were attempting to rebuild lives shattered by war and revolution and disrupted by occupation were very moving.

The ICRC plane was the only flight of the day; a gang of workmen were squatting quietly in the shade of their trucks—very old trucks these—waiting to unload by hand the drugs, the plasma and the food that it would bring. The field was deserted but for one Vietnamese army helicopter and a couple of battered DC-3s, those veterans of the world wars that, in the Lon Nol period, had flown ammunition, food and contraband in and out of the government's shrinking enclaves and now were only gathering rust. The place seemed empty as we lifted slowly off the field, up over the Mekong and away.

In Bangkok two hours later there was a great flock of 747s, 737s, 707s, Tristars, DC-10s, all gleaming in the bright coats of their national airlines, growling impatiently as they waited for space, or roaring in and out of the sky. Outside the airport there was, as usual, a long, noisy, fuming traffic jam as buses, trucks, cars and motorbikes hustled their way through the poor suburbs of Thailand's overcrowded capital.

After a month in Cambodia, the airplanes had never seemed so massive, the noise had never before seemed so invasive, the pollution had rarely appeared more obvious. The contrast between the two neighbors—the one cast into an insane torment redolent of the Dark Ages, the other trussed in the painful coils of what could only be twentieth-century change—was so great as to give me physical shock. After landing in Bangkok I spent several hours trembling at the enormity of the divisions.

In the fall of 1983, almost five years after the Vietnamese capture of Phnom Penh, I returned to Indochina. In Ho Chi Minh City I talked with a former minister of the Provisional Revolutionary Government of South Vietnam, a Communist who, like most other southern Communist leaders, had been excluded from effective office after Hanoi imposed reunification in 1976. I have rarely heard anyone more cogently expose the failures and the cruelties of Marxist Leninism. In Cambodia I was again moved by the courage of ordinary people, including many who worked for the regime. But I was also struck by how little life seemed to have improved, despite the inflow of aid since 1979. Phnom Penh still seemed to be a town in which people were camping precariously. There was more street trading but very little more real production of wealth. The roads around the country were in worse, not better, repair. Hospitals in Phnom Penh still had no water. Once again it seemed that the rice crop would be inadequate—in part because of a very poor monsoon—and predictions of a serious food shortage in 1984 were once again being made by FAO and other agencies.

Even more depressing was the politics. The Khmer Rouge seemed stronger and, at least in the rainy season, were able to reach far across the country; once again they had attacked the heavily armed Phnom Penh-Battambang train, killing many people, and in September 1983 they murdered eight Soviet cotton experts in the eastern province of Kompong Cham. As a corollary, there were reports that the Vietnamese army of occupation had become more brutal in its attempts to suppress opposition, particularly in villages in the western provinces suspected of sympathy with the non-Communist Kampuchean People's National Liberation Front, led by Son

Sann. A massive Vietnamese attack on the camps along the Thai border was expected in the 1983 dry season. (Later, in Bangkok, Squadron leader Prasong Soonsiri, the director of the National Security Council, said that this time Thailand would allow refugees safe haven inside the country.)

In Phnom Penh I found that many more people, including officials of the regime, were prepared to speak of their dissatisfaction with Vietnamese rule. Some Cambodians complained that hundreds of thousands of Vietnamese settlers were moving into the country, and that fish was being exported in large quantities to Vietnam. Officials complained that only those who were most obedient to the Vietnamese obtained promotion. They spoke also of the extent to which their Vietnamese advisers or "experts" dictated almost every decision to them. (Some months previously a secretary to the foreign minister, Hun Sen, had defected to the border and had related in detail the extent to which officials of the regime were controlled by the Vietnamese and the resentment they felt.)

Back in 1979, the Vietnamese Ambassador to Phnom Penh had, with considerable prescience, acknowledged, "It is normal that in a few months or a year the memory of Pol Pot's horror will fade and people will start looking at the Vietnamese with a critical eye. We should certainly not overstay our welcome." In 1983, the horror of the Khmer Rouge was still alive in most peoples' minds, but it seemed to me that dissatisfaction with the Vietnamese was bound to grow and that Khmer nationalism was reawakening. For the Vietnamese themselves the problem would grow worse.

One Cambodian friend who worked for the government said to me, "In the ministries they used to be called advisers. Now they are administrators. They run everything, make all the decisions. People leave for that reason. Those who stay work with clenched teeth. We want to continue to make an effort, so we clench our teeth, but—" he shrugged. He pointed out to me that the President of the National Front had recently instructed the Women's Congress that "their work must be closely linked with those of the Vietnamese experts of whom the experience and directives are always inspired."

Another said, "The liberators are becoming the colonizers. There are thousands of Vietnamese here now, everywhere. They have been settled in every district of Phnom Penh. They have much greater civil rights than us. If a Cambodian catches a Vietnamese thief, he will be afraid to report him to the police. Vietnamese run almost all the commerce in the town, and they are taking our fish from the Tonle Sap." Such feelings must have been widespread; the government had published several papers, in Khmer as well as in foreign languages, on proper relations between Cambodians and Vietnamese residents.

As a result of such pressures and fears, the number of people trying to reach the Thai border was rising once again—by about 30,000 during 1983. Another official in the government asked me many questions about how, if one reached the border, one could ever get resettled in the West. I told him it was very hard. He said, "I do not want to leave. I am a patriot. I want to help my country. I want to stay. But it is becoming more difficult. It is not as bad as under Pol Pot, but some of the methods are the same and are getting worse. We have so much propaganda now. They say religion is free, but it's not. Only old men can become monks, and they are all appointed by the government. No one believes their sermons. But the trouble is that Cambodians do as they are told. We did as we were told under Pol Pot, and we do so now again. Please, can you tell me what will happen? Will there be another war? We are very frightened of another war."

I began this book by referring to what has become widely known as "The Holocaust"—the attempt by Nazi Germany to destroy European Jewry. I did so partly because of my own personal memory of Nuremberg and the way in which that memory was stirred by the sight of the mass graves in Cambodia. And partly because, as I came to write about what happened in Cambodia during 1979 and 1980, I was struck by the frequency with which "The Holocaust" was invoked.

I have always been puzzled by the way in which the term has come to be so widely applied to the murder of European Jewry. The original Greek words *holos* and *kaustos* meant "wholly burnt," and for centuries *holocaust* was used to describe a sacrifice or burnt offering.

Early English translations of the Old Testament used the word to describe Jacob's preparations to slay his son Isaac. The Tindale Bible has Mark 12:33 as "a greater thing than all holocaustes and sacrifises," which in the Authorized Version becomes "more than all whole burnt offerings and sacrifices." In the fifteenth and sixteenth centuries *holocaust* came to embody also the completeness of a sacrifice. Thus, "Very true obedyence is an holocauste of martyrdom made to Cryste"; "The perfect holocaust of generous love"; "While I thy Holocaust remain"; and "We humbly offer our Lives and Fortunes, which is that true Holocaust which all true honest-hearted Scotsmen will give to so good . . . a Prince."

Gradually the word came to incorporate destruction, complete consumption by fire and slaughter as well as sacrifice. Thus Milton compared Samson's victorious death with the rebirth of the phoenix:

> Like that self-begotten bird
> In the Arabian woods embost,
> That no second knows nor third,
> And lay ere while a holocaust,

An eighteenth-century poet wrote: "Shou'd gen'ral Flame this World consume . . . An Holocaust for Fontal Sin." One nineteenth-century writer took it further toward today's usage when he recorded that "Louis VII . . . once made a holocaust of thirteen hundred persons in a church."

The first uses of it to refer to the destruction of the Jews by Hitler are obscure. Hebrew words that are used to describe the disaster are *Sho'ah,* which means catastrophe, and *Hurban,* which means whirlwind. Some Jewish scholars consider *Holocaust* a careless translation of *Sho'ah* that became current in the United States in the fifties and early sixties. But as early as 1951 the Israeli Knesset had named a special day as "The Holocaust and Ghetto Uprising Day"—*Yom ha-Sho'ah.*

In any case, despite what seem to me inapposite implications of sacrifice and burnt offering, *holocaust* now stands in popular parlance almost exclusively for wholesale slaughter and *The Holocaust* for the most barbaric example of modern genocide.

In 1979 *The Holocaust* seems to have lain especially close to the surface of Western consciousness—first in regard to the boat people, then in regard to Cambodia. That summer British relief agencies formed an ad hoc group that sought to pressure the reluctant British government to give asylum to the Vietnamese boat people, who were then drowning in large numbers and were yet being turned away from Southeast Asian shores. References to the *Struma* and other boats of Jewish refugees were then constantly being made. The group discussed at some length whether it could and should use the headline "An Asian Holocaust" over half-page advertisements in national newspapers. In some ways it seemed profane to do so; in others it seemed necessary, to convey an adequate sense of urgency. In the end, and with some apprehension, it was used, and it proved to be an analogy with which the Board of Deputies of British Jews concurred. A few weeks later, the same comparison was constantly made by Vice-President Walter Mondale and other speakers at the Geneva Conference on Indochinese refugees. They asked that the failure of the Evian Conference to give asylum to European Jews in 1938 not be repeated. For a time it was not.

Then, in the fall of 1979, when Cambodia belatedly became a fierce issue throughout the Western world, the holocaust analogy was invoked almost daily. Time and again as journalists, politicians, aid officials and ordinary people strove to come to terms with what had happened and what was now happening inside Cambodia, it was to the murder of the Jews that they referred.

It was an analogy that was used with as much imprecision as passion—and often for purposes of propaganda. The Vietnamese assiduously tried to associate Pol Pot with Hitler, and they had considerable success. Thus, for example, Tuol Sleng, the prison in which the Khmer Rouge tortured and murdered people, was called "An Asian Auschwitz." The museum was indeed derived in part from Nazism, but the prison was not. This distinction seems to me to be important. In the spring of 1979, the Vietnamese, with the help of East German advisers, arranged Tuol Sleng, according to officials of the Heng Samrin regime, to recall images of the Nazi concentration camps. Moreover, in 1983, in preparation for the fifth anniversary of the Vietnamese takeover, the museum was remodeled. The task was carried out in good part by its efficient curator, Ung Pech, who had been one of the few Tuol Sleng prisoners to survive the Khmer Rouge. He was sent to East Germany to visit Buchenwald and Sachsenhausen for new ideas on how to make Tuol Sleng more closely resemble the Nazi "original."

In fact, it is hard to think of two prisons more different than Auschwitz and Tuol Sleng. Auschwitz was a work camp and an extermination camp in which millions of people—perhaps as many as four million—died or were murdered. About half of them were Jews, and they died precisely because of that. In Tuol Sleng, by contrast, about 16,000 people had been killed, most of them because they were members of the Khmer Rouge apparat, or families of such members, on whom the organization had turned in its revolutionary and chauvinistic ferocity. In Auschwitz there was no such thing as a "confession," no "party" to whom disloyalty was alleged and which controlled events. In Tuol Sleng, confessions were meticulously extracted from the tortured victims before they were done to death in the name of the Party they were supposed to have betrayed. Such confessions were vile and paranoid. But they were not unprecedented. The constant invocations of Nazism helped to obscure the fact that the Khmer Rouge were a Marxist-Leninist organization and that Tuol Sleng resembled much more a Stalinist prison than a Nazi concentration camp. ("I have nothing to depend on, I have only the Communist Party of Kampuchea," wrote Hu Nim, the former Minister of Information, in his "confession." "Would the party please show clemency towards me. My life is completely dependent upon the party.") Yet I recall no one describing Tuol Sleng as an "Asian Lubyanka." Stalinist crimes have not been registered upon modern memory to anything like the extent of those of the Nazis.

There are many obvious reasons for this. Some are good. One which is not reflects differences in communications, access and propaganda. The Nazi death camps are preserved by both the Communist and the Social-Democrat societies which took over the wreckage of the Reich, as monuments and as warnings. Indeed, the horror of Nazism is one of the few issues on which Communist and capitalist propaganda is agreed and which each seeks constantly to reiterate.*

* In this cold warring world each side also tends, at least in extremis, to try to associate the other with fascism. Such attempts almost always owe

That is a powerful combination. By contrast there are no similar shrines to the victims of Stalin; on the contrary, the vast *apparats* of the Soviet state and its allies are geared to obscuring rather than broadcasting its reality. The banality of much anti-Soviet propaganda is in no way capable of exposing it.

Propaganda aside, in the fall of 1979 the constant evocation of the Holocaust (either committed by the Khmer Rouge or impending through famine) by those who visited Cambodia—and by those who perceived it only darkly—was surely crucial to the way in which the disaster assumed such international emotional force. It was precisely because of the fear that history was in danger of being repeated that much of the world, especially the Western world, girded itself to undertake the mammoth rescue operation that was launched. There was a genuine determination to show that a lesson had been learned, that "it shall not happen again."

That the murder of European Jewry should be one of the principal, if not *the* principal, benchmarks by which we now judge catastrophe is not surprising in itself. Indeed, it is inevitable. And one cannot but salute any individual or collective determination to prevent its repetition. But some of its consequences are unfortunate. There is a danger that only when something can be compared, perhaps rightly, perhaps wrongly, but anyway plausibly, with the Holocaust will it assume truly disastrous proportions in our perceptions. The use of such images can be coarsening. I asked one Oxfam official why he thought that Cambodia had become such a *cause célèbre* in 1979. He replied, accurately enough, "It had everything—temples, starving brown babies and an Asian Hitler figure—it was like sex on a tiger skin." It was in good part the emphasis on such images by

more to rhetoric than to reality and, as such, they almost always devalue that reality. When the Soviets shot down the Korean 747 in 1983 not only did they refuse to apologize (this was perhaps the most terrifying element in the whole disaster), but they also tried to shift the blame to the United States. In alleging that the plane was spying, one Soviet spokesman declared that the White House was "worse than the Nazis. The passengers were sacrificed by the White House just as innocent people had been destroyed by the Nazis." A few weeks later Mrs. Thatcher, in a burst of anti-Soviet rhetoric, likened the Soviet system to that of Hitler. Such comparisons inhibit understanding.

the press, by aid agencies and—perhaps most crucial of all—by governments on every side of the argument that enabled Cambodia in the fall of 1979 to achieve, after long years of disaster, critical mass in Western conscience. That it deserved great attention is beyond dispute. But the real needs of the country were often obscured by propaganda, by sensationalism and by cliché, as well as by straightforward political controls. As a result, much of the aid was misdirected, much of it was inappropriate, and the Cambodian people as a whole did not benefit from the widespread surge of compassion on their behalf to anything like the extent which they deserved.

The nearest parallel to what happened in Cambodia in 1979–80 is Biafra in 1968–69. Then too *holocaust* and *genocide* were the principal refrains. Then too their constant invocation for propaganda purposes had vast emotional impact throughout the Western world. One of the principal Biafran spokesmen later wrote, "The genocide propaganda was designed to confirm and instill in the public's mind that nothing short of a sovereign Biafra could guarantee security of life and property . . . It terrorized the home public and alerted the entire world, for it conjured up an image of the Nazi regime and its Jewish victims." In Biafra, too, the memory of the holocaust and a determination to prevent it led to some suspension of critical judgment. At the same time, humanitarian aid was used to prolong a civil war and all its suffering.*

* Soon after fighting between federal Nigerian troops and the Biafran secessionist forces began in 1967, the ICRC sent delegates to Nigeria to look after the interests of prisoners of war. It then began to give medical care to wounded soldiers. By the end of 1967 it had also begun to respond to the needs of refugees. As the dimensions of the crisis—and world awareness—grew, forty-three Red Cross societies and nineteen international voluntary agencies placed themselves under the ICRC umbrella on the federal side. ICRC made clear it sought to work in Biafra also.

There were also dozens of private agencies working in Nigeria, many of them under the banner of the "Joint Church Aid" Group. This was a huge and disparate organization, embracing agencies from twenty countries.

Western public opinion began to become keenly aware of Biafra in the spring of 1968, well after the war had begun. But, as in the Cambodian crisis, perceptions of what was actually taking place varied widely. As in Cambodia, no one knew how many people there were in the Biafran enclave—population estimates varied between nine million and four million. Nor was there any evidence as to how much food could be produced locally.

. . .

There is an ominous sense of progression between Biafra and
Cambodia. During the seventies more and more governments seemed
to have understood that they could exploit humanitarianism. In

---

After a visit to Biafra in June 1968, Leslie Kirkley of Oxfam announced
that two million people would die in the next two months if nothing was
done. Significant supplies of food were not imported till three months later.
But, so far as is known, two million people did not die.

Despite Western rhetoric to the contrary, the federal government of
General Yakubu Gowon remained committed throughout the war to allowing
humanitarian supplies through to the civilian population within Biafra.
Gowon did, however, seek to control the way in which aid was delivered. He
wanted it sent overland from Lagos in a controlled breach of his own block-
ade of Biafra. This, for clear political reasons, the secessionist leader, General
Ojukwu, rejected. He insisted that international aid be delivered direct to
Biafra with no federal involvement or supervision whatever. Since he was
claiming that the federal government was intent on the genocide of the
Biafran people, this was not surprising.

After the capture of Biafra's only deep-water seaport, Port Harcourt, by
federal forces in May 1968, the only direct route into Biafra was by air. The
territory's only airstrip was a length of ordinary road, 25 meters wide, outside
the town of Uli. It was, to say the least, inadequate. Ojukwu insisted that all
flights into Uli be made by night. This made it almost impossible for the un-
sophisticated Nigerian Air Force to detect whether the planes belonged to
international relief organizations or to gunrunners.

Relief organizations reacted to these contradictory pressures in accordance
with their relations with other governments, particularly those supporting
Lagos. U.N. organizations, for obvious reasons, found it most difficult to
take actions of which the federal government, a member, disapproved. Only
UNICEF was involved in Biafra. General Gowon did not seek to prevent it.

On the other side, it was the independent church groups who found it
easiest to mount an airlift into Biafra. Catholic groups were especially dedicated—because almost half the Ibos were Catholics, whereas their Hausa enemies were mainly Moslem.

The ICRC tried, as the Conventions require, to work on both sides. But
in May 1968 it launched an international appeal named "SOS Biafra." Since
the federal government recognized no such place, this was hardly prudent.

Through the spring and early summer of 1968 both the ICRC and private church groups flew relief flights into Uli. The churches accepted Ojukwu's
conditions and flew by night only. Since the ICRC was already active on the
federal side, it felt that it had no alternative but to do the same—to preserve
its neutrality. To this General Gowon agreed, though with irritation. In a
letter to Emperor Haile Selassie he complained that ICRC had presented him
with an ultimatum and a *fait accompli* "to fly over positions held by my troops
in taking supplies to rebel-held areas without agreement. . . . This is a fla-

Cyprus, in Angola, in the Middle East, as in Cambodia, humanitarianism has been used either to buy time or to strengthen at least one of the protagonists. The expansion of the International Committee of the Red Cross reflects this painfully. Ten years ago the ICRC would hire about ten new delegates every year; now it has to take on fully

---

grant attempt, against all the conventions and history of the ICRC, to do in an African country what they have never dared to do in many other more disastrous theaters of current world conflict. . . ." Gowon even authorized daytime flights again, but once more Ojukwu rejected them and so the ICRC, as well as the churches, built up a massive nighttime air lift. At this stage talks in Addis Ababa between the two sides broke down—in part, it seems clear, because Ojukwu now felt certain he was to get massive aid.

The ICRC and the private relief organizations quickly upgraded the Uli airstrip. They provided 30,000 square feet of aluminum planking to create a new parking area, landing lights (instead of kerosene flares), radio and navigational equipment. Altogether they raised the capacity of the strip threefold. By October 1968 the narrow road was handling fifty flights a night, some carrying humanitarian aid that would relieve the pain of the war, others military supplies that would prolong that pain.

The spirit of the humanitarian effort is captured in a report written by an American church official: "To stand in Uli in the middle of a dark night . . . is a wondrous experience indeed! One wonders at the might of the Christian Church and the determination that we are our brother's keeper, and to see so visibly and hear so audibly what has been wrought."

The humanitarian agencies publicly claimed that they were feeding only the desperate in Biafra—children and lactating mothers, pregnant women, the sick, the old, the wounded. In fact, the distribution of supplies was rarely supervised. Members of the rebel government and soldiers almost always had first pick of what had been air-lifted in, and each expected (and was expected) to feed his entire extended family. Without such free rations, civil servants simply could not have afforded to stay in the government—during 1968 the price of cassava flour increased to thirty-six times its prewar price.

This is not to say that ordinary Biafran people did not need or did not receive humanitarian aid. They did. But it is also clear that the international relief at least helped to bolster the collapsing Biafran economy and was one of the factors that enabled Ojukwu to turn away from a negotiated settlement.

This happened because, to large sections of Western public opinion, the "reality" of Biafra was close to the line written by Biafra's own Directorate of Propaganda, a brilliant organization established soon after the war began. One of its principal purposes at home was to convince the Ibos that they faced "genocide" at the hands of federal troops if they did not win independence. (The massacres of Ibos in the Northern Region in 1966 gave substance to this claim.) Its task abroad was to convince the rest of the world that the Ibos would fight, literally to the death of the people, unless the federal government was pressured into granting independence.

Passions were especially inflamed in Germany. In the United States too

one hundred and fifty. In 1978 the ICRC had eighteen delegations around the world; by 1983 it had thirty-six. Some senior ICRC officials despair at the implications of such expansion. At the same time some of the basic principles of the Geneva Conventions have either come under attack or under question or are more and more often disregarded.

In 1982 the ICRC took concerted legal action to keep one of its former delegates from publishing a thinly disguised fictional account of his prison visits in El Salvador. His argument was that the ICRC was becoming accomplice to torture; the organization argued that his book threatened to dilute the principle of confidentiality. In 1983 the ICRC issued an unusual public rebuke to the governments of Iran and Iraq for failing to observe the Conventions in their treatment of each other's prisoners of war. Its frequent appeals for a regard for the Conventions in Lebanon were almost all ignored. And in the Cambodia operation the ICRC constantly had to try to defend its concept of neutrality from abuse by all sides. To the ICRC it seems that today more and more governments are abjuring compromise and are seeking to use its offices and those of other humanitarian organizations as a way of postponing, perhaps indefinitely, difficult political compromises in favor of continual, uncompromising, ever-

---

there were countless vigils, fasts, rallies, full-page advertisements, appeals to the President. But the Johnson Administration, recovering from Tet and in its last months before the election, had other priorities. Dean Rusk, the Secretary of State, declared that Nigeria was "a British responsibility."

In Britain an unfamiliar and unusually powerful coalition of churchmen, leftists, humanitarians and right-wing politicians vilified the Labour Government of Harold Wilson for its support of Lagos. In face of the perception of genocide all arguments in favor of the policy seemed contemptible to millions of people. In his memoirs, Wilson described Biafra's public-relations exercise as "a success unparalleled in the history of communications in modern societies." This was both oversimplification and hyperbole. But it is true that the Biafran cause was sustained both by the constant publication in Western newspapers and television of starving babies and—more important, because the currency of starvation has been devalued—by the cry of genocide that echoed harshly around the world in 1968. It was only when that fear receded in 1969 that the high tide of Western support for Biafra also turned. Resumption of West German aid to Lagos was seen there as a triumph. The Gowon government considered Germany to have been especially susceptible to Biafran propaganda, because of "the memories of Jewish genocide which had led them to identify with Biafra . . . to salve their national conscience."

encroaching war. The ICRC performs an essential task, often superbly. But both its expansion and the assaults upon its principles are, truly, terrifying.

At this time in particular it may be a mistake to refer to *1984*, but there is a sense in which one of George Orwell's principal warnings in that book has indeed been realized. War is now always with us, if only—to the fortunate—as distant thunder.

Since 1945, war has been kept out of western Europe, perhaps by the rough balance of superpower rivalry. But there have been literally hundreds of wars elsewhere in the world, in many of which greater powers have intervened on behalf of their various often arbitrary proxies for frequently cynical reasons and often in a careless manner. As I mentioned at the beginning of this book, between 1979 and 1982 six new wars began in the world and only two ended, four million people and forty-five nations were engaged in combat, and unnumbered millions died. Since 1980, the largest and most destructive war in the world today, that between Iran and Iraq, has continued almost unnoticed behind a veil of lies and secrecy cast over it by both sides. At least 200,000 people, many of them conscripted children, are thought to have been killed there. We have come to accept the idea of much of the world in a state of war or extreme distress; it seems now to be a feature of political geography, and today we barely ever pause to ask,

> "Who will remember, passing through this gate,
> The unheroic dead who fed the guns?
> Who shall absolve the foulness of their fate—
> Those doomed, conscripted, unvictorious ones?"

At one point in my research for this book I asked Brian Urquhart, one of the Secretary General's most experienced assistants and a man who is widely credited with managing, single-handed, to keep the United Nations functioning, to introduce me to the U.N. Historical Office. He laughed and said that in that whole vast building with its hundreds of offices, there was no room for such a place. "There is no historian at the United Nations, because no two members here could possibly agree on what has happened, let alone on what should be recorded." Similarly, there will be many who disagree with both the narrative and the judgments of this book. It is a mystery story. I have examined only aspects of it and I do not pretend to have solved it beyond all reasonable doubt. Some may think that I have been too critical of the Thais and their allies, others of the Vietnamese and their allies. Some officials of Western—and Eastern—governments may think I have not subjected the agencies to adequate scrutiny, while many relief officials may feel the opposite. I have also been unable to provide conclusive answers to all the questions I posed in the Prologue.

Another criticism might well be that the fragile state of so much of the world today makes it invidious to concentrate, as I have done, on one particular crisis. The "disasters" which do attract our attention are by no means always the most destructive. Jim Grant of UNICEF frequently speaks of the danger of what he calls "loud emergencies"—like Cambodia—drowning out the continuous "quiet emergencies"—like the death of at least ten million children every year from "causes associated with malnutrition." In 1982, ICRC calculates, about 30,000 children starved to death in Angola and no one noticed. A large majority of the world's people live always in conditions which can only be called "disastrous," yet they are given only minimal aid. In the fall of 1983, Oxfam warned that freak weather conditions had brought unprecedented drought to over forty countries in Asia and Latin America. Oxfam, together with other agencies, warned that unless a huge rescue operation was mounted, agriculture could collapse across a broad swath of the world from Peru through Africa and Asia to the Philippines. But although this disaster may prove to have a catastrophic effect upon scores of third-world societies, it was having little impact upon jaded Western consciousness.

I quoted at the beginning of the book a tiny fraction of the prosecution's evidence at Nuremberg. "The father was holding the hand of a boy about ten years old and speaking to him softly; the boy was fighting his tears. The father pointed to the sky, stroked his head and seemed to explain something to him." In her account of the trial, Rebecca West noted "the living pity" of such images, such memories. The story of Cambodia, as of Biafra, demonstrates that despite the plethora of communications to which we are now subjected, the fast succession of awful images, the world is still capable of responding to such "living pity." We are still able, in Gloucester's phrase, "to see it feelingly." We can still know with the heart as well as the head. The danger is that we do not always respond when response is most needed, that propaganda is now able so much more easily to exploit our compassion for uncompassionate ends, and that our conscience becomes exhausted and thus ever more forgetful.

Nuremberg embodied the rhetoric of progress, but it was even at the time tinged at best with irony, at worst with warning, if only because of the ambiguous record of the prosecuting powers, particularly the Soviet Union. Nonetheless, it is understandable that the judgment of Nuremberg should have been grasped, again in Rebecca West's words, as "a sort of legalistic prayer that the Kingdom of Heaven should be with us." And perhaps it was equally predictable that that prayer would not be fulfilled. Nonetheless, even when the prescriptions laid down at Nuremberg are ignored as cruelly as they have been in Indochina and many other parts of the world in recent years, they cannot be forgotten.

Out of that darkness of the Second World War, the victors and the survivors developed or created many of the institutions a small part of whose work I have attempted to describe in this book. Those institutions are designed to rescue us from our own frailty, to bind the self-inflicted wounds of the world. They are man-made, and they are therefore imperfect. They have high ideals from which they often slip and which, more often, governments prevent them from fulfilling. The criticisms that have been made of them here in no way suggest that their work is not needed. On the contrary, to deny its importance in a world that is more closely interlinked than ever and, at the same time, also more painfully disparate, would be to deny common humanity.

I was tempted to end this book by saying that despite the viciousness of Cambodia's fate, we have to continue both to hope and to trust in the progress of mankind.

But while hope is essential, it is not enough. And while the very existence and much of the work of the humanitarian organizations testifies to a heartfelt desire for progress, this story of Cambodia— which is not atypical today—hardly demonstrates real improvement in international conduct. In the case of Cambodia, the quality of mercy displayed was certainly "twice blessed." But it was also subverted. We have no cause for complacence.

21 ❧ Report from Ethiopia—May 1985

The Ethiopian crisis to which the Western World reacted in the fall of 1984 had a depressing familiarity. Millions of people, it suddenly appeared, stood on the edge of death from a famine caused by a combination of civil war, drought, and agricultural exhaustion. A vast relief program was hastily mounted. But six months later it was embroiled in fantastic difficulties.

Like Cambodia in 1979, Ethiopia in 1984 had already been afflicted by war and revolution for ten years. The country's suffering had by no means gone unnoticed in the West—but neither had it really caused any great furor. For many months in 1983 and 1984 Ethiopia's own Relief and Rehabilitation Commission, voluntary agencies and some United Nation organizations had been warning about the risk of famine; not much attention was paid. (The U.N.'s Food and Agriculture Organization, as so often, read the situation wrong and underestimated the risk.) Then all at once, in the fall of 1984, Ethiopia's suffering burst upon Western imagination and inflamed Western conscience—as the result of one BBC news film.

All this was, in a way, horrifyingly arbitrary. Although the famine in Ethiopia was undoubtedly the most serious in Africa at the time, terrible scenes could have been filmed in several other African countries. Perhaps then Western compassion would have been aroused for Sudan, Mali, Angola or Mozambique, instead of for Ethiopia.

Arbitrary also was the role of the Ethiopian government. Until the autumn of 1984 it was not officially encouraging the idea of famine. True, the BBC had been able to make a first film of famine victims in the summer of 1984, but then access to the starving was delayed until October—until after the regime had celebrated, with great pomp and greater expense (met in part by Moscow) the tenth anniversary of the overthrow of Emperor Haile Selassie.

This point needs to be emphasized. Before the anniversary, Ethiopia's Relief and Rehabilitation Commission had been stressing the urgency of the crisis, but this effort had not been underwritten by the Politburo. Official schizophrenia prevailed in Addis Ababa. Indeed, some foreign relief officials recall that until the tenth anniversary, Ethiopian Relief and Red Cross officials risked being accused by the Politburo of "working for imperialism" or even for the CIA if they discussed the true magnitude of the crisis. As late as October, this accusation was made by a senior ideologist against even the head of the Ethiopian Red Cross, who then sent him a videocassette of the awful scenes of famine-stricken people dying at Korem feeding center. Some relief officials wonder whether or not Politburo members, having insisted on the reality being hidden, really knew the true nature of the disaster.

Another caprice should be considered; the fickleness of both television executives and television viewers in the West. Starving children in Africa are not always considered "a story" by producers. The French paramedical group Médicins sans Frontières failed to persuade French television to make a film about Ethiopia in the summer of 1984. Months before that, an American free-lance producer on assignment for CBS had had his footage of dying children rejected on the grounds that it was not strong enough.

The BBC film broadcast in July 1984 had showed terrible scenes of starvation and, together with an independent television documentary, helped raise £9 million. But it did not change public consciousness as the later, October, film did. In the United States it made no impact at all. Michael Harris, the former overseas director of Oxfam, has one explanation for this. He thinks that the Western public is much more susceptible to appeals for help in the fall than in the summer. In summertime fewer families are sitting around the television together—there are so many other activities. Moreover, people are either on their vacations or saving for them. In the fall, by contrast, families watch television together at home; the children's horror and their questions about the awful images on the screen provoke parents' guilt—as perhaps does the approach of Christmas. The Cambodian crisis reached "critical mass" in the autumn, he points out; so it was with Ethiopia. Moreover, in the summer of 1984 famine faced unusually tough television competition—the United States conventions and the Olympics.

Whatever the reasons, arbitrary or not, the BBC's October film, made by cameraman Mohammed Amin and reporter Michael Buerk, was dramatic and terrifying. "Dawn, and as the sun breaks through the piercing chill of night on the plain outside Korem, it lights up a biblical famine, now, in the twentieth century. This place, say workers here, is the closest thing to hell on earth." A three-year-old child died on camera. All those around looked like death. Many people compared them to inmates of Auschwitz. Television viewers appear to have been most struck by the dignity with which starving Ethiopians waited patiently for food handouts. Why are there no food riots? people asked. The listlessness and passivity which are symptoms of famine are not widely understood in the West.

After the transmission, the Western public awoke and emitted cries of shame, remorse, recrimination and promises to do better. British charities had an extraordinary response. In the first twenty-four hours, Oxfam alone received one thousand calls promising help, including the offer of three airplanes. Within a few days it had become clear that, somehow, Ethiopia was arousing even more concern than Cambodia.

The same thing happened throughout Europe and, even more importantly, in the United States. The BBC film was passed on to NBC and shown immediately by the network across the United States. The response there was also phenomenal. The night of the broadcast the phones of Save the Children (U.S.) began ringing off the hook.

Public outrage was further fueled by the way in which much of the subsequent television analysis focused on the huge grain mountains kept in storage, at great expense, by the EEC and the United States. It would actually be cheaper to give it away to starving

Ethiopians than to store it, so why did governments not do so? aid agency officials and reporters asked.

Under the pressure of this newly awakened opinion, Western governments—which had long had the information on which to act, if not the will to do so—began both to promise and to ship supplies. But many of the first offers had more to do with placating domestic opinion than with meeting the real needs of the famine victims. Airplanes, for example, were in some cases offered for only one month or less.

Famine became good publicity for commercial enterprises. In London, tabloid newspapers such as the *Daily Mirror* and *The Sun,* which had shown scant previous interest in Ethiopia, began to use the famine in their circulation war against one another. Rupert Murdoch's *Sun* ran a SUN TO THE RESCUE campaign, while Robert Maxwell, the new owner of the *Mirror,* began to organize a MIRROR MERCY FLIGHT. Mr. Maxwell himself accompanied this planeload of material; Ethiopian officials describe wryly the way he gave orders as soon as he landed in Addis. The huge *Mirror* headline greeting the arrival of Maxwell and his supplies was THANK GOD YOU CAME. Meanwhile in the United States, NBC ran full-page ads congratulating itself for having awakened Americans and congratulating Americans for their sensitivity: "THE ORDEAL OF ETHIOPIA. THE COMPASSION OF AMERICA. . . . NBC News will continue its special reports on Ethiopia on the 'Today Show' with Bryant Gumbel and Jane Pauley . . . [and on] NBC Nightly News with Tom Brokaw."

Those first few weeks were chaotic. In November and December between twenty-five and thirty new "relief" aircraft were in Addis, and there was not enough food to fill them. Some Western governments demanded that the Ethiopians immediately free the country's ports for a sudden frenzied burst of Western charity. The Ethiopian regime was not prepared to do so. More serious in the long run, no real plan of action, no precise conditions for help, were negotiated with the regime.

Many aspects of the Ethiopian dilemma echoed the Cambodian crisis. Similarly, the government seeking help was a Communist regime aligned with the Soviet Union and anathema to many Western states, in particular to the chief donor, the United States. As in Cambodia, the regime was responsible for creating many of the conditions in which the famine raged; it had abolished feudalism, but had spent very little on rural investment and rehabilitation, except in the state farms it built. Its agricultural pricing and marketing policies were designed to provide cheap food for the cities (its main base of power) rather than to encourage peasants to produce more grain than the minimum necessary to keep their families alive.

Perhaps the single most important similarity to Cambodia—and, together with drought, the most important cause of the famine—was that here also the government was engaged in a bitter civil war. With extensive Soviet help, it was attempting to suppress secessionist rebellion in Tigre and Eritrea. At times it was clear that the regime regarded this as a higher priority than saving the lives of its people. As in Cambodia, the regime was intensely suspicious of the intentions and the effect of Western agencies giving aid to both sides of the conflict. The Sudanese border with Tigre and Eritrea performed somewhat the same function as the Thai-Cambodian border. The International Committee of the Red Cross (ICRC) was the agency most active on both sides of the border.

In November 1984 I asked Jacques Beaumont, who had been the first UNICEF man into Phnom Penh in 1979 and who was now running UNICEF's Disasters Office, what lessons, if any, had been learned from Cambodia and were being applied in Ethiopia?

First, he said, was the importance of gearing relief aid to crop cycles. This had not originally been done in Cambodia. Secondly: plan for at least 15 to 20 months—nothing shorter would be adequate. Third, aim for proper coordination between bilateral aid, multilaterial aid and aid from private agencies. Fourth, and perhaps most importantly, the World Food Program and UNICEF had together asked the secretary general to appoint a logistics coordinator for Ethiopia. The man chosen was Kurt Jansson, who had gone to Phnom Penh to run the Joint Mission's program in the summer of 1980. He became the assistant secretary general for emergency operations in Ethiopia.

That it should be only in 1984 that U.N. agencies concerned with disaster relief recognized the importance of crop cycles might seem astonishing. I asked whether Jansson, who in Cambodia had

been a superbly calm, effective broker between the donors and the
Phnom Penh authorities, would have any power of the purse that
would enable him to cajole the various agencies into working along
a common scheme. Ah, no, said Beaumont, that was asking much
too much of the U.N. In five years' time, perhaps, but not yet.

In early 1985 in London I asked Jannson about the nature of
the crisis in Ethiopia. "The main difference from Cambodia," he
said, "is that there you could not easily starve to death. Nutritional
levels might be low but there was always something. In Ethiopia
there is nothing. I have never seen people in the countryside
starving to death before my eyes before. In Cambodia we were
giving supplementary food, but in Ethiopia we are feeding people
totally. It's much more severe. A real catastrophe." He thought that
between 600,000 and 1 million Ethiopians had already died and
that between 7 and 8 million of the country's 42 million people
were at risk in 1985. This was also the figure given by the Relief
and Rehabilitation Commission. In response, the international
community now planned to ship 1.3 million tons of grain into the
country during 1985—vastly more than was given to Cambodia.
That commitment alone was a fairly remarkable achievement.

By early 1985, many more voluntary agencies were working in
Ethiopia than had been permitted in Cambodia, and the government was allowing them a freedom to operate which was unthink-
able under the Vietnamese. Many of them had excellent feeding
programs, and altogether they carried about one-half of the total
food distribution—they did it themselves and monitored it themselves. "There is much less suspicion of us in Ethiopia," said
Jansson. This was certainly true. Jansson was able to work closely
with the Relief and Rehabilitation Commission, whose chief commissioner, Major Dawit Wolde Giorgis, was widely praised. But it
was also clear that some officials within the increasingly powerful
Ethiopian Workers' Party viewed with distaste the spectacle of over
four hundred relief workers and scores of journalists being given
access to much of the countryside and being able to criticize the
government's efforts.

For the party's Soviet allies the situation must also have been
frustrating. It is not often possible for Westerners to see Soviet
armed forces in action. But in Mekele, the capital of Tigre, I was

able to watch the arming of Soviet helicopter gunships whose Soviet crews pursue the government's Tigrean enemies in the frightful free fire zone which much of Tigre is today.

By this time, May 1985, a new crisis was apparent. Masses of food had arrived in Ethiopia—half a million tons had been imported since December. Hundreds of thousands of lives had been saved with it. But it was not being distributed quickly enough to the people who most needed it. As a result, some children in some of the feeding camps were now at least as hungry as other children had been before large shipments began to arrive six months before.

From the air Mekele looks like a town besieged, which it is. All around it are pitched thousands of white tents—the camps or "shelters" in which are camped the armies of the starving. About 60,000 people were living in the shelters in May. Government policy was to encourage them to go home. But few if any of them had any homes to go to. They had sold their oxen and their tools and finally they had even sold their houses—as firewood. The government constantly promised to give them seed to take home, but there was a critical shortage of seed in the country.

One problem in Mekele in May was cholera; another was food. The government consistently refused to acknowledge that there was cholera in the country, but by early May there were several hundred cases in the Mekele shelters alone. The crisis was made much worse by the government's resettlement program which was spreading the disease around the country. At least in the shelters it could be and was being treated by the relief agencies, under the name of "acute diarrhea." Only Médicins sans Frontières acknowledged the truth of the matter; alone among the agencies it was publicly calling cholera, cholera.

Apart from the 60,000 in the shelters of Mekele, tens of thousands more people, who still had some life in the countryside, were coming to the town for monthly rations of food—set at 15 kilos (about thirty-three pounds) per adult and 7.5 kilos per child. But more and more of them were finding life in the parched and war-torn province impossible, and were camping around the shelters. The government had consistently refused to allow U.N. food convoys into the areas of Tigre which they did not control. The only source of food for many of the people in the countryside was the

Sudanese border—a frightful trek away. In May, the International Committee of the Red Cross (ICRC), which was opposed to the shelter concept except in extremis, opened its own—in frustrated recognition that the need in Tigre was growing.

By this time half the food coming into the country was distributed by the Relief and Rehabilitation Commission and half by the agencies. In the shelter run by the ICRC and in another run by the Catholic Social Action Committee, distribution of fifteen kilos per adult per month was assured. But in other shelters nothing was so certain by May 1985. Hence the starving children being brought to the ICRC feeding program.

The Red Cross had to select, almost arbitrarily, 1500 children every fortnight from out of the thousands pressing to be admitted to the program. Children were fed four or five times a day and their mothers were given full rations for the rest of the family. Some mothers always seemed to be keeping one child especially thin—so that they could have continuing access for themselves and their families to the program.

The reason was simple: not enough basic rations were being distributed by the Relief and Rehabilitation Commission. People in RRC shelters were getting perhaps three of four kilos a month instead of fifteen. Unless basic rations are assured there is no point in supplementary feeding. A child is brought in, fattened for two weeks, and then once out of the program, will relapse.

The same was true farther south in Korem, where the death rate among children under the care of Médicins sans Frontières doubled during April. By May, Save the Children Fund (U.K.) was on the verge of abandoning its supplementary feeding in the camp and opening a soup kitchen instead.

Two principal theories were offered for this state of affairs. The most popular among relief agencies blamed the acute shortage of transport. The other, less popular notion, was that it was the fault of the Politburo—which was diverting resources from famine relief to the war, and to its controversial program of resettling people from the north to the south. Either way it was disastrous.

Singers can make records which can earn millions, schoolchildren can give away their toys, congregations can collect money, newspapers can launch appeals, governments can give grain, the U.N. can charter ships—but in a famine all this is to no avail unless there is a good way to take the food from the ports to the victims. In disaster relief, all the goodwill in the world can be destroyed by rotten local logistics. In Ethiopia the logistics are very hard.

Ethiopia is a huge country—twice the size of France, about the same size as Texas, New Mexico and Oklahoma combined. Its landscape, too, is truely fantastical—in inspiration for Arthur Rackham or Tolkien, a transport nightmare.

Most of the victims of drought, war and famine live north of Addis. When you fly low north out of Addis in one of the relief Hercules, provided by the British Royal Air Force or by the Red Cross, or in one of the relief helicopters provided by Poland, you fly first over a farming plain; there are small villages with little round huts, *tukuls,* gathered inside low stone walls, little clumps of trees, cattle. Suddenly with a rapidity that takes your breath away, the edge of a village will fall away—just disappear in a rush of rock down several hundred, perhaps several thousand feet. Now you will be flying through a different world of gorges, cliffs, bluffs, stone valleys, cataracts, precipices, cathedrals and canyons, with tiny hamlets perched on little terraces carved out of the mountains' sides, scattered and dotted miles up and down from each other. The earth will rush sharply back up and the helicopter will veer around a pinnacle of rock, across another small plain and then the rock symphony will begin again. In profile the countryside must look like a very bizarre heartbeat—all jagged highs and lows with a few calm periods in between.

In between a few of these villages are some roads, but not many and none of them paved—less than half of Ethiopia's roads are paved. As one reaches farther north, into the provinces of Tigre and Eritrea beyond, the mountains become a little less dramatic, but communities are just as remote from one another and from main towns. In fact—this is hard to imagine—over 90 percent of all Ethiopians live more than ten miles from the nearest road. They think nothing of walking two or more days to the nearest market.

Some of the more remote communities just north of Addis were being reached by airdrops mounted, in excellent cooperation, by the Polish helicopters, the RAF Hercules and the West German

Luftwaffe. These provided first-class training for the pilots of all three nations and even better propaganda for their governments—the airdrops made good pictures and a comforting story for some journalists out for a day trip to the famine with their Hilton lunch boxes.

The program undoubtedly reached and helped several thousand people, but many relief organizations argued that it was a very expensive way of delivering relatively small amounts of food. The whole point of the airdrop on which I flew seemed somewhat diminished by the simultaneous arrival of two trucks laden with grain. On the other hand, trucks would not survive such tracks for long. And the political reality was that the British government was prepared to supply the RAF; it was not prepared to spend the equivalent amount of money on tracks. In its airlift to Mekele and other towns, the RAF planes were at least as vital as all the others.

Ethiopia has three seaports of entry—Mesewa, which is Eritrea's port on the Red Sea, Aseb a little farther south, and Djibouti. From Djibouti goods come to Addis on Ethiopia's only rail line; there are not enough rail cars or trains. (Just one of the organizations using Djibouti, Swedish Save the Children, landed ten containers of childrens' clothes in early 1985; by May only three had reached Addis. Dozens of other groups were facing similar backlogs.) From Aseb and Mesewa a small proportion of the food can be moved by plane, but the bulk has to be taken by truck. The trucks have been the problem.

Back in December 1984, when the world geared up to send 1.3 million tons of food to Ethiopia during 1985, Kurt Jansson recommended that Ethiopia's fleet of trucks be enlarged. He asked the donors to provide spare parts for 400 broken-down trucks and to buy 300 long-haul trucks (22-ton capacity) and 400 four-wheel-drive short-haul trucks (6–10 ton capacity).

By May the Germans had sent 165 Mercedes, and the Italians had promised 100 more, but that was all. (The first 50 Italian tractor trailers arrived without trailers and were therefore useless.) Why had the response been so slow? Because Western donor governments find it easier to give large quantities of surplus grain for which there is no other use, than actually to pay for trucks. Jansson's total logistics proposal would have cost $139 million—hard cash.

In December 1984, the plan—or the hope—was to shift 119,000 tons of food every month out of the ports into the countryside. In fact, between December and May less than 50,000 tons a month was moved out of the ports and out of the country's two principal warehouses at Kombolcha and Nazareth.

By early May 1985, almost 500,000 tons of food had been delivered to Ethiopia, but almost 200,000 was still in storage—either at the ports or in the warehouses. Another 60,000 tons were waiting on board ships standing off the ports. At Aseb the crisis was self-evident. Sacks of grain were stacked in the open air, many of them burst. Rainstorms at the beginning of May are thought to have damaged at least 7 percent of them. That would make 7000 tons lost overnight.

Kurt Jansson's office reckoned that, altogether, 1230 long-haul and 1842 short-haul trucks were needed to distribute quickly and efficiently all the food coming into the country. At the moment there were less than half that number of trucks deployed for the relief effort; fewer than 70 trucks a day were hauling grain out of Aseb, and most of these were only six-tonners.

Certainly there was an overall shortage of trucks in Ethiopia, but also important was the fact that the government was deploying many of them elsewhere. First of all, the rest of the economy had to be serviced. Government officials would sometimes point out that 8 million people might be affected by famine, but 34 million others were living ordinary lives. Second, the government was using trucks to support its wars against the rebels in Eritrea and Tigre. Third, they were being used to support its massive resettlement program. That also needs to be looked at.

The government has been resettling small numbers of people from the barren (and hostile) north to the more fertile and underpopulated southwest of the country for several years. In many cases the exercise makes sense. Much of the land in Tigre and Welo had been exhausted by years of overuse, by deforestation and by soil erosion. But most countries have found that for resettlement programs to succeed, they have to be done slowly, with great care and with a lot of investment; in Indonesia, for example, it is said to cost about $5000 per family.

In November 1984, at the height of the famine crisis and

shortly after the Workers' Party of Ethiopia was officially formed, the government announced its intention of moving over 1 million people from north to south during the course of 1985. The vast program was to be under the control of the party, not of the Relief and Rehabilitation Commission. Obviously the resources needed would be enormous. One Oxfam official says "This marked the end of our honeymoon period with the government."

For the first two months no foreign diplomats or aid officials were allowed to examine the operation; it was carried out with Soviet aircraft and trucks by Workers' Party officials. In January, after about 160,000 people had already been resettled, aid officials were allowed to see a few of the new sites; some of them were reasonably impressed. "When you have seen how desperate things are getting in Welo and Tigre, you realize there is no other option," said Brother Augustine O'Keefe, the head of the Christian Relief and Development Association. Others were less sanguine—either on grounds of the diversion of resources from famine relief or on the grounds that force was often being used and families were being broken up, and that many of the new areas could never be self-sufficient anyway.

At first large numbers of people, particularly from Welo, who thought their own land could never be productive again or who dreaded endless life in a shelter, did volunteer. Even so, there were not enough people to fill the quotas set for the Workers' Party in each area. And so in places, force was employed. In some shelter towns, the government simply stopped delivering food to the shelters, while providing people in the resettlement transit camps half a mile away with inflated supplies. Even this did not entice enough people out of the shelters. In February there were reports that men were being carried away from their screaming families by soldiers and Communist cadres and forcibly shipped south. Unnamed relief workers said that hundreds if not thousands of starving peasants (mostly males) were seized from the camp at Mekele and carted off to the airport, packed into Antonov cargo planes without seats, and flown to Addis, where they were transferred to buses and trucks for the drive to the southwest. At this stage, about 10,000 people a week were reported being resettled from Tigre. The ICRC complained to the local Ethiopian Workers' Party about the use of force.

For a time the seizures stopped. But a few days before I arrived in Mekele in the middle of May, government troops had gone round the shelters with Kalashnikovs and clubs and had seized over 400 people, mostly able-bodied men, and taken them away to the transit camp at the airport. (An ICRC delegate had been asked to take all the old, blind or unproductive people to his shelter.) Among those taken had been the Ethiopian field workers of the Catholic Social Action Committee based there; after protests, these men were returned. When I walked around the shelters the following week, it was noticeable how few young men were to be seen. Either they had been resettled already or, scared of the prospect, they had stayed in the dry hills. Relief workers in Korem said that about 10,000 people had recently returned totally destitute to their bare villages, such was the fear of resettlement.

From Addis, I visited one resettlement area—near the south-western town of Metu, in Illubabor province. The local party official courteously explained the details of the program and offered to let us see several new villages. In the event we saw only one, because of the illness of one of our party. The site was exquisite. Only a few round wattle houses, tukuls, perched on the side of virgin hills which looked as the Blue Ridge Mountains must have appeared before they were cultivated—no erosion or deforestation here, not yet. In the eucalyptus trees and above the wild mango and the wild coffee trees played black-and-white Abyssinian Columbus monkeys with long bushy tails, while overhead soared Abyssinian Ground hornbills, spectacular birds with long, white-tipped wings.

About 127 people were living here—Tigreans who had been taken from their village to Mekele by Soviet helicopter. Did they ask to come? "They told us and we happily accepted," said the priest, Kidanu Wolde Amlake, through the government translator. "We had suffered droughts for four years." They were flown to Addis and then bused here; they found the huts already built for them and villagers nearby gave them food. Their only complaint was of a shortage of medicines.

This was a model site, a Potemkin village; it is doubtful

whether these 127 people could be representative of the 120,000 who had already been resettled since November 1984 in Illubabor province alone. (By now, about 400,000 had been resettled since December all told, and latest government statements suggested that the program was being slowed.) Many people were being taken, not to idyllic highlands such as these but to lowlands farther west—and had not come voluntarily.

Ethiopian refugees in the Sudan have confirmed to anthropologists from the Harvard-based group, Cultural Survival, that "settlers" have been seized by troops in Tigre, and often they are not famine victims at all, but healthy young men taken from the marketplace or threshing floor. They speak of dreadful travel conditions, either in the planes or in grossly overcrowded buses, with very little to eat. They talk of the highlanders' susceptibility to malaria in the lowlands—a completely new threat for them. They complain about the collective farming which the government has imposed on many, though not all, of the settlers.

In Addis I met a Swedish aid official who had visited one major area, Gambela, west of Metu. He said that conditions there were terrible; people were living in huge state farms, and although land had been plowed there was at present no food. Children were very sick, he said. Because of the tsetse fly, oxen—which the highlanders have used for thousands of years—were useless in Gambela. Tractors were needed instead. These tractors had been imported from the Soviet bloc and then carried by truck all the one thousand or so kilometers from Aseb. The fuel had to be brought for them as well. So did most other supplies for the settlers.

In Metu I saw dozens of brand-new trucks (the Soviets had supplied about 300 trucks, none of which are to be seen carrying food in the north) loaded with tractors and other covered supplies, presumably food.

In other words, to sustain a few hundred thousand settlers in the southwest the government has had to set up long new supply lines three or four times the distance between Aseb and Tigre or Welo, where the people came from in the first place. The trucks in Metu could have been used to feed—and take development aid to— far more people in the north of the country. Not all of the north is totally depleted for agriculture; much of it could be rescued if the investment were made.

Against this, it has to be said that almost all the aid provided by the donors has been specifically emergency relief aid and not development aid; the United States, citing congressional amendments banning development aid to regimes which do not compensate American companies for assets seized, insisted that none of its aid be used for food-for-work projects such as land terracing or irrigation. The food could only be used for direct famine relief. In the long run such policies are obviously counterproductive and indeed destructive. In May 1985, the U.S. government began to modify this restriction.

But even if development aid had previously been available for the north, the political purpose of the regime was to move people out of the areas contested by the rebels. And so resources were diverted from the transporting of food to people in the famine areas. At the beginning of 1985, for example, fifty trucks were taken south from the drought-stricken province of Welo, leaving the Relief Commission there with only ten trucks at its command.

The effect of such diversion of trucks and other resources was disastrous—and predictable. Save The Children (U.K.) warned as early as January that resettlement should be seen as a long-term solution to a chronic problem, and that "mass resettlement at this time can only be achieved at the expense of the emergency relief effort [and] will effectively cripple relief efforts altogether."

During April and May, Kurt Jansson constantly tried to enlist more trucks for the relief effort. In early April government ministers promised him that 100 army trucks would be deployed on the Assab route to clear the backlog. That promise was broken. Then, in early May he had more success. He flew with Chairman Mengistu to see the extent of the chaos at the port and the chairman too promised military trucks. Like the emperor before him, the chairman is obeyed at once in Ethiopia; the military trucks began to roll. Offtake improved enormously at once—to over 3000 tons a day. Jansson hoped for 4000 tons a day.

At the same time, Jansson appealed to the donor community

to provide $50 million for trucks and spare parts. The only immediate response came from the Americans, who agreed to give $1 million toward spare parts and to provide air transport for spares provided by any of the European donors. By the end of June over $40 million had been pledged; but all of this would take time to come through.

Even with the help of the army and even if new trucks finally arrived, so much was due to be landed in the summer that there was no way in which the stocks at Aseb would be significantly reduced. And so Jansson began to warn that he might have to ask the donors to delay the shipments. Imagine such a thing! When some people were as hungry as they were six months ago, and the government was claiming that the number affected by the drought was increasing to between 8 and 9 million.

Finally one arrives at the most difficult problem of all relief operations—monitoring distribution.

In Cambodia proper, monitoring was impossible, because the government would not cooperate. In Ethiopia the constraints were slightly different—one of them, of course, was the vastly larger size of the country and of the operation.

The government in Addis was far more cooperative with the donors and with the relief agencies. But, as in Cambodia, it provided few figures. For example, Major Dawit Wolde Giorgis, the relief commissioner, addressing the donor ambassadors in April, merely said, "A total of 283,990 tons of cereals and supplementary food has been distributed to 5.74 million drought-affected people in various parts of the country."

Such broadbrush figures excited surprisingly little comment among the donor embassies in Addis. Whereas in Bangkok the donor embassies constantly questioned the figures provided by the Phnom Penh authorities on distribution, in Addis they were remarkably quiescent. As early as February 1985, Jean Pierre Hocke, the operations director of the International Committee of the Red Cross, warned donors that they had a choice: "Either you just want to send a lot of food to the country, or you really want to help the starving. In the second case, what is happening is unacceptable." Not much attention has been paid. Indeed, ICRC officials in Addis were surprised at how reluctant the donor embassies were to accept bad news. There were perhaps a number of reasons.

First was genuine liking and respect for many of the senior relief officials, including Commissioner Dawit. Second was a fear that protest would not only make Dawit's task more difficult but would also strengthen the hand of those ideologues in the Politburo (and the Soviet embassy?) who were rumored to want to cut back Western involvement in the country. Third was the knowledge that protest would arouse great concern at home while not necessarily achieving anything in Addis.

Even the Americans, who had committed about 400,000 tons—one-third of the total food for 1985—were far less aggressive about distribution figures than they had been in Thailand. In Phnom Penh, of course, they had no representation and therefore nothing to risk. In Addis they have a chargé d'affaires, not an ambassador, and their relations with the regime are precarious. By May 1985, none of the U.S. AID officials had been properly accredited, despite the size of the AID program. Earlier in the year an Ethiopian employee of the embassy together with a man from the Relief and Rehabilitation Commission had been beaten up by Workers' Party thugs as they accompanied U.S. officials to the northwest province of Gonder; they were accused of being CIA spies. (The CIA had, by its own admission, taken part in the exodus of the Falashas from Ethiopia to Israel.) Party leaders made constant verbal attacks on the United States and the extent of U.S. aid was never acknowledged publicly. On the contrary, criticisms were denounced by the party as inadmissible interference. It was hard for donor embassies and relief agencies alike to know just how far criticisms of the regime could be pushed; as in Cambodia, there was always a fear that too much criticism could lead to expulsion. In fact, the Ethiopian regime was so dependent on the humanitarian relief program by May 1985, that this seemed unlikely.

The distribution figures were disquieting and helped explain, for example, the continued starvation of children in Mekele. As I have mentioned, about half the food coming into Ethiopia was being distributed by the voluntary agencies, half by the Relief and Rehabilitation Commission. Some of the private agencies, notably the International Committee of the Red Cross and the Catholics, had organized their own systems of transport; the ICRC was able to state categorically that by May 1985 it was feeding 600,000 people a full ration of 15 kilos of grain every month—500 grams (slightly over a pound) a day. What of the Relief and Rehabilitation Commission's distributions? If Major Dawit's figures were correct and 284,000 tons had been distributed among 5.7 million people over the four months between February and March, then 70,000 tons would have been distributed each month and each person would have received 450 grams a day—a cause for celebration and congratulation. But the rising malnutrition in some RRC shelters suggested otherwise. In fact, agency officials in Addis said privately that the Relief Commission was distributing only between 30,000 and 40,000 tons per month to the victims of famine. Two senior relief agency officials in Addis suggested to me that as much as 30,000 tons were unaccounted for each month. This was vigorously denied by Kurt Jansson and by the RRC.

Some relief officials in Addis suspected that a large amount of food had gone to the resettlement areas, although none of the donors had agreed to get involved in the program. American officials said they thought all the 50,000 tons they had given the Relief Commission had gone to resettlement. Other food was probably being stored, against the day when international shipments ceased. Inevitably, stories circulated of the Russians taking food; these were impossible to confirm. Food had certainly been given to veterans and militiamen, particularly in Tigre.

In Addis food abounded—some of it brought from France on preferential terms. Sometimes in the capital, where the regime was concerned to protect its power base, it was hard to believe that there was any famine in the country at all. There were far fewer beggars than in many capitals, there was ample food in the city, and prices were subsidized by the regime. There were excellent restaurants— the most expensive were doing very well indeed serving aid officials and journalists.

Similarly, relief officials reported that in Eritrean towns controlled by the government large quantities of food had been given away, to placate the population and to diminish the attraction of Eritrean nationalism. There was a lot of relief food for sale on the market in Asmara, while in neighboring Tigre there was almost nothing to be had by the very people in the shelters for whom it was originally sent. All in all, one ICRC official thought that every month perhaps only 20 percent of the food in the hands of the Relief and Rehabilitation Commission was going to the real victims of the famine.

I have concentrated here on the shortcomings of the relief effort because when I was in Ethiopia in early May and in June 1985, the hunger in the north seemed to be worsening—because of inadequate distribution. There were also clear indications that famine was spreading in parts of the south. The new crisis promised to get worse still, if only because the months of high summer are always the leanest—the new crop has not yet arrived and the old one is almost exhausted. Despite the large quantities of food now in the country, 1985 promised to be another bad year.

This is not to deny that much had been achieved. Members of the Western public had responded very generously and had pushed their governments into action. Thousands upon thousands of lives had already been saved by the relief effort. And many of the relief organizations had very successful relationships with the government; there were many excellent feeding and even small-scale development programs in Ethiopia throughout this period. But the basic purpose of the emergency relief program—arresting famine in Ethiopia—had not yet been achieved.

That in itself might not be a cause for concern or surprise. But both surprising and worrying was the possibility that the underlying situation was deteriorating, not improving. In this regard, principal responsibility had to be placed on the government itself. The Relief and Rehabilitation Commission often functioned well, but it did not have the full political backing of the Politburo. Famine relief is not the government's first priority.

But many of the problems of the Ethiopian relief program are so similar to those of Cambodia that they call into question many of the ways in which disaster relief operations are now mounted. The principal difference is that in Cambodia the threat of widespread famine was exaggerated by the government for its own political purposes. In Ethiopia it was clearly real—but even so, some relief officials said that the government's claim that 8 to 10 million people were at risk was too high, and that food was clearly being used for political, not humanitarian ends. They suggested it would be much more effective to concentrate all resources on, say, 4 million of the worst affected famine victims.

In each case a Communist government was at first reluctant to advertize the problem to the world. Then, lurid and tragic television film produced an international outcry and pressure on Western governments to act. The United Nations appointed a coordinator—Robert Jackson for Cambodia and Kurt Jansson for Ethiopia—but no one, neither the donors nor the recipient regimes, wanted him to have real powers to direct the distribution of U.N. aid, let alone voluntary agency supplies. In each case large amounts of food were shipped without, at least at first, adequate transport. The food was not distributed as quickly or as widely as Western donors or some relief organizations thought appropriate. The government denounced and tried to prevent distribution of food to civilians in opposition to it.

In each case, initial enthusiasm on the part of both donors and recipient regimes was followed by disappointment, even recriminations. But these were rarely made public. In Addis as in Phnom Penh, individual agency officials felt privately far more misgivings about the problems of the program than they dared to express to the government. They rarely made concerted objections, still less threats. The aid community did not, for example, unite to demand better distribution or to demand proper access to the civilians starving in the disputed areas of Tigre and Eritrea.

One senior relief agency official in Addis in May was so frustrated by all this that he went so far as to describe it to me as "a great scandal concealed by a conspiracy of silence." In that conspiracy he included Western ambassadors as well as many relief organizations and the government itself. The press should also be included—not many of those newspapers or television companies which had expressed such anguish in October 1984, displayed commensurate interest in the spring of 1985. Ethiopia had long been eclipsed. Other officials thought it was nonsense to talk of any conspiracy and argued, as in Phnom Penh, that much had been achieved, and that with careful diplomacy, much more could be achieved. There was always the fear that too much protest would be counterproductive and would lead to fewer rather than more people being helped.

In Cambodia a considerable portion of the aid (it is impossible to say just how much) was exploited for political purposes. Its long-term effect was to build up the Vietnamese-controlled regime on one side and the Khmer Rouge on the other. In 1985 the war between these two was fought more fiercely than ever, and the Cambodian economy remained almost nonexistent. All the passion and the care that had been expended on Cambodia at the end of the 1970s and the beginning of the 1980s had little long-term effect on its predicament. In the mid-eighties its problems remained as intransigent and unaddressed as ever.

It was too early, in the summer of 1985, to pass any verdict on the outcome of the Ethiopian relief operation. Yet there, too, relief had had the effect of freeing the government of onerous humanitarian responsibilities. The government was allowing international (principally Western and some Polish) aid to cope with the famine, while most of the government's own resources, and those of its ally the U.S.S.R., were concentrated on its military and political objectives. So, in Ethiopia as well as Cambodia, humanitarian aid was being used by a Communist regime to underwrite war. As in Cambodia, the rebels against the government were doing the same thing. Peace therefore seemed further away than ever. And without peace there would never be an end to starvation, at least not in Eritrea and Tigre.

In neither Cambodia nor Ethiopia did the ordinary people for whom the aid was delivered benefit from it to the extent which had been intended and which they deserved. Instead aid was being used to prolong rather than to end the disaster.

London, June 1985

Acknowledgments

Much of the material for this book was collected in Europe, the United States and Southeast Asia between 1979 and 1983.

In the United States, and in the U.S. Embassy in Bangkok, many government officials were helpful. I thank them all collectively. But I was not able to employ the Freedom of Information Act to the same effect as with my previous book *Sideshow*. Unlike the Carter Administration, that of President Reagan did not seem anxious to fulfill the spirit of the Act. I regretted this, if only because it has always seemed to me that the Act is a tribute to the self-confidence of American democracy.

There is no freedom of information in Cambodia or in Vietnam today. Nonetheless, officials of both countries were helpful to me when I visited Cambodia in the fall of 1980 and returned to Vietnam and to Cambodia in the spring of 1981. Unfortunately, however, I was not then allowed a visa to visit either country again until the fall of 1983, after this book had been virtually completed. I would have liked to spend more time in each country; my inability to do so was a matter of regret to me.

Thailand today has probably the freest national press between Hong Kong and Calcutta. And although speculation on some subjects, notably the monarchy, is actively discouraged, foreign writers and journalists can work there under comparatively few restraints. Thai officials did not much care for some of my views, but they made no attempt to limit my research or my visits. I thank them. Perhaps as a result of this freedom, I may have been able to make more detailed analysis and criticism of aspects of Thai policies than of Thailand's antagonists across the Cambodian border. I hope that my Thai friends will consider that this is, in an important sense, a compliment.

In Bangkok, officials in the embassy of one of the principal Western donors, not the United States, gave me access to their files on the relief effort. These were very helpful, and I am grateful.

I am also grateful to many officials of many relief agencies for having given me their time and, in some cases, access to their files during a period when they were involved in a relief program of extraordinary political complexity. It is hard to name all those individual officials who helped me, but I would like to thank in particular Sir Robert Jackson, the Secretary General's Special Representative, and, at UNICEF, James Grant, Charles Egger, Jacques Beaumont, John Saunders, Knud Christensen, Robert Walker, Jacques Danois, Maggie Murray Lee, Ulf Kristofferson, Ron Ockwell and Suman Dhar. At UNHCR, Zia Rizvi, Mark Malloch Brown, Martin Barber, Minja Yang, David Taylor, Karen Burgess, Nanda Na Champassak, Bruce Palling, Hanna Sophia Greve, Rob Van Luwen. At the ICRC, which had to refuse me access to the archives on grounds that this would infringe the organization's principle of confidentiality, Jean Pierre Hocke, François Bugnion, Dominique Dufour, François Zen Ruffinen, Jean de Courten, Eamon Frank, François Perez and John de Salis. At the International Rescue Committee, Simon Cornwell and Robert de Vecchie. At Oxfam, Brian Walker, Michael Harris, Guy Stringer, Malcolm Harper, Chris Manning, Marcus Thompson, Roger Newton, Paddy Coulter, Tony Casey, Tim Lusty, Eva Mysliwiec. From the American Refugee Committee, Susan Walker; from the World Council of Churches, Jean Clavaud; from C.I.D.S.E., Honesta Carpene; from Christian Outreach, Robert Ashe. And many others.

For enduring this project and helping me, it goes without saying that, above all, I thank my wife, Michal, and my family, in particular my mother-in-law Leah Levin, who knows the U.N. world far better than I will ever know it. For many different sorts of conversation, help, hospitality or encouragement, I am grateful to Philip Alston, Anthony Barnett, Elizabeth Becker, Jacques Bekaert, Christiane Besse, Tony Besse, Chantou Boua, Ben Bradlee, Sean Brady, the late Wilfred Burchett, David Burgess, Victoria Butler, Margaret Carpenter, Nayan Chanda, David Chandler, Colin Campbell, Derek Davies, Neil Davis, Tony Davies, Patrice de Beer, David de Voss, Karen de Young, Beryl Drinkwater, Bernard Estrade, Faith Evans, James Fenton, Sylvana Foa, Magdalena Gardner-Brown, Michael Gast, Anne Godoff, Denis Gray, Elaine Greene, Ian Guest, Peter Harris, Steve Heder, Jim Hoagland, the late Richard Hughes, Philip Jones-Griffiths, Henry Kamm, Kamolwan Sonsomsook, Stanley Karnow, Ben Kiernan, Roger Laughton, Lek Hor Tan, Michael Leifer, Edith Lenart, Anthony Lewis, Borithy Lun, Samet May, Karl Meyer, John McBeth, Dan Morgan, Birgit Oeberg, Jean Christophe Oeberg, Milton Osborne, Anthony Paul, Yvette Pierpaoli, Roland Pierre Paringaux, Claudine Pittes, François Ponchaud, James Pringle, Peter Pringle, Eleanor Randolph, Paul Quinn Judge, Ranji Satthiah, Christine Satthiah, Ed Schneider, Richard Sennett, Brooke Shearer, Lloyd Shearer, Marva Shearer, Robert Silvers, Carine Slade, Mary Spillane, Judy Stowe, Sutichai Yoon, Strobe Talbott, Barry Wain, Andrew Wilson, and many more—especially my indomitable editor, Alice Mayhew.

London, December 1983.

Sources

Prologue

Satellite News Channel advertisement, *New York Times,* November 12, 1982.

Archibald MacLeish, quoted by James Reston, *International Herald Tribune,* June 21, 1982.

Milan Kundera, *The Book of Laughter and Forgetting* (New York: Knopf, 1980; London: Faber and Faber, 1982).

George Steiner, *Language and Silence* (London: Faber and Faber, 1967).

Chapter One

The Herman Graebe testimony can also be found in Roselle Chartock and Jack Spencer, *The Holocaust Years: Society on Trial* (New York: Bantam, 1978).

Chapter Two

Ben Kiernan's explanation of how he changed his mind about the nature of Khmer Rouge rule is published in *Bulletin of Concerned Asian Scholars,* Vol. 11, No. 4 (1979).

Hu Nim's confession is published in the *New Statesman,* May 2, 1980 in a long article with commentary by Ben Kiernan and Chantou Boua. The confession was obtained at Tuol Sleng by Anthony Barnett.

Chapter Three

The story of the world's failure to rescue the Jews has been widely told. This short account is derived principally from Arthur Morse, *While Six Million Died* (New York: Random House, 1967); Walter Laqueur,

The Terrible Secret (London: Weidenfeld and Nicolson, 1980); and Martin Gilbert, *Auschwitz and the Allies* (London: Michael Joseph, 1981).

The ICRC apologia is contained in *Inter Arma Caritas,* ICRC publications, reprinted (Geneva, 1973).

Noam Chomsky expressed his views about the coverage of the Khmer Rouge first in *The Nation* (New York), June 25, 1977, with Edward Herman. These views were expanded into a book, *After the Cataclysm: Postwar Indochina and the Reconstruction of Imperial Ideology,* 2 volumes (Boston: South End Press, 1979).

The pre-1975 articles on Khmer Rouge conduct: Baltimore *Sun,* March 2, 1974; *Washington Post,* November 24, 1974; *New York Times,* March 9, 1974; *New Statesman,* February 1 and June 7, 1974.

Woollacott's recollections, *Guardian* (London), September 6, 1977.

Daily Telegraph reports of Khmer Rouge atrocities.

New York Times reports, July 9, 1975.

Murder of a Gentle Land (Pleasantville, N.Y.: Reader's Digest Press, 1977).

Cambodia: Starvation and Revolution (New York: Monthly Review Press, 1976).

McCormick statement, *Journal of Contemporary Asia* Vol. 10 (1980). 75–118.

Vietnamese and Soviet bloc praise of Khmer Rouge rule. Hanoi International Service in English, 1000 GMT, April 9, 1977, Hanoi Vietnam News Agency, April 16, 1977; and for other praise, *Nhan Dan* (Hanoi), April 17, 1977; *New Times* (Moscow), October 1977.

An account of the author's visit to the border was published in the *New York Review of Books,* March 4, 1976.

The Ashe correspondence was made available to the author by Robert Ashe.

Lacouture article in *New York Review of Books,* March 31, 1977.

Time Magazine article, July 31, 1978.

New York Times on "unreachable terror," July 3, 1978.

Wall Street Journal and McGovern, August 25 and September 5, 1978.

Chapter Four

Time Magazine comments, January 22, 1979.

Sihanouk's press conference, *International Herald Tribune,* January 9, 1979.

U.N. Security Council debate, contemporary U.N. press releases.

Ha Van Lau remarks to Tommy Koh, author's interview with members of the Singapore delegation.

Khmer Rouge documents published by Phnom Penh, "Some evidence of the plots hatched by the Beijing expansionists and hegemonists against the Kampuchean people," Press Department of the Foreign Ministry of the People's Republic of Kampuchea, Phnom Penh, September 1982. Henceforth, "Some Evidence . . ."

China's invasion of Vietnam and Carter recollections, "Keeping Faith" by Jimmy Carter, pp. 208–9. Brzezinski recollections, *Power and Principle* (London: Weidenfeld and Nicolson, 1983), p. 411.

Malaysian Prime Minister's warning, Bangkok *World,* January 16, 1979.

Thai Prime Minister's warning, Bangkok *Post,* November 28, 1978.

The account of UNHCR's dealings with the Royal Thai Government on behalf of the Cambodian refugees is based upon interviews with members of the High Commissioner's staff and documents supplied to the author by members of the staff.

Interventions of Ambassador Jean-Christophe Oeberg, interviews with the author, 1980 and 1981.

Comments of Ambassador Morton Abramowitz, interviews with the author, 1980 and 1981.

Geneva Conference on Indochinese refugees. The author attended this conference.

Chapter Five

UNICEF and ICRC efforts to establish relations with the new regime in Phnom Penh, UNICEF archives and interviews with officials concerned. On January 12, 1979, Jacques Beaumont in UNICEF's New York headquarters cabled Bertram Collins in UNICEF's Hanoi office, "Re Your tel 106 Kampuchea please register any eventual communication by embassy when delivered and cable extensively UNICEF headquarters for examination Executive Director." In Hanoi, Collins and François Zen Ruffinen of the ICRC made repeated requests for access to and information about Cambodia. Author's interviews with Beaumont and Zen Ruffinen.

Famine reports, Jean Pierre Gallois, *New Statesman,* April 13, 1979; *Far Eastern Economic Review,* April 13, 1979; Henry Kamm, *New York Times,* April 23, 1979.

Oeberg views and cables. Interviews with the author, 1980 and 1981.

Neou Samoun interview. S.P.K. in French, April 23, 1979.

Vietnamese looting. Many Cambodian refugees to Thailand in 1979–80 brought such stories, including one former Heng Samrin official, Borithy Lun, who settled in Britain, and who made available to the author a long paper on his experiences.
UPI report, *Business Times* (Bangkok), May 14, 1979. Keyes Beech report, *Business Times,* May 4, 1979.
Kurt Waldheim's remarks on Hanoi's attitude, May 1979.
The Secretary General's briefing paper, "The situation in South East Asia," Supplement No. 1 HS/nl June 11, 1979.
Wilfred Burchett's reports from Phnom Penh.
UNICEF cable on press discretion, Geneva-Bangkok, July 7, 1980.
Hun Sen letter. The entire text read:

Monsieur le Directeur exécutif,
Au nom du Conseil Populaire Révolutionnaire de la République Populaire du Kampuchéa, j'ai l'honneur de vous exposer la situation alimentaire au Kampuchéa et vous demander une aide urgente pour notre pays. Durant près de quatre années au pouvoir l'ancien régime a systématiquement détruit la société kampuchéenne jusque dans sa cellule familiale. Presque toutes les familles ont été disloquées, toutes les villes évacuées et toutes communautés traditionelles bouleversées. Une armée de 160,000 hommes a été mise sur pied, dépassant de loin les ressources humaines et économiques du pays et des guerres de frontières continuelles ont été déclenchées contre les pays voisins. Des millions de personnes expulsées de leurs anciens lieux de résidence ont été astreintes aux travaux forcés et soumises à un régime alimentaire de famine; la ration journalière était de 2 bols de soupe de siz au sel, soit environ 100g de riz par jour. Ce régime alimentaire conbine à d'autres formes de tortures physiques et morales et des exécutions sommaires ont mis à mort environ trois millions sur les 7.25 millions d'habitants (d'après les statisques officielles de 1969) et laissé la plupart des 4 millions restant dans un état de grave malnutrition et de débilité physique, ce que entrave sérieusement la mobilisation des forces humaines pour restaurer la production agricole. D'autre part après la libération récente du pays, des centaines de milliers de personnes sont encore à l   leurs familles dispersées; ceux qui ont regagné leurs anciens villages se trouvent souvent dans une situation précaire: maisons en ruines, sans outils ni bêtes de trait devant des champs en friche. De ce fait, la culture est retardée et d'importantes superficies cultivables sont encore laissées en jachère. À cela s'ajoute le fait que les débris de l'armée de l'ancien régime sur le chemin de leur fuite, se sont achamée à piller et détruire les silos et les récoltes pour forcer une partie de la population à

les suivre. De ce qui précède, il résulte que la famine ménace plus de 2 millions de nos compatriotes.

Jusqu'ici d'énormes efforts ont été déployés par le pouvoir révolutionnaire pour préserver la sécurité et normaliser la vie de la population et restaurer la production. Dans cette oeuvre nous avons reçu les secours urgents de plusieurs pays amis. Cependant les séquelles sont trop lourdes et les besoins pressants, au nom du Conseil Populaire Revolutionnaire j'ai l'honneur de vous adresser cette réquête pour une aide urgente en vivres et autres produits alimentaires afin de juguler la famine et améliorer la situation nutritionelle de la population.

Les besoins de secours immédiats pour 2,250,000 personnes ménacées par la famine sont les suivants:

> Ris ou farine de blé: 2,250,000 $\times$ 12 kg $\times$ 6 mois = 162,000 tonnes.
> Huile végétale: 2,250,000 $\times$ 0.6 kg $\times$ 6 mois = 8,100 tonnes.
> Sucre: 15,000 tonnes.

Le Conseil Populaire Révolutionnaire de la République Populaire du Kampuchéa s'efforcera de résoudre le tiers de ces besions en vivres, soit 54,000 tonnes de riz. Il demande au PAM d'accorder une aide urgente pour les 108,000 tonnes de riz ou farine de blé restantes et les quantités des autres produits alimentaires mentionnées si-dessus et en même temps d'entreprendre des démarches en vue d'autres aides ultérieures.

Si cette demande est agrée par Monsieur le Directeur exécutif nous proposons que les premiers envois seront effectués dans le plus bref délai possible pour rémédier à la situation. L'Ambassadeur Extraordinaire et Plénipotentiaire de la République Populaire du Kampuchéa en République Socialiste du Viet Nam dûment mandaté par le Conseil Populaire Révolutionnaire en discutera des modalités concrètes et signera, au nom du dit Conseil, avec le Représentant du PAM à Hanoi les documents nécessaires.

Très haute considération,

Hun Sen, Ministre des Affaires Étrangères de la République Populaire du Kampuchéa.

Meeting between Henry Labouisse and Thiounn Prasith, Note for the Record, July 13, 1979.

Chapter Six

The account of the first Joint Mission to Phnom Penh is derived principally from UNICEF archives and from interviews with relief-agency officials.

The account of the trial of Pol Pot and Ieng Sary is derived from documents published at the time by S.P.K., the official news agency of the People's Republic of Kampuchea.

The account of Jim Howard's mission for Oxfam is derived from his own written report and interviews with him soon after his return to England.

Chapter Seven

Thai-Chinese deal over Cambodia. The outline of this agreement has been acknowledged by Thai government officials. Other details of the Chinese attitude appear in "Some Evidence . . ."

The account of the meetings between ICRC and UNICEF officials and the Khmer Rouge in Bangkok is derived principally from UNICEF's archives and from interviews with some of the aid officials concerned, and with Ambassador Oeberg.

American attitudes. From this point in the story onward, the author has had access to the files of one of the principal Western embassies in Bangkok, not the U.S. Embassy. These files contain almost daily cables between the embassy and its foreign ministry and other embassies around the world regarding the international response to the humanitarian crisis in Cambodia. They contain accounts of meetings throughout the world between diplomats of the major donor countries and relief-agency officials. They are an invaluable source of information. Where they are relied upon, they are described in the notes as "donor embassy files."

Egger cable to Beaumont, August 25, 1979.

Saouma meeting, UNICEF archives.

Waldheim-Labouisse meeting, UNICEF archives.

Kriangsak's remarks and Thai Cabinet decision, UNHCR archives.

Jean Pierre Hocke on Siddhi, interview with the author, May 1983.

The account of Beaumont and Bugnion's problems in Phnom Penh is derived principally from UNICEF archives and interviews with the author. François Bugnion's cables and memos were obtained independently of the ICRC.

The account of the UNICEF-ICRC trip to the Khmer Rouge areas along the Thai-Cambodian border is derived principally from UNICEF archives.

Chapter Eight

Pilger articles, *Daily Mirror,* September 12 and 13, 1979, *New Statesman,* September 21, 1979. His film, *Year Zero,* was delayed by industrial action by one of the unions in the British television industry and was transmitted on October 30, 1979.

The account of the meeting between Ha Van Lau and Waldheim's officials is contained in UNICEF archives.

The account of the meeting between Air Vice-Marshal Siddhi and foreign embassies and relief agencies is derived from UNHCR archives.

Waldheim's meeting with Ieng Sary, Memo September 28, 1979, U.N. Secretariat files.

The account of the further problems between the Joint Mission and the authorities in Phnom Penh is derived principally from UNICEF archives and from interviews with many of the aid officials involved.

Labouisse to Waldheim, letter of September 20, 1979.

Waldheim staff visit to Ha Van Lau, memo from Ilter Turkman to Waldheim, October 6, 1979.

UNICEF cable from Bangkok to New York, September 22, 1979.

The account of Air Vice-Marshal Siddhi's meeting with the embassies and agencies in Bangkok derives from UNHCR and donor embassy files.

Kurt Waldheim's meeting with Ieng Sary, memorandum of September 28, 1979, U.N. Secretariat files.

Labouisse memo to Waldheim, October 5, 1979. Labouisse cable to Bangkok, October 6, 1979.

The account of Guy Stringer's mission is derived principally from his own report, "Slow Boat to Indochina," and Oxfam files made available to the author in the fall of 1979. The account of Brian Walker's visit to Phnom Penh is similarly derived from his own report and from Oxfam files.

Waldheim's intervention with the Vietnamese, documents from the U.N. Secretariat files.

Brian Walker's press conference, *The Guardian,* London, October 16, 1979.

François Bugnion on Buchenwald, Agence France Presse, Geneva, October 5, 1979. A.F.P. report from Bangkok, October 4, 1979.

Anthony Lewis articles, *New York Times,* October 6 and October 16, 1979.

Vietnamese and Cambodian denials of famine, A.F.P., Bangkok, October 10, 1979; A.F.P., Hanoi, October 11, 1979; A.F.P., Hong Kong, October 19, 1979.

Chapter Nine

The account of Stringer's voyage derives from his own report, see above. The account of the Beaumont-Bugnion negotiation in Phnom Penh is derived principally from UNICEF archives and from interviews with participants. Phnom Penh's increased estimate for food for 3 million not 2 million people is contained in UNICEF document E/ICEF Misc 328, November 30, 1979).

Oxfam campaign, Oxfam's Kampuchea Sitrep 10.

Bugnion's account of Oxfam, message 58, October 21, 1979.

The account of Stringer's recommendations to Oxford is derived from Oxfam archives.

Mooneyham's discussion with Hun Sen, Mooneyham interview with the author, Bangkok, April 21, 1983.

Stringer's flight out of Phnom Penh, Stringer's report, see above.

Chapter Ten

Much of this chapter is derived from UNHCR archives.

Reuters report on "catastrophe," Bangkok *Post,* October 11, 1979.

Visit of Roland Pierre Paringaux et al. to the border, Paringaux recollections to the author, 1983. Klaus Bratt report to UNHCR, UNHCR archives, including Minja Yang Note for the File October 4, 1979.

Time Magazine cover story, November 12, 1979.

Thai articles on Khmer Rouge chances of survival, *National Review,* October 15, 1979.

The account of Kriangsak's visit to the border, his "open door" policy and UNHCR's response is derived principally from UNHCR archives, from interviews with Thai officials including General Kriangsak and with officials of UNHCR and from the donor embassy's files.

Abramowitz's cables were read in the donor embassy files.

Lionel Rosenblatt acknowledgement, see "Rice, Rivalry and Politics," Linda Mason and Roger Brown, University of Iowa Press, 1983, p. 101.

Hesburgh et al. visit to President Carter, *New York Times,* October 25, 1979.

Rizvi-Abramowitz meetings, UNHCR and donor embassy files. Levin cable, Bangkok 44393.

Mrs. Carter's visit to Sa Kaeo, UNHCR archives and interviews with UNHCR officials.

Chapter Eleven

Speeches and pledges to the U.N. Conference on Cambodia, U.N. press releases.

Socialist bloc food, *Guardian,* November 2, 1979. S.P.K. declaration, November 5, 1979; see also A.F.P., November 4 & 5, 1979.

The account of Labouisse's discussions in Phnom Penh and Hanoi derives principally from UNICEF archives.

U.S. three-page report to NATO, October 30, 1979, from donor embassy files.

Abramowitz cable, "What to do?" November 26, 1979.

Associated Press report, Bangkok *Post,* November 28, 1979.

Nouvel Observateur, November 26, 1979.

Shawcross articles, London *Daily Telegraph,* September 26, 1979, and *New York Review of Books,* January 24, 1980.

Chapter Twelve

The account of life in Phnom Penh is derived principally from UNICEF and Oxfam archives and from interviews with many of the foreign aid officials living there at the end of 1979.

Harper trip around lake, interviews with the author, 1981–83. Bugnion report, December 21, 1979.

James Reston article in *New York Times,* December 12, 1979.

UNICEF New York "any real exposition," Emergency 668945X HQs 006.

Bugnion cable No. 295.

Western perceptions of and complaints about Kurt Waldheim and Australian ambassador's report, donor embassy files.

Jackson's appointment. Interviews with the author, 1980 onward.

Lack of Vietnamese trucks, report by de Bock to Saunders, December 12, 1979.

Guy Stringer's Christmas, from Stringer's own trip report to Oxfam.

Christmas at the Samaki and story of Ung Sophal, interviews with aid officials present, and Bangkok *World,* March 18, 1981.

The allegations about maldistribution of food made by Hieng Mea Nuont are contained in a confidential memorandum written by Paul Mettler of ICRC on December 22, 1979.

Chapter Thirteen

This account of the border is derived from the author's own visit there in February 1980, from UNHCR and UNICEF archives and from interviews with many of those living or working there.

U.S. government paper on food diversions, December 7, 1979, USAID, Bangkok.

Colonel Prachak and the cost of the roads, UNICEF archives.

ICRC report on baby food, "Recommendations on food donations in the Khmer Refugee Relief Operation in Thailand, 1979–80," ICRC, Aran, February 12, 1980.

Egger assessment of border, memorandum of January 7, 1980.

Abramowitz assessment of Rizvi, cable to State, Bangkok 49924, December 5, 1979. State Department cable on UNHCR and border, State 326408.

The account of interagency meetings in Geneva and Bangkok derives from UNICEF and UNHCR files and interviews with participants.

Jackson's meeting with donor ambassadors, donor embassy files.

Meeting between Grant and Siddhi, UNICEF archives.

Chapter Fourteen

This account of life in Phnom Penh derives principally from UNICEF and Oxfam archives, from interviews with many of the aid officials in Phnom Penh at the time, and from contemporary press reports.

Saunders' views of other organizations, UNICEF archives. One of the Oxfam claims to which Saunders objected was contained in the *Far Eastern Economic Review* of January 25, 1980.

Government attempts to stop aid officials talking to people in the street etc., Saunders Note for the File, March 30, 1980.

Malcolm Harper on growing Vietnamese-Khmer suspicions, Harper report April 11, 1980.

World Food Program deliveries to Cambodia, undated WFP tables 1980.

Brito briefing, donor embassy files.

Jackson's concern, UNHCR Note for the Record, March 13, 1980.

Nossiter in *New York Times,* March 21, 1980.

Shawcross in *Washington Post,* March 16–21, 1980.

Meetings between donors and senior aid officials, March 24 and 26, 1980, donor embassy files.

The account of Phnom Penh street life derives from contemporary press reports and from the vivid reports of Pete Davis of Oxfam.

Maurice on malnutrition, Malcolm Harper report, April 11, 1980.

Devaluation of the riel, Pete Davis report, May 13, 1980.

Phnom Penh industry, reports by John Burgess, *Washington Post,* May 17 and 18, 1980.

Maurice assessment of hospitals, a series of reports, April 1980, including April 29, 1980.

Soviet medical teams, author's interviews with aid officials.

Hoefliger and Saunders *démarches* to Phnom Penh authorities, UNICEF archives. Saunders letter to the government complaining of food being distributed to the military, April 2, 1980, to Hor Nam Hong, Vice-Minister, Ministry of Foreign Affairs, Phnom Penh.

Henry Kamm in *The New York Times,* reprinted in *International Herald Tribune,* Paris, April 15, 1980, Denis Gray, Associated Press in Bangkok *Post,* April 15, 1980, John Burgess, in *Washington Post,* May 11, 1980.

Pete Davis on Svay Rieng, report April 17–18, 1980.

Joint Mission on "catastrophic" logistics, ICRC Note for the Record, May 13, 1980.

Joint Mission's *aide mémoire,* April 30, 1980.

Grant and Hocke's visit to Phnom Penh, UNICEF files and interviews.

Bui Huu Nhan complaints to Jacques Danois, Danois letter to Jack Ling and Jacques Beaumont, UNICEF headquarters, New York, June 11, 1980.

Soviet aircraft, Egger cable June 27, 1983.

Chapter Fifteen

This account of the seed program derives from UNICEF archives, in particular from long memoranda for the record by Ron Ockwell, and from interviews with many of those aid officials involved.

Ministry of Agriculture estimate of 1979 rice crop, given to Hans Page, FAO man in Phnom Penh. Paddy production for 1979–80 crops, "Rebuilding Kampuchea's Food Supply," paper by Orlin J. Scoville, so far unpublished. Mr. Scoville was a member of two assessment missions sent by the FAO to Cambodia to determine the country's needs in 1980 and 1981; he is the source of the remark that it was impossible to check whether the Vietnamese ever delivered the seed it promised.

Saunders on land bridge, UNICEF archives, including cable E287, Christensen to Grant, March 8, 1980.

FAO on land bridge, UNICEF archives including Ron Ockwell, Note for the Record, March 19, 1980.

Airlift "costly and insignificant," cable from Farouk Abdel Nabi, World Food Program, Bangkok, to WFP headquarters, Rome, March 21, 1983. Warner initiative, UNICEF archives. Warner arrest, *Washington Post,* September 24, 1980.

Seed articles, *Newsweek,* April 15, 1980 and *Far Eastern Economic Review,* May 2, 1980, Jacques Danois in Bangkok *Post,* May 12, 1980.
American pressure on ICRC, donor embassy files.
Negotiation between FAO, etc., and Thailand's Marketing Organization of Farmers, Ron Ockwell's Notes for the Record, UNICEF archives.
FAO shipments to Battambang, Hans Page interview with the author, October 1980. Battambang province chief's assessment, to Kurt Jansson of UNICEF, UNICEF files.
Heng Samrin/FAO statistics. Figures provided on different occasions often conflicted. For these figures see, for example, Inter Agency Working Group on Kampuchea Report, November 12, 1981, New York; and FAO Assessment Mission Report, December 1982, Rome.
Cable from Rome embassy, Rome 4725, March 3, 1981.

Chapter Sixteen

This account of UNHCR in Thailand is derived principally from UNHCR files and interviews with many of the aid officials concerned. I have also drawn on a study of the refugee population conducted for UNHCR by Dr. Milton Osborne, a distinguished scholar of Cambodian affairs.
Susott memorandum "To all VOLAGS potentially involved in family planning or family-planning education in Kampuchean Holding Centers," August 1980.
UNHCR on food being used as weapon, memo from Minja Yang to Legal Section, February 18, 1980.
John Jensen reports, February 29 and March 17, 1980.
Melbourne *Age,* March 28, 1980.
Zia Rizvi, statement, interview with the author, September 1980.
O'Reilly memorandum, June 10, 1980.
Rizvi on Thach attitude and on confrontation with Kitti, interview with the author, September 1980.
Ha Van Lau meeting with Waldheim, U.N. Secretariat files.
Abramowitz statement, interview with the author.
UNHCR summary on protection, Country summary of Thailand, Regional Protection Meeting, August 12–14, 1981.

Chapter Seventeen

Korb's song, *Southeast Asia Chronicle,* Issue 77, pp. 27–29.
U.N. Human Rights Commission, see *Journal of the International Commission of Jurists,* 1979, 1980, 1981.

Conversations between Deng Xiaoping and Ieng Sary, "Some Evidence . . ." Phnom Penh, 1982.

Henry Kamm stories, *New York Times,* March 1, 1980.

Elizabeth Becker, *Washington Post,* August 2, 1981.

Thirty percent of supplies to Khmer Rouge, Ulf Kristofferson, Khao Din report, February 5, 1980.

Jim Grant attitude, interview with the author, June 1980.

Holbrooke cable, July 2, 1980.

The account of Jackson's mediation is derived principally from the donor embassy files, UNICEF archives and interviews with aid officials concerned.

Hocke views, State Department cable. Geneva 9490, July 9, 1980.

Siddhi views, donor embassy files.

Prasong on boredom, *Focus,* Bangkok, September 1981.

Brian Eads, *Observer,* September 7, 1980.

Elizabeth Becker, *Washington Post,* March 1, 1983.

Chapter Eighteen

This account of the famine derives principally from the records of the aid agencies concerned and from interviews with many of the individual officials involved.

Heng Samrin request for aid, letter from Hun Sen to World Food Program, July 4, 1979.

Joint Mission delivery of food by end February 1980. The Joint Mission was itself unclear exactly how much food had been delivered and distributed, because precise information was so difficult to obtain. Indeed, the World Food Program and the ICRC published quite different figures leading to such headlines as "Agencies Conflict on Amount of Food Distributed in Cambodia," John Burgess, *Washington Post,* March 15, 1980. Some documents produced by the Joint Mission show the amounts of food landed and distributed as even lower than the figures quoted here. These figures were released by WFP in March 1980.

Food being loaded on Vietnamese army trucks, author's interview with Joint Mission officials, confirmed by Sir Robert Jackson.

Arbitrariness of food distribution figures. Author's interviews with Dominique Dufour (ICRC), Werner Schleiffer (WFP), Hans Page (FAO), Phnom Penh, October 1980.

U.S. Embassy calculation, cable from Kampuchea Emergency Group, Bangkok Embassy, February 26, 1981.

UNICEF report, Wendy Bjoerk, August 11, 1980.

UNICEF report on Battambang, presented to donors meeting September 3, 1980, based on trip by Joint Mission officials, August 26–30, 1980.

U.S. Embassy response, Bangkok 39991.

Jansson letter to Robert Jackson, October 8, 1980.

Heder report, "From Pol Pot to Pen Sovann in the Villages," p. 41 of manuscript.

Vietnamese change of position on famine, see notes to Chapter Eight.

Tim Lusty report, November 12, 1979.

Hans Page report, November 13, 1979, and interviews with author, October 1980.

Robert Mister report, undated, December 1979.

François Bugnion report, December 21, 1979.

ICRC Epidemiology Unit report, No. 2, December 3, 1979, and Report No. 3, January 4, 1980.

Mortality in Sa Kaeo, *ibid.* See also paper by Phil Nieburg, M.D., "Public Health/Surveillance Issues in Cambodian Refugees in Thailand, October 1979–May 1980," presented to Workshop on Cambodian Refugee Relief, sponsored by Cambodian Refugee Health Clearinghouse, Washington, D.C., June 10, 1980.

François Perez, interview with the author, November 1980.

Knud Christensen, interview with the author, November 1980.

Kurt Jansson, interview with the author, October 1980.

Charles Egger, interview with the author, November 1980.

Agence France Presse, November 1, 1979.

Soviet failure to supply adequate aid, see for example, *Washington Post,* January 4, 1982. This article, by William Branigan in Bangkok, quoted relief officials as saying that in 1981 the USSR promised to ship 100,000 tons of food aid to Phnom Penh, but in fact sent only 45,000. This concurs with the author's own interviews with relief officials.

U.S. government position on relief aid, memorandum from Desaix Anderson to John Negroponte and Richard Smyser, February 2, 1981.

FAO's ice-making plant, Orlin J. Scoville, February 2, 1981, p. 27.

Chapter Nineteen

UNICEF officials on food to Thai Villagers and Royal Thai Army, unattributable interviews with the author, 1981 and 1982.

FAO 1983 report, by Dr. Wil H.P. Schreurs, Head, Department of Clinical Biochemistry Institute, CIVO, Zeist, The Netherlands, March 1983.

Brian Eads, Observer, May 29, 1983.

Chris Manning, "Oxfam Medical work in Kampuchea," July 1982, and interviews with the author, 1983.

David du Pury report to Oxfam, undated 1983.

Former prisoner on Heng Samrin prison conditions, interview with Amnesty International officials, 1983.

ICRC and children, author's interviews with ICRC officials, Bangkok and Geneva, 1983.

Red Hill, the author, visited the border and Khao I Dang in 1983.

World Health Organization report, "Health Conditions in the Kampuchea-Thailand Border Encampments," based on mission February 4–20, 1983.

ICRC's chief delegate in Thailand, John de Salis, in interview with *CCSDPT News,* Thailand, Summer 1983.

Negotiation between Thai Government, ICRC and UNHCR over Cambodians at Red Hill, author's interviews with officials concerned.

INS attitude toward Cambodian refugees, author's interviews with U.S. Embassy and UNHCR officials. See also Gail Sheehy, Boston *Globe,* February 6, 1983.

Chapter Twenty

Vietnamese ambassador's statement, *Far Eastern Economic Review,* August 31, 1979.

Tuol Sleng–Auschwitz, author's interviews with Ministry of Culture officials and other officials, Phnom Penh, October 1980, March 1981 and November 1983.

Biafra account. This is derived principally from John Stremlau, *The International Politics of the Nigerian Civil War* (Princeton, 1977).

Testimony of Hun Sen's secretary, *Far Eastern Economic Review,* October 15, 1982.

❦ Index

ABOUT THE AUTHOR

William Shawcross, one of the world's most distinguished journalists, won the 1984 World Hunger Media Award for *The Quality of Mercy*. He won the 1980 George Polk Book Award and the 1979 Sidney Hillman Foundation Prize Award for *Sideshow: Kissinger, Nixon and the Destruction of Cambodia*.

Mr. Shawcross has written for *The New Statesman, The Spectator, The New York Review of Books* and *The Washington Post*.

He lives in London with his wife and children.